Claiming the Pen

CLAIMING THE PEN

*Women and Intellectual Life in
the Early American South*

C ATHERINE K ERRISON

Cornell University Press

ITHACA AND LONDON

First published 2006 by Cornell University Press
Printed in the United States of America

Library of Congress Cataloging-in-Publication Data

Kerrison, Catherine, 1953–
   Claiming the pen : women and intellectual life in the early American South / Catherine Kerrison.
      p. cm.
   Includes bibliographical references and index.
   ISBN-13: 978-0-8014-4344-2 (cloth : alk. paper)
   ISBN-10: 0-8014-4344-X (cloth : alk. paper)
   1. Women—Southern States—Intellectual life—18th century.   2. Women—Books and reading—Southern States—History—18th century.   3. Women authors, American—Southern States—History—18th century.   4. Women and literature—Southern States—History—18th century.   5. American literature—Southern States—History and criticism.   I. Title.
   HQ1438.S63K47 2006
   305.48'9630975—dc22   2005016063

Cornell University Press strives to use environmentally responsible suppliers and materials to the fullest extent possible in the publishing of its books. Such materials include vegetable-based, low-VOC inks and acid-free papers that are recycled, totally chlorine-free, or partly composed of nonwood fibers. For further information, visit our website at www.cornellpress.cornell.edu.

Cloth printing   10 9 8 7 6 5 4 3 2 1

For Justin, Sarah, and Elizabeth

Contents

List of Illustrations		ix
Acknowledgments		xi
1.	Toward an Intellectual History of Early Southern Women	1
2.	"The Truest Kind of Breeding": Prescriptive Literature in the Early South	34
3.	Religion, Voice, and Authority	70
4.	Reading Novels in the South	105
5.	Reading, Race, and Writing	139
	Conclusion: The Enduring Problem of Female Authorship and Authority	185
	Postscript	195
	Abbreviations	199
	Notes	201
	Index	259

Illustrations

1. "Fair Lady Working Tambour," London, c. 1770   16
2. "The Conversation Group," English, c. 1775   58
3. "Lady's Toilette: The Wig," English, c. 1802   62
4. "Maternal Advice," London, 1795   113
5. "Correspondence," London, 1760   172

Acknowledgments

Writing is a solitary pursuit. Nonetheless, as I complete this book, I see clearly the imprints of others: questions posed, sources suggested, interpretations pushed, support granted, prose polished, and encouragement continuously offered. Thus I have accumulated professional and personal debts along the way that I cannot hope to repay, except perhaps by following the example set for me by all whom I now have the pleasure of thanking.

I had the inexpressible good fortune to "come of age" intellectually under the auspices of the Department of History at The College of William and Mary, whose rigor, resources, intellectual vitality, and collegiality presented a bountiful smorgasbord to this student who wanted to come back to school to study early America. I offer my profound thanks to James P. Whittenburg, whose numerous teaching awards and legions of devoted former students attest better to his gifts as teacher, mentor, and friend than can any words of mine. I am ever grateful for his expert guidance, warm encouragement, and abiding friendship. I thank Robert A. Gross for introducing me to the history of the book and inspiring this work, and Leisa D. Meyer for simultaneously asking hard questions and supporting my interpretive efforts. James Axtell has set a standard for style and grace in writing that I shall spend a career trying to attain; I thank him for all he has taught me about the practice of history. I thank Blair Pogue, Gail S. Terry, and her husband, the late John Hemphill, for introducing this returning student to the disciplines of research and writing and making the path easier. For conversations outside the classroom as stimulating as any we had within, I am indebted to my colleagues, particularly Richard Chew, Meaghan Duff, Michael Guasco, and Brian McCarthy.

I thank all who have read and commented on portions of this book as it has evolved in conference papers, articles, and chapters: Catherine Allgor, Holly Brewer, Kathleen M. Brown, Richard D. Brown, Stephanie Cole, Joanna Bowen Gillespie, Cynthia Kierner, Charlene Boyer Lewis, Sarah Pearsall, Linda Sturtz, Tatiana van Riemsdijk, and Karin Wulf; particular thanks to Caroline Winterer and Terri L. Snyder for reading the manuscript in its entirety. I have profited enormously from their thoughtful readings and sage advice. I particularly thank Sheri Englund, editor extraordinaire, who shepherded this book through the initial acquisition process at Cornell University Press with remarkable efficiency and grace.

I also thank the archivists and librarians who have patiently taught me so much and who have graciously granted me permission to quote from their collections. I thank the staff at the Virginia Historical Society, particularly Nelson Lankford and Frances Pollard, whose warmth and interest in my work made the Historical Society a research home. I am grateful to the staffs of the Manuscripts and Rare Books Department at Swem Library, The College of William and Mary; the Library of Virginia, particularly Sandra Gioia Treadway and Nolan Yelich; the Library of Congress; the Albert and Shirley Small Special Collections of the University of Virginia; the Southern Historical Collection at the University of North Carolina, Chapel Hill; the Archives and Records Department of the John D. Rockefeller, Jr. Library, Colonial Williamsburg Foundation; the Library Company, Philadelphia; and the Quaker Collection, Haverford College. I thank the *Journal of Southern History* for permission to reprint material in chapter 4 that had appeared earlier in their journal.

I am grateful for the generous funding that has made this book possible: an Andrew W. Mellon Research Fellowship from the Virginia Historical Society and a grant from the National Endowment of the Humanities, which funded the writing of chapter 5. I thank Villanova University for a Faculty Summer Research Grant as well as a sabbatical in which to write. I thank my colleagues in the Department of History, who have offered their support in countless ways, from their first warm welcome to my children and me when we moved north to their helpful advice on all manner of working drafts. I am fortunate to have found in my coworkers the most generous of friends. For his assiduous reading and fact checking of the manuscript, I thank my graduate assistant, Jeffrey Ludwig.

I could not have completed this work without the unstinting encouragement of friends outside academe. I thank Wendy DiTraglia for seeing me through the early years; Wendy Hamilton Hoelscher for providing both quiet respites at the beach and vigorous peptalks, and for her wisdom in knowing which was needed when; Karen Lally for her Irish wit that never failed to elicit a laugh; and Sallie and Joe Cross and Michelle and Bill Brauer for keeping constant a candle in the window to guide and welcome us home.

Finally, I thank my family: my father, Raymond Kerrison, from whom I have inherited a love of words; my mother, Monica Kerrison, who taught me to have faith that everything would turn out just fine; and my children, Justin, Sarah, and Elizabeth Foster, who by their faith and love daily teach me the most important lessons of life. With all the love a grateful mother's heart can hold, I dedicate this book to them.

Claiming the Pen

Toward an Intellectual History of Early

Southern Women

It was one of those delightfully mild days that occasionally grace the Virginia Tidewater in winter. The clear weather on that December day in 1711 beckoned irresistibly to the two women, who left the house together for a walk. Mrs. Dunn had been staying with her friend Lucy Byrd on and off for over a year, seeking refuge from an abusive husband. Perhaps they sought privacy for their conversation, away from the omnipresence of the house slaves. Perhaps Mrs. Dunn confided the fears, resentments, and injuries she suffered living with her clergyman husband who, she said, beat her. In any event, in the temporary respite afforded by the balmy weather and the ear of a friend, the two women lost track of the time. So completely engrossed were they in their conversation that Lucy forgot about preparations for dinner. By the time they returned to the house, they found its master, William Byrd II, hungry and incensed. Later that evening, his pique unrelieved, he punished his wife, refusing her request to take a book out of his library.[1]

Fast forward over one hundred years to 1819. Bookseller Joseph Swan had been working assiduously to fill the order of Lady Jean Skipwith, one of the wealthiest women in Virginia. Packing up her books, he prepared a note to accompany them. "Your Lady Ship will Observe that I have procured all the Books (According to your Order) that is to be found in this town. There is some I am afraid I cannot procure as the Booksellers Here as well as myself Have never had them. However," he reassured her, "I shall Write to New York in my first Order for all that is Lacking. Any Books that you want order them[,] if not to be had I shall write for them." Eager

1

to maintain this lucrative account, he pointed out smoothly, "Your Lady
Ship will observe that those are the latest Publications."[2] By any measure,
Jean Skipwith was an unusual woman: she was single for all but seventeen
of her seventy-eight years; in the post-Revolutionary republic, she retained
the designation of the baronetcy into which she had married; she nurtured a passion for gardening, collecting books on the subject, conducting experiments in her gardens, and exchanging specimens with gardening advocates at home and abroad; and she cultivated a network of
bookseller contacts, ranging from Edinburgh, Scotland, to Raleigh, North
Carolina, to Philadelphia, Pennsylvania, all eager to serve her. By the time
of her death in 1826, she possessed a collection of at least 384 titles (850
volumes) that librarian John Cook Wyllie called "incomparably the largest
and best [library] made by a woman" in the Jeffersonian era.[3]

These vignettes bracket a century of momentous changes that included
the Enlightenment project, which defined man as a rational being capable of entering into contracts of self-government; attempts to overthrow
the *ancien regime*'s hierarchical chain of being; and the colonial American
uprising against Britain and subsequent creation of a republic. The Byrds
and Lady Jean Skipwith have much to tell us about these changes in
America, particularly in the South. In his splendid walnut-encased library
and in his control over his wife's access to it, William Byrd exemplified the
privileges of the old order: his status and gender allowed him to control
the people in his household and fostered his access to books, which im-
parted the knowledge that legitimized his claim to that control. Byrd was
a collector whose library was a potent symbol of the legitimacy of his claim
to gentility and authority.[4] He fairly burst with pride when a visitor, "a
man of learning," surveyed the collection of immaculately bound books—
all gilded by their owner for a uniform appearance—and pronounced
himself "pleased with the library."[5] Handsome as it was, however, Byrd's library was not just for show. By his death in 1744, he had accumulated a library of more than thirty-six hundred volumes. His diaries record his
daily reading of Latin or Greek, philosophy, the sciences, history, law,
drama, and theology.[6] Reading his imported books in his home on the
banks of the James River in Virginia, Byrd considered himself as educated
as any English country gentleman and as comparably situated in the world
of British belles lettres. It was a world at once privileged, powerful, and
male, and in his image of himself as patriarch, in the mold of those of the
Old Testament, a world to which he unquestionably belonged.[7]

By Jean Skipwith's time, however, women's access to books had broadened considerably. They chose what they wanted to read, and their books
were less a mark of their status and more a reflection of their interests.

Certainly Lady Jean also delighted in beautifully bound books, their titles gilded in gold, but rather than serving as a symbolic assertion of authority, her library marked her deep interests in travel, history, geography, and gardening.[8] It is significant, too, that she placed orders herself for books she would use and enjoy, choosing independently of male influence, even, it appears, during her seventeen-year marriage. Both she and Peyton Skipwith ordered copies of *Cook's Voyages*.[9] And of the 384 titles we know she owned, novels, poetry, and drama titles numbered 197; of religious works she owned but six. Jean Skipwith's books signify an enormous shift over the century in women's reading, in their interests, in their access to knowledge, and in the meanings books had for female readers. Her books, then, alert us to an important story about southern life that has not been told until now: the origins of an intellectual tradition of southern women.

REGION AND GENDER IN INTELLECTUAL HISTORY

For generations, American intellectual history had been heavily weighted toward New England; it is a comparatively recent idea that the colonial South even possessed an intellectual life worth studying.[10] Even in the eighteenth century, it was the impression of an unlettered South that helped spur the founding of the Charleston Library Society to counteract it.[11] Noting that the first printing presses in the South were not set up until 1726 and 1730 (in Maryland and Virginia, respectively), and taking too literal a cue from Virginia governor William Berkeley's often-quoted words, "I thank God, there are no free schools nor printing" that would bring and disseminate "disobedience, and heresy, and sects" within his dominion,[12] historians in the nineteenth and twentieth centuries have cast the New England way as prototypical of the American character.[13] Early attempts to shift this center of gravity, such as Philip Alexander Bruce's massive projects on seventeenth-century Virginia, Julia Cherry Spruill's painstaking work to begin to identify southern women's reading, and Louis B. Wright's work on the intellectual lives of eighteenth-century Virginia gentlemen, were impressive in their own right but barely made a dent in the New England bulwarks.[14] Other works appeared, most notably the edited diaries of William Byrd II and Landon Carter, showing the significance of education, reading, writing, and the book trade in colonial Virginia in new ways. With Richard Beale Davis's *Literature and Society in Early Virginia 1608–1840* (1973) and *Intellectual Life in the Colonial South 1585–1763* (1978), the very concept of an intellectual life in the South assumed credibility. More recent studies on education, literacy, reading, and the book trades in the South have resurrected not only the classic work of Bruce, Spruill, and Wright but also essays, lists of books for sale, and inventories of private libraries that languished unnoticed in regional historical publications.[15] But these works (with the exception of Spruill's) have focused on male literary culture. Even those studies that have examined women's lives in the colonial and Revolutionary periods have focused primarily on women in the North, while studies of southern women have relegated women's reading to a single chapter.[16]

In devoting its full attention to southern women readers and writers of the eighteenth century, this book aims to widen further still the scope of southern intellectual history, both chronologically and analytically. Indeed, it stretches for an even more ambitious goal: to supply an important missing piece from the master narrative of American intellectual history prior to 1900. To studies of the great southern literary lights of the twentieth century, recent historians have added women's reading and writing of the antebellum period (1820–60).[17] But I train my spotlight on an even earlier era: on the women of the previous century, in a time when female reading and writing literacy lagged so far behind men's that a women's intellectual history appeared inconceivable. In telling this story, this book considers not only how literacy is directly linked with power and authority (as all intellectual histories must) but other issues specific to the southern experience as well. These include the significance of definitions of race and gender as expressed in law, custom, and practice for white women's understanding of themselves; attention to southern women's reading of their texts (rather than a focus on authorial intent), which opens up new ways of understanding their interpretation and use of their texts; the significant impact of gender on reading, writing, and authority; and perhaps most important, the impact of living in a slave society. How do women begin to exert any intellectual autonomy in a society that depends on the constant articulation of hierarchies in nature to justify its exploitation of slaves? This book focuses on the dynamics of southern women's reading within such a world and on their understanding of the limits within which they might exercise the rights of men by taking up the pen. Ultimately, it reveals women's reading and writing habits as practices of southern femininity.

In spite of all the political, legal, economic, and social constraints that were intended to buttress the hegemony of white men, southern women did find ways to begin writing in increasing volume by the turn of the nineteenth century. To try to understand how and why they did so, I read what they read: the sermons, devotional tracts, conduct-of-life advice, and later, novels, all of which taught them what it meant to be a woman in the eighteenth century. I began to see that it was in the convergence of themes of female virtue in both religious and secular advice literature by the end of the eighteenth century that southern women found the authority to produce their own advice literature and that as they did so, they formulated a model of femininity distinct from that of male advice authors. In the face of tumultuous social and political changes in the eighteenth century that threatened to topple the traditional structures of patriarchy, male advice writers had sought to make more palatable the image of male power. Since these softer images were more cosmetic than real, women seized on new developments in culture, particularly print's increased availability and the rise of the novel, to take an active role as advisers to daughters, wards, and friends. Indeed, by the end of the century, many women had acquired a new consciousness of themselves as agents in creating their own world. This book shows how this happened, albeit at a slower pace than in England or New England, in the most unlikely of places: the slaveholding, patriarchal society of the early American South.

Indeed, a crucial component of my story is the fact that while these cultural developments were common to white women in the Anglo-Atlantic world, southern women experienced them in different ways. It is a tricky proposition to talk about "the South" in the eighteenth and early nineteenth centuries. The residents of the colonies from Maryland to Georgia certainly did not think of themselves as sharing a distinct regional culture. Before the Revolution, colonists thought of themselves as Rhode Islanders or New Yorkers or Virginians, rather than as northerners and southerners. Ironically, a growing consciousness and identification with region would be born in the process of building the infant nation and reaching maturity in the antebellum period.[18] (Therefore it must be understood that I refer to Virginia, North Carolina, and South Carolina as "the South" or "southern" solely to avoid unwieldy sentences and not to impute a regional consciousness in this period.) Nonetheless, visitors to the region even before the Revolution noted differences from England and the northern colonies that in many ways they attributed to slavery.[19] To highlight the ways in which this southern experience was distinctive, ways that they may not have recognized themselves, I pay particular attention to the problem of the intellectual development of women living in a slave society. While southern women's participation in the Anglo-American world of print shows how actively they participated in the life of the mind, this book also argues that the gender hierarchy constructed in the context of a slave society explains why they lagged a full century behind English female authors, whose works appeared in print from the last quarter of the seventeenth century and only increased in volume during the eighteenth.

Yet I also discovered that white southern women engaged actively in intellectual activities even as their education was tightly circumscribed. In a world that offered little structured education for men, much less for women, advice literature comprised the core reading for women in a curriculum whose focus differed sharply from men's. Rather than reading in law or medicine, for instance, women read to understand their female nature (as formulated by natural and divine law) and the inherently female roles those laws dictated. This literature, then, was fraught with meaning for women, for it was the source of their learning, of their understanding of themselves and the way their lives should be lived. We can see this link between life and literature in the ruminations of two young Tidewater Virginia women as they watched the consequences of a friend's seduction by a French officer during the American Revolution.[20] Their responses to her were shaped by what they had learned from the traditional advice literature of women's responsibilities during courtship, yet they rejected its directive to abandon such fallen acquaintances. The lessons of the novels had also taught them how easily innocent young women could be duped by the sweet promises of a suitor. Indeed, one of the chief developments this book traces is how, as Lady Jean Skipwith's library shows us, the novel by the early nineteenth century supplanted traditional conduct-of-life advice as a prominent influence on women's thinking about female virtue and identity. And in a region that developed a code of honor based on the defense of white female virtue, the contribution of southern women toward that regional identity was profound. As the complexity of this tale unfolds, then, it becomes clear that not only is there a story to tell about intellectual life in the South before the antebellum period, but southern women are an indispensable part of it.

PRINT CULTURE IN THE EARLY SOUTH

One of the first ways to begin looking for books is to look for a printing press. That the Puritans of Massachusetts Bay established a press in Cambridge, Massachusetts, as early as 1636 is therefore cited as evidence of the depth of their commitment to their spiritual and intellectual lives.[21] Conversely, Virginia's late start proves what everyone already knew anyway: Chesapeake settlers were a rather superficial lot who were too busy growing tobacco to read, reflect, and write. But the absence until 1730 of a printing press and its small output (relative to that of Massachusetts, for

example) most emphatically did not mean that Virginians were not reading. Seventeenth-century colonists brought as many as twenty thousand
books into Virginia alone.[22] Perhaps about a third of the settlers in the initial settlements around the Chesapeake Bay owned books, although their
household libraries were small, typically less than five books, and generally religious in nature. These were not the cheap prints of English popular culture; rather, the Bible was prominent in these homes, often followed by the Reverend Richard Allestree's devotional work for laymen,
Whole Duty of Man.[23] Virginians treasured these books, sharing in the reading tastes of the middling class in England, and they passed them down
from one generation to the next.[24] Reading tastes were similar in the
Chesapeake, regardless of rank, however. For example, wealthy John
Carter I owned one of Virginia's largest libraries, having brought books
from England with him in 1649, and bequeathed it to his son, John
Carter II. As in the small libraries of his neighbors, religion was prominent in Carter's: fully one-third of his library was devoted to religious and
devotional works. Early Virginians may not have been extensive readers,
but they were intensive ones. And from the very beginning of settlement
in the New World, through their books they nurtured and cherished their
cultural connections to the England they had left behind.[25]

This became increasingly true in the eighteenth century. Southern gentlemen consciously sought to emulate the lifestyle of English country gentlemen, and as in the case of William Byrd, one of the most important
ways in which they forged this cultural connection was in their reading.[26]
To facilitate this connection, southerners established a thriving book
trade with their English factors to supply them with books on all subjects
from agriculture to classical literature to the latest novels. Indeed, by
1770 more than 40 percent of all British books shipped to North America
were destined for Virginia.[27] Not to be outdone, Scottish tobacco merchants also jumped into the book trade. While books were not *the* sub-
stantive part of their cargo, between 1743 and 1760, the two Scottish
ports of Greenock and Port Glasgow cleared 416 hundredweights of
books bound for Virginia, an average of about 2,800 volumes per year.[28]

William Parks, Virginia's first printer, positioned himself to take advantage of the colonial desire for things English. Having founded his first
newspaper in England in 1719, he maintained his English connections
when he emigrated, "by which, upon all Occasions, I [would] be furnished with the freshest intelligence, both from thence, and other Parts
of Europe," for his American ventures.[29] His newspaper, the *Virginia
Gazette*, drew upon English periodicals for material to fill his paper (there
being no copyright infringement laws to prevent him). Fortuitously lo-

cated within convenient walking distance of the Capitol building, Parks's business was enormously successful.[30] The *Gazette* enjoyed a wide circulation from its initial publication in 1736. In October of that year, Parks predicted that "these Papers will circulate (as speedily as possible) not only all over This, but also the Neighboring colonies, and will probably be read by some Thousands of People."[31] It was not an idle boast: by midcentury, the Williamsburg press was turning out a thousand copies each week; by the mid-1770s, in the midst of the pre-Revolutionary ferment, Virginia readers supported three newspapers.[32] Nor was the *Gazette*'s readership confined to subscribers; colonial newspapers were shared by neighbors, over tavern tables, and sometimes stolen outright. Parks complained in 1737 that "several Persons break open the News-papers, who have no Right to them, and after having read them, instead of Sealing and Forwarding them to the Persons they are directed to, have kept or destroy'd them."[33] The account books of the Williamsburg printing office for 1750–52 and 1764–66 show "a sweeping geographic pattern" across the colony of both subscribers and advertisers.[34] Whether over the groaning tables of the gentry or the boisterous tables of the taverns, in modest kitchens or over shop counters, the pages of the *Gazette* were read, shared, and discussed so that neither low income levels nor even an inability to read was necessarily a bar to access to the information contained in them.[35] It is clear, then, that one of the most widely available sources of information in Virginia after 1736 was the newspaper and that a Virginian did not necessarily have to be a subscriber or even be literate to have access to the news.

But the *Virginia Gazette* was more than a source of news; it was also one of the primary means by which English literary culture permeated Virginia's. Nearly every eighteenth-century English journal found its way, "through quotation or allusion" into the *Gazette*, including the *London Evening Post*, the *London Gazette*, the *Universal Spectator*, and the *Westminster Journal*. Excerpts from the *Gentleman's Magazine*, first published in 1731, appeared so frequently during William Parks's tenure as printer that he began to refer to it merely as "the Magazine."[36] English literary greats such as Joseph Addison, Alexander Pope, Jonathan Swift, and William Shakespeare exerted their influence on Virginians. Parks published many of Addison's poems and essays; Pope's poetry accompanied many essays; the struggles of the "Rev. Doct. Swift, Dean of St. Patrick's, defender of Irish political liberties," were followed closely in the *Gazette*; poems attempting to imitate Shakespeare and essays citing his works appeared occasionally as well. Dimmer literary lights also appeared by name, although without any accompanying explanation, suggesting that their names were familiar to the *Gazette* readership. Other pieces, such as "A remarkable Instance of His Majesty's Goodness and Clemency" from the *London Weekly Journal,* connected loyal subjects in Virginia with those in Britain.[37] A shrewd businessman, Parks would have included so much of this literature only if it sold papers to a responsive audience.[38]

Parks also opened a bookstore in the colonial capital of Williamsburg in which he sold imported English imprints. A look at the account books of the Williamsburg Print Shop at midcentury reveals southern reading tastes. When Virginians came to town looking for a new book, they continued to stock up on religious works, pragmatically choosing books they considered useful, to promote the welfare not only of their farms and crops but also of their souls.[39] The bookstore extended its reach even further by mailing books to purchasers;[40] in addition, *Gazette* riders, employed to deliver subscribers' papers, also made money on the side by re-selling books cheaply.[41] Thus books were not restricted to the wealthy. A cursory study of eighteenth-century inventories in Virginia reinforces the point that people of varying degrees of wealth owned some books, even if the only evidence of this is the frustratingly vague notation "parcel of books."[42] This designation was ubiquitous in York County, for example, where in 1706, John Broster's small £34 estate included nine shillings' worth of "a parcell of books." Thomas Gibbins's books, in 1707, were valued together with a "tablecloth, 5 old chairs, 1 little Table, one Case with nine Bottles in it," at £1.15.0 in an estate that totaled £42. Armiger Wade's more substantial estate of £250 included "a parcell of old Bookes and other Lumbar," valued at £1.1.0 in 1709.[43] Henry Tyler, who owned twenty slaves at his death in 1729, owned a "parcell of books" assessed at seventeen shillings.[44]

More ostentatious private libraries in the colonial South reflect their owners' desire to create on the American side of the Atlantic the same genteel culture that existed in England. In contrast to those who owned only "a parcel of old books," some southern elites took pride in their ownership of books, arranging them on shelves with meticulous care. In an unusual early case of inventorying a library, the executors of Anglican minister Thomas Teakle's estate on Virginia's Eastern Shore cataloged his 333 books in 1697, before dividing them among his son and two daughters.[45] The library of Ralph Wormeley, numbering 375 volumes in 1701, shows the early development of Virginia gentility; William Byrd's library of 3,600 volumes forty years later dramatically illustrates the significance of books to cultural authority in just two generations.[46] Edward Moseley of New Hanover County, North Carolina, compiled a catalog of his law books "of my Own hand Writing, in a Marble Cover book."[47] When New Jersey tutor Philip Vickers Fithian resided at Councillor

Robert Carter's Nomini Hall plantation on the Northern Neck of Virginia, he "took a Catalogue of the whole of his Books," and learned that another 458 volumes more remained in Carter's town home at Williamsburg. "An overgrown library" Fithian judged, surmising (and perhaps disapproving of) its social rather than purely intellectual function.[48] Yet these wealthy bibliophiles were generous in loaning their treasured books. Numerous ads in the *Virginia Gazette,* requesting books be returned to their owners, attest to this practice. When the family of John Mercer of Fredericksburg attempted to put his library up for sale after his death, they were forced to publicize only a partial list of his twelve hundred volumes, since an ad placed almost three years earlier had not yielded the missing four hundred volumes.[49]

With its wealth of navigable shorelines along the rivers that flowed into the Chesapeake Bay, as well as its rich soil, Virginia's topography enabled the stream of imported books to the colony.[50] North Carolina, however, was not as fortunate. The approach to the colony was impeded by the treacherous Outer Banks; without a safe, natural port, North Carolinians looked north to Virginia or south to Charles Town for their imports, incurring further expenses for the costs of overland transportation. Nor was its sandy soil as hospitable to tobacco farming as its northern neighbor's. Indeed, North Carolina never developed a staple crop, and as late as the 1770s, even contemporaries referred to the colony as "Poor Carolina."[51] Such a striving economy hardly bode fair to support a printer; indeed, James Davis, the first to make the attempt after an apprenticeship with William Parks, did not arrive in New Bern until 1749.[52] Yet North Carolina too was home to libraries reflective of the culture its people shared with England. The more spectacular examples are those of attorneys John Luttrell and James Milner. Luttrell's library was heavily weighted towards law books but also included ancient and modern history, poetry, the novel *Tristram Shandy,* and the popular literature that was a direct link to English coffeehouse culture, the *Tatler,* the *Spectator,* the *Idler,* and the *Rambler.*[53]

James Milner's library was considerably more extensive, almost 650 titles, 182 of them law books.[54] It was a library of a gentleman, including history, philosophy, belles lettres, music, and numerous reference works, all encased in walnut bookshelves. Milner also provided books specifically addressed to women for the women in his family: there were two copies of the fashionable *Fordyce's Sermons for Young Women, Memoirs of Several Ladies, Letters to Married Women, Lady Mary's Letters,* and *The Lady's Magazine.* Instructional works included *The Young Man's Companion, Paths of Virtue,* and *Conversation and Behavior,* in addition to mainstays such as *Rudiman's Grammar.* Thirty-four Latin books attest to the quality of his children's ed-

ucation. Prayer books, Bibles, and sermons appeared in his inventory, although only marginally.[55] Milner may have lived in the cultural backwater
of North Carolina, but he went to great expense to fashion himself and
his family in the mold of English gentility, actively cultivating its intellectual life and ensuring that link for his children as well.

Still, elites were not the only people able to access English culture.
Studies on popular culture have demolished assumptions that an inability
to read created an unbridgeable chasm between the mental worlds of the
unlettered and the educated.[56] Literacy studies have shown that the skills
of reading and writing were not always taught together; thus the inability
to write did not necessarily denote an inability to read (this was particularly true for women). One early study of literacy in colonial New England
revealed that while two-thirds of white males in seventeenth-century New
England could sign their names, by the mid-eighteenth century almost all
men had achieved signature literacy. New England women lagged far behind, however: only one-third could sign their names by the late seventeenth century; by the mid-eighteenth century, that number had only
climbed to 50 percent. In the South, white men did not attain even two-
thirds signature literacy; women's literacy levels always remained lower
still.[57] Nonetheless, it is important to remember that reading illiteracy did
not have to signify exclusion from information.

LITERACY AND POWER

The broad reception, then, of English culture by all ranks of colonial society through print indicates colonial acceptance of the cultural authority
of the London metropolis. It also reinforced the legitimacy of claims to
rule made by those most deeply immersed in it. Elites pointed to their
books, displayed in polished walnut shelves, not to emphasize the number
but to note "the[ir] symbolic potency in the life of the community."[58] To
be illiterate in this society, David D. Hall has commented, was to be culturally inferior and excluded. Thus, the literary culture in eighteenth-
century Virginia buttressed hierarchical social differences. William Byrd
II's satirical description of the uncivilized North Carolinians who populate his *Secret History of the Dividing Line* described the great distance between gentry and common folk that he, as a gentleman, wanted to find.
The language and classical allusions in the *Virginia Gazette* were the code
of an exclusive "club" of gentlemen who grounded their authority in their
reason and learning.[59] In all these respects, William Byrd II illustrates
what it meant to be male, white, and wealthy. His reading was crucial to
his sense of himself and of his authority; his tight discipline of both read-

ing and record keeping in his diary configured him as a person of reason, control, education, and taste—all marks of the English gentleman he believed himself to be. This is why he believed himself entitled to recognition as an equal during his trips to England, to the governorship of Virginia, and (after Lucy's death) to a wife from the ranks of the English aristocracy.

Learning not only separated gentlemen from nonelite men, but it also marked boundaries of race and gender. As the mistress of nineteenth-century slave Frederick Douglass learned when her irate husband happened upon her teaching Douglass to read, "Learning would *spoil* the best nigger in the world. . . . It would forever unfit him to be a slave."[60] Indeed, runaway notices in the colonial period attest to slaves who could write well enough to forge travel passes and pass as free.[61] In 1740, in the aftermath of the Stono rebellion, South Carolina was the first to forbid teaching slaves how to write.[62] But some slaves did learn to read, predominately through Anglican missionary efforts in both Virginia and South Carolina that had established schools to teach slave children to read the Bible.[63] Even as South Carolina legislated against slave writing, Anglican commissary Alexander Garden successfully petitioned a grant of £1,500 from the Society of the Propagation of the Gospel in England to build a school for slave children in South Carolina and furnish it with two slave teachers.[64] But masters were reluctant to send their slaves. The trustees of the Bray school in Williamsburg reported that "Planters urge it a sin & impolitick to enlarge the understanding of their Slaves, which will render them more impatient of Slavery."[65] A skill that could confer freedom of body as well as of mind, slave literacy would eventually be outlawed by the antebellum period. North Carolina forbade teaching slaves in 1830; Virginia outlawed teaching them to read and write in 1831; South Carolina followed its law of 1740 with one in 1834 that forbade teaching slaves to read. Nat Turner's rebellion in Virginia in August 1831 prompted the legislature to forbid preaching by slaves or free blacks.[66] All these laws were a formal recognition of literacy as a critical tool of political power that must be restricted to whites. So effective were they that fewer than 5 percent of former slaves interviewed by the Federal Writers Project in the 1930s could remember being taught to read.[67] Even in the colonial period, literacy was coming to be defined as a privilege of whiteness. As a writer in the *South Carolina Gazette* noted, lacking "judgments, Wit, Vivacity . . . and knowledge of Books," a man with aspirations to gentility might be dismissed as a "Molatto gentleman"—that is, his ignorance would preclude any aspirations to that status as forcefully as a drop of black blood precluded whiteness.[68]

GENDER, LITERACY, AND POWER

Though women did not face such stringent bars to literacy, those who had a propensity to display their learning and wit would find their "masculine minds" denigrated or their chastity questioned, since such behavior crossed gender lines. In fact, the respective educations afforded boys and girls prepared them scrupulously for the gendered roles they were to fill when they grew up. The three R's did not obtain as a universal basic standard of education. Instead, colonial educations imitated the English model in which all boys learned reading, writing, and vocational skills, while wealthier boys added Greek and Latin; female education focused on domestic skills with the addition of polite accomplishments for wealthy students. Young as she was, eleven-year-old Virginian Betty Pratt recognized the discrepancies as she wrote in 1732 to her brother, who was in school in England, that "you write better already than I can expect to do as long as I live; and you are got as far as the Rule of three in Arithmetick, but I can't cast up a sum in addition cleverly, but I am striving to do better every day. I can perform a great many dances and am now learning the Sibell, but I cannot speak a word of French."[69] Even in New England, where an emphasis on the reading of Scripture had propelled the highest reading literacy rate in the colonies for both men and women, Abigail Adams complained to her husband in 1778, "You need not be told how much female Education is neglected, nor how fashionable it has been to ridicule Female learning."[70] The situation was worse in the South, where formal education was a haphazard affair for all but gentry sons, who frequently were sent to England for their schooling. Nor did wealth guarantee a steady program of education. Virginia planter Robert Carter of Nomini Hall, who built a schoolhouse on the grounds of his plantation, was unable to provide consistency in his children's instructors, hiring a succession of three tutors in three years.[71] And although his sons and daughters gathered in the same schoolroom, the curriculum split along gender lines: Latin and Greek for the boys and beginning arithmetic, letter writing, and reading for the girls.[72] Indeed, the very arrangements of the great houses of the southern gentry reflect the relative weights they assigned to the cultivation of an intellectual life for men and women. George Washington's extensive additions to Mount Vernon included a south wing that housed his library on the first floor and a bedroom on the second connected by a stairway; his wife had a writing table in her bedroom.[73]

Overall, a range of private tutors, in-town classrooms, and makeshift field schools provided a range of schooling for only the most fortunate of southern girls. When Benjamin LePetit opened his school on Market Square in Williamsburg in 1773, he accepted boys in that public venue but offered to wait upon the girls in their homes.[74] Mrs. Neil's exclusive boarding school for girls offered reading, needlework, music, dancing, and writing.[75] Middling parents, such as silversmith James Geddy, also hired tutors for their children. Polite accomplishments for the daughters of the household were emphasized at this rank as well: Anne (Nancy) Geddy learned how to play the spinet so well that an ode to her talents appeared in the *Virginia Gazette*.[76] Other parents structured and supervised their children's study themselves. Eliza Ambler copied lessons her father prepared for her, "written in the fairest hand by him self—short, but always containing a lesson on piety; or an elegant moral quotation."[77] In rural areas, poorer white farmers often pooled their resources, built a small community school in an abandoned tobacco field, and hired a teacher. Boys and girls attended during the summer months, between planting and harvest, receiving lessons in the basic rudiments of reading, writing, and arithmetic. Education was a priority for parents. In 1751, Virginian Mary Horton took James Pinckard to court to enforce the contract she had made with him that the apprenticeship for her daughter, Elizabeth Mason, would include "Reeding . . . soen [sewing] & knit as a woman ought to do." Horton clearly recognized the long-term benefits of an education for her daughter; she was not interested in a cash settlement. She petitioned the court to order "the Said James Pinckard Sattisfie the Said Elizabeth mason for hir Learning." At least Elizabeth Mason had a mother who acted as her advocate, but absent a parent's watchful eye, an orphan could not expect to acquire even "the rudiments of learning."[78]

Writing was also gendered. Boys learned different hands, or styles of writing, but all were marked by clean, bold, and neat strokes; a masculine hand with "movement" was much admired as well. By the eighteenth century, masculine hands were differentiated further by rank and trade. Thus, a gentleman would use an italic hand, which was distinguishable from the more workmanlike round hand of his secretary or a merchant.[79] Male students of the middling class prepared for their future station in life by copying business documents such as receipts, ledgers, and bills of lading, learning the hands linked to commercial pursuits. Girls likewise learned a hand thought to reflect the female body and station: female handwriting was more ornamental, smaller and "easier" than men's, and more decorative, signifying their status and leisure.[80] A prospective teacher in Norfolk made this point explicitly, crafting her curriculum of needlework, painting, reading, and writing particularly "for the Amusements of Persons of Fortune who have Taste."[81] In sum, then, one's hand, whether male or female, was as crucial a form of self-presentation as one's dress and telegraphed as much information about the sex and status of the writer. This is not a small point, given the legal and societal constraints that governed both. Sumptuary laws forbade the camouflage of low rank by a rich cut of fabric or lace trim; satirical renderings of women dressed in men's garb ridiculed women who attempted to perform such masculine activities as preaching or endorsing political actions.[82]

Access to the tools of handwriting was also gendered. Writing students had to learn how to craft a pen from a variety of bird quills with a penknife. A poorly cut pen precluded perfection in forming one's letters; uneven nibs scratched paper, dispensed the flow of ink unevenly, and made impossible the pleasing aspects of hair-stroke ascending lines alternating with broader descending ones. This was not a skill conveyed to most girls. Even in Philadelphia Deborah Logan was frustrated by her pens that were "so rascally bad that they make me deface my book sadly." Although she had one of the best teachers in colonial Philadelphia, Anthony Benezet, she mourned that he did not insist "on my acquiring the art." [83] Making ink was a domestic task that drew from materials found in most colonial kitchens. Writers could also buy powders that needed only the addition of water. But the deprivation of the skill to make the tools necessary to write was an overt way to retain control over not only the form and content of the writing but indeed of its very production.

Last, handwriting as a skill was also gendered in the way female writing was viewed as an outgrowth of needlework. Since the very qualities prized in female handwriting were identical to those so esteemed in good needlework, instruction in both was usually offered in tandem. A *Virginia Gazette* advertiser searched for "A Well bred woman of Character, capable of teaching young Ladies the Degrees of Needlework, together with Reading and Writing" but probably did not find anyone qualified; writing instructors were almost always male.[84] The owner of Mount Pleasant in Norfolk, seeking to open a school in her home in 1772, could offer classes in needlework and reading herself, but hired a "Master properly qualified" to teach writing and arithmetic.[85] The conflation of needle and pen was explicit in a popular saying, "Then let the Fingers, whose unrivall'd Skill, Exalts the Needle, grace the Noble Quill."[86] The needle is barely distinguishable from a pen in "Fair Lady Working Tambour." Her posture, too, is precisely that required of a female writer: straight back, head slightly bent, needle held as a pen, and facial expression marked by "an easy but graceful attitude."[87] Both verbal and pictorial depictions of female expression make clear its limits: it should be ornamental and pleasing.

Printed for CARINGTON BOWLES, Map & Printseller. The FAIR LADY working TAMBOUR. at Nº 69 in Sᵗ Pauls Church Yard, LONDON.

Fig. 1. "Fair Lady Working Tambour" (London, c. 1770). The conflation of needle and pen is apparent in the pose struck by the needle worker; for elite women of the eighteenth century, both sewing and writing were understood to be ornamental accomplishments. Courtesy of the John D. Rockefeller, Jr. Library, Colonial Williamsburg Foundation.

Gendered in these ways, then, education underscored the different functions it was meant to serve for boys and girls. A boy's education taught "self-control, endurance, striving, and athletic prowess," while the point of female education was "subservience and to combat vanity and pride."[88] The overall impact of such haphazard attention to female education was low literacy rates: from below 20 percent in the early seventeenth century the rate rose to only 50 percent by 1850.[89] By the Victorian era, rather than improving, attitudes about female writing literacy had deteriorated further still. As Tamara P. Thornton explained, "If character formation [which she defined as masculine self-mastery] was an inherently male process, then, and if writing meant forming characters, then only men were truly capable of writing. The male gendering of handwriting in the nineteenth century thus functioned on a much deeper level than it had in the colonial period, for it suggested not merely that women do not usually write but that women in the profoundest sense *cannot* write."[90]

THEORETICAL CONSIDERATIONS

The conclusion previous historians have drawn from such an abysmal educational record is that southern women, few in number (compared with northern colonies) and preoccupied with farm rather than domestic duties, left so few writings behind as to make an intellectual history impossible.[91] But in asking different questions, this book shifts ground from traditional ways of thinking about education (that is, descriptions of education for boys) to new vistas. For example, what if we looked for intellectual activity in different places than colleges or schoolrooms? What if we identified other venues of learning? What if we reconsidered the criteria for a program of study? It is clear that regardless of economic rank, girls' education in the colonial South was substantially different from that of boys, so we need to look in unconventional "classrooms" where most young women acquired their education. In their homes and in apprenticeships they learned housekeeping and medicinal, sewing, and other skills that equipped them for their futures as matrons in their own homes. There, too, young women learned their catechism and devotions, how to behave in socially acceptable ways, and how to attract, please, and keep a husband.[92] The books they read in preparation for their future as wives and mothers thus take on a new significance because they were the canon, the whole of what a young girl needed to know. Therefore, we need to see this reading as critical to female education. A typical lesson young southern girls learned, for example, was that females are subordinate to men, taught by Richard Allestree's *Whole Duty of Man*, which reinforced teachings about proper male and female relationships. The essential distinctions between male and female articulated in the advice literature (such as the male capacity for reason that complemented the female capacity for feeling) explain why William Byrd was master of his world and why he could forbid his wife his books.

Prescriptive Literature for Women

This literature was not peculiar to the southern colonies. Most of what southern women read was generated in England, and thus they, too, shared in an Anglo-Atlantic culture of print, for the Atlantic Ocean served more as conduit than obstacle to the flow of ideas about what it meant to be female. A sample from the front page of the *Virginia Gazette* in May 1737 illustrates the general tenor of advice to women on both sides of the ocean. An essay entitled "Rules for the Advancement of Matrimonial Felicity" skillfully blended flattery with prescription. In an article that mingled appeals to the readers' vanity, the laws of nature, and the authority of the church, the writer invoked the gendered discourse evident in much of the advice literature for women in the eighteenth-century Anglo-American world. Nature had blessed women with "an alluring Eye, sweet Voice, and beautiful countenance," he believed, but for women to take advantage of their gifts and "lord it over their Husbands" was "odious to Mankind, indeed to the natural order." For women of faltering resolution, he urged "Read often the Matrimonial Service, and overlook not the important Word OBEY." [93]

Eighteenth-century prescriptive literature that explained such differences between men and women understood those differences to be grounded in divine and natural law. The compliant submission required of women of all ages to their fathers, brothers, and husbands was rooted in the belief of women's spiritual inferiority as inheritors of Eve's sin and in science's conviction of female physical weakness as an immutable natural phenomenon. These themes were ubiquitous in all the literature, whether the work had a decidedly religious cast or a secular one. The most popular of these works (measured in terms of availability in print shops and private and subscription libraries) were the Reverend Richard Allestree's *Whole Duty of Man* (1658) and *The Ladies Calling in Two Parts* (1677), George Lord Halifax Savile's *A New Year's Gift to a Daughter* (1688), Reverend James Fordyce's *Sermons for Young Women* (1765), and Dr. John Gregory's *A Father's Legacy to his Daughters* (1774). Raised on the words of Allestree, Halifax, Fordyce, and the anonymous others who echoed them in the southern presses, female readers understood how God and nature had marked out the parameters of being female. Failure to be properly modest or circumspect by a display of their learning, for example, was a rejection of their very nature. Many women would have understood completely Massachusetts's Eliza Southgate Bowne's conclusion, as she sought to defend female education: "I believe I must give up all pretension to *profundity*, for I am much more at home in my female character."[94]

Of course, the crucial question is what southern girls and women made of what they read. While it is true that the availability of the printed word increased exponentially in the eighteenth century, it is also important to heed historian John Brewer's reminder that "the expansion [of print] increased the availability of traditional works and old forms as well as new types of literature." This is true in men's libraries in the colonial period, as William Byrd's collection of 174 books on religion shows; it was also true in the modest increase of female literacy, which only strengthened and widened the influence of traditional advice literature.[95] Richard D. Brown concluded in his study of Lucy Breckinridge in Virginia that, as late as the 1860s, she was reading primarily English authors who "reinforced American conventions" of gender roles.[96] This was precisely the case for many women of the colonial South as well. "Britain led in discussions of female character and place [in the eighteenth century]," Nancy Cott has said, "setting sex-role conventions for the literate audience."[97] But reading in the isolation of plantation life and lacking the physical freedom of British urban centers (in the streets of which respectable women strolled, shopped, and visited) or the intellectual encouragement of literary salons of London or Philadelphia to challenge or even discuss those conventions, many southern women conformed to the teachings of traditional advice literature.[98]

The "Colonization" of Southern Women Readers

It is a mistake, however, to assume that prescription dictated behavior; that is, the advice books probably tell us more about men's ideas of women's proper behavior than about how women actually behaved.[99] Nonetheless, it is true that gendered education reinforced a hierarchy of being in which women were taught that their subordinate status was instituted by divine and natural law and that because of their natures, they were best suited to domestic duties. One way of looking at the gender relations this system of education perpetuates is to think of it as a colonial relationship, a model, as P. Joy Rouse explained, in which the colonized are assumed to be inferior; the education system is controlled by the dominant group; the history of the colonized is denied; the content of the colonized education is different from that of the colonizer; and the colonized identify, as a result of the education system, with the oppressor and see themselves as the colonizer does. The crucial point here is that female-specific education colonizes female identity.[100]

While Rouse used this model to understand nineteenth-century female education, it is equally suitable to the eighteenth century. As we shall see throughout this book, southern women learned to identify with the "colonizer" in many ways—that is, they saw their interests aligned with those of male family members rather than with those of other women, and certainly with whites rather than blacks. For instance, we will see southern women's acceptance of the flaws that rendered them inferior to men. Maria Carter's commonplace book is one example of how young women absorbed advice of various types.[101] Despite their innocuous name, commonplace books were repositories of treasured words culled from wider readings. On scraps of paper, Carter collected items such as proverbs, poetry, an elegy to a dead wife, even the words of seventeenth-century Anglican Archbishop Tillotson. In her neat hand, two years before her marriage, she copied sayings about human nature, love, and courtship that she kept for her lifetime.[102] Reflections of traditional advice appear in her notations. From "Mr. Pope's moral Essays," she recorded an illustration of the ridiculous extremes female vanity could reach. Preparing a corpse for burial (appropriately enough, in life her name had been Narcissa), one woman instructs another, "One would not, sure, look frightful, though One's dead; And—Betty—give this Cheek —a little—red."[103] Female inconstancy is the subject of another verse, in which Chloe, swearing eternal Love to Damon, "on a Leaf the Vow imprest." Zephyr, however, distracted her, and "Love, Vow & Leaf blew quite away." And in a tacit acknowledgment of the double standard that placed the responsibility for men's sexual behavior on women, she copied a ubiquitous warning to eighteenth-century women: "Passions are the gales of life, and it is our part to take care that they do not rise into a Storm." She borrowed from *The Spectator* the only description of marriage that appears in her book, from which we can infer her view of the components of a happily married life. "A happy marriage has in it all the Pleasures of Friendship, all the Enjoyments of Sense & Reason and indeed all the Sweets of Life," she wrote, choosing a definition that had at its center the congeniality of friendship, moderated by the intellect. "A marriage of Love is pleasant; a marriage of Interest easie," she continued, concluding, "and a marriage, where both meet, happy."

Not surprisingly, southern women's letters are marked with self-deprecating elements, even when they are writing to one another. In 1756, Maria Carter responded to a request for a "merry & comical letter" describing her days. Although she did not feel that she could satisfactorily perform the task, she began by saying, "Now I will give you the History of one Day, the Repetition of which without variation carries me through the Three hundred & sixty five Days which you know compleats the year."[104] Carter's airy dismissal of the importance of her daily life was meant to be amusing, but her wit did not hide the frequently mindless repetition that marked the lives of women, young and old. Instead, that one sentence revealed much about how insignificant she thought the tasks of her daily life.[105] Closing a long letter to her friend Eliza Lee in 1806, Ann Stuart caught herself: "How I rattle on, regardless of your patience, which if you are not descended from the immediate family of Job must now be quite exhausted."[106] A cousin of Ann Eaton Johnson of Franklin County, North Carolina, begged her "pray dont let any boddy see this peace of nonsense but your self and mother."[107] All these letter writers assumed that their scribblings, reflective of their thoughts—indeed, even of their daily lives—were frivolous, unimportant, and even nonsensical. Even in a private diary for which she was the only audience, Judith Anna Smith bemoaned the "foolish thoughts" she struggled to fight off during a religious service.[108]

However, another prominent theme of colonialism is resistance. Women all over the Anglo-Atlantic world—in England, New England, and the southern colonies—developed new paradigms of the female intellect and education. That there was resistance to the principle of masculine superiority is apparent as early as the seventeenth century, in Richard Allestree's complaint that in England "the Duty of Obedience, which Wives ought to practice towards their Husbands . . . is of late become rather a matter of Jest than of Doctrine."[109] It is clear also in the masses of writings by seventeenth- and eighteenth-century Englishwomen who spent their considerable talents pleading for the right of access to the same kind of education men enjoyed. It was educational deprivation, rather than their inherent nature, they argued, that explained their inferior capacities. Mary Astell was prominent among these thinkers. Her *Serious Proposal to the Ladies for the Advancement of Their True and Greatest Interest* (1694) laid out a plan for a female seminary to which women could retreat, to learn in an environment of Christian love and community. Freed from the gender conventions of the world, Astell's school would focus on internal beauty, on the life of the mind and the soul, neither of which was as vulnerable to the ravages of age as external beauty. "Since God has given women as well as men intelligent souls," she asked pointedly, "why should they be forbidden to improve them?" Women were not naturally inferior to men, she saw, but had been "from their very infancy debarred those advantages, with the want of which they are afterwards reproached."[110] In her insistence on women as rational creatures, endowed by God with an intelligence equal to men's, Astell identified reason and religion as central to her program. But the nascent feminism of these early writers, dubbed "reason's disciples" by Hilda Smith, died almost as soon as it had been born, submitting over the course of the eighteenth century to a view of women as feeling, rather than reasoning, creatures.[111] Still, these early writers had produced a substantial body of work addressed to questions of women's intellect and education. It was no accident that writers such as Allestree, Halifax, and Fordyce were popular in the colonial South while the writings of these late-seventeenth-century English women writers were almost completely absent.[112]

A full hundred years after Mary Astell's work appeared, New Englander Judith Sargent Murray presented the case for female education in America. Compiled in *The Gleaner* (1798), Murray's essays passionately asserted women's intellectual equality with men and proposed a curriculum of female education that would lead to economic self-sufficiency.[113] Mercy Otis Warren kept up a correspondence with close friend Abigail Adams, in which they discussed political issues at length; after the war, Warren wrote the first history of the American Revolution.[114] Adams had also been vigorously interested in politics. Writing from Massachusetts in March 1776, she penned her now famous petition to her husband to "Remember the Ladies" in the new code of laws to be written for the new nation, in which she advocated legal protections for married women (heretofore, nonentities before the law, under coverture). Never happier than when reading and writing about politics, Adams fully expected her daughter also to share that passion. "You cannot be a descendant from the spirit of '76 to be totally indifferent to what is passing," she exclaimed.[115] In their writings, these New England women proved the fallacy of the popular wisdom of female intellectual incapacities by achieving that which was allegedly impossible for females.

Judith Sargent Murray's *Gleaner* was one of the most explicit American statements on the intellectual equality of men and women; she was also insistent that women's education prepare them to be economically self-sufficient. Indeed, these two points were intimately related. An educated woman could not be divested of her intellectual property, Murray knew, even if financial adversity deprived her of material goods. "THE SEX should be taught to depend on their own efforts, for the procurement of an establishment in life," she argued, looking forward to the day when the term "*helpless widow* might be rendered as unfrequent and inapplicable as that of *helpless widower*." Endowed, like men, with the capacity to reason, well-educated women could make themselves useful to their society and their families, superseding the dependence that normally marked their sex. Like England's Mary Wollstonecraft, whose *Vindication of the Rights of Woman* (1792) had made a similar argument, Murray had suffered economic reverses because of her husband's financial incompetence, and both writers determined to help other women avoid the consequences of such cultivated female helplessness. Though their stories differed in the details, they agreed on the main themes: the narrow vocational choices open to women, the humiliation of financial difficulties about which women remained ignorant until too late, and the perpetuation of female helplessness.[116]

In Philadelphia's Quaker culture, the trope of female dependence was rejected explicitly in female praises to the single life. Even before the Revolution, Philadelphia women produced commentaries, poetry, and essays on life, gender relations, and marriage, frequently praising the single life and circulating manuscripts on the subject among one another and their female students in Quaker-run schools. In her commonplace book, Milcah Martha Moore preserved the lively verse of her friend Hannah Griffitts: "I've neither Reserve or aversion to Man, / (I assure you Sophronia in jingle) / But to keep my dear Liberty, as long as I can, / Is the reason I choose to live single. . . . The Men, (as a Friend) I prefer, I esteem, / And love them as well as I ought / But to fix all my Happiness, solely in Him / Was never my Wish or my Thought."[117] Griffitts's sentiments would have met with empathy and approval from her friend Susanna Wright and aunt Elizabeth Norris, both unmarried themselves. Indeed, wealthy and well-connected Norris kept her family estate of Fairhill as a kind of retreat home for single women (three of her spinster cousins accepted her invitation to live with her there) and for hosting traveling Quaker women preachers.[118]

Highly unorthodox in the embrace of female participation in church government, teaching, and preaching, these Quaker practices derived from their belief in an "Inner Light," the presence of the Divine in every human being, a theology that ultimately demolished notions of natural hierarchy. Frequently excoriated for these eccentricities that ran counter to prevailing gender conventions, Quakers might not seem to offer the most persuasive comparison with southern mores.[119] But the creation in Philadelphia of a female literary culture was not limited to Quakers. One of the most well-known female literary figures of eighteenth-century

Philadelphia was Anglican Elizabeth Graeme Fergusson, whose work also appeared in Martha Milcah Moore's commonplace book. Fergusson stood at the center of a literary salon that attracted men and women of ideas and—deserted by her loyalist husband, whom she never saw after 1779—she also wrote poems in praise of female friendships.[120] In addition, the wider Philadelphia literary scene of newspapers and almanacs also contained numerous critiques of gender inequities in marriage, and while they could be scornful of spinsters, they could also be sympathetic. "The History of Amelia Gray," for example, which appeared in a 1775 issue of the *Pennsylvania Magazine*, complimented Amelia's choice of a purposeful single life devoted to serving the needy over an empty marriage to a man attracted only by her fortune. This story even noted the benefits of the leisure afforded by single life: time to "range in the flowery fields of literature, and to contemplate the wondrous works of the celestial architect."[121] Like Quaker Elizabeth Norris, the fictional Amelia Gray would command herself, body, mind, and soul.

There is even evidence of some resistance in the southern colonies, as in the verses of "The Lady's Complaint," published in 1736 in the *Virginia Gazette* and in 1743 in the *South Carolina Gazette*. Protesting the double standard, in which "They [men] freely can their Thoughts disclose, / Whilst ours must burn within; / We have got Tongues and Eyes in Vain, / And Truth from us is Sin," the writer concluded, "Then Equal Laws let Custom find, / And neither Sex oppress; / More Freedom give to Womankind, / Or give to Mankind less."[122] More commonly, however, southern women acquiesced to notions of female inferiority, not surprising perhaps when we consider the quick reply of a South Carolina gentleman who attributed the female writer's indignation to the lack of a "simply homely Swain, [who would] ease you of some Anguish."[123] But in the years after the Revolution (an experience that for many women had contradicted conventional truths about male protection and female ineptness), they would struggle with the same questions their English ancestors had about the female intellect, although in an entirely different setting. Englishwomen certainly faced stalwart resistance to their efforts for education, publication, and political participation, yet they wrote, published, and participated in a developing salon culture as the rapid urbanization of eighteenth-century Britain allowed them to expand the boundaries of female respectability.[124] Southern women had no such context as they grappled with the same contradictions that Englishwomen had a century earlier. Largely unfamiliar with Mary Astell's *Serious Proposal* or Bathusa Makin's *An Essay to Revive the Antient Education of Gentlewomen in Religion, Manners, Arts and Tongues*

(1673), they struggled to reconcile the lessons of the literature with those of their experience.[125]

INVENTING FEMININITY IN THE SOUTH

This book argues that the significance of southern women's writings by the latter half of the eighteenth century—that is, their letters and their first attempts to compose manuals of advice—must be understood in this context. Surrounded on all sides and in every way (physically, legally, and economically) by a form of patriarchy that depended for its survival on keeping the distinctions between male and female, black and white, uniformly rigid, and unaware of the ways in which Englishwomen had attempted to deal with these questions one hundred years earlier, southern women had to invent for themselves a new notion of femininity in a setting far more restrictive than existed in Britain or New England and the mid-Atlantic.[126] Three key elements were instrumental in this project of reinvention: the novel, evangelical religious revivalism, and the Revolutionary separation of church and state.

The Novel

None of the women in this book would have labeled themselves nonconformists; all were concerned deeply with their reputations and respectability. Yet many not only ignored the vociferous condemnations against reading novels but understood their books to be another form of advice in which they found the authority to refashion what they read into a new model of respectable, Christian, southern femininity. Southern women's reading had become more varied, over the century, as they, too, tapped into English literary culture. Women read the *Spectator* and the *Tatler,* both bastions of polite bourgeois conversation in the male culture of London's coffeehouses.[127] English writer Eliza Haywood even named her short-lived periodical *The Female Spectator,* banking on its namesake's popularity with women. In Virginia, the "Monitor" was the *Virginia Gazette's* attempt to emulate the writers of the *Spectator,* and, as we have seen, many short pieces in colonial newspapers can be traced to their English journal origins.[128]

But probably the most significant change in southern reading patterns was the increase in recreational reading prompted by the publication of Samuel Richardson's novel *Pamela* in 1740. Together with the novels of Henry Fielding, Tobias Smollett, and Laurence Sterne, "as well as the deluge of imitations," Richard Beale Davis observed, "the matter and degree of recreational reading changed markedly, and in no place more than in the later eighteenth-century South."[129] The account books from the *Virginia Gazette*'s bookshop certainly reflect this interest. Regardless of the newspaper commentaries, including the *Gazette*'s, that severely censured novel readers (more severely in America than in England), the *Gazette* print shop in Williamsburg continued to advertise novels, and the adjoining bookstore sold them, eager to tap into the profits they promised.[130] Even dissenting minister Samuel Davies recorded reading *The Memoirs of the Fortunate (Country) Maid, a Romance* in 1753, although he chastised his congregation for reading romances rather than the Bible.[131]

The novels' chief appeal to female readers was that they featured women at the center of the plotlines. *Pamela* is the story of a servant girl who, resisting the many attempts of her master to seduce her, wins his admiration and love and becomes his wife. In her story, women learned that rather than relying on men to protect their virtue, they must rely on themselves. Against the thrilling plotlines of deceit and seduction, traditional advice literature such as Fordyce or Allestree rather paled in comparison. Moreover, the novels implicitly questioned the legitimacy of a patriarchal order that insisted on the subordination of women to the physical, intellectual, and spiritual superiority of men, who clearly did not live up to the obligations of their rank. As novels illuminated the contradictions within patriarchy, traditional advice lost some of its power to persuade women of their obligation to be submissive to men's higher authority.

Even more significant than the novels' critique of patriarchy was the way they allowed women to imagine themselves as heroines. In American Hannah Foster's *The Coquette* (1797), for example, women readers recognized themselves, talking to one another, confiding, and advising, in a narrative that put women at the forefront.[132] Furthermore, the focus after the American Revolution on women's increasing literacy allowed them access to a "republic of letters" in which readers, for the first time, were aware of being part of a national public readership. They read themselves into public conversations about politeness and virtue that "potentially limitless others" were also reading.[133] Reading Foster's *Coquette* for example, in which the villain was a model of politeness but hardly virtuous, women joined a national dialogue about the importance of individual virtue for the public good. It was a long way from the private, fatherly direction of seventeenth-century English advice manuals. As we shall see, southern women read novels, ordering them from their English contacts, borrowing them from friends, or stealing surreptitiously into a father's library to sample the forbidden fruit.

Evangelical Revivalism

Evangelical religion also provided a way for women to resist notions of their inferiority. Indeed, it is perhaps here that women were most successful both in their resistance and in their creation of something new, as they played upon ideas about female piety and feeling to usurp moral authority in their homes. In the insistence of evangelical preachers (first the Baptists, then the Methodists) on the development of an individual relationship with God, cemented by an abject remorse for sin and the ecstatic realization of grace, women discovered a new locus of authority: feeling. Unlike Anglican preachers, who were expected to have a university education and ecclesiastical ordination, evangelical Christians required only the experience of conversion and grace. In the inward journey to cultivate their relationship with God, women discovered selfhood, distinguished for the first time from the person whose function remained subordinated to the needs of her family. Hannah Lee Corbin was able to resist the considerable exertions of her family (the eminent Lees of Virginia) to repent of her conversion to the Baptist fold (her brother, Richard Henry Lee, sat on the local county court that cited her for nonattendance at the Anglican Church in 1764).[134] Her evangelicalism may even have spawned an incipient feminism by demanding of her brother that women property holders be eligible to vote for the property assessors who would determine their tax liability.[135] Even staunch Anglican Elizabeth Foote Washington, who wanted no truck with "Baptistical notions," profited from the evangelical emphasis on individual authority.[136] She assumed the responsibility of her slaves' religious instruction decades before the antebellum period in which historians have more commonly located this development.

Disestablishment of the Church

In the post-Revolutionary era, the disestablishment of the Anglican Church (reorganized as the Protestant Episcopal Church of America in 1789) had profound consequences for southern women. Formerly a bastion of male authority and power as an arm of the state in the colonial period, the Church occupied a new kind of ground between public (increasingly defined as the masculine polity) and private (increasingly defined as the feminine domestic). Although no longer a part of the polity, the Church nonetheless remained a public, nondomestic space. Into this structure, now private (that is, nongovernmental) yet still an institution, women began to pour their time, resources, and considerable

energy, filling the vacuum left by men for whom the Church had out-
lived its secular usefulness. From Virginia to the Carolinas, women
propped up sagging Episcopal churches, funding restorations of build-
ings, hiring pastors, and faithfully attending services. Bolstered in many
cases by this empowering experience, southern women ventured further
still, into the streets, gathering orphans and penniless women on whom
to shower their benevolence, and even into state legislatures, incorporating their charitable associations to force state recognition and protection of their efforts.

From our vantage point in the twenty-first century, these changes may
not seem consequential. But the scope of this transformation should not
be downplayed, for in spite of the changes in women's experiences, there
had also been a great deal of continuity, even through the Revolutionary
era. Conduct literature had continued to form the corpus of women's educational literature in the eighteenth and early nineteenth centuries, re-
inforcing traditional gender conventions. And even after the Revolution,
education for men and women retained its gendered purposes; that is,
men were groomed for assuming public and civic responsibilities while
women were prepared to be mistresses of their households and good social companions. But on the eve of the Revolution, southern women were
already better educated than any generation that had gone before,[137] and
their increasing literacy after the war fostered an evolving sense of com-
petency as they read and reconciled the varieties of advice with their own
experience. The letters and journals of the women in this book show that
they derived a sense of their own authority from religion earlier than has
been documented previously, and that the increasing popularity of sentimental fiction was a crucial component of that development. The convergence of themes in novels and devotional literature that identified sensibility of feeling with women, and religion with emotion, gave southern
women the ideological foundation from which to alter conventional notions of femininity. Their writings and religious and charitable work,
then, were the tangible outgrowth and expression of their thought.

Just as religion, virtue, and respectability were bound together in a way
that could not be disentangled in the literature, so, too, were they en-
twined in daily living. Martha Laurens Ramsay of South Carolina had used
religious rhetoric as she sought to combat a depression brought on by her
helplessness at her husband's indebtedness.[138] Other women turned notions of female piety to their advantage in different ways. For example,
Elizabeth Foote Washington took this understanding as her moral authority to write an advice manual to teach her daughter, even in absentia
in the event of her death. By the end of the century, educated southern

women thus created their own form of feminine respectability, culled selectively from the advice they read and refined by their experience.

READING AND WRITING IN A SLAVE SOCIETY

A final consideration in my study of women's intellectual activity in the South is the context in which they read and wrote: a largely agricultural, slave society. Even though slaveholding families were the minority in the South (only 25 percent as late as 1860), the ways in which the southern legal, economic, political, and social systems developed bear witness to the enormous weight of their cultural authority. Indeed, this is a crucial consideration with which anyone studying the South must contend. In *Rethinking the South,* historian Michael O'Brien listed the arguments made by previous historians who have attributed the lack of a vibrant intellectual life in the South to that cultural authority, offering a rebuttal against each. To those who cited the isolation of planter life as a deterrent to the development of ideas, he replied that planter life was irrelevant, since most antebellum southern writers were city dwellers. To those who characterized the southern mind as obsessed with slavery, he pointed out that slavery was not the only subject about which southerners wrote. To the argument that slavery suppressed freedom of thought, O'Brien observed that a regional consensus about slavery did not preclude disagreements about other issues.[139]

But O'Brien's apologia for a thriving antebellum intellectual life in the South assumed male writers; his responses to the old historiography, then, demand further elaboration when we think about the writing lives of women. In fact, white southern women *were* isolated on far-flung plantations—as late as 1840 only 6 percent of Virginia women lived in cities—and lacked the mobility men enjoyed.[140] Although their movements varied depending on their trade, men traveled from their homes to represent their families in business and legal and political matters. A carpenter was more likely to travel to different homes for work; a small planter was more closely bound to his land, while a prominent planter had the widest range with frequent trips to courthouse, tobacco warehouses, and other planter homes.[141] By contrast, in the colonial period, women typically did not range farther than a five-mile radius from their homes, bound as they were by the demands of nursing infants and small children. Some scholars have even argued that women's mobility diminished after the Revolution as their writing literacy increased and they could rely on letters to maintain their bonds of friendship.[142] Plaintive ob-

servations on loneliness and the tedium of plantation life are common
themes in southern women's letters, and the writers took palpable comfort from imagining the presence of their correspondents as they wrote.

O'Brien is correct that an obsession with slavery did not block out considerations of other topics of conversation. Indeed, what I have found so
remarkable is the almost total silence on that subject in southern
women's writings in this period.[143] Nonetheless, it is clear that slavery, or
more precisely, living in a slave society, circumscribed white women's
reading, thinking, and writing in significant ways. Mindful of the hierarchy that separated master from slave and white woman from black, elite
southern women understood the advice literature differently. Gender
and racial hierarchies were mutually supportive: the "natural" subordination of wife to husband was often cited as the proof of the naturalness of
other hierarchies, particularly racial. To question gender categories,
then, threatened the racial categories on which southern society had
based its economy, polity, and society and, by extension, threatened the
limited privileges afforded white women in that societal structure. The
consequences could be more direct and emphatic, however, for a woman
who, contesting those categories by her outspokenness or desire for learning, deprived herself of the protection of white men. In a culture that developed a finely honed code of honor, white women exposed themselves
to ridicule, ostracism, and even sexual assault when they refused the protection of men. The ready sexual availability presumed of black women
could just as easily be applied to an unescorted white woman.[144] This
code, whose ostensible purpose was to protect the virtue of white women
against the assaults of black men, thus operated to control independent
expressions of female thought (verbal and written) in a far more insidious
way than it did men's.

In paying particular attention to this problem of intellectual development in a society built on oppression, this book spotlights the overlay of
race and slavery on white women's reading and writing. For them, freedom of expression was not only about content, as it may have been for
men, but about something far deeper: their position in a hierarchical
order designed by God and nature. In this order, in which obedience to
authority was a paramount value, southern women would take much
longer to claim their authority by taking up the pen; to do so was, as Amy
L. Wink remarked of nineteenth-century women writers, to "prove their
own intellectual power in the face of potentially overwhelming external
experiences."[145]

Yet I have found that by the end of the eighteenth century, that is precisely what they did, as they began to compose their advices for their pos-

terity. Drawing on the changes of the latter part of the century, they refined the advice they had read, bringing it into a closer alignment with
their own experiences. The model of womanhood they created, however,
reflected the limits imposed by their colonization. Profoundly influenced
by the context of the slave society in which they lived, they could not challenge the conventions of natural hierarchy, especially since southern configurations of race elevated their own status. The claims southern women
made for their education, then, were not calls for economic autonomy, as
they were for Mary Wollstonecraft and Judith Sargent Murray, but rather
for moral authority, based on a different idea of female usefulness and industry. In their configuration of what it meant to be female, we can see the
emergence of a model with a distinctive southern cast, the construction of
which was significant to the evolution of southern regional identity.

The letters of Ellen Wayles Randolph Coolidge, granddaughter of
Thomas Jefferson, reveal this paradigm of the intellectual world of early
southern women, showing both the influence of the slave society in which
she had been reared and her clear recognition of its regionalism by the
mid-1820s. Raised at Monticello, she was educated by her mother, Martha
Jefferson Randolph. A willing and able student, Ellen read avidly, dutifully taking "notes & extracts [which had] been the employment of years."
When she moved to Boston in 1825 to marry Joseph Coolidge, she dis-
dainfully noted her in-laws' preference for another daughter-in-law, noting that "the daughter of an orthodox and federal family, who is believed
to have received a *useful education* is really more welcome than a *blue-stock-
ing Unitarian democrat* could possibly be."[146] Already North and South
seemed to define female usefulness in different ways. Martha Jefferson
Randolph had educated her daughter to be industrious in her intellectual
pursuits, following the example of her mother and grandfather, who were
"always busy . . . reading or writing . . . always doing something."[147] Ellen
was proud that she was a "bluestocking," a female intellectual, and less
concerned about the lack of a "useful" education designed to prepare her
for domestic tasks.[148]

In the South, of course, the association of industry with intellectual pursuits rather than manual labor was a clear marker of both whiteness and
gentility. At Monticello, education was meant to prepare Ellen to use time
in an efficient, orderly, and rational way—qualities to which, the daughters and granddaughters of the author of *Notes on the State of Virginia* knew,
enslaved blacks could never aspire. So girls learned to understand their
whiteness as a marker of authority, even while maintaining the conventions of gender. The regionalism of this perspective of female education,
industry, and identity is abundantly clear in the letters Ellen wrote back to

Monticello from her new home in Boston. Commenting on her sister's plan to make do with a skeletal staff of slaves, Ellen warned, "You will be obliged dear Virginia, to adopt Yankee habits if you follow Yankee fashions." In Boston, Ellen explained, "the [servant] women should never be called from their regular business to do a second time in the day what they have already done. . . . The young ladies of the family if they put a thing out of place take care to set it back again." Unlike southern girls, northern ones "take care to require from the servants no running about from place to place and leave no clothes tossed about no drawer open, combs, pins, curls, ribbons, trinkets here and there on the dressing table, shoes in the middle of the floor, and so forth." Both Ellen and her mother feared that Virginia's plans "str[o]ve to unite two incompatible things, the domestic economy of the north, with the habits and manners of the south." Genteel, white, female industry meant reading, writing, drawing, or music, but most emphatically not manual labor, since, as Ellen believed, "there are always plenty of people all the better for having something to do, and who are infallibly idle if you do not find them employment."[149]

Ellen Wayles Randolph received her education at her mother's knee, but through the antebellum period, the growing numbers of female academies denote at least a tacit acknowledgment of the legitimacy of southern women's claims to a formal education. Together, elite southern girls learned to read the classics, comment in journals and letters to friends on the novels they had read, and even publish—in quantity—their own novels and advice literature. In their schools, they cultivated networks of female friends, cementing relationships that would survive their dispersal back to their plantation homes and marriage. Supplied by the voluminous letters, diaries, journals, and school composition books generated in those academies, others have written histories about those later years.[150]

My story, however, supplies the prequel: how southern women claimed the pen. Having outlined here a sketch of literacy, literature, and education in the southern colonies, I examine in the next chapter the ways early Virginians sought to establish authority in the New World and the role of religious and devotional advice literature in that project. In spite of rising rates in book imports and female literacy, this literature operated as a powerful instrument for the perpetuation of women's subordinate status. However, religion could also have the opposite effect. Chapter 3 explores the impact of evangelical religion and the post-Revolutionary separation of church and state on women of both established and dissenting religions, and the ways women used religion as a springboard for their claims to an authority previously accorded only to men. Chapter 4 demonstrates the ways women read novels, an entirely new form of advice, interpreting them in new ways to formulate for themselves—and future generations— a new model of femininity. While the distinctiveness of the southern experience is a constant theme throughout the book, chapter 5 presents a case study set in Baltimore (a city that has always defied easy classification as either northern or southern). The contrast with a society with slaves makes clearer the impact of life in a slave society on the intellectual autonomy of women.[151]

Lacking the generous archival legacy that antebellum historians enjoy, I have found other ways to approach my story. Working with collections of family papers in southern archives, I have identified southern reading materials through inventories, wills, account books, receipts, journals, and letters. Court records also yield information about book ownership in wills and inventories. Analyses of bequest patterns point to gendered ideas about reading and education, to different preferences in men's and women's reading, and to the books women treasured and bequeathed to the next generation. Account books and receipts reveal colonial Americans' habit of buying books from their English merchant friends and partners, while the extant copies of the *Virginia Gazette* enabled an exploration of the wider public circulation of ideas of gender, race, and society beyond those that appear in private family papers. Letters written by both men and women illuminate women's attitudes toward their own intellects and abilities, in addition to their behavior in their roles as daughters, wives, and mothers.

Indeed, more than any other sources, their letters and journals show us how women reflected on, accepted, rejected, or refined the lessons of the advice literature. Their wit and wisdom, playfulness and pain, limitations and depth, are evident on every yellowed page, in hands bold or delicate, labored or flowing, written in haste or leisure. Their writings have let me see something of their humanity, from the nobler aspects of their intelligence and compassion to the darker side of their racism and elitism. As we recall Amy L. Wink's reminder about the "potentially overwhelming external experiences" that shaped them, let us attempt to meet these women on their own ground. Imagine a world in which an omnipotent (and male) God has placed men above women, white over black, free over enslaved; and then let us ponder how a white southern woman could possibly consider taking up the power of the pen to transform it.

"The Truest Kind of Breeding"

Prescriptive Literature in the Early South

In 1770, Mary Ambler traveled to Baltimore from Fauquier County, Virginia, with her two children to be inoculated against smallpox. She recorded her experiences in a diary, together with as complete a list of her expenses as she could recall. Then, as if her attention was suddenly diverted, she finished with words she hoped would guide the days of her daughter's life that lay ahead. "From Mr Fordyce's Sermons to Young Women," she inscribed the passage, "this Paragraph is transcribed for the use of the Copi[e]st & She begs her Daug[hte]r to observe it well all her Life."

> If to Your natural softness You join that christian meekness, which I now preach; both together will not fail, with the assistance of proper reflection and friendly advice, to accomplish you in the best and truest kind of breeding. You will not be in danger of putting your-selves forward in company, of contradicting bluntly, of asserting positively, of debating obstinately, of affecting a superiority to any present . . . or of neglecting what is advanced by others, or of interrupting them without necessity.[1]

The trip had been a trying one. Unable to persuade her sister (who easily mustered ample arguments against voluntary exposure to the pox) to accompany her, the widowed Mary Ambler had set out alone with her two young children for the three-day journey to Baltimore. Then there had been the several unsuccessful attempts at inoculation: wasted weeks, wait-

34

ing for the telltale fever and pockmarks to emerge; anxious nights, as the mother watched over the high fevers of her children; miserable days, when she herself was sidelined with fevers and purges; and finally home, after almost two months. Yet after such an ordeal, both tedious and harrowing, it was not a pious reflection on the perils of this life and the promises of the next to which Mary Ambler turned. Instead, she was taken by a recipe for good breeding, a formula that appeared to survive, intact, its Atlantic crossing.

Mary Ambler's excerpt from the Reverend James Fordyce's *Sermons to Young Women*, first published in London in 1765, is as apt an example as any of the eighteenth-century Anglo-American recipe of womanhood that drew from natural science, theology, and manners to construct an image of what was properly female.[2] Begin with the softness with which women were endowed by nature, mix it with the Christlike virtue of meekness, and, Fordyce was sure, the "truest kind of breeding" would result. Fordyce was a Presbyterian clergyman from Scotland, yet his *Sermons* resonated with an Anglican mother who lived an ocean away in colonial Virginia. Indeed, as Mary Ambler's journal makes plain, the Atlantic Ocean served more as conduit than obstacle to the flow of ideas about what it meant to be female. Her views of womanhood conformed entirely to the most current statement of genteel English teachings. If she had ever entertained any doubts before, her travels certainly confirmed the importance of appearance and demeanor in opening the right doors to the right circles, where she had been accepted and assisted by the right people. In an age when the word "widow" was invariably preceded by "helpless," Mary Ambler must have felt that her survival of her ordeal had been utterly dependent on her ability to attract the necessary assistance for her family.

By the eve of the Revolution, gentility most certainly mattered—even on the outer margins of the British empire.[3] Mary Ambler's record of Fordyce's wisdom is but one indicator of the success of the project to Anglicize the southern colonies, for it shows her acceptance of structures of authority that had acquired normative status there, in which the place of women was a crucial component. Fordyce's words took on a double authority, coming as they did from a clergyman and confirmed by her own experiences. Ambler compounded their weight further still when she copied them for her daughter, her maternal approbation obvious in her plea that her daughter "observe [them] well all her Life."[4] Print and literacy, therefore, were important tools in the Anglicization of America. In Mary Ambler's notation we see the reach of British culture to the colonial South, female reading and writing literacy, the spread of print, and the dispensation of advice from southern mothers to their daughters. But as much change as these developments might portend for women, they could also work to entrench even more deeply the old gender order. And indeed, in Mary Ambler's journal we can see the clear impress of the colonizer in her views on female education, an ocean away from its source.

COLONIAL CONTEXT: SETTLEMENT, RELIGION, AND AUTHORITY

While the hegemony of the colonizer (male master) never went undisputed in the colonial period, the social stability achieved by the mid-eighteenth century signaled a resolution of the problem of authority that had characterized the early days of settlement in Virginia. In seventeenth- and eighteenth-century England, an overlay of institutional authority reflected centuries of accepted wisdom about natural hierarchies and the respective places of men and women in society. From monarch and Parliament to the local justices of the peace, from a national network of bishops to the local vicar, from paternal government to marital, English men understood their place in political and social structures, while women were governed at every turn by men whose institutions had garnered strength and legitimacy from their very longevity. A very different prospect, however, awaited women in Virginia, the first permanent English settlement in the New World. Efforts to re-create on new ground the institutions of the old, with all the authority and deference that was their due, were complicated enormously by the conditions of life in the Chesapeake region in those early years.

The stories of the first two women who arrived in 1609 are typical of those of many immigrants to Virginia. Mistress Anne Burras, who had traveled to join her husband, died almost immediately; her maid, freed from servitude, married quickly thereafter. Indeed, the first fifty years of settlement in the Chesapeake were characterized by disease and death and by a skewed sex ratio (six men to one woman in 1630, for example), a combination that was a formula for social dislocation. One historian has estimated that while approximately 155,000 English men and women migrated to the Chesapeake between 1635 and 1680, the population of the region in 1680 did not exceed 55,800. Overcome by malaria and dysentery, and weakened in the heat and humidity of Virginia summers, settlers succumbed by the hundreds during the "dying time," between May and October.[5]

Under such conditions, authority and leadership—which in England were predicated on a combination of rank, land ownership, and age—perched precariously in Virginia on the shoulders of those who managed to survive the longest and to accumulate the most land and servants (by fair means or foul) to work it.[6] Discovering that the road to riches in Virginia lay in tobacco leaf, wealthier settlers invested in the acreage required by that crop, whose voracious appetite stripped the land of nutrients, forcing frequent field rotation. And since land without workers was useless, they also invested heavily in labor. As many as 75 percent of the immigrants in those early years were men who arrived as indentured servants, bound to a master for a term of five to seven years (if they survived that long) before being freed to strike out to make their own fortunes.[7] This pattern of migration, dictated by the requirements of the colony's staple crop, had eased somewhat by the turn of the eighteenth century, as Virginia's planters, frightened by the rebellion in 1676 of so many freed servants, made the gradual commitment to enslaved labor instead.[8] Not until the first quarter of the eighteenth century would the colony's demographic oddities of an unbalanced sex ratio and early death be overcome,[9] although the overall pattern of an agricultural society and slavery would characterize Virginia and the Carolinas until the Civil War.

These developments had a profound effect on women's lives. Though the skewed sex ratio assured women of husbands and may have even enabled social mobility as competing offers presented a choice of suitors, the appalling mortality rates of the first seventy-five years wreaked havoc on the stability of family life.[10] Early deaths led to an array of blended families: "now-wives" caring for stepchildren, stepfathers supporting children related to them by marriage rather than blood, children who survived a series of parental and stepparent deaths that left them in a household headed by an adult to whom they had no blood ties.[11] In such precarious circumstances, many Chesapeake fathers sought to ameliorate the economic impact of their deaths on their children by devising their estates to their widows, giving them full legal control over land and, in many instances, legal guardianship over their children as well. Unusual in the English common law experience, in which estates generally settled on a male heir, pausing only to support a widow until her remarriage or death, many Chesapeake widows enjoyed economic independence and even some legal authority. Such deviations from English norms spelled neither a new way of thinking about gender and authority nor a freedom distinctive to the American experience, but rather were temporary expedients for dealing with a demographic crisis.

That this was true is clear in the ways the picture changes in the eighteenth century. As settlers became increasingly "seasoned" to their tidewater environment and lived longer, they were able to accumulate greater wealth, shore up family and kin networks, and consolidate power in a cohort of emerging gentry families, governed by powerful planters.[12] The principle of natural hierarchies found renewed life in this stabilized society; indeed, it was its strongest prop. Probably the most powerful social cement in the eighteenth century was the elaboration of race, designating black slaves as a permanent underclass over which all whites governed. Virginia's overhaul of its slave code in 1705 (largely patterned after South Carolina's code of 1696) legalized this social formulation of black inferiority that elevated the status even of poor white men and all white women.[13] Over the drama of court days, the excitement of militia musters, and the choreography of Sunday morning church services, the gentry presided, explicitly demonstrating their authority even as they courted the deference of poorer Virginians, wooing them with implicit assurances of their common interests as whites.[14] The development of slavery and racism, then, was one key solution to the problem of authority in the seventeenth-century South.

The developing influence of the Anglican Church was a second solution; its story mirrored that of this emerging society. Although it was the established church in all the southern colonies, it, too, was weak in the early years, suffering from the tenuous nature of authority in the Chesapeake's demographic disaster. Clergy were in short supply and would remain so for the entire colonial period, since there was no bishop in America to ordain Anglican priests on site. Consequently, all candidates for ordination were forced to sail to England for their studies and to take orders there. The southern colonies' geography also limited the church's initial influence. Living on widely scattered farms, colonial Virginians found the distances required to travel to church discouraging. As one minister complained, "divers of the more remote Families being discouraged, by the length or tediousness of the way, through extremities of heat in Summer, frost and Snow in Winter, and tempestuous weather in both, do very seldom repair thither."[15] Other southern colonies fared little better. As late as 1765 in North Carolina, there were only six priests to serve the colony's population of one hundred thousand. One historian's description of the church in South Carolina as "merely the low country planter aristocracy at prayer" suggests the paucity of clergy in that colony as well.[16]

By the eighteenth century, the Church had adapted to its colonial environment. In Virginia, for example, colonists created a system of "multi-congregational parishes," in which several chapels served a single parish.[17] Some planters, such as William Byrd II at Westover, built chapels on their plantations.[18] The result was a church that had a stronger lay government than its English parent, which boasted a stronger ecclesiastical establishment. Each parish vestry, comprised of leading gentlemen in the parish, oversaw such parish business matters as church construction and maintenance, clergy hires and salaries, discipline of members, placement of orphans, and assistance to the needy.[19]

How effective a church it was in its colonial configuration has been a matter of debate. Fairly or not, many historians have followed the earliest assessments of John Winthrop, Puritan founding father of the Massachusetts Bay colony, that the infant colony of Virginia was "given up of God to extreme pride and sensuality, being usually drunken, as the custom is there."[20] Others have portrayed the Anglican Church of the southern colonies as an institutional prop of grasping gentry authority, its clergy subservient to the hiring whims of lay vestries, its liturgy dry and devoid of soul, and its Sunday services offering more social than spiritual sustenance to its attendees.[21] More recently, however, historians have stressed the high quality and longevity of colonial clergy, the beauties and significance of the church's *Book of Common Prayer* from which services were read each Sunday, and the religious vitality of a church whose attendance records must include the many outlying chapels in addition to the larger churches.[22] Indeed, the eighteenth century was a period of sustained growth for all colonial churches, including the Anglican Church, which founded more than one hundred new congregations in the South between 1750 and 1776.[23] This fact alone indicates that as a governing institution that regulated community behavior and oversaw matters of social welfare, the Church fulfilled a necessary function in the organization of southern life.

There are significant indicators that it provided a necessary spiritual function, as well, in the ways southern colonists practiced their religion in their churches and even daily in their homes. Attempting to assess religious commitment is always tricky, and counting the numbers of church members or baptized or communicants is a reassuringly concrete way to try to plumb the depths of souls.[24] But such quantitative methods do not take into account the nature of faith and belief, private as well as public devotions, or the reconciliation of theology, worldview, and practice. Anglicanism of the seventeenth and eighteenth centuries was a religion that eschewed the passions that had resulted in the convulsions of religious wars of previous centuries; talk of hellfire and damnation seemed out of place in an enlightened age. Rather, Anglicanism was an orderly religion, expressive, in one historian's words, of a "low-key, but deeply felt piety."[25] Not for Anglicans was the agonizing descent into despair or the exultant realization of God's saving grace (crucial steps in the Puritan conversion process) or the "prying into adorable Mysteries" of Catholic theologians.[26]

Instead, Anglicans concentrated on living the moral life, each individual responsible for performing his or her duty to God and to others, believing that a strict adherence to dogma that lacked a care for human need was an empty religion indeed. As William Byrd saw it, "religion is the Duty which every Reasonable Creature owes to God, the Creator and Supream [*sic*] Governor of the World."[27]

Virginians and Carolinians received their instruction in their duty at Divine Service, the literal high point of which was the sermon, its importance underscored by its delivery from a pulpit positioned high above the congregation's heads. Not many Anglican sermons remain from this period, but those that do emphasized a universal order, compliance with which ensured harmony on earth.[28] Central to that order was obedience to those God had placed in positions of authority—king, cleric, master, father, and husband—and so Anglican preachers had a particular message for women. Believing the daughters of Eve still had the power to upset that order, Virginia-born Anglican minister Devereux Jarratt wove his understanding of the Fall (the expulsion of Adam and Eve from Eden) into his sermons. From the pulpit, he chastised "every female art of dress and frippery, ornament and beauty, that could tend to captivate, and insnare the incautious beholder," seducing men away from God.[29] Like Fordyce, he blamed women for their attention to such superficialities, even as he admitted that "their education consists a great deal in the art of dressing." And after she has prepared herself in a manner calculated to please men, "what presents itself to our view," Jarratt asked, "but an *empty trifle*—glaring without, but within void of all solid worth, and destitute of piety—the love of God, and the ornaments of a meek and humble spirit."[30] From such explication of the Scriptures, southern women learned the dangers of attention to superficial matters and the threat they posed to the spiritual and moral welfare of men if they did not cultivate piety and humility.

Sermons were an important way to inculcate the tenets of Anglicanism for both the illiterate and the lettered. Certainly weekly sermons provided an important education in faith and morals for people who could not read, but they were also significant for the highly educated. William Byrd's periodic attendance (every other week) at his chapel's Sunday services can be explained by the clergyman's absence: no minister, no sermon. On off Sundays, he stayed home instead and read seventeenth-century archbishop John Tillotson's published sermons.[31] Sermons were significant to women as well, and some preserved memorable teachings in notes and journals. Martha Laurens Ramsay, raised an Anglican in South Carolina, was, in her husband's words, "a constant and devout attendant on divine service; [she] steadily recorded the text, and occasionally made a short analysis of the sermon."[32] Frances Baylor Hill of King and Queen County, Virginia, recorded reading sermons and "a great many chapters in the bible" in her 1797 diary, and on several occasions, commented favorably on the sermons she had heard.[33] Edmund Randolph described his wife Betsey's devout Anglicanism in terms of her "unremit[ting]" attendance at church and at the sacrament [Communion]." Her private worship matched her public in regularity as she addressed her prayers to the "throne of mercy" and placed unquestioning trust in the "sacred truths."[34] In 1788, Joseph Eggleston urged his daughter Jane to attend Mr. Craig's service of the "blessed Sacrament of the lords Supper," saying that her mother "Before Marriage always receiv'd it, and never Mis'd, when She had an Oppertunity afterwards." Even the demands of motherhood were not to keep Jane from keeping "the positive Commands of our holy religion," to keep the Sabbath holy.[35] In their attentiveness to a discipline of devotional reading and church attendance, southern women heard constant reminders of what Holy Writ had to say about the nature of woman and her function on earth.

DEVOTIONAL LITERATURE

The practice of religion was not limited to attendance at a public service each Sunday. Though the laws of the colonies required at least bimonthly attendance, and the weekly repetition of the familiar words of the Book of Common Prayer enabled even illiterate worshipers to participate in the rites, Sunday services were not the complete expression of an Anglican's religious devotion.[36] Perhaps as a result of the difficulties they experienced in the lean years of seventeenth-century settlement, Virginians had learned to nurture their religious lives outside the institutional structures of the church. Vestrymen led the service of Morning Prayer in the absence of clergy; both men and women noted their private devotional readings, especially if they did not make it to church for Sunday worship. In the 1760s, Devereux Jarrett discovered both his faith and his vocation for the ministry outside the formal structures of the church.[37] In fact, it is when we look outside those structures into their private devotions that we can see how colonial Virginians reinforced for themselves the precepts of order taught from the pulpits.

Books were key to devotional lives outside church. While historian Edward Bond has observed that "books became substitutes for ministers who could not properly serve their parishes," it is clear that the colonists' reliance on religious texts was not limited to Sundays.[38] From the seventeenth century, inventories reveal that about one-third of Chesapeake settlers owned books. These were not great libraries but treasured Bibles they had brought from home and perhaps one or two other religious books.[39] And while seventeenth-century libraries contained twice as many religious titles as libraries of the eighteenth century, the Bible continued to be the one book everyone owned throughout the colonial period. Indeed, there were frequently more than one, even in small libraries.[40]

Related to the Bible were the many devotional works and commentaries that gave Virginians assistance in the practical application of the Bible's lessons to their lives. What is so striking about these supplementary books is both their popularity and the breadth of Virginian tastes. Puritans John Milton and Richard Baxter and Presbyterian James Fordyce were well represented in addition to Archbishop John Tillotson, Richard Allestree, and Lewis Bailey, Anglican writers one might expect to find in Virginia. Even writers from the Roman Catholic tradition, such as St. Augustine, Thomas à Kempis, and Erasmus, appear in these libraries. *The Adventures of Telemachus*, a work by French Catholic François Fénelon, was ubiquitous.[41] Next to the Bible, these religious commentaries were the "most popular books in all Colonial Virginia."[42] The presence of these books and the ways in which colonists in the South treasured them make several significant points: religion was important to them; beyond the requirements of Sunday church attendance, Virginians sought ways to broaden their understanding of the lessons of the Bible; and they did not feel themselves bound by a particular religious discipline but rather cast their devotional nets broadly, choosing those texts that suited them best and crafting their own disciplines. In short, through their books, we can perceive an active intellectual engagement in their pursuit of religion and its application in ordering the daily lives and relationships of men and women.

By far the most popularly represented of these devotional works was Richard Allestree's *The Whole Duty of Man*, a mix of prayers, moral lessons, and practical advice in daily living. This was followed by Lord Halifax's *The Lady's New Year's Gift*. *The Whole Duty of Man* was found in bookshops and private libraries throughout the thirteen colonies.[43] William Byrd's copy was bound proudly in "black morocco, gilt and blind tooled."[44] Daniel Parke Custis (whose wife later became Martha Washington) owned four books by Allestree.[45] Prominent Maryland planter Daniel Dulany the Younger (1722–97) displayed his family's copy (along with Allestree's *The Lady's Calling in Two Parts*) in his dining room.[46] Even in the North Carolina backcountry, a region far removed from the more accessible coast, it was standard fare that successfully staved off challenges in the mid-eighteenth century from an exciting new genre, the novel.[47] In his will, John Yeates of Nansemond County, Virginia, arranged for his executors to buy books, including *The Whole Duty of Man,* for "the poorer sorts of inhabitants."[48] Printer William Parks of Williamsburg, who usually restricted himself to the guaranteed profits of government-commissioned work, even printed it in 1746.[49] Printer Elizabeth Timothy advertised it for sale in the *South Carolina Gazette* in 1739.[50] Despite its mid-seventeenth-century provenance, then, it remained as popular throughout the eighteenth century in Virginia as the frequent publications indicate it was in England.[51]

Women, too, had access to all types of devotional literature and read deeply in it. John Carter II bequeathed his copy of *The Whole Duty of Man* to his fifth wife in 1690.[52] George Hickes recommended it in his *Instructions for the Education of a Daughter,* published in 1707.[53] In 1716, *The Whole Duty of Man* was among the titles bequeathed by Virginian Mary Degge to her nieces, in addition to *The Ladies Calling* and Halifax's *The Lady's New Year's Gift.*[54] (All three works enjoyed great longevity; they were still being advertised for sale in Williamsburg, Virginia's colonial capital, in 1775.)[55] Catherine Dulany Belt of Maryland cherished a copy of the deathbed letter her grandfather wrote to her mother, in which he "earnestly recommend[ed] . . . the strict observance of your duty to God, yourself and your neighbours the particular of which you will find laid down in the "Whole Duty of Man," and the other writings of that pious and learned Author whose works I have in one volume, and do this day freely and absolutely give to you."[56] In 1745 Edward Moseley of New Hanover County, North Carolina commanded the executors of his will to buy for his daughter, Ann Humphries, "the work of the Auther of the whole Duty of Man." He also bequeathed to his widow, "3 volumes in folio of Archbishop Tillotsons Works, [and] four volumes in Octavo of Dr. Stanhopes on the Epistles & Gospels."[57] North Carolinian James Milner owned an extensive library in which he also provided his female family members with books specifically addressed to women, including *Memoirs of Several Ladies, Letters to Married Women, Lady Mary's Letters, The Lady's Magazine,* and two copies of *Fordyce's Sermons.*[58] William Byrd owned *The Whole Duty of Man* and *Lady's New Year's Gift* and had his wife, Lucy, read aloud to him from Tillotson's sermons.[59] In 1763 teenaged Maria Carter copied some of Tillotson's advice that was later gathered into a commonplace book, a collection of sayings she culled from her readings of English writers from Puritan poet John Milton to Alexander Pope.[60] At mid-century, Hannah Lee Corbin, sister of Richard Henry Lee, copied in her own hand an Anglican tract that filled 860 pages in four volumes.[61] Virginian Elizabeth Foote

Washington believed that "there is no real happiness without religion."[62] Late in the century, South Carolinian Martha Laurens Ramsay read *The Whole Duty of Man* very closely, modeling her spiritual life according to its directions.[63]

How can we understand the broad appeal of Allestree's ideas in such different contexts as the colonial South and England? From the first, Allestree intended a wide audience, addressing his book in its title to "the Meanest Reader," and he enjoyed immediate success: between 1660 and 1711 there were probably enough copies printed to supply every tenth family in England.[64] Surely one explanation for the book's success was its nostalgic appeal to a traditional way of life that seemed gone forever. He wrote *The Whole Duty* in answer to the tumult of civil war and the interruption of monarchical rule that had shaken England in the 1640s and 1650s. Seeking to restore the old order, Allestree sought to promote a view of the human condition that, before the war, had been widely held but not fully articulated: the hierarchy implicit in the Great Chain of Being, in which God invests His authority in select persons ordained to govern others while the remainder perform their duty by obeying. Allestree, a Church of England clergyman, would have agreed with political philosopher Sir Robert Filmer, whose *Patriarcha* (1656) argued that since men have been born into families from the beginning of time, the family structure was not a human creation but original to the state of nature. The subordinate status into which all people are born, then, was itself proof to Filmer of the natural model that government must follow. Armed thus with both divine and natural law, Allestree believed that the restoration of the monarchy at the political level and of patriarchal authority at the familial was the surest way to return English life to normal, and sought to cement those notions in his writings.[65]

A key component to the restoration of the old order was women's subordinate place within it. Allestree's *Whole Duty* devoted an entire chapter to this aspect of family relations, paying particular attention to women readers with his advice regarding love and marriage. Love, Allestree explained, was "that special end of the woman's creation, the being a help to her husband, Gen. ii.18." Within marriage, the wife owed her husband obedience, commanded "by the apostle [Paul], Col. iii.18, Wives submit yourselves to your own Husbands, as it is fit in the Lord." He condemned the "peevish stubbornness of many wives who resist the lawful commands of their husband, only because they are impatient of this duty of subjection, which God himself requires of them." Neither could wives plead that the bad behavior of their husbands forced their disobedience: "[No] Faults, or provocations of the Husband, can justify their frowardness,"

Allestree asserted of English wives. The best way to win his approbation was with "gentleness and sweetness." Indeed, Allestree pushed his point further, admonishing wives not to let their anger at their husbands be the occasion of their mates' sinking into sin. "How many men are there that, to avoid the noise of a froward wife, have fallen to company-keeping, and by that to drunkenness, poverty, and a multitude of mischiefs? Let all wives therefore beware of administering that temptation," he warned.[66]

Allestree expanded his advice to women to book length in his tract *The Ladies Calling in Two Parts* (1673).[67] Although it was published anonymously, its authority was established on the title page: "by the Author of the Whole Duty of Man." Historian Anthony Fletcher has called it "the first coherent account of female gender construction" published in England.[68] The first part of the work delineates feminine virtues and attributes, frequently with a comparison to the masculine. For example, Allestree enjoined meekness upon both men and women as a Christian virtue, but he believed that it was particularly enjoined upon women as a "peculiar accomplishment of their Sex."[69] Other feminine virtues he urged on his female readers were piety and devotion, pointing out that women were "somewhat more of a predisposition towards it in their native temper" than men; affability and "courtesie, which as it is amiable in all, so it is singularly so in women of Quality, and more universally necessary in them than in the other Sex"; and compassion because "the female Sex, being of a softer mold, is more pliant and yielding to the impressions of pity." Patience and obedience, ubiquitous themes in women's advice literature, are prominent in Allestree's work as well, particularly with reference to wifely duties.[70]

The most indispensable trait for a woman, however, was modesty. Modesty should be apparent in the face, in a woman's look, in her manner, all of which should point to a "humble distrust of herself; she is to look upon herself as but a novice, a probationer in the world." Without it she not only forfeited her womanhood, but she lowered herself to the level of a brute—"nay," Allestree says, she is worse. Such women are beneath the brutes themselves, "an acquired vileness is below a native."[71] To us today, this may seem rather strong language for women whose demeanor did not quite measure up, and in fact, for Allestree and other like-minded writers, the term "modesty" comprehended much more. Seventeenth-century sensibilities equated female modesty with chastity; it referred, Allestree explained, not only to "the grosser act of incontinency, but to all those misbehaviours, which either discover or may create an inclination to it." The smallest misstep could lead to disastrous consequences, and the vigilant young woman guarded herself against "every indecent curiosity, or impure fancy."[72] As historian Angeline Goreau explains, modesty "had its roots in concrete circumstance, it was interpreted by contemporaries in an abstract, or symbolic, fashion, and then reapplied to the circumstances of everyday life—thus enlarging its sphere of influence to cover the whole experience."[73] A bold, impudent woman who disregarded such warnings was "as a kind of monster, a thing diverted and distorted from its proper form," a monster, who having rejected her femaleness, was unclassifiable.[74] In the early modern lexicon, then, "the words 'modesty,' 'honour,' 'name,' 'fame,' and 'reputation' [which for a man would refer to his qualities as a man of business], took on the same specifically sexual sense" as 'chastity' for women.[75] With sexual significance thus firmly attached to "modesty," it was no wonder that the conduct manuals of the seventeenth and eighteenth centuries devoted such meticulous care to every aspect of womanly demeanor, manner, speech, dress, and behavior, and that any woman who deviated from the standard would be labeled a monster.[76]

ADVICE TRANSPLANTED IN THE SOUTH

Advice about manners and demeanor may seem, at first glance, to be largely superfluous in the chaotic conditions of life in the seventeenth-century South. Yet Allestree's works, published in the 1650s, had crossed the Atlantic at least by the 1690s.[77] One explanation for their steady popularity in the southern colonies throughout the colonial period would have been their mutually supporting religious and political sympathies. In a region that declared its adherence to Anglicanism as its established state church, Allestree's measured approach to the duties Christians owed their fellows made sense. For Anglicans, living the Christian life was not a matter of trying to discern and follow a preordained plan of an inscrutable God (as it was for the Puritans) but was the responsible fulfillment of one's duties to God and one another. Allestree's attempt to reinvigorate the English gentry's sense of responsibility and duty toward society and religion played well in a region in which aspirations to govern could not necessarily rely on one's birth or pedigree, since Chesapeake diseases recognized no such distinctions. And, unlike the colonists in New England, disenchanted Puritans who had migrated more than a decade before the outbreak of hostilities between the Anglican king Charles I and his Puritan opponents, colonists in the South were largely predisposed toward the monarchy. The order of society that Allestree labored in his works to reinstate made sense to Anglicans trying to establish a toehold of legitimate authority. By the mid-eighteenth century, southern gentry men understood the deference accorded them to be due recognition of the performance of their responsibilities to the lower orders.[78]

Allestree's defense of natural hierarchies would have had an additional layer of meaning for southern colonists, as they struggled to define their relationship with the African slaves they were importing to work their tobacco, rice, and indigo crops. Though Africans comprised only 6.9 percent of the Virginia population by 1680, the Virginia House of Burgesses (Virginia's legislative body) had been addressing questions of racial interaction and status from the 1630s.[79] From denying Africans the right to bear arms, to forbidding interracial sexual relations and marriages, to allowing whites to maim or kill runaways with impunity, Virginians (like South Carolinians before them) fixed in law and society a "natural" hierarchy of race with which Allestree's worldview was quite compatible.[80] Indeed, Allestree's devotional works imputed to this configuration the endorsement of Scripture.

The place of women in the social order, so central to Allestree, was also a key question for the colonial South, the resolution of which cannot be understood apart from the construction of race. By the antebellum period, southerners had fully formed a justification for slavery in the precedent of the natural subjugation of women to men. But they began to forge that link in the colonial period, as southern legislation increasingly differentiated white women from black. In Virginia, for example, black women were counted as tithables, a designation previously reserved for men sixteen years of age and older who were able-bodied workers in a plantation's tobacco fields. This 1643 law, refined in 1668 to make clear its application to all black women, free or enslaved, embodied English ideas about the proper role of women: white women performed domestic duties only, while black women, regarded as bestial and less than female, were suitable for the physical exertions of field labor.[81] But in 1662, addressing "whether children got by any Englishman upon a negro woman should be slave or free," the legislature declared that the "condition" (free or enslaved) of a child would follow that of the mother, in its most significant demarcation of race and gender. In a single stroke, the burgesses reversed the patriarchal conventions that had obtained in England from time out of mind, in which the status of family members derived from that of the father. The consequences for slave women were devastating: slavery became a hereditary condition; the impregnation of slave women would actually profit a slave holder; and, it was clear, the conventions of chastity that were so crucial for the reputations of white women would have no application for blacks, leaving enslaved women completely vulnerable to the assaults of their masters. In such a hierarchical system, where race and gender were so inextricably connected, white women could scarcely afford to ignore the boundaries that divided them from black.[82] Indeed, it has been said that the portraits of the wives of prominent Virginians, Hannah Ludwell (Mrs. Thomas Lee) and Laetitia Corbin (Mrs. Richard Lee II), captured all that Allestree valued in women: refinement, a certain shyness and reserve, and delicacy.[83] Any behavior that suggested a rejection of social mores of their sex threatened to reduce them to that unprotected status of black women. Legislation defining the status of black women, then, by implication also marked out the boundaries for white.

Given these considerations of life in the colonial South, the popularity of advice texts written an ocean away for entirely different circumstances becomes more comprehensible. The legal codes seemed to make the distinctions between white and black, male and female, definitively clear, but as the anxious patriarchs of the eighteenth-century South realized, those divides were tenuous despite their appeals to divine and natural law. Sermons and devotional texts that reinforced divine imperatives for the ordering of society, therefore, found a receptive audience in the aspiring gentry of the South. The household of William Byrd II is a perfect example of the dynamics of authority in early-eighteenth-century relationships: the repeated assertions of the patriarch, the resistance of the subordinate, and the patriarch's resort to books for a rationale for order.

The story of the tempestuous yet passionate marriage of William and Lucy Byrd has been well documented: the urbane man of the world, educated in London and newly returned to Virginia to take over the lands he inherited at his father's death, and his younger wife, Lucy Parke, by all accounts beautiful and headstrong, the daughter of a man notorious for his desertion of his Virginia wife for an English mistress.[84] The couple's turbulent marriage in 1706 unfolds in the pages of William's secret diary. Lucy resisted William's attempts to control her: she threatened to stay home from the governor's ball in Williamsburg if he would not allow her to pluck her eyebrows; she raised his ire at her mounting purchases from England; she had the temerity to discipline slaves in the presence of visitors to their plantation. His struggles to contain her took many forms, also described in the diary, usually followed by the satisfied comment, "But it was soon over by her submission."[85] Their reconciliations were often punctuated by sex, a physical symbol of his mastery over her. What is rather unusual—even for Byrd—is his pairing of such reconciliations with reading in the sermons of Archbishop John Tillotson, one of the most admired Anglican preachers of the seventeenth century and one of William's favorite authors.

Like Allestree, Tillotson worked to craft a brand of Anglicanism in the post–Civil War period that combined a reasoned approach to faith with practical exhortations to living the moral life. For Tillotson, "the great business of religion is to make men truly good and to teach them to live well." Throughout the eighteenth century, Tillotson's unadorned and straightforward prose was cited as a model worthy of emulation even by secular writers such as Richard Addison, and the clarity of his teachings recommended them as suitable even for the more limited understanding of women.[86] We do not know which segments William directed Lucy to read to him; with the poignant exception of his comment, "read a sermon in Dr. Tillotson about angels" two weeks after the death of his infant son, he never specified the subject. Still, after the "little quarrel" that was resolved with a flourish on the billiard table (itself a competitive venue for a battle of strong wills), he might have had Lucy read the passage in which Tillotson urged his hearers to "still all the murmurings of our spirits" when they understood that the ills they thought "as coming only from men," emanated in fact from "the hand of God."[87] Or possibly William consoled Lucy with Tillotson's empathetic sermon on "The Difficulty of Goodness," in which he exclaimed, "How next to impossible is it . . . to maintain that evenness of temper and not to be sometimes peevish and passionate! And . . . not to be apt to say with Jonah, *We do well to be angry!*"[88] Two days after another quarrel with his wife that left him in "but indifferent good humor," he again "took a flourish with my wife and then read a sermon in Tillotson." Harmony restored, he concluded his day with "good health, good thoughts, and good humor."[89] From our perspective today, the great issues of religious controversy that dogged England in the latter half of the seventeenth century might seem remote from Virginian life, but on the banks of the James River, William Byrd called upon Tillotson on at least two occasions to underscore the legitimacy of his rule over his wife.

SECULAR ADVICE

Not all advice literature in the colonial South was religious in its language, tone, and import, however. *The Lady's New Year's Gift; or, Advice to a Daughter* (1688) was a practical manual for women written by George Savile, Lord Halifax, a canny politician who had served as a privy councilor and successfully navigated through the reigns of three kings, his influence and power intact.[90] Fearing the corrupting influence of degenerate men who sought their fortunes at court and preyed on innocent and naïve young women, he wrote *The Lady's New Year's Gift* to equip his daughter to detect and rebuff such cads (and, not incidentally, to protect his own fortune). The intimate father-to-daughter tone of the manual, first published in 1688, made surrogate daughters of his readers and gave his words the strength of parental authority.[91] So successful was this literary strategy that Halifax's letter was reprinted in England throughout the eighteenth century, enjoyed a wide readership in the American colonies (including the South, as we have seen), and even crossed the English Channel for four editions in French and one in Italian.[92]

Halifax's work differed from Allestree's in content as well as tone and style. Although religion was the first topic Halifax addressed, he dispensed with it in relatively short order (devoting only six of eighty-four pages to the subject) before proceeding to more practical concerns of husband, family, behavior and conversation, and friendship.[93] Although he sympathetically owned it a disadvantage to women that they were seldom allowed to choose their husbands, he quickly revealed his thinking about the relative merits of men and women. "You must first lay it down for a foundation in general [that is, you must first take it for granted]" he began, "that there is inequality in the sexes, and that for the better economy of the world the men, who were to be the lawgivers, had the larger share of reason bestowed upon them." This, he believed, justified women's "compliance that is necessary for the better performance of those duties which seem to be most properly assigned to it [the female sex]."[94] Halifax's reliance on religious or scientific arguments for his position was ambiguous. Whether God or nature bestowed the larger share of reason on men, he did not specify, nor did it much matter. He rested confidently in the assumption of male superiority as a universally acknowledged truth.

Yet Halifax was well aware of the double standard that existed in Restoration England. While admitting that the "laws of marriage run in a harsher style towards your sex," his purpose was to show his daughter how to make the best of things. Since law and custom were not going to change, her best bet was to be forewarned; alerted to the perils that beset English marriages, she would know how to "cure your husband's mistakes and to prevent your own."[95]

The primary hazard to marital bliss was infidelity. Again, while admitting that what was seen "in the utmost criminal degree" if committed by women, "passeth under a much gentler censure" for men, he nonetheless urged her to turn a blind eye to her husband's indiscretions. An "indecent complaint," Halifax argued, "makes a wife more ridiculous than the injury that provoketh it." The best way to handle such situations was with "discretion and silence," which he believed would be the "most prevailing reproof."[96] Deprived of any legal identity, much less legal recourse, within marriage, a wife had to take to the moral high ground, relying on the virtuous influence of her example.

Her husband's failings could have their bright side, however. For example, a husband who was overly fond of wine would fail to notice housewifely lapses, as his drunkenness "will throw a veil over your mistakes, and will set out and improve everything you do that he is pleased with." A weak husband was a perfect foil to his wife since she would "make the better figure for her husband's making no great one." A smart wife could get around a witless husband by "do[ing] like a wise minister to any easy prince; first give him the orders you afterwards receive from him." A faultless husband would be more of a nuisance anyway, since he "hath an eye so piercing" that everything would be "exposed to his full censure."[97] Halifax moved in the highest circles of the Restoration court; he saw everything. Knowing full well the inequities of law and custom, the best he could do was advise his daughter how to put the best face on her situation. Women were not without options, he was suggesting, if they but knew how to exercise influence.

As Allestree had before him, Halifax saw a woman's behavior as indistinguishable from her modesty. It could be a bit tricky to walk a line that intimated neither forwardness nor rudeness. In an impossibly vague prescription, Halifax warned Elizabeth and his other "daughters" to avoid "looks that forbid without rudeness," and to cultivate those that "oblige without invitation." It was crucial that a woman not be overly loud in her conversation, laugh boisterously, or display any learning, but neither was she to affect shyness. She must acknowledge a man's superiority of judgment yet not be led by a "compliance which may betray you into irrecoverable mistakes . . . [that] hath led your sex into more blame than all other things put together."[98] Courtship, of course, was fraught with opportunities for irrecoverable mistakes; "it is as safe to play with fire as to dally with gallantry," Halifax warned. It was all too easy for a woman to mistake the humble posturings of men for love, particularly at the Restoration court, but Halifax knew that a suitor's "fair appearance[s] have generally less respect than art in them." The design of the compliment, rather than the lady herself, was the object of the effort. The discerning woman could recognize pure flattery when she heard it, and a practiced reserve in her behavior was her best guard against it.[99]

The care a woman exercised in courtship was equally necessary in her choice of friends, for her virtue was judged not only by her demeanor, manners, and deportment but also by the company she kept. No friends are perfect, Halifax granted, but at least, he instructed his daughter, "be sure yours may not stray from the rules." The common inclinations implied by association became problematic when a friend fell from innocence. This delicate situation called for scrupulous judgment so that one neither joined hastily in the censure nor defended her with suspicious vigor. The danger was that with the "vexation that belongeth to such a mistake you will draw an ill appearance upon yourself." In the end, the priority had to be saving one's own reputation, by severing the friendship although "without breaking too roughly."[100]

Halifax began his book with an assumption of the inequality of the sexes. That was why a wife must submit to male authority and patiently forbear her husband's faults (if not be grateful for them). Yet it is clear that he also recognized some of the tensions within a patriarchal system, not the least of which was the contrived logic on which it was founded.[101] He could see that the weaker sex, far from finding protection from his, suffered injustices inflicted by men. He acknowledged the double standard and the problems posed by exceptional women who rose above the level of their sex and therefore were entitled to "a mitigation in their own particular of a sentence which was given generally against womankind."[102] He also recognized, briefly, that the best he could offer was a way for clever women to use their powers of moral suasion to get around the strictures of law and custom. Even so, with the pragmatism of a court politician who supported the Stuarts until James II himself fled the struggle for the throne, he surveyed the world as he knew it, accepted its immutability, and was satisfied with stating the obvious: "[Y]ou must take it for a foundation . . . that there is an inequality in the sexes." So he constructed an advice manual that reinforced ideas of female inferiority and the necessity of cultivating a virtuous demeanor of submissiveness, obedience, and deference.[103]

A common thread for women in all these writings, of course, was the essential difference between male and female natures as both God and nature dictated and the preservation of that gender hierarchy. The recommended reading for "ladies" discussed the sins of pride and vainglory and the virtues of meekness, obedience, and temperance in pleasure seeking. These themes were intermingled in religious and secular literature. Lord Halifax's *Lady's New Year's Gift,* for example, had carried religious themes into his secular work.[104] Fordyce's *Sermons for Young Women,* on the other hand, offered advice about decorous female behavior packaged in the weighty trappings of sermons. First published in 1765, Fordyce's *Sermons* set the tone for advice writings aimed at countering what Fordyce viewed as the considerable freedoms British women were enjoying. Freer to move about in public, writing protests against the limitations on their education, and, later in the century, conducting salons in which they could display their wit, Englishwomen did not conform to the prescriptions set for them by Halifax or Allestree to remain quietly at home.[105] The distinctions that John Locke's writings had made between a masculine public, which comprehended government and business, and a feminine private to be found in domesticity, seemed clearer on paper than on city streets, where a new, sociable public was taking form.[106] For wealthy women, eighteenth-century cities offered theaters, lending libraries, visiting circuits, and salons; for poor women, the hope of employment. Women's very visible presence in the urban centers of London, Edinburgh, and Glasgow prompted both the trotting out of old advice and the generation of new to meet in various ways these challenges to patriarchal authority. Fordyce's *Sermons* was the most notable of the new advice books. Enormously popular, the *Sermons* underwent at least fourteen editions in England by 1814; was found in many early American private and circulating libraries; and, Jane Austen knew, carried such instant name recognition that she could assume that the readers of her *Pride and Prejudice* were as familiar with it as were her fictional characters.[107]

Although a clergyman, Fordyce moved comfortably in the aspiring genteel circles of both Edinburgh and London (his brother was banker Alexander Fordyce) and so knew how to target his sermons to the worldly lives of those he met there.[108] While Fordyce began by declaring immediately his "unfeigned regard for the Female Sex," his sermons actually reinforced the King James Biblical image of women as "the weaker vessel," whose thoughts and speech, mobility and deportment, must always remain within bounds set by men.[109] Both God and nature, he believed, placed women in the protection of men. God impressed upon men "so high an esteem for every indication of chastity in women," he argued, that they were bound to protect women. Nature, too, committed women to the protection of men. "They [women] are timid, and want to be defended. Nature says to men, "O do not take advantage of their weakness.' "[110] The female nature, inherently endowed with virtue, modesty, and softness, was markedly different from the male, which was characterized by strength, courage, and wisdom. But, Fordyce asked, was this not "Nature's intention?" "Such difference of sex, which she [nature] has marked by characters no less distinguishable than those that diversify their outward forms," he explained, merely proved those "mental and moral" differences between men and women.[111]

While men might supply knowledge, wisdom, and counsel to women, women were fashioned by God and nature to soften the rough edges of masculine temperaments, to ease life's burdens with a steady cheerfulness, and to earn the approval of all society, but more particularly, of the one man to whom she would devote her life. Fordyce's sermons showed women how Scripture delineated their functions in life—to tame and please men, to marry, to raise a family—and how daily work was to be apportioned between husband and wife, all duties restricted to the context of marriage and home. Women's "ability to . . . to melt into tears at the sight or hearing of distress, [and] to take the care of children" fully suited them to domestic life.[112] On the other hand, the male "constitution of mind, no less than the body, is for the most part hardy and rough. By means of both, by the demands of life, and by the impulse of passion, they are engaged in a vast variety of pursuits, from which your sex are precluded by decorum, by softness, and by fear."[113] Weaker in mind and body, women were excluded from "outdoor affairs," a common eighteenth–century phrase that so effectively denoted a compendium of centuries of scientific and religious thought.

Whether discussing a woman's virtue, grooming, dress, deportment, conversation, or role in life, Fordyce guided his female readers to the ultimate purpose of attending to these many details: the approbation of men. "The male heart is a study, in which your sex are supposed to be a good deal conversant," he declared pointedly, "To gain men's affections, women in general are naturally desirous."[114] Indeed, he asked, "Does it not seem agreeable to the purposes of Providence that the securing of this [male] attention, and these regards, should be a principal aim?"[115] Couched in the context of a sermon, based on scriptural and divine imperatives, and buttressed by the immutable laws of nature, the powerful message to women could not be ignored: the very goal of her life was to secure the favorable attentions of men.

Dr. John Gregory likewise brought the authority of his position, professor of medicine at the University of Edinburgh, to bear upon his understanding of the female nature. His *A Father's Legacy to his Daughters*, published in 1774, was an immediate hit on both sides of the Atlantic. In America, it went through sixty-nine editions. When William Aiken printed it in Annapolis, Maryland, in 1775, he incited local demand by advertising that five thousand copies had sold in London in three weeks.[116] Gregory showed how female virtues were linked to female biology: female modesty could be measured by the depth of a woman's blush, for example. Modesty, in turn, would "naturally dispose [women] to be rather silent in company," an important consideration for a doctor who believed that "Wit is the most dangerous talent you can possess." Gregory was unusual, however, in his views about women and marriage. While Fordyce could not envision women outside the bounds of matrimony, Gregory "knew nothing more despicable than [a woman] thinking it essential to her happiness to be married." Indeed, he told his daughters that "the ease and independence of a single life" was to be preferred to living as "slaves of a fool's or tyrant's caprice." These deviations notwithstanding however, Gregory joined Fordyce in his abhorrence of witty, informed, unreserved women. When in company, he advised his daughters, they should keep their learning "a profound secret, especially from the men."[117]

In some ways, Fordyce and Gregory seem to be echoing the familiar themes that Allestree and Halifax had promoted: female submission, obedience, and silence. But, in fact, the eighteenth-century writers began from a different vantage point than their predecessors had. When Fordyce explained to his female readers, for instance, that "Nature appears to have formed the faculties of your sex for the most part with less vigour than those of ours; observing the same distinction here, as in the more delicate frame of your bodies," he was articulating the new eighteenth-century understanding of sex and gender.[118] By midcentury, the older notions of a "one-sex" model that had obtained since the time of Aristotle had given way to a "two-sex" model. Aristotle, and all the European authorities who followed him, believed men and women shared the same sex, separated only by degree; that is, though both sexes possessed the same reproductive organs, the female body was an inferior, incomplete version of the male's. Women were distinguished by their frailty, coldness, and inferiority; men by their strength, heat, and superiority. Their very anatomy proved the truth of these beliefs: unlike male fetuses, females lacked the heat necessary to expel their genitalia. However, "sometime in the eighteenth century," historian Thomas Laqueur believes, "sex as we know it was invented." For the first time it was possible to speak of the "opposite sex" as scientists discovered and named women's internal reproductive organs, noticed differences in male and female skeletons, and understood sex and gender in new ways. Biology now bore the weight of understandings of gender; in the enlightened eighteenth century, with its emphasis on empiricism, what mattered most was "the immovable foundation of physical fact: sex."[119] Sex and nature, as observed in the different bodies of men and women, justified the ordering of social relations. Ideas about women's incapacities remained, but what was different was the empirical foundation that upheld them. No longer reliant on the thought of the ancients, the modern world of eighteenth–century science discovered an immutable ground—the female body—for its social order that, in Anthony Fletcher's apt phrase, "was entirely consonant with the central theological tenets of women's inferiority."[120] Fordyce built on these new understandings, linking the inferiority of the distinctly different female anatomy to female intellectual capacities, as well.

He was not alone in drawing these conclusions. The great minds of the Scottish Enlightenment, including Adam Smith, David Hume, and Henry Home (Lord Kames), applied the scientific findings of the female body to a theory of history in which women played a prominent but subordinate role. Posited as a four-stage process, man's development had evolved from primitive hunter to sophisticated man of commerce. At each stage, the softening, civilizing influence of women increased, refining male passions as it did so. Since these thinkers saw the family (rather than the individual, as in Locke's thinking) as the pivotal social institution in which men and women learned the skills necessary to build a successful society, their thought highlighted the importance of the mother's role.[121]

With their civilizing influence on the family, mothers occupied a prominent societal role for these thinkers.[122] This social function did not translate to a political one, however. Despite Scottish emphasis on the necessity for female education and even occasional references to female "equality," it was clear that the freedom that women enjoyed in the eighteenth century was relative, not to the men with whom they lived but to women who had suffered through the first three stages. Having emerged "out of slavery," according to Kames, women now "possess[ed] the elevated state they [were] justly entitled to by nature." For Kames that meant refining men: "where-ever women are indulged with any degree of freedom, they polish sooner than men."[123] In this pursuit, Fordyce and Gregory taught, women had to be content with exerting influence privately. Scientists and physicians explained why women could not be admitted to equal political participation with men. When naturalist William Smellie noticed that female birds and humans shared the same loquacious tendencies, he emphasized greater differences between men and women over those between animals and humans.[124] There was not much difference between her inability to control her tongue or her desires; female passions could never hope for a masculine rationality or restraint. In the milieu of the Scottish Enlightenment, clergyman, physician, political theorist, and scientist agreed that the nature of woman was best suited for mothering and the refinement of manners from within the boundaries of domesticity.

These were the ideas that resonated so with Mary Ambler. They were part of a genre of English prescriptive literature for women that had been forged in the fires of civil war in the seventeenth century and refined in the enlightened world of the eighteenth, as advice authors of all stripes sought to rein in the social and cultural upheavals of their times. As historian Paul Langford has pointed out, "Underlying the delight in the accomplishments of eighteenth-century woman was a pronounced fear that liberty might turn to license, and indeed that women might demand of right what they were granted by way of liberties."[125] The outpouring of male conduct-of-life advice such as Fordyce's and Gregory's meant to counter these liberties and to delineate clear lines of public and private (read, male and female) spaces. The separate domesticity, idealized by the middling sort, who understood their household and labor arrangements to be morally superior to those of a licentious and self-interested aristocracy, refuted the streets as a place for women.[126] Unlike the public space of the court, where men and women intermingled and jockeyed for royal favor and position, the private space of the middle-class home was a feminine sanctuary in which to take refuge from the harried world of business. A mouthpiece of this new middle-class culture, Richard Addison's *Spectator* observed that a woman undertook forays into city streets only to be reminded of "the superior attractions of domesticity."[127]

The "Conversation Group" shows how these ideas permeated the English middle class, as the portrait both reflects the family's adherence to respectable gender conventions and perpetuates them.[128] Mother and daughter occupy the left side of the painting, distinguished by the light color of their clothes and the fragility of their sex: the child is keeper of the flowers, symbols of beauty, delicacy, and genteel femininity. What the men bring to the table—so to speak—are skills and property; arrayed on the other side of the portrait, they are confident and sure of themselves, their world, and their place in it. The father and patriarch is plainly of the professional class. Pen in hand, he administers the family business, perhaps even writing the will that will serve to convey his property to his sons. His elder son stands beside him, fully confident of his future as his heir, while his younger brother proudly displays the ancestral home he will one day inherit. These "conversation" pieces, or family portraits, which became such a popular genre in eighteenth-century Britain, are pictorial genealogical statements: the line of succession and inheritance is clear and defined by gender. Tangential in every way, the demure females (the daughter so physically small that she would be easily overlooked) neither

Fig. 2. "The Conversation Group" (English, c. 1775). "Conversation groups," or family portraits, were a popular genre in eighteenth-century England. Gender roles are inscribed and perpetuated in the very arrangement of males and females on the canvas: status, money, and power are clearly conveyed on the right; marginalization (indeed, the daughter is barely even visible) mark the pair on the left. Courtesy of the John D. Rockefeller, Jr. Library, Colonial Williamsburg Foundation.

face the table around which their men are gathered nor share the concerns or the privileges of manhood.[129]

ANGLICIZATION OF GENDER IN THE SOUTH

Different as this urban British world was from the American South, its advice literature was prized by eighteenth-century southerners. We have seen the appeal of its articulation of an organically ordered society: William Byrd's copy of *The Whole Duty* was bound luxuriously and displayed in his impressive library; Daniel Dulany of Maryland displayed his copy in his dining room; and James Milner of North Carolina supplied the women of his family with *two* copies of Fordyce's *Sermons.* The popularity of *Telemachus, Son of Ulysses,* a novel written by a French Catholic and sold in both English and French in Dixon and Hunter's Williamsburg print shop, is explained by its plot: the expedition of Telemachus after the Trojan war to find his father, restore him as rightful patriarch of the family, and protect his mother against the lascivious suitors, who would transgress his father's prerogatives.[130] These books not only supplied the blueprint and scriptural imperatives for the proper societal structure, but they also pointed to the legitimacy of a household governor's claim to rule. They symbolized the patriarch's subscription to enlightened British ideals and his ability to follow them to maintain order (no doubt one reason why William Byrd had Lucy read to him from Tillotson after quarrels). Significantly, even the ideas of the Scottish Enlightenment thinkers reached a wider audience than upper-crust elites. In the pages of the *Virginia Gazette,* the "Essay on Women" argued that the sexes complemented each other: "women soften and polish men." The "2 sexes ought to be perfected by one another," the writer pointed out, "If men did not converse with Women, they would be less perfect and less happy than they are."[131] In their subscription to the advice literature of genteel British culture and in their prominent display of their books, then, men of the southern colonies claimed both status and authority.

Gender ideology and geography combined to render women's access to books and their meaning considerably different than men's. As the example of William Byrd shows, men often mediated women's access to books: deciding what they would read and when. As late as the eve of the Revolution, Virginians believed (again, if the *Virginia Gazette* is any indication) that "Female minds, overwhelmed with Trifles, would languish in Ignorance, if Men, recalling them to more elevated Objects, did not communicate Dignity and Vigour."[132] As the intellectual superiors of women, therefore, men properly functioned as their teachers and governors. As household heads, men also kept a tight rein on money; lacking men's discretionary spending power and their geographic mobility over the agricultural landscape, women were further disadvantaged in their reliance on men to supply them with books and newspapers purchased at such various regional centers as Williamsburg, Petersburg, or New Bern, North Carolina. Despite her location on the navigable Rappahannock River, Sophia Bland complained of the lack of books in Port Royal, Virginia, in 1799.[133] Nor did the companionate marriage of Frances Bland and St. George Tucker resolve the problem of geographic mobility. Marooned on her plantation, she relied on him to supply her reading materials from Williamsburg, as her playful yet urgent appeal makes clear: "I beg you would regale us by sending the Monitor [Virginia's equivalent of Richard Steele's *Spectator*]. You promised me. Do not deny me this request my d[ea]r St. George. I wou'd give half I am worth for it."[134]

These are particularly significant points, as a visit to the Williamsburg print shop and bookstore illustrates. John Dixon and William Hunter published a long advertisement on page one of an edition of the *Virginia Gazette* in 1775, hoping to entice visitors and mail orders (Hunter was also postmaster).[135] A quick glance at the shelves assesses the display: 6 titles in folio, impressive in their size, weighty in their import, and the most costly; then, in descending order of size, 18 titles in quarto, 154 in octavo, and 163 in duodecimo. Though there was no standardized measurement for each size, we can still imagine the choices presented to colonial customers. Folios were the largest (at least 17 by 20 inches), heavy, and calculated to invoke ceremony in their display and use. Dixon and Hunter had copies of the Bible in folio, as well as *The Laws of Virginia* and Jacob's *New Law Dictionary*. Thus, the texts that were most fundamental to ordering colonial life were printed in the most grandiose form. Edward Moseley of North Carolina owned Tillotson's *Works* in folio; it must have occupied pride of place in his home. Indeed, its size would have dictated that some ritual accompany its reading; one does not resort to such a book for a quick reference. His widow, to whom he bequeathed the books, would pull a volume off the library shelf where it was displayed, seat herself near a window, or place it on a table and light a candle in preparation to read. The next size was quarto—literally, one quarter the size of folios. They could be as large as 15 × 11 inches or as small as 7 × 6 (depending on the size of the original sheet).[136] These books were also authoritative on important aspects of colonial Virginian life: William Blackstone's *Commentaries on the Laws of England*, for example; *The Complete Farmer: Being a general Dictionary of Husbandry in all its branches*; or Foster's *Discourses on all the*

Principal Branches of Natural Religion and Social Virtue. They would be crucial reference works for gentry justices of the peace, up-and-coming lawyers, planters, and all households wishing to inculcate order based on religious principles.

Folding the original sheet of printing paper further still yields the smaller octavo, a size that frequently denoted a cheaper and thus more widely available book. At Dixon and Hunter's shop, the choices were considerably more varied in this size: titles in history, travel books, farming, law, medicine, cooking, political treatises, devotional works, and Shakespeare. A prosperous planter or merchant would head straight to this section, since it answered his need for practical information (how to doctor his wife, children, and slaves, for instance), for the kind of literature in which a well-educated Englishman would be versed, and for the educational needs for his sons. Moseley bequeathed his four octavo volumes of Stanhope's *Epistles and Gospels* to his widow; she probably found these books easier to reach for than the heavy Tillotson folio, and more companionable when she needed a Scripture verse or explication for encouragement, guidance, or comfort during her widowhood.

After making his selection for himself, our planter might then turn to the smallest and cheapest books, the duodecimos. This size was small enough to be held easily in one hand or carried about in a pocket, but its diminutive size did not necessarily denote insignificance of subject. While many of these books were meant to amuse—*The Entertaining Fabulist, containing a Variety of diverting Tales and Novels,* for example—the cheaper price of this size also enabled less wealthy families to stock up on devotional literature such as Baxter's *Call to Unconverted Sinners* or Fordyce's *Sermons,* or Richard Steele's *The Ladies Library.* Tucked in one's pocket, these books could serve as a ready reference, a steadying hand, or an understanding friend during the course of the day. Indeed, though it did not evoke the kind of ritual or preparation the elaborate folios did, in the intimacy of daily use, the humble duodecimo was probably the most read, loved, and cherished of all. This category held the titles that would have been most relevant to the lives of southern colonial women, and the smaller investment of money for duodecimos might have rendered the purchase more palatable as the planter weighed the possibilities for his wife.

Indeed, most (but not all) book purchases at the Williamsburg print shop were made by men, a fact not at all surprising when we consider the difficulties of travel for women, and the limited purposes and radius of their travel. The cost of the books could also be prohibitive for women without access to a discretionary allowance. The cost of even a cheap

LADY'S TOILETTE.
The Wig

Fig. 3. "Lady's Toilette: The Wig" (English, c. 1802). As this satire makes plain, all the feminine beauty aids in the world (wig, perfume, makeup, and dress) will not disguise the mannish inclinations of women who read serious-minded books. Courtesy of the John D. Rockefeller, Jr. Library, Colonial Williamsburg Foundation.

schoolbook could be the equivalent of two pairs of leather shoes, while the price of a luxury edition of Smollet's *History* could furnish 180 pairs (or six head of cattle or thirty hogs).[137] As the colonial capital, Williamsburg was certainly a cultural center for Virginia. Even so, the prominence of the bookstore as an important conduit of British ideas and culture did not outweigh another source of books: the private purchases between planters and merchants and their agents or factors in Britain. But here again, women readers were at the mercy of men, who acted as intermediaries even at their own docks, between ship captains, factors, and British print culture. Widowhood released women from this constraint, as we shall see with Hannah Lee Corbin in the next chapter. Still, the picture of William Byrd scolding his wife for her extravagances is the prevailing image for southern women's access to the consumer goods of the eighteenth century. As the satire "Lady's Toilette" shows, dresses, combs, and perfumes were understandable enough as objects of female acquisitiveness; books were most emphatically less so.[138]

What southern women made of what they read is yet another question. Though few women commented explicitly on their reading, we can nonetheless see, with some imagination, the effectiveness of the colonizer on women's ways of thinking about gender. For example, we can see female acceptance of a divine designation of male superiority in many of their writings, particularly in their commonplace books. Sometimes these were scraps of paper of differing sizes, bound together years after they were penned, as was Maria Carter's in Virginia in the 1760s. Sometimes they were beautiful books, leather bound and gilded, that evoked a sense of importance, as was Mary Abigail Willing Coale's in Baltimore in 1800. Commonplace books had long been part of the formal educational training for boys. Collecting fragments of great writers' works, students in ancient Greece had learned to reproduce the Greek rhetorical tradition in their own school exercises. While this manner of using commonplace books persisted throughout the centuries (that is, adopting the ringing words of the ancients in one's own written expression), the humanists of the Renaissance era introduced another use: building character. Choosing from recorded experience—or "places" in the public mind—one formed one's character by drawing selectively from this common fund of societal wisdom.[139] Indeed, commonplace books could be even more selective than more private writings (such as letters and diaries), precisely because they incorporated a wider world of experience into a personal one. "Beneath their surface sheen of public knowledge," Kenneth Lockridge has written of William Byrd's commonplace book (itself a small, simple stitched notebook), "these are profoundly instruments of personal identity."[140] Reading and copying on the shores of the James River, the Virginia-born Byrd carefully cultivated the genteel identity he believed he shared with English gentry on the other side of the Atlantic, since he followed their program of reading.[141] By the mid-eighteenth century, elite girls, too, had begun keeping commonplace books as part of their education. Admittedly, female students were not trained in the art of rhetoric (self-expression was not part of a colonial girl's education), but the practice was intended, as for boys, to cultivate character.

Maria Carter's commonplace book is one example of the female use of these books: it contains a satire from Alexander Pope on female vanity and inconstancy, a warning from Tillotson about being the object of slander, and the prescription that "Gentle replys to scurrilous language, is the most severe Revenge."[142] Whether she chose these fragments herself or copied them as a handwriting exercise, they reveal the important lessons Carter was learning in her girlhood about being female: the necessity for reticence, spotless reputations, and quiet submissiveness. On the eve of her wedding in November 1779 to Lund Washington, Elizabeth Foote prayed that "my gracious God [may] direct & influence my heart & its affections, that I may make it my study to please my husband in every thing that is not against the divine Laws . . . may it be one of my daily petitions to the throne of grace to conduct myself as a dutiful obediant wife."[143] Several years into her marriage as she looked forward to setting up her own household (apart from her in–laws), she hoped to conduct her family with "great peace & quietness . . . am also sure it is Mr. Washington's desire,—& that alone would make me so endeavour after it—if I did not [also] feel a principal of religion in me that causes me to desire it."[144] So even as these women adopted a discipline that had been understood as masculine since antiquity, they placed it at the disposal of the prevailing gender order. As Christian Moore (first wife of Virginian Episcopal Bishop Moore) admitted to her husband a few months before her death, "your affection has always been my greatest happiness."[145]

Martha Laurens Ramsay of Charleston, South Carolina, "was well acquainted with the plausible reasonings of modern theorists, who contend for the equality of the sexes," her husband David Ramsay wrote after her death in 1811, "but she yielded all pretensions on this score, in conformity to the positive declaration of holy writ."[146] Indeed, she had decided as a young woman that she would devote herself to the study of religion as her brother would to politics.[147] Several texts formed the basis for Martha Ramsay's concession: the Genesis prescription that, as a result of Eve's transgression, "thy desire shall be to thy husband, and he shall rule over thee" and Paul's instruction to the wives of Ephesus to "submit yourselves unto your own husbands as unto the Lord." Martha Ramsay derived "a knowledge of her true station" from the Bible, her husband wrote in his memoir of her, so that "in practice, as well as theory, she acknowledged the dependent, subordinate condition of her sex . . . consider[ing] it as a part of the curse denounced on Eve."[148] She never relinquished this view, despite her husband's financial incompetence that kept the family in a constant state of indebtedness from which they never recovered during Martha's lifetime.

Ramsay's reference to the curse pronounced on Eve is striking, given the transformation of Eve's image that had taken place in the eighteenth century north of Virginia.[149] There both ministers and the popular press had been won to the view of Eve portrayed by Puritan poet John Milton in *Paradise Lost.* A divine beauty whose sweet company persuaded Adam to risk the terrors of life outside Paradise with her rather than remain in solitude in Eden, Eve no longer represented the seductive route to perdition. Instead, Milton made clear, man was created to live in concert with woman, with whom perfectibility was possible; indeed, with her, heaven could be realized on earth. Benjamin Colman, prolific eighteenth-century minister, preached Milton's vision of Eve from his pulpit at Brattle Street, Boston.[150] Mrs. Charles Apthorp of Boston chose to sit for her portrait with her copy of *Paradise Lost* on her lap, opened to the precise passages in which Adam glorified Eve.[151] Late into the century, magazines from Baltimore to Boston borrowed from Milton's Eve to construct a new model of partnership in marriage suitable for men and women of the new republic.[152] In 1792, Anna Maria Coale of Baltimore copied Milton's most famous description of Eve into her copybook, "Grace was in all her steps. Heaven in her eye. In every gesture dignity and love."[153] Milton's *Paradise Lost* was available in the South as well, but readers there seem to have arrived rather later at the idealized version of womanhood, as Ramsay's remark indicates.[154] Not until the nineteenth century would magazines in Charleston and Richmond adopt Eve as "A Vision of Female Excellence," but even then it would be to stress the differences between women and men, refuting any notion that such views would lead to an equality between the sexes.[155]

In the South, it was modesty and a quiet demeanor that won the approbation of men. Tutor Philip Vickers Fithian concluded of Priscilla Heale, a visitor to Robert Carter's Virginia plantation, "that her Modesty is invincible." He had tried in vain for two days to coax her into conversation and judged from her reticence that "[s]he is far removed from most of the foibles of Women." Similarly, he approved of Jenny Washington in her emulation of Fordyce's advice: "[S]he is not forward to begin a conversation, yet when spoken to she is extremely affable, without assuming any Girlish affectation, or pretending to be overcharg'd with Wit."[156] Edmund Randolph praised his wife, Betsey, who had "such an unchangeable and undiminished fund of delicacy . . . she never used to me an expression, which if over heard ought to have produced a tinge in her cheek." A model of modesty, she was a stranger to "subjects of indecency or indecorum." The "infantine purity" of her manners that sprang from her "unsullied female heart" was manifested as well in her "personal neatness [that] was never surprised."[157] Her childlike quality confirmed the gender hierarchy in their household. Perpetual cleanliness, an attribute prized by such disparate men as James Fordyce and Thomas Jefferson, was a reflection of the physical cleanliness to which neither slave nor nonelite women could aspire. Betsey Randolph's genuine interior purity could neither be affected nor caught off guard.[158]

When Peter Vivian Daniel wrote a memoir of his wife, Lucy (daughter of Edmund Randolph), he described her "pure and delicate sensitiveness of heart" and her "solemn piety," which combined to form "a being which a virtuous and generous nature . . . would be disposed almost to idolize." He admired her timidity, which "shone out with an attractiveness that was irresistible," and the "correctness of her opinions," which he believed were in perfect conformity with his. This daughter of Edmund Randolph, who had memorialized her mother in much the same terms, was a devout Anglican who clearly had internalized Scripture–based ideas of femininity. Yet although Daniel was well aware of Lucy's "settled principles, and of her warm & humble feelings of piety," he was "comparatively uninformed of the solemnity and ardor of her devotion" until after her death, when he discovered her diary. In spite of their forty years together, he was oblivious of the thinking that informed her religious practices and her acceptance of the scriptural imperatives that kept her subordinate to him.[159]

That at least two of these women kept their spiritual journals hidden from their husbands is telling. In spite of a confessional culture that is broadcast daily on television, we think of journals today as intensely private documents, the repository of innermost thoughts and a safe space in which to reveal the true self. Whether Lucy Randolph Daniel or Martha Laurens Ramsay viewed their journals in that way and kept them with unflinching honesty, however, is doubtful. Interestingly, Daniel's has not survived, although one would expect such a document to have been treasured all the more after her death. Similarly Ramsay's has also disappeared; her husband edited her writing, publishing that which he thought presented a paradigm for young women of the republic to follow. But unlike Daniel, Ramsay had revealed its existence to her husband on her deathbed, perhaps in hopes that it would be distributed at least to family members. Indeed, if she had always intended such publication of her diary, it would surely have shaped the choices she made about the record kept there. If either diary contained cries of anger, resistance, or outright rebellion, we can neither know nor deduce from the testimony of the husbands, whose praise of their wives did not betray whatever dismay such words may have caused them. More likely, a lifetime of self-editing lay in those pages, the outward self-control reflecting thoroughly ingrained lessons of female delicacy, piety, and submission. Certainly that was true for Elizabeth Foote Washington, who admitted that she could not keep a "more perticular" journal of her life "without speaking of all the ill treatment I [ever] met with, & that I did not wish to hand down."[160] If either Daniel or Ramsay achieved a sense of identity apart from her role in the family, she did so in the only safe place she could carve out for its cultivation: in secret.

"Truest Kind of Breeding"

All of these women were Anglicans, that is, members of a church known for its formality in prayer and preaching and its adherence to principles of hierarchy and order. Indeed, their expressions of religion could well have been designed to meet expectations of their gender, as Edmund Randolph made plain in his strident declaration that "a woman in the present state of our society without religion is a monster."[161] For both Allestree in seventeenth-century England, who had described a bold woman as "a kind of monster, a thing diverted and distorted from her proper form," and Edmund Randolph in late-eighteenth-century Virginia, women who resisted male prescriptions for their behavior were, quite literally, monstrous.[162] As the passage inscribed by Mary Ambler shows, the lines between religious and secular advice about religion, nature, manners, and deference had blurred to produce the perfect southern woman. Ambler lived in a society in which her accord with ideas of natural hierarchy was demanded as a religious duty, to which every aspect of her outward behavior should conform. And in the colonial South, the epithet "monstrous" would have had a special significance: in its application to black women as something less than fully human, it was all the more abhorrent to white women. Barred from any semblance of higher education or pretensions to authority, Ambler and other southern women were not in much of a position to contest the truth of these teachings.

Instead, Ambler's ordeal had probably proven to her the truth of
Fordyce's words, and thus what initially strikes a reader as an afterthought
was instead a commentary on her whole experience. Ambler had been
widowed just two years before her trip to Baltimore. Her wealthy and well-
connected husband had inherited the Ambler family's venerable holdings in Jamestown; by 1770, they were already an old Virginia family.[163]
But his death had left her in sole charge of four children, and the death
of an infant daughter following closely on the heels of her husband's demise left her terrified of losing the others. She had waffled agonizingly
over the question of inoculation; as she inclined toward the procedure,
she met Thomas Lawson, a gentleman esteemed by his friends as "the
most deserving of men," whose knowledge of Baltimore kept her from losing her nerve and eased her entry to that town. He wrote to the doctor
about his inoculation schedule, arranged for respectable lodgings, and
even offered to escort her there. His acquaintance with the roads, ferries,
and hospitable homes along the way not only relieved her of most of the
anxieties of travel but made it more comfortable as well. Her account was
filled with gentlemen who came to her aid: doctors who were so concerned when the inoculations failed to take; Captain Margacking [Maga-
chen], an acquaintance of her brother-in-law, who called frequently to
"ask how we did & make a tender of every service in his power" and who
"showed an Hundred Civilities" to her "since she came to Baltimore
Town"; and Colonel Carlyle, who found replacements for a harness that
had been stolen, allowing her the "prospect of get[tin]g home" again.[164]

In spite of the ordeal of inoculations, purges, fevers, and the tedium of
waiting, Ambler never forgot the importance of appearances, decorum,
and connections. Fearing her good clothes would be contaminated by the
pox (she had probably read warnings in the paper),[165] she had left them
at home, so when Sunday arrived, she could not go to church because she
had nothing suitable to wear. Even the usually plain Quakers, whose
meetinghouse was "as much frequented as the Church," were well
dressed, she noticed. Ambler remained conscious of her class status even
while traveling. While Lawson had identified Mrs. Chilton as a respectable
landlady with whom a widowed mother with two young children could
safely stay, he arranged for Ambler and her children to take their meals
separately from the "Mess," a "large Comp[an]y of Gent[tleme]n [who]
dine at Her House every day." She passed the time at home with her
"Books & knitting"; it was at Mrs. Chilton's home that she encountered
Fordyce's *Sermons.* Her genteel occupations were easily set aside when
prominent women came to call: Mrs. Contee, a widow with "a great estate
in Calvert County"; Mrs. Smith, Mrs. Boze, and Mrs. Brook, all women of

Baltimore who visited several times and on whose kindness Ambler repeatedly remarked. On her return home, she graciously acceded to Martha Washington's request to linger at Mount Vernon to dine before completing the last leg of her journey.[166]

So the placement of her *Sermons* excerpt probably should not be interpreted as the last-minute jottings from a book she read during her Baltimore stay. More likely, in her chosen excerpt she found a mirror image of her experience. Her manner, deferential deportment, and dress were critical to her very survival, attracting the solicitous Lawson, who ensured her safe arrival and lodgings; the doctors who worried over her and her children; and Carlyle, who rescued her when she was stranded. A woman of the "truest kind of breeding," Ambler would not have put herself forward in company or contradicted bluntly the men who offered help and friendly advice. Instead, she recognized her vulnerability and dependence, was grateful for the many kindnesses she received, and never "affect[ed] a superiority to any present."

That Ambler advocated a natural softness and Christian meekness to her daughter even as she had courageously taken her children to Baltimore to undergo a controversial treatment underscores the effectiveness of the colonizer's program of education. The increasing availability of print, the rapidity with which English works reached the colonial South, and the increased literacy of women by the end of the colonial period did not always result in forward thinking or the discovery of the self (much less the stirrings of feminism), as we might have expected. Rather, the reverse was often true: the immense popularity of the steady sellers of religious and female advice, and the ways in which women acquiesced to it, showed the power of traditional religion and devotional works, resting on the authority of Scripture, to perpetuate women's subordinate status. Even a woman such as Mary Ambler, privileged with money, education, status, and connections, remained convinced that the best course for women was to learn how to inveigle the protections of men.

THREE

Religion, Voice, and Authority

The women we have met thus far were Anglicans, members of the established church in the southern colonies and of elite families. As such, they had an interest in upholding the social order in which they were prominent. Nor is it accidental that they should figure in the historical record: they were more likely to be able to write than women of lower economic ranks, and their elite social status would encourage the preservation of their papers (even if not nearly in the same quantity as men's papers). But the Anglican Church faced two serious challenges to its spiritual authority in the eighteenth century: evangelical revivals in the 1740s, known today as the Great Awakening, and the American Revolution three decades later. Both events shook the assumptions of hierarchy on which Anglo-American society rested, and both events affected southern women in profound ways. The rapid proliferation of dissenting sects in the wake of the Great Awakening cracked the veneer of conformity to Anglicanism, as thousands found themselves drawn to the evangelicals' emotional messages of repentance and forgiveness. As churches divided, so too did southern women, disagreeing over the efficacy of various established and dissenting religions. Nonetheless, by century's end they had concluded that religion allowed them to appropriate to themselves a measure of authority that the prescriptive literature had previously accorded only to men. And in the void left by disestablishment in the aftermath of the Revolution, women of all religious tempers found a new space in which to flex their newly acquired moral muscle.

GENDER IN THE JUDEO-CHRISTIAN TRADITION

In a country that today prides itself on the separation between church and state, it may be difficult to understand the significance of religion in ordering basic social relations, and why writers such as Allestree and Fordyce commanded the authority they did. In fact, however, they stood on the shoulders of centuries of Judeo-Christian scriptural interpretation and tradition that had made clear the functions of men and women. In the book of Genesis, literally "the beginning," we find the definitions of male, female, and gender relations that permeated religious prescriptive writings on both sides of the Atlantic. Christian interpretations of the ancient Hebrew stories of the creation of male and female and of the Fall (the sin and expulsion of Adam and Eve from Eden) were largely responsible for the shape of gender relations in eighteenth-century Anglo-American culture. To understand the weight of that tradition on southern women and how deeply rooted it was (and arguably remains today), it is helpful to look at some of the most frequently cited biblical passages and the ways in which Christian theologians have interpreted them.

There are actually two creation stories in Genesis. In the earlier (and perhaps more familiar) version, God created Adam from dust, then put him into a deep sleep, extracted a rib, and created a woman to be his companion. The later version is much shorter, however, and reads in its entirety, "God created man in his own image, in the image of God he created him; male and female he created them."[1] The later passage conveys no sense of female subjugation or distinction; both men and women are understood to have been created in the image of God.[2] Christian writers have tended to conflate the two stories, however: the simultaneous creation story represents the state of perfection humanity knew before the Fall but has been unable to regain since. The story of the Fall was different, however. Presented as a chronological sequence, it provided the proof that God sanctioned the subordination of women as punishment for Eve's sin. It showed how woman was created after and for man; it is significant that man was given the power to name her as he had named all the other creatures that inhabited the earth.[3] Then when Adam and Eve encountered the serpent in the garden, it was Eve who led Adam astray: "[W]hen the woman saw that the tree was good for food, and that it was a delight to the eyes, and that the tree was to be desired to make one wise, she took of its fruit and ate; and she also gave some to her husband, and he ate."[4] The New Testament writer of the first letter to Timothy in the first century CE crafted an interpretation of this passage that resonated with most male Christian theologians in ensuing centuries: "For Adam was formed first then Eve; and Adam was not deceived, but the woman was deceived and became a transgressor."[5]

Tertullian, a North African convert to Christianity in the late second century, took the story of the Fall to warn his "sisters in Christ" that they "are the devil's gateway . . . you are she who persuaded him whom the devil did not dare attack. . . . Do you not know that every one of you is an Eve? The sentence of God on your sex lives on in this age; the guilt, of necessity, lives on too."[6] Attempting to reconcile both stories in the fourth century, Augustine of Hippo explained that "the woman together with her husband is the image of God, so the whole substance is one image. But when she is assigned as a help–meet, a function that pertains to her alone, then she is not the image of God." Following the writer of the epistle to Timothy, Augustine believed that Eve was more easily tempted, and therefore, it was she who was "the frailer part of society."[7] Thomas Aquinas, a leading medieval theologian, believed that women's sole purpose was procreation. Greatly influenced by Aristotle, whose work he attempted to incorporate into Christian theology, Aquinas believed men were the more rational and superior of God's creatures. He urged children to follow the example of their fathers since "[t]he father is more to be loved than the mother because he is the active generative element, whereas the mother is the more passive."[8]

Protestant reformers thought of women in somewhat more positive terms—elevating marriage and motherhood over the celibate state, for example—but John Calvin still believed woman was "in the second degree" although created in the image of God. And while he wrote that "Adam was taught to recognise himself in his wife, as in a mirror," he still thought that "Eve, in her turn, [was] to submit herself willingly to her husband, as being taken out of him."[9] While Martin Luther incorporated the later Genesis story to support his assertion that Eve was not rendered inferior to Adam because of her sin, he nevertheless claimed that her descendants were relegated to "stay at home and look after the affairs of the household as one who has been deprived of the ability of administering those affairs that are outside and concern the state."[10]

Of course, Christian theologians did not create patriarchy. The system of male hegemony took nearly twenty–five hundred years to complete, beginning with the development of agriculture in the Neolithic period, during which women were "exchanged" both to cement alliances and to produce children to work the fields. The commodification of female sexuality and male control over female labor became landmarks of civilization with the rise of agricultural societies, urban areas, and city and na-

tion states.[11] Ancient philosophers such as Aristotle strengthened this already–established hierarchy with an elaborate system of thought that positioned males as the standard of perfection. Sex existed solely for procreation. In Aristotle's scheme, the male represented the efficient cause, the
female the material—that is, the male supplied the sensitive soul, without
which the body was no better than a corpse; the female supplied the cor-
ruptible body. Second-century physician Galen of Pergamun believed
both a man and a woman contributed "seed" to produce a child. If each
partner produced strong seed, they would create a boy; weak seed resulted in a girl. Always, however, Galen understood that to be female
meant to have weaker seed, not as an empirical matter (he devised no experiment to prove so) but as a logical one.[12] The greatest teachers of both
Roman Catholic and Protestant traditions had thus incorporated the
thought of the ancients into the revealed truths of Scripture. Aquinas's
Summa Theologica, for example, was the result of his life's work to apply
Aristotelian principles to interpreting Scripture. This combination of reason, science, and revelation gave new strength to centuries–old ideas
about sex and gender.

Perhaps no phrase unites these ancient and early-modern views of
women as effectively as William Tyndale's "the weaker vessel" in his 1526
translation of the New Testament.[13] Carried into proverbs, sermons, the
King James Bible (1611), and later advice literature, this phrase links ancient ideas of the body with Christian teachings about gender. Weaker in
body, intellect, and character, women were passive vessels in their divinely
ordained function of childbearing. Well into the eighteenth century,
Fordyce asked, "Does not the apostle Peter expressly style the woman the
weaker vessel?"[14] Fordyce's young readers were, of course, the descendants of Eve who had inherited all the womanly frailties and weaknesses
of their biblical mother. This core belief in the inherent weakness of
woman's nature was the springboard for a host of related traits that were
considered peculiarly female. Echoing Allestree, Fordyce believed that
modesty, reserve, virtue, piety, and softness were but a few virtues essential
for young women to cultivate to compensate for their inherent weakness.
The enduring usage of the term "weaker vessel" through the centuries tes-
tifies to its power and appeal, particularly to men who grounded their
claim to authority over women in such biblical directives and produced
the advice books from which women should derive their understanding
of God's ordering of their world.

Given the collective weight of the pronouncements of centuries of
philosophers, teachers, scientists, and theologians, we might find it easier

to understand the deference of Mary Ambler and other Anglican women to wisdom they judged greater than theirs. Nonetheless, even they gradually began to realize the authority religion offered them when as mothers, they took to themselves the responsibility of teaching their children. In the colonial period, Helen Calvert Maxwell Read recalled that her mother took her to church every Sunday and "was always setting me to read the Bible, which I always loved better than any other book."[15] Eliza Jaquelin Ambler Carrington recalled listening as a child to her "Mothers [Rebecca Burwell Ambler's] rapturous account of her early devotion to her Maker." Orphaned at age ten, Rebecca Burwell had sought refuge from the noisy tumult of her adoptive household (William Nelson of Yorktown, Virginia) in "a retired spot in the Garret, where she erected a little Alter to worship at; there with her Collection of sacred books, she spent her earliest and latest hours." Rebecca's books, her spiritual guides in her orphaned childhood, instilled in her a confidence in her spiritual identity that she conveyed in her teaching. Eliza was so taken with the power of her mother's teaching that she sketched a verbal portrait of it for the next generation to read and emulate.[16] Catherine Dulany Belt of Maryland credited her mother for the benefits she derived from religion that enabled her to bear the news of her brother's illness. As she confided to her sister-in-law, "My ever dear Mamma instilled these sentiments in my mind and I feel the advantage of them so powerfully."[17]

But such apparent conformity to gender norms did not connote unthinking acceptance of them. Elizabeth Foote Washington, who believed that she would never get to heaven if she did not "cultivat[e] humility, meakness & patience within [her] heart," confessed the struggle to do so: "I have been used extremely ill in time past . . . and wonder'd how I could bear such treatment,—but I must."[18] Elizabeth Nicholas Randolph may have won her husband by "the best of all graces, cheerfulness, good sense, and benevolence," and "anticipated the means of gratifying even [his] caprices" during the course of their marriage. Nonetheless, she revealed an iron will as she refused to receive deists Thomas Jefferson and George Wythe when they visited her home. And, her "infantile purity" notwithstanding, she was the one who decided to whom the family's charity was meted out and which slaves must be sold when her husband's "tenderheartedness" rendered him unable to do so.[19] Indeed, female piety could undergird female resistance. When, despite the pleading of her family, Hannah Lee Corbin rejected her Anglican roots to join the Baptist communion, she showed the subversive potential evangelical Christianity afforded for female spiritual autonomy.

EVANGELICAL CHRISTIANITY

The arrival of Anglican minister George Whitefield in 1739 signaled the beginning of the evangelical revival in the colonies. Historians debate the intensity and influence of the Great Awakening everywhere but particularly in the southern colonies.[20] Indeed, by 1810, fewer than 20 percent of southern whites had joined the Baptist, Methodist, or Presbyterian churches (those most closely identified with evangelicalism), although they had built twice as many churches as had the Anglicans in the two decades before the Revolution.[21] Sects dissenting from the Anglican Church had been present in the South long before Whitefield's first visit. Quakers had been living in Maryland and Virginia since the 1660s; German immigrants brought several evangelical strains with them; Scotch-Irish immigrants were largely Presbyterian; other English immigrants were Baptist.[22] And in Northampton, Massachusetts, Congregational minister Jonathan Edwards had launched a revival within his own congregation in 1735.[23] Still, Whitefield lit a firestorm of fervent conversions. His long blond hair and mesmerizing voice captivated men and women alike; his open-air preaching up and down the eastern seaboard was a completely new style of religion that refused to recognize boundaries of colony, denomination, or even church building; his message of a loving God, ready to forgive and save the repentant sinner, struck a deep chord in many colonial Americans.[24]

The appeal of evangelical Christianity was its emphasis on the individual's personal relationship with God. This view of religion dispensed with the necessity of preachers schooled in English universities and equipped with degrees in theology. Presbyterian Samuel Davies found slaves much attracted to his preaching in the 1750s; when attempting to evaluate the genuineness of their conversion, he finally relied on their "conduct and temper" as indicators rather than on their knowledge of doctrine. Indeed, for all evangelicals, the evidence of true conversion was the range of emotions experienced between the realization of one's guilt and then of one's salvation. These experiences were marked by torrents of tears, deep anguish, and fits interspersed with exhaustion. The conversion experience was the first central characteristic of evangelical Christianity; the other was the imperative to share the knowledge of God derived from it.[25] The very experience of God's grace authorized the telling and preaching of the story, and evangelicals published their narratives and preached them from makeshift wood platforms, in barns, in the parlors of homes, and in letters to one another. The gulf, therefore, between evangelicals, who looked to emotion for divine revelation, and the Anglican establishment, which relied on a dispassionate reading of the Scriptures, could hardly have been wider.

Evangelicals presented a challenge to the social and political order as well. The growing Baptist sect, for example, attracted great numbers even as it condemned such amusements as gambling, drinking, horse racing, and dancing, all cherished pastimes of the gentry and, even more important, crucial symbols of their authority. By reframing these activities as morally wrong, Baptists implicitly questioned the legitimacy of gentry claims to that authority. Moreover, the Baptists opposed slavery, the economic system on which gentry wealth rested, and even incorporated blacks into their congregations, disrupting racial alliances gentry leaders had attempted to forge among whites of all ranks.[26] Anglicans met these challenges by means legal and otherwise. Baptists were prosecuted for sedition, fined, and jailed; preachers were hauled off their preaching platforms and beaten; services were broken up by mobs bearing sticks and clubs, even in some cases a live snake or a hornet's nest.[27] Even Presbyterian Samuel Davies, the "ideal apostle of dissent to the decorous Virginians," who had dutifully applied for (and been granted) permits to preach in the colony, incurred the ridicule of some Anglicans who sneered at the "great numbers of poor people, who, generally, are his only followers."[28] In the years before the Revolution, then, evangelicals endured ridicule and worse from Anglican elites who sought to repress their gatherings and criticisms of their gentry betters.[29]

Women, too, were caught up in the revival, as different evangelical sects had varying appeals to them. Isaac Watts and Philip Doddridge, influential English evangelicals who, in one historian's assessment, were "the two men who were largely responsible for defining and disseminating affective religion," took a middle way between the rational and emotional that appealed to many women, particularly in Virginia.[30] Isaac Watts's works, especially his hymns, were staples in colonial American churches and homes, and Doddridge's influence was transmitted to Virginians in his *Principles of Christian Religion* (1754) and through the preaching of Samuel Davies, who admired him greatly.[31] Other women were more interested in the ways that evangelicals legitimated their personal experiences of God. In their exploration of their relationship with God, some women used increasingly intimate, even erotic, language. Methodist Sarah Jones, for example, described her "sacred banquet" with Jesus, in which she was "drunken with my beloved, until I am sick of love, and roll in tumbling oceans of bliss immortal."[32]

As the Great Awakening began to reshape the religious landscape in the South, southern women responded to the evangelicals' emotional appeal to the heart. One of the few elite converts to the Baptist sect before the Revolution was Hannah Lee Corbin. The daughter of Thomas Lee, president of the Governor's Council and the builder of Stratford Hall, one of the finest homes in colonial Virginia, she was born into wealth and position. She also married well. Gawen Corbin was a justice of the peace in Westmoreland County, a member of the House of Burgesses, and later of the Council.[33] They had one child, Martha. But in 1759, at the age of thirty-one, Hannah Corbin became a widow. Corbin's will bequeathed to his wife all of his estate of Peckatone, which was to be divided in half upon their daughter's marriage (provided she followed her father's instructions and did not marry before age twenty-one). And in his final decree, Corbin forbade the remarriage of his widow, under pain of losing all but one-third of the estate.[34] Thus far, the evidence is clear; it becomes considerably less so during Corbin's widowhood. She fell in love with the physician, Dr. Richard Hall, who attended her husband in his last illness. He owned a small estate in Fauquier County, but he came to live at Peckatone in Richmond County with Corbin. Their first child, Elisha Hall Corbin, was born in March 1763, followed by a daughter, also named Martha.[35] There is no record of a marriage between Corbin and Hall, which is not surprising because a legal marriage in the colony would have deprived Corbin of a portion of her legacy. For the rest of her life she signed her name "H. Corbin."[36]

The details of the conversion of this high-profile Lee to the Baptist sect remain a bit murky. Baptist histories claim that Dr. Hall was already a Baptist and that he and Corbin were married in a Baptist ceremony, a dissenter marriage that would not have been legally recognized in Anglican Virginia.[37] Others, citing her feisty spirit, have argued that Corbin thumbed her nose at Northern Neck society and her husband's wishes, living without benefit of marriage with the man of her choice after Gawen Corbin's death.[38]

There is no proof, however, that Hall was ever a member of a Baptist community; nor, before 1771, is there a record of Corbin's membership. There is plenty of evidence later in the 1770s of Corbin's Baptist affiliation, but dating her conversion to support the theory of a Baptist marriage is troublesome. Both she and Hall were cited by a grand jury for nonattendance at the Anglican Church in 1764.[39] This may indicate Baptist sympathies, but there is no hard evidence that they had converted by then, although it is possible. David Thomas, a well-educated, talented Baptist preacher, had moved from Pennsylvania to Fauquier County in the Northern Neck, where he founded Broad Run Church in 1762.[40] That twenty-three people were baptized the day after its organization suggests an interest in the Baptist church that Corbin might have shared.[41] Thomas's evangelism in Corbin's neighborhood brought forth much fruit. Broad Run Church spawned many smaller congregations—most notably for this account, Chappawamsic Baptist Church and its offshoot, Potomac Church.[42] In 1771, granted letters of dismissal to form another congregation, several former members of Chappawamsic Baptist Church founded Potomac Baptist Church. After setting out their covenant with their God and with one another, the clerk affixed their names to the register. The ninth name is that of Hannah Hall.[43] Here, within the Baptist community, is the name she used nowhere else. It appears as a quiet affirmation of her marriage and status as Hall's wife by a congregation that punished by excommunication far lesser sins than fornication.[44]

Her family was appalled. Upon hearing the news of her conversion, her brother Arthur Lee had written from London an impassioned plea to their brother, Richard Henry Lee, to "recall her . . . persue, try every gentle, winning Art to lure her to herself. He, for whose Honour you are laboring will prosper the good Work & bless its Undertaker."[45] In 1778, she wrote to her sister, Alice Shippen, defending her defection from Anglicanism. "I am not surprised that you seem to have a mean Opinion of the Babtist religion," she acknowledged gently. "I believe most people that are not of that Profession are perswaded we are either Enthusiasts or Hypocrites. But my Dear Sister the followers of the Lamb have been ever esteemed so. this is our Comfort—And that we know in whom we have believed."[46] And so she remained serenely firm in her new profession, committed enough to host meetings on her plantation in the face of the hostility to which evangelicals were subjected.[47]

It is clear from Corbin's defense of her faith that she followed the evangelical prescription to get things right with her God rather than with men.[48] She described her dependence on the Divine, her love for and profound joy in God, in a way that makes plain a deeply personal relationship:

> I hope I shall never live to see the day that I dont love God, for there can nothing I know befal me so horrible as to be left to myself. I have wofully experienced what a mangled situation when I desired to be in my own hands. And surely never poor Mortal had so much reason to sing Free Grace as your Sister, that my exalted Redeemer should mercifully snatch me from the Fire when so many Thousands infinitely better by Nature have been permitted to Sin on till they have sunk to endless misery. Glory be to my God for his Pardoning Grace His redeeming Love.[49]

Corbin's description of her faith contains all the elements of the evangelical formula: awareness of human frailty, the acknowledgment of her sin, and the "Free Grace" granted by a forgiving God. The serenity that followed her conversion is palpable in her letter; she had experienced her Redeemer and knew only the comfort that sustained and strengthened her against her Anglican family's opposition.

By the time Judith Anna Smith of Henrico County resolved to keep a "memorandum of the daily ocurrances of my life, and of the goodness of God towards [me]," emotion had become a prerequisite of true faith. Smith began her diary in 1789 at the age of twenty, resolving to be more watchful "as becomes a creature that must soon appear in Judgment." She recorded all the ups and downs of her devotional life: on the same day, she was pleased with herself for her meditations during a stroll in the woods, for her attendance at Mr. Lacy's sermon, and for her way of passing another Sabbath, yet discouraged when she "had to fight with a hard heart and foolish thots" during divine service. "But," she concluded, "God is kind, I trust he was near me this evening." Then, looking back over the first day of her resolution to be God's, she wrote anxiously, "I hope I felt solemn."[50] Another day, she first sought a female friend's advice on religious exercises, then talked with a male friend who raised her "thots towards Heaven." Both encounters were agreeable enough; indeed she was "charmed" by the latter, and her "heart quickened to press on towards the gates of the Heavenly Jerusalem." The exertion proved too much, however, for her next words read "much fatigued. Could not feel so enlarged in prayer as I hoped."[51]

Smith measured her success in achieving communion with her Lord by the emotional depths she was able to plumb. On day three of her new regimen, she felt herself a failure at prayer precisely because she felt so "unaffectd . . . O where is that broken heart and those flowing tears I hope I once experience at such times, and wich should always accompany such solemn duties."[52] Surely thoughts of human sinfulness and the imminent prospect of death must conjure up tears of repentance—solemnity, at the very least. Yet public rather than private worship, and talks with friends rather than solitary rambles in the woods, produced more desirable effects: conjuring emotions or quickening her heart. Her need for external prompting suggests a soul searching to respond appropriately to the evangelical preaching it has heard. Eager to respond to the call, understanding that she could not reach God without first acknowledging and bewailing her sinfulness, she looked in vain for the sins that required such grief.

Smith's struggle was not unlike that of Mary Avery Browder, who was so taken by Devereux Jarratt's preaching that her sisters wondered if she had not been "Jarratifyed." Her letters to her Methodist minister testify to her unease about the state of her soul. For all of her efforts at reasoning through her conversion process, she could not be sure of God's forgiveness until she had actually felt the despair of her sinfulness. "I had not suffered enough," she explained to him. "I could neither feel the burden of sin nor know that my sins were forgiven."[53]

Like Browder's letters, Smith's diary tracks the peregrination of a soul; it is a record of her constant notations of God's mercies, her failings in resolution, and her impatience that the much-awaited transformation did not occur faster as a result of her concentrated efforts to be good. On day five, she puzzled, "I am concerned to think that after all cultivation I should still remain the same unfruitful creature I have always been."[54] Her entries broke off for the summer, and in September she resumed, despairing that despite "all the lively scenes of nature together with the frequent attendance on the blessed Gospel, as well as every other privilege of reading praying, conversing and meditating," nothing had produced the desired "warm affections to God" that were the barometer of true faith.[55]

Although she had no use for any evangelical sect, Anglican Elizabeth Foote Washington was also keenly aware of the nature of human frailty, the need for repentance, and the hope of salvation (all key aspects of evangelicalism); indeed, this awareness colors her entire diary. However, she approached these issues in a typically Anglican way: with an overlay of reason. She was puzzled by the caprices of human nature, "for it has ever appear'd to me," she thought, "to be the greatest contradiction in the world to be call'd after his name & at the same time not to walk in his steps . . . by cultivating humility, meakness & patience." Still she acknowledged her own difficulty at controlling her temper when "ill–used"; only because God had "possess[ed] my heart with a sincere desire to please him," was she able to keep her "evil nature from making such answers sometimes as would [have] been severe." Yet even she was not completely untouched by the appeal of emotionalism in evangelical religion. While she prayed to have a "truly religious family—not led away with Baptistical notions" she also wanted "a religion that effectually touches the heart."[56]

The struggles of all these women—even the reserved Washington, who wanted "no outside shew"—illustrate how evangelical sermons that stressed a religion of the heart changed the way women responded to their faith.[57] The primacy of the emotional experience of conversion for evangelicals legitimated feeling as *the* means by which God reveals the divine to humankind; evangelical Christianity thus forged a strong link between emotion and ultimate Truth. No learned degrees, no ability to write lengthy theological discourses, not even a license or church pulpit were required to preach the Truth derived from the raptures of a conversion experience. Barred from the formal institutional apparatus of min-

istry and consigned to the world of feeling that was understood as a female province, many women found in evangelical Christianity a unique
invitation. In their experience of God's grace, they realized a dawning
sense of their spiritual autonomy and confidence.

Evangelical ministers encouraged women's discoveries of their own
worthiness and significance before God, even supporting their choice to
convert in the face of opposition from their husbands. Women were able
to speak publicly in promiscuous—that is, mixed sexed—Baptist settings,
and to bring grievances against fellow members, their "brothers" as well as
their "sisters."[58] This was even true for black women before the Revolution. In these ways, within the enclaves of their congregations, Baptists acknowledged the legitimacy of female spiritual authority and eased somewhat, even if only temporarily, the gender and racial hierarchies of
southern society. It was an upending of the old order that Anglican
Robert Carter Nicholas could not abide. "Suppose . . . every Man was allowed . . . *Freedom of Judgment*," he sputtered, "instead of that Uniformity
of Doctrine which our Church has formerly been blessed with, what a
Babel of Religions should we have amongst us?" Surely the lower sorts of
men (let alone women and African Americans) could "rely with greater
Safety upon the glorious Luminaries of our Church [than upon a] private
Preacher" to interpret and teach true religion.[59]

What the evangelicals began to create, then, was a powerful sense of the
significance of the individual, buttressed by the strength and sanctity of a
conscience shaped by a loving God who had revealed himself in a conversion experience. It was, quite literally, a spiritual and intellectual awakening for both men and women but with different consequences for each.
In the groundswell of the Awakening, some scholars have seen how the
search for spiritual autonomy laid the groundwork for the struggle for political independence thirty-five years later.[60] In their view, the claim the
Declaration of Independence made for the right of each individual to
life, liberty, and the pursuit of happiness was facilitated, in part, by the
awakening of colonial Americans to their individual worth before God.
When Thomas Jefferson advised his nephew Peter Carr to "shake off all
the fears and servile prejudices under which weak minds are servilely
crouched," and to "fix reason firmly in her seat, and call to her tribunal
every fact, every opinion," he was warning Carr against the claims of each
sect to the possession of divinely revealed Truth.[61] Yet his advice, as applicable to judging an office seeker's speech as to a preacher's sermon, underscores a signal eighteenth-century development: the emergence of the
individual's right to form his own judgment. This right was understood to
be a male prerogative, of course; and while both Jefferson (a Deist who

had little use for institutional Christianity) and evangelicals applauded that right, Jefferson relied on reason to form that judgment, while evangelicals relied on feeling.

The other difference, of course, was that the ability to reason remained understood as masculine throughout the century. The Constitutional Convention did not consider women viable participants in the polity, since women's susceptibility to passion rendered them incapable of making the rational judgments required of voting citizens.[62] Of course, not even all men realized their claims to participation in the polity that would come incrementally over the course of the next two centuries. The unrest that boiled over in violence in the backcountry of Massachusetts, Pennsylvania, and Maine signaled the disparity in views between the Founders and rank-and-file farmers about the meaning of liberty.[63] Free black men everywhere were gradually disenfranchised by 1840, even as white men's rights expanded.[64] Nonetheless, the Revolution had begun a process of democratization that diminished the relevance of Nicholas's "Luminaries" and enhanced the significance of individual men.

LEGACIES OF THE REVOLUTION

Claiming the Self

The legacy of the Revolution was very different for women. Excluded from the formal workings of government, women located their civic duty in their homes, charged with the responsibility of instilling in the children of the republic those civic virtues guaranteed to preserve it. This duty, called Republican Motherhood, required a more thorough education than had been provided before the war. Female education thus took on greater ideological significance in the postwar period, a marked gain for women, as many young girls entered more institutionalized programs of learning than the haphazard field school or occasional tutor arrangements of the colonial period.[65] However, historian Linda Kerber believes that the most significant legacy of the Revolution for women was the erosion of their dower rights, which by English law and custom provided a widow with the use of one-third of her husband's estate for her maintenance and support. After the Revolution, state courts increasingly divided estates equally among widow and children, frequently reducing widows to abject dependence on their sons.[66] In short, a revolution fought for independence for men only confirmed women's *de*pendence, as women of the republic remained in the same legal category of dependence as children and the insane.[67]

Though the Revolution's impact on women may have been ambiguous, its implications for the relationship between church and state were certainly clear and momentous. In a series of debates in state legislatures, the proposal and disposal of various configurations of church and state relations, and finally the adoption of various bills of disestablishment, Americans worked out their fears about how to maintain order without the staying hand of an established church. While some states proposed ways in which freedom of religion would be guaranteed, even enabling citizens to direct their tax dollars to the church of their choice, it was Virginia's passage in 1785 of Thomas Jefferson's "An Act for Establishing Religious Freedom" that completely severed churches from any state sponsorship, effectively guaranteeing freedom *from* (rather than of) religion.[68] The other states followed Virginia's lead. With the Anglican Church thus effectively sidelined as a competitor, the leading evangelical churches (Baptist, Methodist, and Presbyterian) grew by leaps and bounds. No longer persecuted and marginalized, these churches gained both respectability and, by the mid-nineteenth century, a majority of the southern white population.[69]

When we evaluate the Revolutionary legacy for women, therefore, disestablishment merits a closer look. For while the disestablished Anglican Church, like all churches, ceased to operate as an arm of the state in the South, it did not cease to exist as an institution. Consequently, the churches of the early republic occupied a new kind of space, simultaneously public and private: public in the sense that they were nondomestic meeting places for both men and women, requiring organization and money for their perpetuation, yet private in their legal separation from state control and support.[70] As they changed from civic power to voluntary association, the churches' appeal to men and women also changed, because power in the church was no longer a measure of secular power. This was both bane and boon for all churches, particularly the Anglican Church. For while men's interest in the churches declined, no longer seeing them as institutions of power and influence, women's interest increased, as they recognized the churches' potential to accomplish good in the early republic. Women resurrected the Episcopal Church out of the ashes of the Anglican, and they raised money for church support, education for girls, the care of orphans, Sunday schools, and a host of other benevolent activities.[71] In short, in the vacuum created by men's abdication, women became a power in the church because there was little fear that power would make itself felt outside the church's boundaries in the secular world.

The impact of these developments—the Revolution, defining liberty and citizenship, and disestablishment—on southern women's intellectual identity was momentous. Certainly, during this period, men were learning to think of themselves as individuals, free to settle where they would, free to pursue personal enrichment and happiness, and entitled to all the rights of citizenship in a republic. That is, they were taking themselves seriously, as *subject*. One of the curiosities of advice literature, to this point, however, was how devoid it was of women as individual subjects.[72] Instead, *woman* was continually presented as a single type or being, a universal; indeed, Fordyce had warned women in his sermons against the dangers of perceiving themselves as a subject. A woman "that affects to dispute, to decide, to dictate on every subject" would become an "object of aversion." A woman who displayed a "certain briskness of air" he thought "approach[ed] too near" the posture of a prostitute. A woman who has broken through the "domestic enclosure," freely "ranging at large the wide common of the world," would be considered "lawful game, to be hunted down" by men.[73] Women appropriating masculine privileges simply could not expect protections accorded to properly behaved females: outspokenness could lead to exclusion, a confident demeanor to a slandered reputation, mobility in the streets to sexual assault. In every way, Fordyce sought to suppress any desire to be a subject.[74] But in the creation of a third sphere, neither public nor private, that resulted from disestablishment women in post-Revolutionary America found a way to excavate and nurture that subject self. As possessors of souls, American women of all religious stripes learned to claim their human and spiritual rights.[75]

Learning to Write

One of the most important ways to manifest the claim of self is by writing, a process that gives voice to one's thoughts and that is tangible and able to be treasured and preserved, unlike the ephemera of tea-table conversations long forgotten. As Dale Spender has explained, "To write was to be; it was to create and to exist. It was to construct and control a worldview without interference from the 'masters.' "[76] No wonder writing was a secondary educational priority for colonial American girls; there was little reason to encourage a means of self-expression in the sex who was taught to be deferential, if not silent altogether. But in their post-Revolutionary assertion of moral and spiritual agency, southern women began to write. The significance of this development for them is more readily appreciated when we consider the practical obstacles that had stymied female writing: the lack and deficiency of instruction, the scarcity of paper and other supplies, and the demands of household and parenting obligations on their time. That eighteenth-century homes did not dedicate any household space to female reading and writing further underscores the ways gender ideology was impressed on all aspects of southern life.

Writing masters had always been at a premium in the early South despite the legislation of the Virginia House of Burgesses commanding the education of southern children. Under such circumstances, girls' writing literacy remained consistently lower than boys'. But the project of writing was not easy, even for those girls fortunate enough to have learned how. First, they required paper. Here again, as in their access to books, their isolation and lack of mobility hampered them. Advertisements in colonial newspapers show writing paper was available for purchase in regional centers (the *Virginia Gazette* regularly advertised paper for sale in their own offices in Williamsburg as well as other outlets in town, and in Petersburg and Fredericksburg, for example), but wives and daughters largely relied on their men to make their purchases for them.[77] William Hunter's daybook between 1764 and 1766 showed that most customers who came into his store were men, and they spent almost twice as much on stationery (paper and blank forms) as they did on their *Virginia Gazette* subscriptions.[78] Paper was always precious; Philadelphian Benjamin Franklin was a major supplier of paper to printer William Parks, until Parks established a paper mill in Virginia in 1743 (with Franklin's assistance).[79] During the course of a forty-year association, Franklin also supplied the Timothy family printers of Charles Town with books and paper; Elizabeth Timothy advertised "several sorts of Writing Paper" and other writing supplies in her shop in the city.[80] Letter writers made the most of every inch of space, sometimes writing sideways up the margins as their words overflowed the borders they had originally allocated. When Catherine Dulany Belt of Maryland feared that her recent marriage was the cause of her friend's silence, Peggy Murdock reassured her, "[D]on't think, my dear, that because you are a married woman, I mean, to have no farther *kinnections* with you, I would not give you up as correspondent, for any consideration . . . [but] How cou'd I write without paper & I had not an inch, to save my life."[81] Even into the nineteenth century women complained of a lack of paper, as Mary Abigail Willing Coale replied to her sister, "You desire me to write on long sheets of paper I have none therefore have written this small and rather *close*."[82]

Likewise, pens were indispensable for writing, and here, too, women labored at a disadvantage. While boys were taught how to shape and sharpen a quill to effect the most precise and exquisite hand for their business papers and personal correspondence, girls were not. Although she was educated by one of the best teachers in the north, Anthony Benezet, Philadelphian Deborah Logan complained that he had not taught her to make her own pens.[83] Virginian Frances Tanner Archer begged her grandmother Jane Cocke to excuse her bad writing as "I am in a great hurry and the pen is very bad."[84] Women would also depend on men to furnish the other necessities for writing: ink powder, bottle, and stand, penknife, pounce (to prevent the ink from soaking into the paper), and ruler and pencil. A poorly prepared ink could fade before the letter could be read; as Charlotte Balfour cautioned Eliza Whiting, "you must be cautious what kind of Ink you write with—Yr. Lettr. Had been open'd before I recd. It—owing I doubt not to the direction being almost effaced—indeed 'twas with the greatest difficulty I cou'd read the contents within."[85] Preparing to write was a process in itself, consuming time of which women already lacked a ready supply.

Indeed, the lack of time to write is one of the most common complaints in southern women's letters. They wrote late at night, when family demands had temporarily ceased, and they raced to beat the tyranny of the melting candle to its final flicker of light. Jean Blair hoped her sister Mary Braxton could read her writing, since she "wrote it in a great hurry."[86] Young Cortenay Norton signed off her letter to her father earlier than she would have wished because "the light from the candle occasion[ed] a weakness in [her] eyes."[87] They set up portable lap desks, writing with one hand, while tending to a child with the other. As Peggy McHenry wrote to her husband in 1789, "I am afraid you can scarcely read this, but I have not time to copy it—it was wrote on a stool on my lap in [daughter] Polly's room and I was up and down frequently while about it."[88] Her letter reveals yet another time-consuming practice of female letter writing: making a fair copy of an imperfect first draft, conscious always of self-presentation, even to a husband. Women of "leisure" also complained of lack of time, squeezing short missives between callers and their own obligatory visits. As Mary Coale explained to her sister, while on a visit to Philadelphia, "I have inclination to write to you every day, but Father Time and I are always quarreling he goes so fast in this Town . . . however this morning I have caught his Lordship but perceive by his provoking finger that I shall have him at my command only for fifteen minutes—as then commences visiting hour."[89]

Finally, the very architecture of homes, even (or rather, especially) of the very wealthy, discouraged women's writing. The small homes of most eighteenth-century southerners, a story and a half high, consisting at best of two rooms on the first floor and sleeping or storage space on a second floor, would have been cramped quarters enough for the average family of five or six people. These houses lacked the luxury of space dedicated to specialized pursuits of any kind, let alone reading or writing; a chair moved to the window would have sufficed. Although the gentry's prosperity in the eighteenth century permitted such elaborated space, of course, it is significant that it was devoted pointedly and entirely to male intellectual pursuits. The library was a male retreat and the locus of splendid display and power, access to which the owner controlled, as we saw with William Byrd. Even as homes became increasingly larger, with more rooms serving particular functions, women never enjoyed ownership over any space. Men and women mixed in parlors and dining rooms, but talk in such company would rarely deal with such subjects as politics, science, or philosophy. As Eliza Key wrote of her visit to the Eastern Shore in 1780, "The great politeness of Ladies & Gentlemen could not fail to be agreeable. . . . They seem, at least those I was most with, indifferent about politics, or rather perhaps from politeness silent on that subject; so that had I not carried any anxiety concerning them with me, I should have returned without any, for it never could have originated there."[90] The most significant conversations took place in the library, from which women were excluded. The bedroom, lowest in the hierarchy of rooms, was private space for women, but only at the sufferance of husbands, who also shared that space. In every way, then, architecture, furnishings, and social uses of space trivialized the import of female thought and expression.[91]

Chronicling the Soul

In spite of all these obstacles, southern women began to write in earnest in the latter half of the eighteenth century, first keeping secret journals, meant for their eyes only, but then daring to write for others in journals, memoirs, and letters they hoped would serve as guides for succeeding generations. Lamenting that she had "too long neglected to keep a memorandum of the daily occurrences of my life," Judith Anna Smith began her journal in 1789, resolving "deliberately to be more engaged in religion." Clues in her journal suggest that she was inspired by the Presbyterian revival (the first since Samuel Davies in the 1750s) generated by students of Hampden-Sydney College in Prince Edward County, Virginia. Possibly the Alexis who had raised her "thots towards Heaven" was a student there; on their walks together to the college, during which they "conversed all the way," Smith could have prodded him to learn of the teachings taking place inside the college walls. Excluded from that scholarly community because of her sex, Smith nonetheless eagerly sought its lessons, talking with Alexis, attending revival sermons, and conferring about "religious exercises" with other women such as "P," who "appears much engaged."[92]

"P" may well have suggested keeping a journal as a way for Smith to become more engaged herself; Philip Doddridge, who had been such an influence on Samuel Davies, recommended that Christians keep a journal, and Presbyterian preachers may have followed suit, urging their hearers to so as well.[93] In addition, since the Presbyterian ministry in the eighteenth century was better educated than the Baptist or Methodist, it is hardly surprising to find a revival of the sect within a college. In such a setting, it makes sense that Smith would turn to writing as a way to probe for evidence of grief and remorse for her sins. Her faults would come to light in her daily memoranda; her writing would reveal her identity: the very essence of her soul. And in writing the story of her salvation, she was the central figure, the self worthy of scrutiny, the recipient of God's "mercy and long forbearance," "the clay in the hands of the potter," waiting to be "fashion[ed] after [his] own gracious image."[94] Her journal was a private one—there is no indication that she ever shared it. But she did preserve it, a precious memento of her interior journey to her true self: an image of God.

In a marriage to which her husband's tribute suggests deep emotional intimacy, Lucy Randolph Daniel nonetheless concealed from him the journal of her spiritual journey. Lucy Daniel had hand-copied her father's tribute to her mother, Elizabeth Nicholas Randolph, to read the account of her mother's life as she would any conduct-of-life advice book. As a child, Lucy had suffered from "an unusual delicacy of Constitution," which together with her "apparent timidity, shone out with an attractiveness that was irresistible" to her prospective husband. However, her husband's observation that even the rack could not dissuade her "from her homage to truth as revealed in the conclusions of her own conscience" suggests the presence of an indomitable will, not unlike her mother's, in spite of her delicacy. He often remarked on her "alacrity and earnestness in preparing to attend public worship," yet he had not known of her journal. Her journal contained prayers for her family's growth in religion (to overcome their recalcitrance?), a justification for infant baptism (perhaps her own theological rebuttal against the evangelical practice of adult baptism?), and "extracts and sentiments" from her reading, in addition to her "reflections on the progress of her religious affections." Lucy Daniel was born in 1790 and came of age in a time when women were assuming more overt leadership in the churches than had previous generations. Yet it is telling that she still concealed the development of an interior self that was focused on something other than her family and that her journal does not survive in the Daniel family's papers, while her husband's writings do.[95] Despite its cast as a spiritual journey, and southern men's general approbation of religious women, Daniel's journal may have revealed too much of an individual will and identity to be disclosed to a husband who had found her timidity so alluring.

Catherine Fullerton of Charleston, South Carolina, was in her twenties when she began her journal in June 1798. The diary was for her own use, since she was certain that "my actions cannot be interesting to any one," and that it would be "vanity to think they can be improving." Its purpose was to serve as a record of her life, so that she could "take pride in endeavouring to improve . . . [and] distinguish the Evil, and determine me to act with as much propriety as is consistent with human nature." In typical Anglican fashion, she disdained passion; thought predestination "question[ed] the justice of God" (could anyone really believe, she argued, that "he creates for the sole purpose of wantonly punishing us?"); and was thoroughly Arminian in her conviction that "we are free agents, and will, in different degrees, be rewarded or punish'd according to Good or Evil Actions."[96] Anglican in her theology, she applied its ethos of hierarchy and order to gender relations in the world around her, remarking with distaste on "Women [who] think the Wife shou'd command & the Husband obey." Like Mary Astell one hundred years earlier, she looked askance at the marital bond, rejecting a suggestion that she would "marry a Rich Old Miser who will be polite enough to die soon after and leave all the money to [her]" (it was not worth it, she thought) but firmly believing that once chosen, marriage and its gender conventions must be honored.[97]

Regrettably, Fullerton kept her diary only through the summer, and so we do not have her account of the momentous changes in her life shortly thereafter: her marriage to Dr. Armand DeRossett, her move to Wilmington, North Carolina, and her conversion to Methodism. But in her family letters we can glean hints about the shift in her theology and in her ideas about gender relations in marriage. Methodism arrived in North Carolina in the 1790s and had, as elsewhere, initially attracted both the lower orders of whites and slaves and the opposition of the elite. But in the first decade of the nineteenth century, the lowly churches in Edenton, New Bern, and Wilmington began to attract genteel women, among them the highly respectable Catherine Fullerton DeRossett.[98] She did not disown her Anglican roots entirely, for she still applied the powers of her intellect to her faith; but now, convinced of the necessity for the spiritual rebirth of the conversion experience, she earnestly wondered why "reasonable Creatures, who know . . . that God will bring all to judgment, should rest satisfied without knowing whether they have the 'Spirit of Christ' or not."[99] Like evangelicals everywhere, she could not understand why the revelations of the Spirit were not apparent to everyone. When she brought her zeal home, she encountered both admiration and resistance. While her husband admitted that he "shudder[ed] . . . to think of the life we might have led, but for your example," he nonetheless remained "utterly opposed to . . . persons who continually endeavor to weaken the attachment of our young people to, & withdraw them from the church."[100] In the void left by the demise of the Anglican Church, the Methodists had snapped up wives, daughters, and slaves, creating divisions in households, not only of denomination but of authority as well. Many men shared Armand DeRossett's dismay at this turn of events. Not coincidentally, they began to shore up the sagging Episcopal Church to reassert their patriarchal authority, and indeed, for all of Catherine's efforts, Armand remained resolutely Episcopalian.[101]

Martha Laurens Ramsay kept a spiritual diary for about fourteen years that she, too, hid from her husband until just before her death. She had written out a covenant with God when she was fourteen that set out her life's purpose, from which she would not be diverted. "She had inwardly determined to become as expert in religion," her biographer, Joanna Gillespie, observed, "as her older brother John was in political and civic affairs." She used her document as a touchstone throughout her life, coming back to it repeatedly to see how she measured up. But it was the confluence of financial, family, and spiritual crises in 1795 that prompted her increasing reliance on her diary, which received the outpourings of grief, doubt, and evidence of deep depression that she shared with no one else.[102]

Born into one of the most prominent families in South Carolina (her father, Henry Laurens, was a merchant, slave trader, and one of the four commissioners appointed to negotiate the peace to end the Revolutionary War), Martha Laurens was raised an Anglican. The legacy of her childhood religion was a deep proclivity for the rational, which, in the midst of her 1795 "dark night of the soul," warred with the flood of emotions that had thrown her into a spiral of depression. But perhaps an even greater influence on her religious development was the books that were guides, and even surrogate parents, for the motherless girl during her father's long absences from home.[103] In her determination to make religion her province, she delighted in the hours she spent in her father's library, in which she learned, in Gillespie's words, "to see herself as utterly unique in God's eyes, her own independent Self." There, in her closet devotions, she met Philip Doddridge, the evangelical writer, in whose *Rise and Progress of Religion in the Soul* she would find the formula for the covenant she would imitate. On "December 23, 1773, Being This Day Fourteen

Years and Seven Weeks Old," Martha Laurens carefully subscribed her pledge to God: "I *avouch* [vow] and declare myself this day to be one of his covenant people." For his part, God promised her a place "in the embraces of [his] everlasting love."[104]

Exactly when she began her diary is unclear, but it is certain that it was the key to her survival in the dark year of 1795.[105] Coping with the threat of bankruptcy, a family scandal, the deaths of two infant daughters, and her own unnamed "most easily besetting sin," Martha Laurens Ramsay sank into a "darkness" that was to envelop her for almost a year. Her diary bore her catalog of afflictions, her desperate cries to a God who seemed deaf to her pleas, and finally, her resolutions for the future as the skies broke and she could discern light. Her diary was her lifeline: there she tried to understand the adversities God had sent her, to calculate his displeasure with her, and to bridge the chasm between her tortured soul and a distant God; there she poured out her agony. She, who had "had a mandate to be religion's successful representative," perched precariously on the edge of failure in this period; perhaps, biographer Gillespie suggests, her "most easily besetting sin" was a Laurens pride in refusing to accept failure in her chosen work.[106]

As crucial as her diary was to the charting of her spiritual identity, Ramsay never revealed the nature of her "most easily besetting sin"; nor was her puzzled husband, reading her diary fifteen years later, able to identify it. Perhaps it was the pride of a woman who expected to adhere without failure or flaw to the covenant of her childhood. Or perhaps it was the frustrated pride that was the occupational hazard of being an educated, elite woman in the eighteenth century, when all the advice literature and sermons and religious tracts taught her to sublimate herself to her husband and family (Ramsay had read Fordyce as well as Allestree). But Ramsay was an exceptional woman in an exceptional family. She had been privileged in her education, picking up Latin and taxonomy, for example, in addition to traditional female subjects. She adored her father and her elder brother, both men of status and ambition: her father had endured imprisonment during the Revolution and her brother's "love of military glory" resulted in his death in a minor skirmish in the days between Yorktown and the final peace of the Revolution. But their heroism had propelled her to seek her own: "the heroism becoming a woman of an honest and pious heart." How difficult submission must have been for a woman born to privilege, with openly ambitious male family members, yet married to a man whose medical practice yielded a sporadic income and whose incompetence in investments lost not only his earnings but her inheritance of $25,000. In their republican marriage, her "language of submission" was not that of subordinate wife; it was a loyal silence about the lowered standard of living to which she, a Laurens though she was, had to accommodate.[107]

Whatever the nature of her sin, it is a curious omission from a diary that held so many other confidences, until one remembers Martha's spiritual guide: Doddridge's *Rise of Religion*. Martha's covenant had come from his book; so, too, had the recommendation to keep a journal. But Doddridge saw an additional purpose for a journal: a record to publish as a guide for future generations. David Ramsay had not known of his wife's diary, but when Martha told him of it as she lay dying, she ensured its publication— at least to her family. She may well have harbored hope for its print publication one day, even in 1795, as she crafted the self who would appear in those pages. Martha may not have been willing to entrust that deepest secret to her diary, as intimate an account of a soul as it was, for fear it would later discredit her as a teacher and guide.

Unquestionably, Martha Laurens Ramsay's sense of herself was intimately tied to her status as a Laurens. But her life's project of "achievement in religion" distinguished her as an individual within that family. Her diary was a permanent record of that process, her writing both reflecting and shaping her soul. With her children, she would turn her writing outward. A true republican mother, she had been responsible for the education of her children and had written many letters of advice, particularly to her eldest son when he was in college. David Ramsay included some of these letters in his *Memoirs* after her death; so apt were they that a fashionable Charleston woman recommended them to her son.[108] It is likely, then, that Martha imagined herself writing for future generations as she charted her spiritual journey in her diary, not out of earthly pride but as one who had gone before. In writing the story of her soul, she realized her voice to teach others.

Similarly, while Elizabeth Foote Washington began to keep her journal to chart the moral course of her own life, she, too, expanded her sphere of influence by writing for the child whose birth she was awaiting. She took this step intentionally, plainly stating "shou'd I have children, & especially Daughters—it can be no disadvantage to them for to know something of my general conduct in my family." As she wrote her rules of life, she believed that "whatever Legacy in advice a dead Mother leaves her Daughters, must have great wait [weight] with them."[109] Her first daughter died after eleven months; when in September 1788 another girl was born to her, she began her advice journal again. "There is no real happiness without religion—a religion that effectively touches the heart," she wrote to her infant Lucinda. "Endeavor to live in peace & friendship with every creature,—intertain a good will and fellow feeling for all mankind, be kind & good to everyone who is in want, never say or do anything that will give another pain, though" she added, no doubt casting back to her own experience, "your evil nature should want to do it."[110]

True, the strains of traditional advice literature are apparent in both the content and mode of Washington's teachings to her daughters. On female subordination to men, for example, she was quite emphatic, "I blame my sex most . . . —our mother eve when she transgress'd was told her husband should rule over her,—then how dare any of her daughters to dispute the point."[111] Religion also underlay her advice about dealing with her slaves, as she tried to "perswaid my servants to do their business through a principal of religion." When teased by a male relative that she "only effected to conform to my husband's will, to be thought an obediant wife," she objected strongly. It was not appearance that motivated her, she insisted, but "Scripture direction."[112] We should not be surprised that, like the English women memoirists historian Felicity Nussbaum studied, Washington's writing "mimick[ed] the dominant ideologies of themselves," or that she adopted the same direct, straightforward mode of traditional advice.[113] We have already observed numerous other examples of the effectiveness of the colonizer's educational program for the colonized. Washington herself insisted that she never "thought it degraded my understanding—to give up my opinion to my husbands. . . . I think a woman may keep up the dignity of a wife & mistress of a family—without ever disputing with her husband."[114] But in her reading of Scriptures and advice literature, she began to derive a sense of her authority and responsibility to teach her family (a term that, in the slave South, encompassed slaves as well as the white nuclear family) and picked up her pen.

Further, she anticipated that her writings would be read as intensively as any advice she had read. Her own books were too big to carry about with her during the day, so she "wrote some small manuscripts that I can conveniently carry in my pocket to peruse occaisionally,—which I have receiv'd great comfort from."[115] This intensive reading was what she had in mind for her daughter. But the words that daily would guide and strengthen Lucinda would not be those of an English cleric, but of her mother. "Should I leave my dear child before she arrives to the year of discresition—I hope she will read this manuscript more than once," Washington prayed, "& what ever other manuscript Books I leave behind."[116] In writing her own advice for Lucinda, Elizabeth Foote Washington asserted an authority that traditional prescriptive works never ceded to a woman, writing a book she meant to serve in her place, if necessary, and laying plans for future books.

Eliza (Ambler) Carrington wished to lay the memory of her beloved parents' example before their grandchildren, who had not been able to know them. In a series of letters to her sister, Ann (Ambler) Fisher, she sketched out their characters as devoted Christians, describing her mother's devotional practices and the lessons in moral teachings they had learned in the books and writing exercises prepared for them by their father. Carrington was explicit about her purpose in supplying these written memoirs: that they "may in a degree be serviceable to our dear Jenetta [Fisher's daughter] . . . [and that] she will endeavor to imitate the character that I so faintly have delineated." "From time to time such communications as these shall be made," Carrington promised, "with the hope that hereafter they may be read by our child."[117] Absent in death, her grandparents nonetheless would teach Jenetta Fisher, as Carrington's writings kept them forever in the family eye.

Caroline (Burgwin) Clitherall's memoirs of her parents describe how such writings could, in fact, work as surrogate parents. Her English mother died in 1787, just three years after her arrival at her husband's North Carolina plantation, when Caroline herself was just three years old. Yet, as Caroline grew up, reading the courtship letters of her parents, she learned lessons about faith that were as powerful as if she had learned them at her mother's knee. Separated by an ocean during the Revolutionary War, her parents wrote to each other of their resignation to God's will and of their lack of fear "whilst we . . . are treading the Path of Virtue."[118] As Caroline Clitherall in her turn wrote her memoir of her mother, addressed, of course, to her children and grandchildren, she exclaimed, "Dear Dear Father—dear dear Mother . . . Gone,—before your loving hearts, and bright example cou'd lead them thro' this briery path of existence..and [how] to apply the all healing balm of Religion—[it is] only from *letters*, & *repetition*, they can, borrow the *images* such produce." And, as had Elizabeth Foote Washington, Eliza Burgwin had also understood her authority to extend beyond her own children; during her brief life in North Carolina, she "held Religious instruction a duty . . . and read the Scriptures" to their slaves every Sunday.[119]

These women's writings in the post-Revolutionary period sound a different tone than letters from the colonial period precisely because of the sense of authority that was a consequence of evangelicalism's influence. The midcentury letters of Richard and Elizabeth Ambler to their sons studying in England offer a comparison in the ways women viewed their teaching responsibilities. The letters of the father are lengthy admonitions on character, study, and spending habits and even include a recommendation to read Addison's and Steele's *Spectator* for an example of

how to write with "great beauty and Correctness in the Stile."[120] Their
mother, however, simply chided her son for his "neglect in not writing
oftner . . . but one letter from you for more than a year." Her single request of him was that he "make a proper use" of the purse she sent him.[121]
Ambler's letter to her son was very different from manuscript books to be
carried in a daughter's pocket all day or from the letter in which Martha
Laurens Ramsay hoped to impress a "laudable ambition" upon her
college-aged son "to attain science, and fit you hereafter to rank among
men of literary and public consequence."[122] Catherine Dulany Belt wrote
a long, solicitous letter to her dying brother, urging on him devotional
books such as Philip Doddridge's *Extracts* to ease his mind in his last days.
She was unapologetic about dispensing her advice on reading, "In writing
on these points I do not feel like a *vain* woman, for never was I more sensible of my weakness, than when I undertake to advise you—but I am so
confident that you might be happier than you are and so truly anxious
that you should be so that I cannot forbear to give my opinion."[123]

In taking up the pen, these later women assumed the twin mantles of
reason and authority, whether they were dissenters or Episcopalians. They
wrote with intentionality and without artifice, with authority and without
apology, refuting Fordyce's slight of women's writing as any "composition
that may fall from her pen."[124] In their writings, they scrutinized their experiences of God, they examined themselves as the objects of the love and
attention of the divine, and they began to see themselves as *subject.*

Disestablishment: Turning Outward

This dawning sense of their own subjectivity was an exceedingly important
development in the early republic, as, fortified by this new intellectual
identity, writing women began to turn their attention outward, beyond
their families, to their churches. Revolutionary thinkers saw the preservation of the republic as dependent on the virtue of its citizenry, who were
willing to sacrifice their own self-interest for the common good. Since time
out of mind, however, exhortations to virtue (and discipline for backslid-
ers) had been the responsibility of the established church, which, acting as
an arm of the state, had helped maintain order. Now that this relationship
was severed, many worried how order, much less virtue, would be maintained in the republic.[125] Perhaps recalling Reverend Miles Selden's belief
that if worship took place only "in private houses, there would soon be an
end of religion," Virginia men petitioned their legislature for continued
state sponsorship of their churches. Not unwilling to rely on the virtue of
their fellow citizens, men from Essex County feared the Church's fate if it

had to "solicit the cold hand of charity" for its support.[126] Their petition failed, of course, as did so many others, and with disestablishment, Episcopal priests and bishops began to appeal to their wealthier parishioners to set an example of generosity and virtue.[127] And indeed, the money began to pour in, and from an unlikely source: women.

Although excluded from formal government, many women did not view themselves as immune to patriotic sentiments or exempt from the project of building a nation.[128] The war had demonstrated their capacity for courage, patriotism, hard physical labor, and even the management of "outdoor affairs," their phrase for the business affairs of men.[129] Having taken over at the helm of the *Virginia Gazette*'s presses after her husband's death, Clementina Rind had published two essays from women from Virginia and South Carolina, urging women to support the boycott on tea after the British government had closed the port of Boston.[130] Virginia women responded in their resolution "never more to use it till the oppressive Act imposing a Duty thereon be repealed."[131] (Not all women sympathized. Alice Lee of Maryland "saw the Brig Peggy Stewart consumed before our Windows on acc[oun]t of the tea, a spectacle that shocked me much[.] Mr S. offered to make all proper concessions yet the merciless Mob would not spare his property—I begin to be out of Love with Patriotism.")[132] A Virginia wife whose husband was away fighting urged other women to support the men in arms.[133] In Massachusetts, Abigail Adams had applied to her husband, John Adams, for congressional attention to greater legal protections for women. Her friend, Mercy Otis Warren, published a three-volume history of the war. In the 1790s, Judith Sargent Murray stressed women's intellectual abilities and the necessity for women's education to prepare them for economic self-sufficiency.[134] In 1801, a "Female Advocate" from Connecticut put the question bluntly: why should men "teach . . . construe [and] govern without the voice of women, or the least regard to the judgment or assent of the other sex?"[135] While southern women did not go to press with such ideas, the letters of Eliza Wilkinson of Charleston, South Carolina, to her sister-in-law resound with passion for her country. "The Land of Liberty! how sweet the sound," she wrote in 1779, "[that] raises a generous warmth in every bosom capable of discerning its blessings." She disputed Homer's prescription that women mind "domestic concerns . . . and leave affairs of higher nature to the men." While she conceded women's physical weakness in comparison with men's, and she was loath to "meddle in what is unbecoming female delicacy," nonetheless she insisted that "our thoughts can soar aloft . . . and have as just a sense of honor, glory, and great actions, as these 'Lords of

Creation.' "[136] In the infant nation, like-minded women answered Hannah Adams's pamphlet "Women invited to war," to fight irreligion, licentiousness, and poverty by rehabilitating ailing churches and aiding motherless orphans (especially girls) and war widows.[137] In their exclusion from government, southern women would hear and follow a higher calling: the preservation of the nation's virtue through religion.

They began with their churches. A committed Episcopalian, Eliza Ambler Carrington faithfully sought to keep afloat St. John's Episcopal Church, Richmond, the church whose walls had reverberated with Patrick Henry's ringing declaration, "Give me liberty or give me death."[138] In her view, the dearth of public worship had reached a critical stage by 1792, as she reported to an English friend that "we [have not] left in our extensive state three Churches that are supported decently." She fully backed the efforts of St. John's vestry (which included both her father, Jaquelin Ambler, state treasurer, and her husband, Edward Carrington) by attending "with a Choice few" the services which the "old church on the hill" managed to hold, and by "contributing our Mite [to] endeavor to preserve the Religion of our Fathers." The enemy, she thought, were the Deists, "Modern Philosophers . . . the enlightened as they call themselves . . . [William] Godwin, [Thomas] Paine &c," who had little use for institutional religion, and she begged her friend to repair to Virginia to add her "persevering zeal in this good cause" to restore the Church against them.[139] Other women funded the building of new churches or the restoration of old ones. Unwilling to go without services while a new church was being built, Virginian Hannah Washington refurbished a house in 1787 and suggested the congregation rent it for the interim; in 1824 Mrs. Jane Hope launched a campaign to restore an old church, worn and deteriorated from its use as an army barracks and barn. An unknown number of similar campaigns, begun or financed by women, are lost to the historical record, since many women were loath to publicize their individual contributions, preferring feminine anonymity to the spotlight.[140]

As Carrington shows, zeal informed Episcopal women as much as it did women of the more evangelical Protestant sects. Probably the best example of the evangelicalism of Episcopalian women was Virginian Ann Randolph Meade Page (b. 1781). Her childhood faith was nurtured by her mother, Mary Meade (b. 1753), an Anglican who attended church only sporadically yet taught her children prayers, catechism, and hymns. When Ann's brother, William, went to Princeton, his mother's letters followed him out into the world, as both she and Ann prodded him toward the ministry.[141] Mary Meade also had a profound influence on Ann's life.

Married in 1799 to a wealthy planter, Ann Page spent her married life trying to counteract the frivolous tendencies of gentry life, fervent in her adherence to the faith she had learned from "maternal example and instruction."[142] Undoubtedly the influence of both mother and sister
prevailed in the spiritual education of Ann's younger brother, William,
who brought his evangelicalism to his diocese in Virginia when he became bishop.[143] In one historian's assessment, the children of Mary
Meade "became the center of Virginia's Episcopal evangelical energy in
the antebellum era."[144] That energy infused the church with the vitality it
needed to survive and grow in those bleak years after the Revolution, and
Miles Selden's fears notwithstanding, it was the practice of worship at
home, rather than public worship, that prepared the Meade children for
the work of restoring their church.[145]

Clearly evangelicalism and Episcopalianism were not mutually exclusive in Virginia; this was true as well in North Carolina, although the combination worked differently there. Since North Carolina had never had a
strong Anglican base, the Church was dealt an almost fatal blow with its
disestablishment in 1776. Indeed, elite male parishioners lost interest in
the Church, most of them persuaded by Deist thinkers; Episcopal parents
were not even baptizing their children. A shell of a Church, it could no
longer hold its female parishioners, who were increasingly drawn to evangelical churches, both the more genteel Presbyterian and the less fashionable Methodist. Intrigued in spite of themselves at what they witnessed at
these churches, women began to develop a discipline of reading and devotions at home: Episcopal women like Rebecca Cameron were reading
English evangelical writer Hannah More and recommending her works to
their friends. In an effort to counter the evangelical persuasions of their
wives—and, not coincidentally, to restore male authority in the household—men began to fund the rebuilding of Episcopal churches and to
hire clergy for them. Women's preferences prevailed in the choice of
clergy, however, as they sought pastors who would nurture their spiritual
growth rather than the administrators or teachers men preferred. In this
circuitous way, women restored the vitality of the Episcopal Church, instilling the evangelical fervor that made their Church competitive with
the Presbyterians and Methodists. By the antebellum period, women were
the spiritual leaders of their churches, outstripping men in zeal, membership, and activism, while husbands provided the financial support.[146]

With the resuscitation of their churches, southern women began to
build on their spiritual authority as they attempted to resolve problems
being ignored by the new republic's government. Although, like Hannah
Adams, southern women were willing to concede the rightful leadership

of the battle against social ills to men, they were no less willing than Adams to pick up the fallen standard and charge into the field. This was particularly true in urban areas. One of the first priorities for the new generation of educated women was the rescue of those less fortunate, many of whom were forced to resort to prostitution to keep body and soul together. As early as 1787, the women of Charleston, South Carolina, had organized their Society for the Relief of Widows and Orphans of the Clergy of the Protestant Episcopal Church.[147] In Petersburg, Virginia, women founded the Female Orphan Asylum in 1811, a venture in which they organized a governing board, located and purchased a building, hired staff, raised and managed funds, and applied to the legislature for incorporation. This last was enormously significant, for it allowed the board members—married women who possessed no independent legal standing—to act for the asylum, which did. Once incorporated, the asylum was able to appear in court and enter into contracts (privileges denoted as masculine), sure and certain steps into the public sphere.[148]

In Richmond, Eliza Ambler Carrington and her network of prominent friends also founded an asylum for poor white girls. Although she was childless, Carrington's passion for female education and her religious sensibilities undoubtedly underwrote her role as a founder of the Female Humane Association of Richmond for the Relief of Female Orphans.[149] The association was first organized in 1805 by Jean Moncure Wood (wife of governor James E. Wood), Mrs. Philip Norborne Nicholas (wife of the Virginia attorney general), and Carrington.[150] In 1807, the women drew up and adopted a constitution and bylaws to govern their meetings and work; by 1810, their impressive success caught the attention of a Major William Duval, who donated two lots on which to build a "seminary of brick and stone" to house indigent females.[151] To be able to accept his offer and hold title to the land, the association applied for and won incorporation in 1811.[152] The association suffered financially during the Panic of 1819, however, and forced to retrench, it narrowed its objectives to "the maintenance and instruction of destitute white female children" and reduced the numbers of orphans it housed.[153] Undeterred by the lack of benefactors during the recession, the women decided to raise their own funds, instituting an annual fair in 1829.[154] Modest as it was, the Richmond Association represented the entrance of women into a public sphere that heretofore had been the exclusive province of men, answering a need government had ignored. By building the asylum, the women of the association stepped in to save poor and orphaned girls from a life of poverty, providing them literal asylum in a world where it was dangerous to lack male protectors.[155] That this project was close to Carrington's heart is revealed in the words she gave to a character in a novel that she started to write years later: "[T]here is nothing earthly that interests me so much as helpless little female orphans."[156]

Carrington's work is but one example of many charities organized by women in the first two decades of the nineteenth century. Fredericksburg women had established the first female charity in 1803, a boarding school for girls, and they gained legislative permission to run public lotteries to finance it. Charity schools later appeared in Norfolk and Alexandria as well. Women founded Bible societies, distributed religious tracts, and established and taught Sunday schools, and by the 1830s had expanded their activities to temperance as well. Historian Elizabeth Varon, who charted the growth of urban female activism in Virginia, observed that "while the image of benevolent women as apolitical beings had some basis in reality in the early years of the 19th century, by the mid-1820s, it was fast becoming a fiction, as . . . [women] took up the banner of moral reform."[157] Yet in their intense interest in the education of poor women, these early female associations were taking up a critical political issue well before the 1820s. The ideal citizen in Thomas Jefferson's mind was the educated, self-sufficient yeoman farmer. Ignorance bred violence, which would lead to the fall of the republic. To avoid that possibility, he founded the University of Virginia, a school intended to serve as a model of public education everywhere and of which Jefferson was so proud that he included it in his epitaph. Ironically, however, his own party's unwillingness to vote the funds necessary for public education left a void that women recognized and attempted to fill.[158] In doing so, they took up an eminently political issue that emphasized the cultivation of reason and the intellect for the good of the republic. And, not incidentally, they served as true guardians of fatherless women who were otherwise vulnerable to the passions of unscrupulous men.

In the wide expanse of the agricultural South, however, urban women were a tiny minority; most women lived on rural farms and plantations.[159] The geographic distance between them certainly inhibited the kind of growth of female associations and societies that obtained in the North but did not forestall it altogether.[160] One of the best examples of rural women's activism was the work of Virginia women in the American Colonization Society, founded in 1816.[161] The daughters of Mary Meade were particularly prominent in the effort to educate and convert their slaves in preparation for their new life in Liberia. Episcopalians Margaret Mercer (daughter of a Maryland governor), Mary Lee Fitzhugh Custis (wife of George Washington's adopted grandson, George Washington Parke Custis), and her daughter, Mary Custis Lee (wife of Robert E. Lee), were also active in the movement, as were Presbyterians Louisa Cocke and Anne Rice. Women of the Colonization Society took seriously their ministers' urging to teach the Bible to their slaves to extend "the empire of God." They organized fund-raising fairs and sewed to raise money for their slaves' transportation and establishment of their new homes. Of course, the project of preparing their slaves for a free Christian life in Africa never seemed to reach fruition, and many privileged women, unable to imagine running a household without their slaves, would have agreed with Mary Lee that the "mighty work of carrying the light and Christianity to the dark heathen country" would have to be continued by the next generation.[162] But this work was perfectly suited for women, since it was contained in a philanthropic frame; indeed, they deliberately used the language of charity and religion. The issue would become a secular one eventually, with petitions for the abolition of slavery (signed by men only) sent to the Virginia legislature during the slave debates in the wake of Nat Turner's 1830 rebellion, none of which rested on a religious foundation. Yet evangelicals like Bishop William Meade and his sisters never understood the project except as a Christian imperative.

When Anne Royall traveled the South in the 1830s, she was critical of female activism, charging that women were motivated not by religion but by vanity's desire to see their names reported in the local paper.[163] While her comment certainly underscores the way women could use religious activism for their own self-interest, to accept Royall's judgment on its face is to miss the larger point: religion could also afford women a strong sense of their significance before God and of their individual identity, particularly in its varied evangelical forms, and could influence women's thought and work. True, the work of colonization was deeply flawed. It was marred by the racism of men and women who thought the intellect of blacks inferior to that of whites and therefore in need of strenuous preparations that rarely met with success, and by the owners' self-interest that kept slaves from ever seeing their promised freedom, even as (some) mistresses acknowledged the evil of slavery. Still, it was their realization of their individual significance, and of the commission that significance conferred, that propelled southern women into these public spheres, expanding their influence far beyond their own homes and plantations. In rescuing destitute girls, establishing boarding schools, appealing to legislatures, raising funds, and working within statewide colonization organizations, early-nineteenth-century women greatly amplified the initial efforts of isolated individuals such as Elizabeth Foote Washington a generation earlier.

By the 1830s, then, the early searching efforts to forge a place for southern women in the new republic would coalesce into a clearly articulated the-

ory of what Donald Mathews has called "evangelical womanhood," which explained women's natural predisposition to piety and the resultant charge to
teach by word and example at home and abroad.[164] Evangelical womanhood
clarified the position of women in their society. By the turn of the nineteenth century, southern evangelical churches knew that they did not care
to remain churches of the disenfranchised (women, youth, and blacks) and
so had begun, in a number of ways, to appeal to southern men. Itinerant
preachers sought the permission of masters before preaching on their plantations; Methodists pragmatically retreated from their threat to excommuni-
cate all those who had not divested themselves of their slaves within two years
of their acceptance into the church; ministers began to preach to their female congregants on obedience as a spiritual pleasure.[165] In short, southern
evangelical churches eventually achieved respectability by honoring the
gender conventions of southern men: promoting patriarchal authority and
muting female voices.[166] Dispersed over a wide landscape, southerners continued their colonial practices of centering religious observances on their
plantations rather than in their churches, emphasizing the "household as
the center of Christian community." As the moral center of that household,
women's status certainly benefited, but ultimately the household as a Christian community remained under the control of the patriarch. Evangelical
womanhood was a creative response to these developments, allowing
Methodist women especially, "a unique social world, one in which female association predominated, separate from patriarchal family structures and
community ties alike." As historian Dee Andrews writes, in Methodism
women "found their place apart from the claims of family loyalty."[167]

There was nothing inevitable about this triumph of patriarchy, even in
this apparently softer form. Both Anglicans (later, Episcopalians) and
evangelicals had encouraged private reading and individual devotions,
particularly as a way to counter clergy shortages in the South.[168] Women's
introspective journeys had revealed to them a rational, as well as emotional, self; and even in the South, women of the post-Revolutionary period struggled to be recognized as such. Jan Lewis has argued that the rational piety of Anglicanism appealed to men and not to those on the
periphery of power.[169] Yet despite the literature's insistence on women's
innate sensibility of feeling, it is clear that women also claimed as theirs a
competence to reason. Perhaps none chafed so much at the restraints of
gender as Eliza Wilkinson of Charleston, who hated being viewed as the
"*earth worms* these authors make us! They won't even allow us the liberty
of thought, and that is all I want."[170] Wilkinson's blunt outburst is unique;
a sense of authority founded in religion may be more typical. Elizabeth
Foote Washington's Anglican faith was in the forefront throughout her

advice book as it informed her struggles to cope with her servants and the deaths of her children; its rationality also helped her to temper her resentful feelings that threatened to overwhelm her. Martha Laurens tried to impose rationality on her depression as she attempted to reconcile financial and personal crises with her faith. When Mary Ellis of Virginia tried to cope with the miseries of her marriage (she had already run away once), she tried to moderate her feelings by the "united efforts of Reason and Religion."[171]

Ultimately, however, southern women conceded reason as masculine and claimed for themselves instead the emotive powers of religion. They had a compelling reason to do so: with moral authority (understood as a privilege of whiteness) as the prize, the struggle to redefine female as rational (which pitted them against men) gave way to the more important struggle over race (which pitted them against blacks).[172] Writing about English women writers of this period, historian Hilda Smith observed that they understood that they had interests, rather than rights, and that they needed the protection that could be afforded only by men.[173] White southern women likewise understood their interests very well: an alliance forged with white males made infinitely more sense than one forged with other women, who were equally subordinated (or, in the case of black women, more so). Nor was female autonomy desirable. No woman anywhere in early America was encouraged to think of developing the self, although northern Quakers allowed for the individual gifts of all their members, even permitting women to preach.[174] But in the South there was no tradition of female authority or female preaching. Rather, southern women lived in a tradition of misogyny, against which, Christine Heyrman pointed out, "many women had become schooled, as their best defense, in habits of submission."[175] Since their education was controlled by men, it makes sense that women would begin to see themselves as their "colonizers" did: dependent and unable to protect themselves.[176]

Yet we have also seen that despite the aim of female education to keep women passive, women's reading and writing, informed by religion, could foster activism.[177] Even Joan Hoff Wilson, who has never seen any positive benefits for women resulting from the American Revolution, believes that "religion still provided the best opportunities socially and culturally for women."[178] Elizabeth Foote Washington's rules of conduct for herself and her infant daughter are most significant viewed in this light. True, she accepted her fallibility as a daughter of Eve, but if Washington reminded herself constantly of the virtue of humility, it was not to prostrate herself on the altar of male superiority but to exert Christian self-control to cope with the frustrations of living in her in-laws' household, dealing with recalcitrant slaves, and incidents in which she had been "used extremely ill indeed."[179] Her writings charted the formation of a self and developed into a guide for her children. Similarly, religion inspired and sanctioned the writings of Caroline Clitherall and Martha Laurens Ramsay and the Randolph women.

Certainly this literary output cannot be compared, either in volume or mode of publication, to that of northern women like Warren or Murray. "Publication" of these modest writings—that is, their dissemination—was limited to small circles of family and friends, who read them intensively and who treasured and kept them through the centuries. Moreover, the appearance of this advice literature was a full century behind the writings of Restoration Englishwomen who were publishing letters, essays, advice, plays, and novels. Seventeenth-century Englishwomen circulated letters, poems, and other texts in manuscript form (including advices to children) to avoid the stigma that associated appearing in print with sexual promiscuity,[180] but by the eighteenth century, they were appearing in print, usually novels—a "natural" outgrowth, it was thought, of the exploration of emotion in the relationships they nurtured through their letter writing.[181] Elizabeth Foote Washington's book for her daughter was an early American version of the scribal publication that existed in England a century earlier. But encased in a hierarchy that was dominated by white male heads of households, southern women had even less opportunity than English women writers to escape their inferior position.[182] It took over a hundred years for this scribal culture to begin to take form in women's writings in the early American South, and even the few examples we have would not approximate the kind of circulation that had made English poet Katherine Philips the most admired female poet of her century.[183] Elizabeth Foote Washington's book may have echoed many of the more traditional ideas about womanhood; still, it is significant that she took up the pen, actively documenting her sense of herself.

Applying the literature's notion about their innate piety and the moral power it gave them in their families, women sought also to apply their powers of reason to their faith. In this appropriation of reason, women like Washington, Clitherall, and Ramsay may also have been a last gasp of the Enlightenment in the brief window of opportunity after the Revolution, before reason dissolved into the sentimental model of nineteenth-century true womanhood. In their appropriation of authority derived from reason and religion, women in the South began a full century later to follow the lead of their English sisters, sharpening their quills, dipping them into the ink, and forming the words they intended to guide the lives of future generations.

FOUR

Reading Novels in the South

"**B**egan a very clever Novel—Evelina it was call'd," Frances Baylor Hill recorded on a late October day in 1797. She had spent most of the previous week looking after a household of sick children, her nursing chores interspersed with sewing projects. She was ready for the diversion of a good read and more than willing to slight her needlework. "Knit a short piece," she explained, "for I was reading the best part of the day." *Evelina* (1778) had claimed her; she finished the first volume in three days. In mid-November, she picked up volume 2, finished it in four days, and immediately began volume 3. Her perpetual sewing duties, company, and a funeral slowed her reading of the last volume, however. Still she stole time for almost a week until November 28, when she noted triumphantly, "I finish'd reading Evelina it is a very good Novel and very entertaining."[1]

By the end of the eighteenth century, the novel as a genre was firmly planted on American soil. William Hill Brown had published *The Power of Sympathy*, regarded as the first American novel, in 1789, but English novels had permeated the colonial literary scene decades earlier.[2] Frances Baylor Hill's absorption in *Evelina* is characteristic of novels' appeal to female readers, whether they read in England, New England, or the eighteenth-century South. Featuring women at the center of dramatic plots that turned on disguise and deceit, seduction and betrayal, rebellion and reconciliation, the novel delivered moral lessons in a style unmatched by traditional advice. Frances Baylor Hill dutifully read James Blair's *Sermons* (1740) when she could not get to church, regarded Dr.

John Gregory's *Legacy to his Daughters* (1774) "a very good Book," and regularly read "letters on education."[3] But none of them captivated her as her novels did. Her reading exemplified the coexistence of devotional, traditional, and educational works and the persistence of that literature as the canon of female education late in the century. The addition of novels, however, is a telling portent of the change we will see in Virginian Lady Jean Skipwith's library by 1825, in which novels would supplant traditional advice.[4] Novels never dominated eighteenth-century southern reading, but their presence in southern libraries merits attention, for their influence can be detected in the ways that women thought about female virtue, friendship, and identity. Indeed, in the novels' discussions about virtue, southern women would find a convergence of religious with secular themes, from which they would draw crucial lessons about the nature of womanhood and how to live their daily lives.

NOVELS IN THE SOUTH

In our own century we tend to think of novels as recreational reading, and undoubtedly they served that function in the eighteenth century as well. But novels were more than diversion; they contained moral lessons, crucial in the education of southern women, both maid and matron, and this literature comprised the core readings of their education. We have seen how little formal education was available to females, but if we rethink our concept of a curriculum's texts to include novels and their core teachings about life and love, virtue and debasement, triumph and disaster, we open an entirely new avenue to women's intellectual history and see the ways in which white southern women were very much integrated into the flow of ideas in the eighteenth-century Anglo-American world.

The traditional advice books that formed part of their curriculum underscored girls' identity as Eve's daughters, whose paths in life had to be monitored constantly. Allestree's *The Whole Duty of Man* and Halifax's worldlier *The Lady's New Year's Gift* continued to enjoy a wide readership in eighteenth-century America.[5] Indeed, as we have seen, local newspapers disseminated their advice further still: in Virginia, for example, a 1737 essay on "Matrimonial Felicity" echoed Halifax's advice to be a quiet wife. "Never dispute with him, whatever be the Occasion," the writer urged, so that "Animosity will sooner cease."[6] Another essayist wrote, "Smiles and sweet compliance are the most convincing Arguments to win the heart," trying to persuade his women readers, "to yield is the only way to conquer." When wives offered their husbands willing compliance and patient forbearance, they succeeded in the "business of her Life . . . keeping her husband's love."[7]

But by midcentury, novels began to supplement the traditional conduct-of-life literature. Dale Spender has argued that "when women were denied access to formal education, women's novels were a welcome substitute."[8] More than "substitute," I believe, novels were a crucial component of female education. Their appeal seemed universal, cutting across class lines. As a writer in the *Virginia Gazette* complained in 1772, "This contagion is the more to be dreaded, as it daily spread through all ranks of people; and Miss, the Tailor's daughter, talks now as familiarly to her confidante, Miss Polly Staytope, of Swains & sentiments as the accomplished dames of genteel life."[9] Nor were larger cities the only places where novels were available. Riding the success of their book sales in backcountry Orange County, North Carolina, partners William Johnston and Richard Bennehan ordered the most popular English novels, in an attempt to bring their clientele into the transatlantic intellectual orbit. Importing only tried-and-true works, they had assembled an inventory by March 1774 that included *Tristram Shandy* (1760), *Peregrine Pickle* (1751), *Roderick Random* (1748), *Gil Blas* (1732), *The Vicar of Wakefield* (1766), *Tom Jones* (1749), *Fables by Mr. Gay* (1727), and *A Sentimental Journey* (1768).[10] So widely available were novels by the beginning of the nineteenth century that Alice Izard, of cosmopolitan Charleston, South Carolina, could look down her patrician nose in the tiny town of Fredericksburg, Virginia, and sniff, "Is it not droll to find new novels in such a little out of the way spot?"[11]

Even at that late date, English novels continued to dominate the American market, as they had throughout the previous century. The same transatlantic currents that had brought traditional advice literature to American shores brought novels as well. Early settlers brought treasured books to Virginia with them: Matthew Hubard of York County, whose will was probated in 1670, owned *Astrea: A French Romance.*[12] Arthur Spicer of Richmond County, who died in 1699, owned some fiction, including Lady Mary Wroth's *The Countess of Montgomery's Urania* (1621).[13] Most inventories, however, did not itemize books, even when noting the larger libraries of wealthy colonists.[14] Typical of such notations were the inventories of Elizabeth Banks of Northumberland County, who left "28 books" in 1720; Mary Swan of Lancaster County, who owned "32 old books, [valued at] 15 sh[illings]" in 1724; and Barbara Tayloe's modest collection of "3 Bibles and a parcel of old books" in 1726.[15] Where men's inventories list novels, male-authored ones are more popular, although the novels of Samuel Richardson, particularly *Pamela* and *Clarissa* (1748), Laurence

Sterne (*Tristram Shandy*, 1760, is truly ubiquitous), Tobias Smollett (*Peregrine Pickle*, 1751), and Henry Fielding (*Tom Jones*, 1749) were much more in evidence than Defoe's *Moll Flanders* (1722).

Novels enjoyed increasing popularity among men over the course of the century. Men collected books on a wide variety of subjects; nonetheless, libraries full of history, natural science, religion, government, law, philosophy, and the classics usually had at least one of the above novels, even earlier in the century. Belletristic books are more numerous than novels, however, with Alexander Pope, John Milton, Jonathan Swift, John Dryden, William Shakespeare, and Geoffrey Chaucer the most popular. Of the *Tatler, Rambler, Spectator,* and *Idler,* at least one, if not more, was found in most large libraries.[16] The four thousand–volume library of William Byrd II, of course, is exemplary of a gentleman's library, although he owned almost no novels. The books that most closely approximate novels were Delariviere Manley's *Court Intrigues, in a collection of original letters, from the island of the New Atalantis* (1711), which features examples of the sexual indiscretions of the aristocracy, and Alain René Lesage's *Gil Blas* (1749).[17] Robert Carter of Nomini Hall in Virginia is likewise typical of this profile.[18] Even the 1736 inventory of Charles Pasture of Henrico County, comprised almost exclusively of classical, divinity, and historical works, shared this belletristic culture with the inclusion of the Restoration era's "Behns Plays."[19]

In North Carolina, James Milner's inventory reflects the same pattern as those of Virginia gentlemen. *Don Quixote* (1712), *The Vicar of Wakefield* (1766), *Tristram Shandy* (1760), *Pamela* (1740), *Sir Charles Grandison* (1753–54), and *Telemachus* (1699) all appear in his enormous inventory of several properties. He also read Pope, Swift, Smollett's *History of England,* and Rosseau's *Eloisa.* John Luttrell's collection of books, as they appear in the inventory compiled by his wife after his death in 1782, is considerably smaller but reflects the same profile of the English gentleman: law books, dictionaries, Smollett's *History,* Pope's and Addison's *Works,* the *Spectator, Rambler,* and *Tatler,* and one novel: *Tristram Shandy.*[20] Englishmen in Virginia or North Carolina could be as worldly and well read as any gentlemen in England.

Cosmopolitan Charles Town, South Carolina, was more receptive to novels than was the North Carolina backcountry. The fourth largest city in the colonies, it had a thriving port; an elite who constructed a glittering life of balls, plays, concerts, horse races, and other amusements rivaling anything found in Europe; and a slave system that supported it all.[21] Further, the *South Carolina Gazette* was twice run by women printers, Elizabeth Timothy and Ann Timothy.[22] The former advertised *Pamela* for sale in her print shop in the 1740s.[23] South Carolinian Eliza Lucas (later Pinckney) read and commented perceptively both on Richardson's construction of the novel and on the character of Pamela herself.[24] Readers may have hoped for wider circulation of novels when they read about the formation of a society that published in 1750 "Rules of the Society for erecting a Library" in Charles Town.[25] Those hopes would not begin to be met until after the Revolution, however; in the colonial period, the Society ordered books on government, law, and philosophy, all geared to propping up white male authority in the colony.[26] But by late century, the Charleston presses were publishing English novels for distribution in America, including Hannah More's *The Inflexible Captive: A Tragedy* in 1774. In 1800 the *City Gazette* solicited subscriptions for the "celebrated novel" *The Beggergirl and her Benefactors* by Agnes Maria Bennett.[27]

Indeed, since some books could be had cheaply, they were no longer the preserve of the elite. The 1760 inventory of Mailana Drayton of Middlesex County, Virginia, illustrates the point: eight (unspecified) volumes were valued at £3.7.4 and eleven volumes of French books at £3.2.4; her "parcel of novels," (unfortunately, also unspecified) was worth only two shillings. As American printers were discovering, books printed in America in abridged form sold more cheaply than the full-length volumes printed and bound in London; adding a counterfeit London imprint made it even more attractive for buyers, who enjoyed an expensive-looking model for a lower price.[28] Jean Skipwith's copy of *Manners: A Novel*, printed in New York in 1818, does not make nearly as impressive a presentation with its rough-edged, irregularly sized paper as her elegantly bound and gilt five-volume set of *The Anchoret* (1773), with its London imprint.[29] Inexpensive as cheap or abridged copies may have been, less affluent readers could have avoided the expense altogether by borrowing books from wealthier neighbors. Evidence in the *Virginia Gazette* in the form of advertisements requesting that borrowed books be returned suggests that planters' libraries may well have served the same function as the subscription libraries of the northern colonies.[30] Women lent books to one another as well. In 1778 Anne Blair used "the occasion I have to remind my Dear Mrs. Randolph of the Poetry I lent her" to introduce to her an acquaintance.[31]

It is not difficult to account for the increasing popularity of the novel in the eighteenth century. For men, novel reading was a way to share in the literary culture of all well-bred Englishmen. For women, however, novel reading served a very different purpose. Because novels more closely paralleled their thoughts, feelings, and sympathies than did traditional didactic literature, reading them was a form of resistance to their colonization.[32] Novels offered an alternative reading on women's lives other than that dished up by traditional advice literature. While Halifax's *The Lady's New Year's Gift* had advised women to overlook the infidelity of their husbands, for example, women's novels universally condemned it.[33] Similarly, Eliza Haywood's periodical, *The Female Spectator*, was filled with stories that warned women against relying on the honor of men to preserve feminine virtue and dignity. Her stories subverted traditional advice as they portrayed men as unreliable protectors and urged women to assume responsibility for their own reputation and virtue.[34] Furthermore, in their depiction of intelligent women, novels subverted the tenets of traditional advice that prescribed unquestioning female submission to superior male intellectual prowess. These heroines had to be treated seriously in their own right rather than as mere appendages to men.[35] It is important, then, to see the novels, short stories, and serials (especially by women writers) as advice literature in their own right. Warning against the dangers of the world to which women fell prey, novels exposed both the insufficiency of the typical female ornamental education and the failure of the "Lords of Creation" in their duty to protect women.[36]

In exposing men as predators rather than protectors, the novels implicitly and explicitly critiqued the double standard from which all women suffered; such tales offered precisely the kind of education the colonizer wanted to withhold. To seek out and read novels, then, was to engage in resistance, as men well understood and sought to suppress. For example, the seriousness of mind with which women in the eighteenth century approached their reading no doubt informed the satire of female reading in "Lady's Toilette" (see fig. 3 in chap. 2).[37] Seated before her mirror, awaiting her maid's final ministrations to her toilette (the addition of her wig), the lady reads *Delphine* (1802), a novel written by Germaine de Staël. Earlier an admirer of Rousseau's ideal of woman (his *Eloise*, on the lady's bookshelf, was trained to a life of domesticity), de Staël's later works, *Delphine* and *Corinne* (1807), criticized the social order of Napoleonic France that could not countenance women of ideas.[38] Her hair cut mannishly short, the reader attempts to disguise her masculine cast of mind with her wig, but all the perfumes, cosmetics, and elaborate clothes cannot make a lady of her. Like the novel itself, the lady is literally self-reflective; the ideas with which she fills her head cannot begin to be countered by the application of a few external beauty aids.

In spite of such efforts to intimidate, however, the writings of eighteenth-century southern women make clear that they were well versed in this new literature. The reflections in the 1780s of two young Yorktown, Virginia, girls, Betsey Ambler and Mildred Smith, on the seduction of their acquaintance Rachel Warrington, were dominated by ideas about education. Raised by a well-meaning but inept aunt, the orphaned Warrington received an education that, Smith noted, "sacrificed every solid virtue . . . [and in which] appearance and *effect*, is everything."[39] Educated for innocence, Warrington was an easy mark for the attentions of a French officer, who had arrived in Yorktown in 1781. Unable to distinguish false appearances from true, she was duped by the flattering addresses of the Frenchman. Ruminating about the meanings of her fall from virtue, Smith and Ambler refrained from following Halifax's advice to "make a fair and quick retreat from such a mistaken acquaintance."[40] Instead, they concluded, a right education, such as Ambler had received from her father, might well have saved Warrington from the disastrous consequences of her naïveté.[41] Their assessment of the cause of Warrington's seduction underscores the significance of Cathy Davidson's observation that "[v]irtually *every* American novel written before 1820 . . . includes . . . a discourse on the necessity of improved education (often with special attention to the need for better female education)."[42] And they would have agreed with the correspondent to Eliza Haywood's *Female Spectator* who argued in 1744 that men need "to be more careful of the education of those females to whom they are parents or guardians! Would they convince them in their infancy that dress and show are not the essentials of a fine lady, and that true beauty is seated in the mind."[43] Indeed, Smith sympathized with the "disadvantages [Warrington] labored under, in being deprived of parents . . . [at a] very early age" and she was "certain [the path] pursued by [her] present patron is a very erroneous one."[44]

Novels, then, more than the conduct-of-life advice written by such men as Allestree or Halifax, enabled a community of reading—and writing— women to share information and ideas. Women's novels may have been trivialized as romances, but they gave women opportunities to imagine a world different from the one they knew.[45] "If a woman sought to learn how other women coped with reality," Linda Kerber observed, "she had few printed resources other than fiction to which she might turn. . . . To deny women access to novels was to deny them access to a rich imagery of what women were and what they might hope to become."[46]

GENERATIONS OF READERS

Young southern girls read and learned and imagined. Frances Baylor Hill read *Louisa the Lovely Orphan* and traveled to Turkey with *Mrs. Montague's Letters* (a travel account, rather than a novel) in addition to reading

Evelina.[47] Though no novels appear in the diary of Catherine Fullerton of Charleston, South Carolina, she did note that *Doctor Moore's Travels* "had afforded [her] infinite amusement lately, and, I hope I may add, some improvement." He wrote in the "most easy, elegant style that can be imagined, relates a variety of Annecdotes of several illustrious characters, and makes some of the best observations on Men & Manners that ever I read," she concluded. For less adventurous readers like Catherine Fullerton, travel accounts (the verisimilitude of many—since that of Sir John Mandeville—are doubtful) offered a safer, more acceptable form of fiction; geography was certainly a respectable interest for young ladies.[48]

Younger readers seemed to be less ambivalent than older women about their novel-reading practices. Rosalie Stier (later Calvert), the sixteen-year-old daughter of wealthy Belgian émigrés, found country life in rural Maryland too dull for her taste. To while away her days, she frequented Annapolis bookstores (which she apparently found well stocked for the reading tastes of the locals) and exulted in January 1796 that she "was up to her eyes in romances—at the moment I have eleven in the house." Her mother was equally absorbed. On the same day, Rosalie complained to her brother that their mother had appropriated a novel Rosalie had been reading and would not put it down, even on Sunday. Mrs. Stier protested that she was reading the novel not "for the pleasure of the very tender English amours, but in order to learn English."[49] If Richard Sheridan's play *The Rivals* is any indication, novels clearly interested young girls more than traditional advice literature, and they were quite resourceful about indulging their taste for them. Early in the play young Lydia frantically tries to evade discovery, urging her maid Lucy to hide her forbidden reading and display the recommended instead: "Here, my dear Lucy, hide these books. Quick, quick! . . . —put the *Innocent Adultery* into *The Whole Duty of Man* . . . and leave *Fordyce's Sermons* open on the table."[50] Indeed, Lydia's lines reveal a great deal: the generation gap between what parents considered suitable and what daughters wanted to read; the enduring popularity of the traditional steady sellers, in Sheridan's assumption that his audiences would recognize the titles; and the increasing disdain younger women had for the traditional advice (*The Rivals* was a comedy, popular in England and America). Mothers' determined efforts to teach their daughters from the old school often fell on deaf ears, as the image "Maternal Advice" makes clear. The fashionable daughters are bored (center) and impatient (right) with their mother's explication of the text from which she has just read. Holding her muff in one hand and a flower (from a waiting suitor?) in the other, the daughter on the right frowns at her mother's caution that "Ten thousand oaths sown, but not one of them

MATERNAL ADVICE.

To Reason my Children assert your pretence,
Nor hearken to Language beneath common sense;
When Angels men call you, and homage would pay,
If you credit the tale, you're as faulty as they.
Ten Thousand gay scenes are presented to view,
Ten Thousand oaths sworn, but not one of them true;
Such Passion, O heed not unless to deride,
Lest victims ye fall to an ill grounded pride.

E'en Hymen's fond slave is oft heard to complain,
Joys founded in love are but airy and vain;
While friendships recorded in truth's sacred page,
The rapture of youth, and the solace of age.
Praise we the dictates of virtue to sound;
True bliss never yet without goodness was found;
Leave folly and fashion, misguided, or youth,
And sink to their opposites wisdom and truth.

Fig. 4. "Maternal Advice" (London, 1795). The generational gap in reading tastes is clear in the mother's earnest teachings of the traditional advice literature and her daughters' obvious boredom and impatience. Courtesy of the John D. Rockefeller, Jr. Library, Colonial Williamsburg Foundation.

true"; has no interest in preferring the "dictates of virtue" to the sweet words of her suitor; knows that what is "misguided" in her world is to prefer "wisdom and truth" to fashion; and is just anxious for her mother to finish so that she can leave.[51]

Understanding the importance of these fashionable books to young women, Sarah Allen of North Carolina bequeathed her collection to her grandnieces. While her 1761 will bequeathed to the women she held dear her most precious belongings (her wedding ring, gold watch, and a silver tea set), to her two grandnieces she left "all the books of Modern taste . . . to be divided between them as equally as setts can be." That these were no "parcell of old books" (the usual notation in colonial inventories) but treasures, is revealed in Allen's instructions for their long-term preservation. The books were not "to be lent out and by that means the Sets may be broke before they can use them." To another niece, she left a writing stand, "quite new[,] to encourage her in that part of her Education, in which she seems to be making great progress within these late months," and which her aunt wanted to promote.[52]

Other women seemed to recall the romances of their youth (whether in novels or their own) with wistful pleasure but from the perspective afforded by experience and more sobered judgment. As Helen Calvert Maxwell Read of Norfolk, Virginia, reminisced about her courtship days, she framed her story as a tale of sentiment. Although she concluded it sensibly enough, her delight in her beaux and her regret in relinquishing the attractive gallant for the safer choice colored her tale. As she remembered the passage of her girlhood until her marriage in 1767 at age seventeen, the passion of novels infused her stories. There was a Mr. Smith, a lieutenant in the British Navy, who "would have given his eyes for me if I would have taken them" and who swore "he would live single for my sake." More than twenty years later, in a chance encounter with an English stranger on a stagecoach to Richmond, she was informed "that he had kept his word, and was still a bachelor for your sake." "There was romance for you," Read recalled with pure satisfaction. Then there was the love of her young life, Bassett Moseley, who "loved me dearly and wished to marry me." But her parents preferred James Maxwell, arguing that he was "honest, sensible, and industrious," even if she did not think him "handsome, at least not like Smith or Bassett Moseley." Protesting that "I do not say that you shall not have him [Moseley]," Maximilian Calvert nonetheless offered his daughter a choice: a portion of five hundred pounds and nothing further if she married Moseley or a thousand pounds and more during her marriage if she took Maxwell. "I reflected accordingly," she sighed, "and soon

made up my mind to take Mr. Maxwell with my parents' favor, rather
than poor Bassett without." Years later, however, her sentimental mem-
ories notwithstanding, Read concluded, "I cannot help thinking that if
young girls would follow their parents' advice instead of their own foolish fancies in the choice of their partners for life, it would often, if not
always, be much better for them." Like so many other readers of novels,
Read indulged in her flights of fancy, relishing her experiences of love
and passion, but ultimately returned to her more prosaic existence
while reassuring herself of the rational grounding of her choice.[53]

Indeed, the discomfiture we see in reading women of the South is typical of that in reading women throughout the colonies. They were self-
conscious about the time they spent with their books. Like Frances Baylor
Hill, who carefully noted the chores she had completed daily in addition
to her novel reading, Philadelphian Elizabeth Drinker felt guilty about
her reading. "'Tis seldom I listen to a romance, nor would I encourage
my Children doing much of that business," she wrote in her diary in 1795,
even though she was doing her needlework while her daughter read
aloud.[54] In New Jersey, Esther Edwards Burr, taxed to find "one vacant
moment for my Life," borrowed and read, over the course of a month,
Samuel Richardson's *Pamela.* Initially angered by his portrayal of women
("he has degraded our sex most horridly"), she finally decided that "there
is sertainly many excellent observations and rules laid down [so] that I
shall never regret my pains."[55] As Linda Kerber has cogently observed,
"leisure does not happen, it is made"; and even as women sought to justify
the time they spent reading, the important point is that they understood
its value enough to make time for it.[56]

Accepting the novels' teachings, whether implicit or explicit, on the
importance of female education, some women understood their reading
as lessons on female virtue and fully engaged the subject. Running her father's six-hundred-acre plantation in South Carolina, nineteen-year-old
Eliza Lucas (later Pinckney) incorporated reading into her daily schedule, reading from her father's library from five until seven each morning.[57] *Pamela,* published in 1740 and immediately in vogue on both sides
of the Atlantic, had not escaped Lucas's notice. Returning the copy she
had borrowed from a friend, Lucas used the opportunity of her cover letter to critique the book. In a paradoxical mix of outspoken criticism and
feminine deference, she illustrated the ways in which the various forms of
conduct-of-life literature shaped her thinking about herself, women's capacities generally, and proper feminine behavior.

Lucas engaged the character of Pamela first, speaking of her as she
would an acquaintance. "She is a good girl and as such I love her dearly,"

she began, taking Pamela and her story into her own experience. "But I must think her very defective and even blush for her while she allows her self that disgusting liberty of praising her self [by] repeating all the fine speeches made to her by others," she continued, in a mirror reflection of traditional writers on feminine modesty. Better if the source of Pamela's praises "had come from some other hand," Lucas believed. Begging indulgence for her "presumption for instructing one so far above my own level as the Authour of Pamella," she nonetheless proceeded to advise the author on ways to accomplish the same end, without placing the offensively self-serving words in Pamela's mouth. Not yet twenty, Lucas was taking on a formidable writer in Samuel Richardson and she knew it. No sooner had she pointed out his deficiency than she "acquit[ted]" him. "He designed to paint no more than a woman," she excused him, "and he certainly designed it as a reflection upon the vanity of our sex that a character so compleat in every other instance should be so greatly defective in this." This she thought made the character true to "nature . . . for had his Heroin no defect the character must be unnatural."[58]

Pamela was both creature of Richardson's fertile imagination and real friend to Lucas. However much she criticized Richardson's literary creation, showing that she could distinguish between fiction and reality, Lucas nonetheless found Pamela to be very real. "I love her dearly," Lucas wrote immediately in her letter to Mary Bartlett. Passionate in her censure of Pamela's unfortunate proclivity to sing her own praises, Lucas ached to counsel her. Did not Pamela realize those compliments could have been the fond phrases of very partial friends? Or perhaps, Lucas suggested further, they were meant "with a view to encourage her and make her aspire after those qualifications which were ascribed to her."[59] In any event, Lucas responded with the compassionate wisdom of a friend to a fictional character in a way reminiscent of tearful visitors at the turn of the nineteenth century who sought the grave of the fictional Charlotte Temple in the yard of New York's Trinity Church.[60]

So real was Pamela to Lucas, that she emboldened Lucas's criticism of Richardson. "I have run this farr before I was aware for I have nither capacity or inclination for Critissism," she confessed, "tho' Pamela sets me the example by critisizeing Mr. Lock [John Locke] and has taken the libirty to disent from that admirable Author."[61] That a woman in print should dissent from the Oxford-educated philosopher was inspiration enough for Lucas; it mattered little that she was a fiction. In spite of Pamela's lapse into female vanity, she had been lauded for the virtue that strengthened her resistance to the persistent "Mr. B." The printed words of a virtuous woman carried within them the power that freed Lucas to speak her mind, at least for a few lines of her letter.

This is just the sort of deeply personal reading some people feared, and they were vociferous in their condemnation of novel reading. Colonial newspapers are an important index to the response to novels. In 1752, a contributor to the *Virginia Gazette* decried the "wickedness of a prophane or libidinous Writer" as "much more atrocious and detestable than that of the hot Libertine or drunken Ravisher" since the writer committed his crime "with a cool deliberation."[62] A generation later, another essayist wrote that novels "falsify the understanding because never being founded upon truth, and only on Illusions, they warm the Imagination, weaken the Modesty, disorder the heart, and, if the young readers are of delicate feelings, hasten their disposition and precipitate them headlong into Errors."[63] The novel was a "literary opium" in another writer's opinion and had "contributed, more than any other cause, to debauch the morals of the Young of the Fair Sex."[64] (Notwithstanding their publication of these essays in their newspapers, pragmatic printers of the *Virginia Gazette* continued to engage in the lucrative business of selling novels from their print shop.) The novels' increased availability further worried critics, who observed the drowning of distinctions of class in a sea of sentiment, a prospect that was regarded with particular horror in the South.[65] Novels made common cause among all women, regardless of class, as the *Virginia Gazette* writer had recognized, in their interest in "Swains & sentiments."[66]

The problem, as some saw it, was that novels contributed to a culture of heightened expectations of marriage as women chose their own spouses, even in the face of parental disapproval. While material considerations remained crucial in bargaining over these matches, more and more women in the eighteenth century began to anticipate marriages that provided not only bed, board, and marital peace but companionate affection as well.[67] Parents and children could differ sharply on which should prevail. In what must have been a formidable showdown, Judith Carter of Richmond County, Virginia, defied the express wishes of her father, Landon, on the subject of her choice. Landon Carter felt justified by reason of his age and experience in "only Claiming a right to dispose of my children as I ple[ase]." But in a rebellious scheme that Landon Carter was sure involved the "devilish influence" of his son Robert Wormeley Carter, daughter-in-law Winifred Beale Carter, and friend William Beale, Judith Carter married William's son Rueben Beale. The marriage, Carter raged, occurred "against her duty, my will, and against her Solemn Promise." Carter thought his daughter totally deluded on the subject of love. "How easily that poor girl is made to believe her distant happiness when I am certain she sees nothing but misery," he commented, "but possibly it was with her All for Love or the world well Lost." She was, he had observed in February 1774, "a mere slave to her affection." Judith had been a much-favored child, and her decision to defy him rankled for the rest of his life. Four months before his death in 1778 he continued to lament that she "chose to go out of the world from her father."[68]

Male advice writers were not the only ones concerned with the pernicious effects of romantic ideas on impressionable young girls. Late in her life, Virginian Nancy Johns Turner wrote "The Imaginationist," in which she described her girlhood introduction to novels, her fall into an imprudent marriage and then divorce at age sixteen, and her subsequent redemption in her education and teaching and second marriage to a minister. The daughter of a Presbyterian preacher, she had been cruelly disappointed in her hopes for a fine boarding school education (she was the fifth child of ten). Left to her own devices at home, she perused her father's library. "Unfortunately for me I now spied in a corner, where they seemed to have been placed merely to fill up a vacancy; about half a doz. Novels, such as Peregrine Pickle, Roderick Random, Gil Blas, and others," Turner wrote. She had seen them there before, but not until that "fatal morning" had she ever been so drawn to them. "While conscious of the sin," she confessed, "I opened & read them, one after another until all were perused. . . . when I had read the last, I almost wept that there were no more to read." "Why my good and pious father suffered such vile books as these surely were to encumber his shelves, I *never could imagine*," Turner wrote, nor could she summon the courage to ask him, even years after her "reformation."[69]

The novels were responsible for the romantic dreams Turner expected to be fulfilled in her rash first marriage: she titled chapter 5 of her memoir "My first peep into novels, and its consequences. Heartrending disappointment." Just as many novels warned their readers against reading novels, Turner also advised her readers "in your proper sphere, [to] try to render [this world] less miserable by acts of usefulness but *never* sit down supinely & fold your hands and dream yourself away into the regions of fancy until a new and fairy world arises under your creative hand. If you do; depend upon it you will reap the bitter reward . . . if your life be spared." When a friend applied to her for advice about a love affair, she cautioned, "[I]f either of you should turn out to be in love with a creature of your own imagination—a perfect being . . . you will surely reap your reward in disappointed hopes, & consequent misery." Of her own experience, she admitted ruefully, "[M]y notions of love have been quite visionary I suppose; & old folks say I have not got hold of the right thing yet."[70]

Turner took to heart the fatal consequences potentially attendant on the romantic notions novels inspired: she was fortunate her life had been spared. In the meantime, novels could cause immediate detrimental effects: "Many a little Miss just entering her 'teens have I seen stealing to her solitary room. . . . I have seen these wandering about the house, with a broad grin and vacant look of the idiot," utterly forgetful of their domestic duties.[71] That she herself had "not got hold of the right thing yet" testified to the enduring ill effects of the novel on a woman's imagination.

But not all readers were young, impressionable women. When Mary Jemima Balfour had her portrait (jacket) painted in Virginia in 1773, she made sure it depicted her as a woman in tune with the intellectual currents of the Anglo-Atlantic world. She was the wife of wealthy James Balfour, a merchant respected on both sides of the Atlantic (with Benjamin Franklin, he had appeared before Parliament in 1766 to appeal for the annulment of the Stamp Act) and eulogized in 1775 as a man of "humane and benevolent heart" who could not be bested in his devotion to "the cause of America."[72] Her lavish gown and stylishly upswept and bound hair reflect the latest British fashions, but unlike the idle aristocracy, she is busy with her intellectual pursuits. Indeed, she appears slightly impatient at the artist's interruption of her reading, and marking her place with her thumb at page 92, she anticipates her momentary return to the more important activity. It is unlikely that she is reading the stodgy Allestree or the genteel Fordyce; neither would countenance the proud portrayal of a woman of ideas that Mary Jemima Balfour's clear-eyed, straightforward gaze and open book shows that she was. Profiting in every way from her husband's mercantile connections, she embodies the twin themes of the flow of ideas across the Atlantic and a new construction of southern femininity.

Hannah Lee Corbin was already widowed when she was ordering her novels; her story allows us to see the ways in which older women also read novels into their lives. Despite her conversion to the Baptist Church, Corbin disregarded both secular and religious proscriptions and avidly read novels. Fraught with moral lessons, her novels dealt with questions of love, marriage, identity, adultery, and honor. And she ordered at least a dozen of them between 1764 and 1772.[73] It is only one of the many puzzles of Corbin's life that she did so, since this indulgence ran counter not only to the dominant male literary culture, which vociferously condemned the reading of novels by women, but also to the dissenting religious one (which she had joined) that condemned many such idle gentry pastimes. Yet she ordered *The History of Charlotte Summers*, the tale of an orphaned girl who, preserving her virtue through a series of perilous situations before discovering the truth of her birth and rank, was reunited with her father and happily anticipated the reward of marriage with the man of her choice. *True Merit, True Happiness* is the "autobiography" of a rather rakish man who tells of his misadventures with women until finally he marries respectably and finds true happiness: the point of the story, as we are given to understand by its title.[74]

Particularly intriguing is *The History of a Young Lady of Distinction*, a novel about love, both faithful and faithless, and the power of religion.[75] It is the story of a young woman who, through a series of letters, relies on the judgment of her mother to guide her through the trials of the marriage arranged for her by her father. Her husband, the Marquis "de***," takes her from her "peaceable and innocent life" at home to the worldliness of his court life. Dismayed that "the pride of his rank, the lustre of his riches and the seduction of company, have obscured a thousand good qualities," the new marchioness asks her mother how she might awaken those "happy dispositions which are only laid to sleep." Her mother's advice was familiar to all eighteenth-century readers: "Your first care ought to be to win the heart of your husband. . . . Shew him daily, and in the smallest matters, that you have no greater satisfaction than in obeying him."[76] (Indeed, Corbin's sister, Alice Lee Shippen, gave precisely that advice to her daughter in the first year of her disastrous marriage to the philandering Henry Livingston.)[77]

Letters continue to fly between the mother and daughter in the tale, as the marchioness becomes more deeply entangled in the affairs—quite literally—at court. Her husband's best friend, a count, falls in love with her. She discovers her husband's adultery with a young girl she has taken in for charity. She fears for the safety and virtue of a sister who has joined her. Again her mother directs her, with the advice most familiar to eighteenth-century readers, to ignore her husband's dalliances. Mother assures young wife of her husband's love (after all, has he not attempted to keep the knowledge of his affair from her?) and urges her to behave in all ways virtuously so that all will turn out well.[78]

In fact, throughout her letters, the marchioness attempts to apply the principles of religion that have always guided her to this new life with the marquis, but she despairs that the "four theological virtues" at court are "faith, hope, charity, and hypocrisy." "This last is in great request here," she laments. Religion is indeed merely a "masque," her mother sympathizes in reply. But the marchioness's next letter shows how seriously her mother has misunderstood the court. Relating an account of a notorious assassin who conducted business and eluded arrest from the refuge of a church, the marchioness shows that religion does not even have the status of a masque; it is held in complete contempt.[79]

Hannah Corbin's life certainly did not have the high drama of the marchioness's life, nor did life in eighteenth-century Virginia resemble life in the court of Turin. Or did it? Much has been made of the worldliness of Anglican Virginian culture: how the established Church propped up the gentry's social, economic, and political dominance; how Anglican clerics danced, drank, gambled, and worse; how Sunday worship was a social occasion rather than a spiritual one.[80] How much more godly was life in the gentry circles of Virginia than in the aristocratic ones of Turin?

Within their respective worlds, the two women faced dilemmas that were similar in terms of reconciling the desire for love and the obligations of family life with their own religious imperatives. The high-minded marchioness struggles with her husband's adultery, worrying less about its consequences for her than about "the injury he does *himself.*" Stricken as she reads one of her husband's love letters to his mistress, she realizes that he has not loved her, his own wife, with such passion. Yet she never succumbs to the corrupting influence of life at court to retaliate. Clinging always to the advice of her mother, to "expect his return to his duty at the hand of God," she prays to find a way to recapture her errant husband's love.[81]

Well placed within the Virginia aristocracy, Corbin could empathize with the temptations of mammon and the flesh. Certainly she recognized the passions described within the fictional world; after all, she lived with Hall and had two children with him. The "young lady of distinction" showed how faith and goodness could prevail, even in such a godless place as Turin. She was a powerful example to Corbin of an educated, aristocratic woman whose marriage was of critical importance, who lived in and was of the world but who kept God at the center of her life. Hannah Lee Corbin was also a woman for whom religion was more than form. That it had substance for her is borne out by the fact that she hosted Baptist meetings at her plantation in spite of threats of violence; that she raised her children with Hall in her new faith; and that she could write joyfully to her sister of the ridicule to which Baptists were subjected, "This is our comfort!"[82] The marchioness showed how to cling to faith in a faithless world; Hannah Lee Corbin could not do any less.

Baptists may have opposed the reading of novels precisely because of their belief in the efficacy of the Word.[83] Yet Corbin's own words reveal they need not have feared; an older, more experienced reader, she drew moral lessons that outweighed the deadly potential novels may have held for younger women. And, as the mother of the young marchioness shows, the novels could contain the kind of traditional advice of which Allestree, Halifax, and Fordyce would all approve: the efficacy of prayer to redirect a straying husband back to the marriage bed, for example. (Indeed, it was frequently the only recourse white southern women had against their husband's nocturnal visits to the slave quarters.) While such strategies were largely ineffective, implicitly revealing the deep entrenchment of the double standard, readers young and old could cite such passages as justification for their novel reading.

Although the library of Lady Jean Skipwith shows the growing importance of novels over traditional advice literature, her novels, too, were heavily infused with religious themes; and though her papers are distressingly few, two items remain that suggest the importance to her of both religion and novels. Raised in Virginia until she was twelve, Jean Miller had been living in Scotland for twenty-five years when her sister's widower, Sir Peyton Skipwith, persuaded her to return to Virginia. When he urged her to marry him, he called on the authority of the church to resolve whatever doubts she had about the legality of their marriage. He enclosed a copy of a letter written by the Reverend John Cameron, a well-respected Anglican clergyman, and (probably not coincidentally) a Scot.[84] The enclosure, Skipwith hoped, would "determine you imediately to compleat a Union on which my future happiness so much & so immediately depends." He also had letters, he told her, from "the most eminent Characters in the Law equally favorable to our purpose," presumably to serve as a backup argument, but he sent the one he knew would carry the most weight.[85] The law might allow their marriage, but Jean Miller wanted the church's sanction more.

Sir Peyton Skipwith died in 1805. How much comfort in her mourning Jean Skipwith derived from her devotional texts we do not know. But on the back of a receipt, dated 1807, are the words of the fictional Agnes De-Courci:

> They pursued the same studies, "and like two artificial gods, creating with their needles, both one flower, both on one sampler, sitting, on our Cushion, both warbling of our Song, both in our key; as if their hands, their sides, voices, and minds, had been incorporate: so they grew together like to a double cherry, seeming parted, but with an union in partitions."—When she recollected all the counsel that they two had shared, this sister Vows, the hours that they had spent, when they chid the hasty-footed time that was to part them.[86]

Jean Skipwith's search for the words to describe her marriage to Sir Peyton ended in a novel. It is interesting that she chose a depiction of love between two women. United in mind, work, and soul, the couple had transcended the barriers that gender conventions had erected. It was a remarkable tribute to their marriage, in an age that assigned so meticulously by sex intellectual capacity, religious duty, and most certainly, labor.

Neither Corbin nor Skipwith wrote explicitly about the novels they had assembled for their libraries, but their books' influence can be inferred from the types of novels they selected. Throughout this period, most novels southern women read were English imports, and of those, their novels of choice were those authored by women.[87] Far from being monolithic in style, content, and message, these books had changed over the course of the eighteenth century. The early novels from late-seventeenth-century England experimented with flouting gender conventions; mid-eighteenth-century novels accepted feminine sentiment as a quasi-religious dictum; late-century novels simply tried to find a way to invest feminine sentiment with religious and moral authority.[88] The ways in which women's relationships with men were portrayed differed throughout the century as writers' thinking changed about questions of virtue, an increasingly relevant issue for women as the term was being redefined from a political sense to a sexual one.[89] But they all exposed the inequities of gender relations as hardened by custom and institutionalized by law and sought ways in which women might cope.

It is clear from Hannah Lee Corbin's 1783 inventory that it was the midcentury novels that had particular appeal among elite women. In addition to *The History of a Young Lady of Distinction*, she also owned *The History of Charlotte Summers, The Fortunate Country Maid,* and *Country Cousins*.[90] Receipts from her London agents supplement the list with *The Rival Mother* and *True Merit, True Happiness*, which were shipped in October 1766, and *Vicar of Bray, The History of Mrs. Somerville,* and *The Curate of Coventry*, shipped in June 1772.[91] Her choices show a preference for those novels in which women authors forsook the issue of sexless minds and souls of the Restoration-era tales and instead embraced sentiment as peculiarly feminine. These works reflected an England that had settled down to a gendered social hierarchy that was firmly in place after the upheavals of the previous century. Even as William Blackstone's *Commentaries on the Laws of England* (1765) stressed the legal inequality of men and women within marriage, novels written in this period, suffused with sentiment, do not so much protest these inequalities as advise how best to endure them. As Lady Pennington wrote in her *An Unfortunate Mother's Ad-*

vice to Her Absent Daughters (1761), "Should the painful task of dealing with a morose tyrannical temper be assigned to you, there is little more to be recommended than a patient submission to an evil which admits not of a remedy."[92]

Similarly, Skipwith's library was stocked with women authors, although of the next generation of writers. One of her favorite authors was Maria Edgeworth, who published late in the century and into the nineteenth. The heroines of Edgeworth's novels who encounter happy endings were those women who understood most perfectly a woman's domestic role.[93] Among the fourteen Edgeworth books Skipwith owned were *Belinda* (1802), *The Absentee* (1812), and the *Moral Tales for Young People* (1801), all of which praised the enlightened domesticity in which mothers feature prominently as teachers of their children.[94] Skipwith's library included six novels each of Agnes Bennett, Regina Maria Roche, and Jane West, in addition to those by Anna Maria Porter, Amelia Opie, Fanny Burney, Ann Radcliffe, and Clara Reeve.[95]

The reading of both women presents an interesting counterpoint to the books available in 1775 at the Williamsburg print shop. To the extent that the evidence allows us to see, when women bought or shared books, they tended to favor female authors rather than the male authors found in the print shop (although Richardson's *Pamela* was popular among women as well). Since printing books was a precarious business, catering to a reading public would seem to make good business sense. But with the exception of the overtly religious Elizabeth Singer Rowe or Eliza Haywood's *Female Spectator* (a work more in line with sentimental novels than her earlier works had been), the shop stocked few women's works.[96] Perhaps male printers did not see women as writers or southern women as part of a reading public, interested in acquiring books. Corbin and Skipwith show their miscalculation. Corbin skipped the Virginia middleman altogether, ordering her novels directly from England. While Jean Skipwith began her sizable library in Scotland before returning to Virginia (perhaps foreseeing the physical and intellectual isolation of life on a Virginia plantation), she continued to add to it during the course of her marriage and widowhood, calling on booksellers in Petersburg, Norfolk, and New York.[97]

The variety of advice literature found in bookstores and private collections is instructive: rather than a neat linear progression over the course of the century, we see some writers who strained in different ways against the dominant culture, others who found ways to make the most of the virtues allocated to women, and still others who resisted mightily any change at all. Images of women did not replace one another; they coexisted.[98] This complexity was evident in the diary of Frances Baylor Hill, with whom this chapter opened. Hill read Catherine Macaulay's *Letters on Education* (1790), which contains a well-known passage urging that chastity be an ideal for both men and women, as well as Frances Burney's *Evelina*, a classic example of sentimental literature, in which chastity is understood to be solely a female attribute.[99] From this perspective, then, the Revolution itself seems not to have had a noticeable impact, save for the increased emphasis on female literacy that followed, enabling an even wider audience for novels than the "tailor's daughter . . . and accomplished genteel dames" of whom the 1772 *Virginia Gazette* writer had complained. The widening availability of print was a process that had begun long before the Revolutionary era; a larger audience meant the wider influence of all types of advice.[100]

NOVELS AND THE REVOLUTION

Because advice writing offered competing messages, readers responded in different ways to their reading, particularly in the context of the Revolution. Themes of virtue and religion certainly had broad appeal, generating the benevolent activism we saw in chapter 3. But for women connected to Revolutionary elites, reading may well have encouraged an incipient political activism as well. Corbin is probably best known for a letter she wrote to her brother, Richard Henry Lee, the Virginia delegate who presented the proposal for independence on the floor of the Continental Congress in May 1776. The contents of her letter, now lost, can be deduced from her brother's reprise of it: "You complain that widows are not represented," he reviewed, "and that being temporary possessors of their estates ought not to be liable to the tax." Indeed, Lee must have found her argument arresting, for he replied as thoughtfully and systematically to her query as he did to any of his brothers' during the Revolutionary period, although he allowed he was "illy able by letter to give you the satisfaction I could wish on the several subjects of your letter." Beset with worries both political and personal (his political enemies' attempts to implicate him in the Conway cabal, a conspiracy to depose George Washington, and the rapidly deteriorating health of their brother, Thomas Ludwell Lee), Lee lamented that they could not enjoy a "few hours' conversation" about her queries. He proffered a few possible explanations for women's status in American and British law: "Perhaps 'twas thought out of character for women to press into those tumultuous assemblages of men where the business of choosing a representative is conducted," he suggested. Or maybe it was "considered as not so necessary, seeing that the representatives themselves, as their immediate constituents, must suffer the tax imposed." In any event, he could not dispute the legitimacy of her grievance at being disfranchised. "The doctrine of representation is a large subject, and it is certain that it ought to be extended as far as wisdom and policy can allow," he agreed, "nor do I see that either of these forbid widows having property from voting, notwithstanding it has never been the practice either here or in England." Completely acceding to her point, he "would at any time give my consent to establish their [property-holding single women's and widows'] right of voting."

He did, however, parry her clever argument that, since most widows did not enjoy outright ownership of lands they inherited (thus keeping estates intact for transmission to sons) they should be spared the burden of taxation on it. A credit to the razor-sharp mind that produced it, her idea clearly intrigued her brother, who would have relished the opportunity for several hours' conversation about it. As it was, he settled for pointing out that woman suffrage would not alter the "mode of taxation" she complained of, since the taxes assessed the land's annual profits rather than its ownership. "A very considerable part of the property I hold is, like yours, temporary for my life," he assured her, "yet I see the propriety of paying my proportion of the tax laid [on it] . . . so long as it remains in my possession and I derive use and profit from it." Even when we look at her through her brother's words, Hannah Corbin is eminently visible. She was a formidable woman: intelligent and fearless in her expression of her ideas and enormously respected in spite of the unorthodox choices of her life. While her mother's portrait mirrored Allestree's model of female virtue, Hannah Corbin's loving relationship with her brother, who would have gladly spent hours in her company talking politics, utterly skewered her own generation's model (Fordyce) of respectable womanhood. Her family connections, her reading, and her religion combined to produce a model of female intellect heretofore unseen in Virginia.[101]

The ways in which Mary Jemima Balfour of Virginia and Sarah Middleton Pinckney of South Carolina (daughter-in-law of Eliza Lucas Pinckney) chose to be portrayed in their portraits also bespeak a political sensibility. Disparaged in the local press and traditional advice, the "learned lady" was a reputation few southern women would willingly court. But Balfour was married to a man in the very center of transatlantic trade and commerce, whose guns welcomed royal governor Lord Botetourt in 1768, and whose signature on the Non-Importation Association agreement two years later appeared in print in company with those of Virginia luminaries

Thomas Jefferson, George Washington, and Richard Henry Lee. Living on their plantation of "Little England" in Hampton Roads, Balfour was no isolated Virginia provincial. Her elegant self-assurance as a thinking woman is unmistakable in her portrait, and in her claim to an intellectual life, her portrait offers an icon of what Revolutionary Virginia woman-hood could be.[102] Sarah Middleton Pinckney's portrait, done roughly contemporaneously, is even more direct in her assertion of her place in the polity.[103] She is dressed in the classic garb of a Roman matron, a book open on her lap; we have interrupted her reading, and she raises her head slightly from her hand where it had been resting, squarely meeting our gaze. Classical garb was the sign of intellectual women in British por-traiture in this period, as they eschewed the artificiality and discomfort of high fashion for the natural simplicity of the ancients' dress.[104] In the con-text of pre-Revolutionary America, however, Pinckney's dress would have taken on even deeper meaning, as women publicly supported nonimpor-tation resolutions, holding spinning bees and making their own, simple clothing instead of importing luxury dresses from England. If historian Stephanie Grauman Wolf is correct that portraits in economically and so-cially mobile colonial America became the "means rather than merely the sign" of status, rank, and gentility, then Pinckney's chosen pose was her way of creating a political niche for women of education, rank, and virtue.[105]

For elite young women, novels comprised the "core curriculum" of an education designed to prepare them for their entry into genteel society and the marriage market; for adult women, they facilitated their contin-ued participation in social rituals that assumed increasing importance over the course of the century.[106] In a society in which men read their way to models of English gentility (William Byrd II, George Washington, and Thomas Jefferson come readily to mind), it is not surprising that women, whose literacy rates gradually rose, should pursue the same course in reading. In the post-Revolutionary age, genteel women would attempt to parlay their status and accomplishments into a strategy for participation in the civic rituals of the republic.[107]

The growing appeal of novels must be linked also to the increasing cul-tural importance of motherhood over the century, particularly in the post-Revolutionary period. Although the ideal of companionate marriage acquired greater currency in England and America during the eighteenth century, its wider acceptance did not signal any fundamental change in the balance of power within marriage. The firm exclusion of women from the franchise in the infant nation heralded a further weakening in women's legal status.[108] The notion of republican motherhood, however, enabled a "cultural enfranchisement" for women in which they acquired learning applicable to their domestic labor, particularly to their children's education, a crucial public service.[109] Mothers' authority to teach their children in the post-Revolutionary period was augmented by the spiritual and moral authority conferred on them by both evangelical Christianity and the secular presses, which increasingly ascribed piety and virtue, rather than seduction and vice, to women. Observing women readers in their novels, southern women took novels as guides for their own behavior and as vehicles for conveying their own teachings to the next generation.

Taking Up the Pen

From their reading, southern women understood the importance of education and their responsibility to succeeding generations, and it was in the wake of the Revolution that they began to extend their advice beyond admonitions on living the spiritual life. North Carolinian Anna Cameron prayed for her son Duncan that God "never leave you my dear without a faithfull guide to direct you" but then added her own advice: "O my Child never lose sight of the virteous education your dear father gave you when you fall in the Company of Wild Young men wich sometimes you must let none of their doings saings nor sentements stick by you."[110]

Alice Izard of South Carolina guided her son's secular, as well as religious, education. Ralph Izard had solicited his mother's advice, begging for "long letters of advice for you know my faults much better than I do myself." Delighted with the reports of his conduct that had filtered back from Boston (where the young Izard awaited posting to a naval appointment), his mother instead supplied him with suggestions for his reading. "I wish you have a good general knowledge of ancient, as well as modern history. Mr. Rollins's ancient & Roman history is the best I know, & it would give me great pleasure to send it to you. . . . The french edition is much superior to the translation," she added, "& I believe you sufficiently master of that language to understand a book so well written."[111] The confluence of the experiences of novel reading and the Revolution are apparent in this shift from religious advice to secular; it was not on a sacred conception of Christian womanhood that Cameron and Izard relied but on the new configuration of virtuous republican mother.

But they did not confine their interest to the education of sons; southern women also took a deeply personal interest in the education of young women. Jane Randolph described her efforts to rescue a young woman from exactly the sort of misguided counsel that had led the fictional character Charlotte Temple to her demise. "You, my friend, are a mother," Randolph wrote in 1805 to Mary Harrison, "you have [a] daughter, you will know how to appreciate the effort to rescue an exemplary young female from the danger of evil counsellors; to screen in some slight degree from unexampled calumny, an object, whose chief error was generated by the guileless simplicity of her heart, & the unequalled easiness of her temper."[112] The education Randolph proposed to provide was the education for identity that was so critical for eighteenth-century women. But the substance of such an education was changing; the "guileless simplicity" of heart that was so quintessentially feminine to advice writer Reverend James Fordyce in 1765 was no longer a goal, although training a woman in virtuous conduct still was.[113] Innocence that was simultaneously childlike and feminine could lead all too often to disaster, as Randolph's ward and Rachel Warrington had discovered. Indeed, Susannah Rowson's *Charlotte Temple* could be understood as a call to older women to be protective of naïve young women as well as a warning to younger women.[114] Unlike the villain Mademoiselle LaRue who led Charlotte to her ruin, Randolph intended to screen her charge from "evil counsellors." Randolph took seriously Eliza Haywood's complaint from her 1744 *Female Spectator* that men ought "to be more careful of the education of those females to whom they are parents or guardians!" No longer willing to rely on men to protect and educate them, women took the educational reins themselves and embraced their roles as teachers.[115]

Indeed, it is in their taking up the pen to teach that we perceive the most dramatic impact of novels on southern women. For it was the novel, and not Allestree or Halifax or Fordyce, that inspired by example: of the approximately two thousand novels written in eighteenth-century England, at least six hundred books were written by women.[116] This is a significant development considering the reticence required of a respectable woman, not to mention the limitations on women's education. Of course, women wrote to uphold the gender order as well as to undermine it. But there is no question that by the end of the century the genre was most certainly gendered, for in the novel, as Juliet Mitchell said, "women create themselves as a category: women."[117] It was in the novel that women became subjects. For the first time they were the main characters of a book; the important issues of their lives—friendship, courtship, marriage, and child rearing—carried the plotline; and as a series of conversations with other women, novels helped women readers begin to realize that the dilemmas with which they struggled were not idiosyncratic to their own experience but symptomatic of the social arrangements under which they all lived. Nonetheless, regardless of their place on a continuum of radical to conservative, by setting forth their thoughts in this most public forum, writing women provided dubious models for the daughters of anxious patriarchs.[118]

Elizabeth Foote Washington's writings are modest in this light; she did not aim for a wider audience than her daughter and she wrote in the direct, straightforward mode of traditional advice as well. But her writing for her unborn child was as intentional as any Englishwoman's.[119] Eliza Ambler Brent Carrington realized full well the value of letters written from one generation to another: "[A] door of improvement would be opened that might prove advantageous," while tales of a "departure from rectitude . . . would fill the virtuous mind with horror" and prompt the alternative, honorable behavior.[120] But she also chose the medium even more appealing to younger women—novels. Late in her life, as she perused the letters of her Revolutionary girlhood, Carrington would begin to transform the story in which she and Mildred Smith had been so absorbed into a novel entitled *Variety or the Vicissitudes of Long life.* Bearing the most transparent of disguises, the real-life characters from Carrington's early life entered her novel: parents, friends, French soldiers, unwary innocents, and experienced counselors. Carrington never completed her novel. Yet it was clear to her that the story recounted in those letters of her past was the stuff of which novels were made. As she read and reread her correspondence, she could vividly recall the heady days of her girlhood, when her novels were so real to her that she and Mildred adopted romantic names for themselves in imitation of their heroines (she could not decide among Bessie, Jacquilene or Sophia; Mildred took Millia).[121] And as she read, she herself was transformed from reader to producer of a story she felt compelled to write. It was surely no coincidence that she chose the genre beloved by young women of the early republic to bequeath her teachings to the next generation. Indeed, her attempt to fashion her own work of fiction demonstrates her faith in the novel, both as a legitimate literary form and as an effective way to communicate important moral lessons to her nieces.[122]

A generation later, Caroline Burgwin Clitherall's reading of her parents' eighteenth-century courtship letters inspired her to write a text that would serve as a conduct guide for her descendants. Her parents' story began when Eliza Bush, a young English Quaker, met North Carolina planter/lawyer John Burgwin during his stay in England in 1777. Burgwin was a widower considerably older than Eliza Bush, and his suit was complicated by the war, particularly by his need to return to protect his Carolina estates threatened with confiscation.[123] In the exchange of their letters until their marriage in 1782, Burgwin assured Eliza Bush during the course of a wartime separation with no foreseeable end to "fear not then . . . whilst we . . . are treading the Path of Virtue" and he urged her to be "resign'd to [God's] will, and rest upon his arm for support . . . mercy and goodness." Eliza's replies were "the index of a heart which knew no double covering" and the best source for her daughter Caroline's essay. Read as intensively as any advice literature, the mother's letters gave her daughter a view of courtship that could be read against popular novels: a view that relied on trust in providence while maintaining the highest standards of virtue.[124]

This example stood Caroline in good stead when during a sojourn in England, she fell in love for the first time. He was a soldier in the British army, the brother of one of her English friends. "Love, *first love*," she wrote in an echo of fictional sentimentality, "no matter what may be future circumstances, *never can* be driven from a warm and feeling heart." Her friends disapproved of the match, however, and Caroline made no promise to him. Instead, obedient to a pledge to her father, she returned to North Carolina, leaving her suitor behind.[125]

At her father's plantation, however, time "pass'd in dreary solitude." It was perhaps that loneliness that allowed the cautious overtures of a North Carolina planter to interest her at all. George Clitherall was "unlike in mind or manner to the few Gentlemen I met," she observed, "the frequency of his visits, the approbation of them by my Father, all conspir'd to render them so pleasing." With the memory of her passion and close call with her British admirer fresh in her mind, she judged that this slow wooing was indeed love. "As true love is timid," she reasoned, "so were his approaches to a declaration." Novels taught the perils of trusting passions and instinct; better to rely on reason and the approbation of an experienced father. Still, her heart was heavy as she "felt the truth" of her father's dismissal of her first love. "My father said 'twas all romance, & he was very glad I had made no engagement, so absurd, & so hopeless.' "[126]

Caroline turned her attentions to George Clitherall's plodding suit, agreeing to an engagement and sagely persuading herself that she had chosen wisely and well. It would take a dramatic downturn of events to engage her heart, however. One day, in a scene of high drama, her father returned from a trip to Wilmington in a fury. "Where is C[litheral]l?" he thundered at his daughter. "Drive him off—See him no more—he shall no longer be in my house—he is a deceiver." Like many fictional heroines, Caroline "felt like fainting." Summoned to her father's study, Caroline was bidden to read an anonymous letter "with the most gross, & cruel accusations of Mr. C." Clitherall robustly denied the charges, pointing to the letter's anonymity as a "proof of their falsity," and invited the "most minute investigation" of his character. Nothing moved, Burgwin "refus'd to do so, & disannul'd our engagement forever."[127]

The scene left Caroline's mind in a whirl. Reviewing the whole, she enumerated the elements of the drama: "the humiliating and cruel position in which he was plac'd; the sudden dash from happiness to sorrow; the mysterious agency of the slanderer, . . . [and Clitherall's] hopeless situation." Samuel Richardson himself could not have brought more sensational elements to his novels: the stinging insults to masculine honor, the incalculable plunge in emotions, mystery, and a hero trapped by forces he could neither identify nor fight. The pathos of Clitherall's plight brought to Caroline's heart "a rush of love, and a promise that I wou'd receive no other to my heart." It was the last element to make the story complete: a heroine who, though stricken by an unforeseen revelation, realizes the truth of her passions and fervidly pledges herself to her wronged suitor.[128]

Caroline Clitherall's virtuous courtships stood in marked contrast with those of contemporary novels. Resisting the strength of passion with her first suitor, responding to the wisdom of true friends, and obedient to the call of a parent, she was unlike the young women who heedlessly left family and friends to rely on a dashing (usually uniformed) suitor's promise of love. While acknowledging that the blandness of her life might have made her more receptive to the overtures of an uninspired suitor, Caroline had worked hard at persuading herself to accept a sensible man. It was not a particularly satisfying choice, but at least it was respectable.

Caroline Burgwin Clitherall's story differed from that of novels in another significant respect. Unlike the machinations of novels, where secrets and deceit drive the main characters, Caroline's hero depended on the exposure of truth. Indeed, full disclosure was critical to each of the main characters in her story. The only way George Clitherall knew to clear himself was a vigorous investigation, in which he invited Burgwin to write to all who knew him for character references, making of his life an open, unabridged book. Similarly, Caroline had opened herself to Clitherall in the early days of their courtship. Resolving that she "wou'd not consent to receive him as a Suitor until he knew the whole," she had shown him all the letters she had received from her English suitor.[129]

Such standards of virtue were strikingly different from the secret alliances and messages, forbidden meetings, and shadowy pasts on which most novel plots depended. That the heightened romantic expectations produced by novels affected Caroline Burgwin, however, is also clear. Like every child who thinks her parent impervious to (or forgetful of) passion, she expected her father to dismiss the "romance" of her love for her

English soldier. She may have been forced to relinquish her soldier, but she did not have to abjure her "sincere affection" for him. She carried his letters, the cherished talismans of their love, across the Atlantic and kept them long after she had given up hope of their union. George Clitherall may have been a sensible choice, but until the stranger's melodramatic intervention, he never met her romantic expectations or replaced Caroline's first love.[130]

The epistolary form in novels such as *Pamela* was a compelling literary device that drew the reader into the plot as it unfolded; Clitherall shows why that form was so effective. As she transcribed her parents' words, she imagined how they must have received the missives of the other: "How often were these lines read—how treasur'd—how waited for by hopes and fear." The letters drew her into the uncertainties of their wartime world, as "copy[ing] the sentiments of [her] Father," she wondered, "have all their hopes met fruition? Have all their fears past away? *Have* they been join'd together as one?—was the wide ocean cross'd, & the stranger land their home?"[131] Clitherall read the letters in as much suspense as any reader anxious for the preservation of Pamela's virtue. It was only suitable that she should choose that form to convey the power of her story to her descendants.

The "publication," or dissemination, of these modest writings, was limited to small circles of family and friends, who read them intensively and who treasured and kept them through the centuries. As we have noticed before, the appearance of this advice literature was a full century behind the writings of Restoration Englishwomen who published letters, essays, advice, plays, and novels, both scribally and in the press. But the timing of its emergence was not accidental. Tentative and late as southern women's writings may seem, they signaled a fundamental change effected by both the Revolution and the widening reach of the novel. The post-Revolutionary experience of disestablishment, together with the elaboration of a theory of republican motherhood, gave southern women both religious and secular foundations for their awakening sense of identity. Conditioned by their increased exposure to novels, it was to the medium of the novel (or a novelistic memoir patterned after the various "histories" such as Hannah Lee Corbin had read) that southern women turned to dispense the wisdom born of their experience.

Just as Englishwomen had begun writing novels in the epistolary style out of their letter writing, there are the faintest suggestions that Virginia women tried their hand in their letters at the richly detailed descriptions that were the hallmark of novels' "realism."[132] Shortly after the Revolution ended, Jane Hunter Charlton of Williamsburg received an eager request from an English correspondent. "O how I long to have an account from your descriptive Pen of all the events that you have experience'd both of Publick and private nature," she added, dissatisfied with the accounts she had read in the English press. Nor would she confine Charlton's pen to domestic events, demanding to know her view of public ones as well. She was confident that Charlton's reply would satisfy her: "You have the power of making the merest trifles interesting and then when you have such ample matter do not fail soon to gratefy me with a relation of all you have undergon in the season of dreadful War."[133] Charlton had a story to tell, the talent with which to tell it, and the perspective (female) from which her English friend wanted to hear it.

Similarly, young Mildred Smith was eager to have her friend Betsey Ambler write up the tale of her flight from the invading British army from the environs of Yorktown, through the hills of northwestern Virginia to Winchester, and then doubling back south to Richmond in 1780. Their journeying included several anxious episodes of alarms of approaching soldiers and sleepless nights. "As soon as the bustle & fatigue [of] moving is over," however, Mildred Smith wanted a "long letter."[134] Ambler obliged, sending Smith a "specimen of my powers at the descriptive" that began with a romantically stylized introduction: "On a fine summer morning early in June, e'er the rose tints of m[orn] were lessened by the sunbeams of summer"[135]—and so on. Schooled in the language of sentimental novels, Ambler bestowed on them her highest praise: emulation.

This literary output, ranging from Charlton's letters to Ambler's novel, derived from educations steeped in conduct-of-life literature in its many forms. Novels especially influenced literate women's lives: women responded to them, identified with them, and found fictional characters real enough to embolden their own words. Corbin ordered them from England, although it was hardly proper for a Baptist woman to do so. Eliza Lucas's reading of *Pamela* proved the very point that critics feared most: the problem of women whose weaker intellects rendered them incapable of distinguishing fiction from fact. Although childless, Eliza Carrington (Betsey Ambler) nonetheless found both the form of the novel and the real-life story she witnessed so compelling that she began to record Rachel Warrington's story into a novel to ensure it would be read by her nieces. While Carrington learned lessons about how *not* to behave, Caroline Burgwin Clitherall gleaned from her parents' letters positive lessons about virtuous courtship. But though those lessons were strong enough to guide her choices, they did not counteract entirely the influence of novels that made her yearn for the passion of a foregone love. Incorporating her own decision to place duty and reason over passion as she left her British soldier behind, Clitherall's autobiography told a story of even more drama, in which honor and virtue contributed toward a happy ending. In a straightforward narrative directed to her descendants, Clitherall wrote a history of honorable conduct that was a direct response to fictional heroines who realized too late the error of their choices.

SENTIMENT AND RELIGION

In 1822, two years before her death, novelist Susanna Rowson reviewed her writing life and proudly observed that "among the productions of my pen I have never promulgated a sentence that could militate against the best interests of religion, virtue, and morality."[136] Her reflections on her career, in their focus on female virtue, mirror the convergence of religious with secular themes. John Richetti's reading of English fiction in the early eighteenth century revealed a "structure [that] tends to take the form of a dramatic confrontation between two opposing attitudes to experience" that he loosely termed "secular" and "religious."[137] But as the century progressed, both the secular and devotional literature depicted women as ideally suited by their very nature to be models of virtuous behavior. By midcentury the lines between the two kinds of literature had blurred: religious works gave women practical lessons in daily living, while secular advice stressed virtue. Religious literature that elaborated on the sublime—that which raised one's thoughts to heaven—had so been diluted by sentimentalism that, as Kevin Hayes has explained, the "notion of sublimity began to be applied to anything in art or nature which strongly excited the feelings."[138] Emotion, then, had become a necessary prerequisite to faith and to the discovery of truth. Understood to inhabit the world of sentiment, women were therefore innately endowed with a new authority that religion and even the secular presses acknowledged: they were keepers of truth. By the beginning of the nineteenth century, the secular and religious had made their peace in sentimental fiction, as virtue and feeling came to be understood as female, private, and sexual, rather than male, public, and communal.

Historian Jan Lewis has observed that women's writings in Jeffersonian Virginia "convey little sense of religious community; they more often discussed their personal trials than church or shared religious life."[139] Though the women here may not have had the same kind of institutionally based religious communities northern women had, their writings reveal a lively sense of their daily interaction with God's will. Clearly, then, there had been a shift in their understandings of religion and its expression and application in their lives. Just as the old authoritarian forms of institutional religion had given way to increased female sponsorship, influence, and participation, so, too, the traditional advice was giving way to the new. The ideal woman—feeling, pious, and nurturing—was as recognizable to proponents of evangelical womanhood as to readers of secular novels. Therefore, the shift to novels for advice by the early nineteenth century does not necessarily indicate a decline of interest in religion, but rather a renewed interest in a subject that had acquired new—and much more engaging—packaging. However complicit they were in the construction of southern white womanhood, women learned from novels how to appropriate a religious and moral authority that did not leave them powerless. This was particularly significant in a society in which individuals, both men and women, were thought "to represent the collective order itself . . . the most personal concerns . . . were swollen with general significance."[140] Both novels and religion contained elements communitarian and individualistic; both taught women ways in which to live a virtuous life that would benefit the common good (their slave society) and at the same time produce individual happiness.[141]

It was precisely in this conjunction of virtue, the republic, and women's place within it that women found the authority to create their own codes of respectable feminine conduct. Cultivating this aspect of her nature, a well-read woman acquired an education and developed her character. Evangelicals even began to condone reading novels, embracing the character lessons they taught, if not their form.[142] An education founded on the study of virtue combined with woman's innate emotion and piety never made her superior to men, but it licensed her—to a degree unknown before—to construct her own codes of conduct and even to judge which men were worthy of her deference and obedience, all without straying outside the boundaries of respectable behavior.

Nonetheless, the sentimental model of femininity that united religious with secular was not without its costs, for while it embraced the new style (novels), it retained the old content. That is to say, while women from Frances Baylor Hill to Jean Skipwith found sermons less compelling than the more entertaining format of the novel, the content of the sentimental model reinforced a definition of femininity in which feeling prevailed over reason. This definition suited southern cultural purposes better anyway, since it allowed women to participate in the polity in a way that challenged neither white men nor the slave system on which planters and their families depended.[143]

Yet like female readers everywhere in the Anglo-American world, southern women were heartened by their recognition of their reflected selves in the books they read. Though women were absent from history, philosophy, science, and religion books, they did find the concerns of their lives mirrored in novels, where they found connections with other women. So even in the solitary act of reading, within the physical isolation of plantation life and the emotional isolation of a patriarchal hierarchy, women drew on the shared experiences of other writing and reading women.[144] Knitting together a female community was particularly important in the plantation South, where women were dispersed over the century into increasingly defined, privatized spaces, both geographic and ideological. Both republican ideology and evangelical Christianity shaped a culture of domesticity that infused women's roles as mothers with greater significance even as it excluded them from participation in the polity and isolated them from one another in households scattered across the agricultural landscape.[145] But it is clear that, despite their geographic distances from each other, southern women sought out female connections in any number of ways. Eliza Lucas used the return of a book as an occasion to critique Samuel Richardson; women as different as Hannah Lee Corbin and Lady Jean Skipwith collected the novels of women authors; teenagers Mildred Smith and Betsey Ambler did not let the Revolution's arrival or Ambler's hasty flight from their neighborhood deter their correspondence; Elizabeth Foote Washington wrote for her unborn child, while Eliza Carrington and Caroline Burgwin Clitherall wrote for the succeeding generations they knew. Of course, the novels were as varied as their readers: the court of Turin was not eighteenth-century Virginia, and Lucas, who ran her father's plantations and would later develop indigo as a viable export crop in South Carolina, was no servant girl. Nonetheless, in their shared reading southern women found a commonality of experience that held all the more significance for them precisely because of their isolation.

Ultimately, then, while southern women participated in a public world of letters recognizable to elites on both sides of the Atlantic, they certainly read and understood it in very different ways. On one level, reading was necessary to divert southern eyes and minds from the very system they had created: a slave society. As Theodorick Bland wrote to his sister Sophy, "When I look around me too and see even in Free America that thousands of my fellow creatures . . . are born to no inheritance but Slavery . . . the greatest source of delight . . . is my Books. . . . Nothing in my opinion so effectually dissipates sorrow."[146] "Reading is the best relief from the toils, & cares of life," Alice Izard of South Carolina advised her son Henry in 1807. "When you have attended for some hours to Rice thumping &c &c you will be delighted to dwell on more pleasing themes & be charmed to see, of what the human mind is capable."[147] Surrounded by slaves, white southern readers read in the midst of an isolation about which they complained mightily. Their minds functioned within a sea of humanity whom they tried to keep mindless. On a deeper level, the lives of southern women living in an agricultural slave society were vastly more circumscribed than that of urban British women.[148] Even their entertainments, held in plantation homes under the watchful eye of the patriarch, were not so much "sociable" as "hospitable."[149] The salons of London and even Philadelphia that facilitated the civilizing influence of conversant men and women found no counterpart in the plantation South; there gender conventions only calcified. In such a society, novels could pose a significant threat to the gender order, particularly the fictions of British writers such as Aphra Behn and Eliza Haywood, whose works circulating early in the eighteenth century allowed their heroines to enjoy sexual freedoms without suffering ruinous consequences.[150] By the latter part of the century, however, the novels read by southern women conformed more to patriarchal ideology. Carroll Smith-Rosenberg believes that the principal occupation for early-nineteenth-century American novelists was trying to discover how "independence and individual happiness [might] be made compatible with social order."[151] Reading their novels as secular catechisms, southern women resolved that dilemma by forsaking the notion of independence and finding happiness in guiding future generations.

FIVE

Reading, Race, and Writing

Even as southern women enjoyed increased reading and writing literacy, as well as access to the genteel print culture of the Anglo-Atlantic world, their understanding of what they read nonetheless differed from other women's. We have seen several circumstances peculiar to the southern experience that help explain why: the ways that climate and terrain influenced the colonists' choices of tobacco and rice economies, and the social orders that resulted; the struggles to define and assert authority; and the isolation of living on an agricultural landscape. They differed as well in their writing, which never matched other women's in quantity (either private letters or print publication) and contrasted greatly in content. Even though developments in religion and print culture had given women new ways of thinking about their authority, as we saw in chapters 3 and 4, the distinctiveness of the southern experience shaped their written expression of these ideas in significant ways.

Indeed, questions of authority were central concerns in an age of Revolution. With Thomas Paine's *Common Sense*, the Revolutionaries had rejected the old organic model of a social order dictated by birth rank. At the helm of government after the overthrow of the king, however, southern slaveholders became more comfortable with idea of organic order, even as Revolutionary rhetoric and postwar emancipation legislation in the North began to reject that view.[1] In the early nineteenth century, then, we witness the irony of emerging regional identities even as Americans of the early republic were shaping a national one. Women were crucial in the development of the Southern ethos, for in upholding a racialized vision of the social order, they helped create the southern regional identity that was so evident in the letters of Ellen Randolph Coolidge. By the 1820s, women had realized, racial superiority could be mustered to offset gender inferiority.

But it was a costly strategy, particularly in the circumscription of their intellectual autonomy. The comparison with northern women writers such as Hannah Griffitts of Philadelphia or Judith Sargent Murray of Massachusetts is one way to illustrate this point. But a more effective way to demonstrate the consequences of southern women's acquiescence to the colonizer is to seek out a comparison with a place that has elements of both regions, such as early national Baltimore. Unlike northern states, Maryland never enacted general emancipation laws, and thus slavery remained legal there until the Civil War (indeed, its legislature rejected Abraham Lincoln's offer for compensation as late as 1862).[2] Unlike the plantation society of the South, however, Baltimore never knew the cultural hegemony of an entrenched slaveholding gentry. The letters and commonplace books of two young sisters, Anna Maria and Mary Abigail Willing Coale, thus show how it was possible to question ancient paradigms of gender in a city in which blackness was not so rigidly affixed to enslavement. The contrast they present with most of the women who have populated this book thus far makes clear the impact of slave society culture on women's thinking and self-expression in their writing. This chapter will look first at the ways in which southern women negotiated the parameters of authority erected in their society and then more particularly at the limits of their intellectual autonomy in the contrast presented by the Coale sisters of Baltimore. Ultimately, white southern women identified with the colonizer, hoping to secure the privilege of their race while blunting the sharp edge of their gender inferiority. But it was a process that took time: eighteenth-century women did not call themselves "southerners," but by 1824, Ellen Randolph Coolidge was clear that was exactly what she was.

SLAVERY AND REGIONAL DISTINCTIVENESS

Regional distinctions did not seem to have been identified as readily by colonial Americans as by Americans today. Indeed, James Madison seemed to have been taken aback during the Revolutionary period as those distinctions emerged. When Madison recorded the debates of the Constitutional Convention, he noted to his surprise that the delegates did not see their interests served in alliances of large versus small states but instead split along regional lines.[3] The southern commitment to slavery appears to be the obvious difference between the two regions, yet it is well to remember that on the eve of the Revolution, slavery existed in all thirteen colonies. Even as late as 1790, for example, 20 percent of white households in New York City held slaves.[4] Indeed, in his most recent study of slavery in the United States, historian Ira Berlin wondered when, prior to the Emancipation Proclamation in January 1863, the "North became a free society."[5] With the exception of Vermont and Massachusetts, northern states emancipated their slaves only gradually: the laws did not free anyone in bondage but rather freed children born after the acts' passage, and even then, only when they became adults.[6] So although all northern states had enacted some form of emancipation statute by 1804, slavery was not eradicated completely for decades: in New York and Pennsylvania, for example, it continued into the 1840s.[7]

What is significant, however, is that the Revolutionary era made slavery a regional, rather than national, institution, as the number of free blacks in the United States increased dramatically after the war. The moves toward emancipation in the North and rising manumissions in the Upper South dealt heavy blows to the idea that slavery was a feature of a natural and divinely ordered hierarchy in which skin color dictated rank. In Virginia, for example, a contemporary estimated that perhaps two thousand blacks (1 percent) in the state were free in 1782; by 1800, however, that number reached twenty thousand.[8] Slave manumissions were probably most dramatic in Delaware (which remained a Union slave state throughout the Civil War), where the free black population stood at 75 percent by 1800, and in Maryland, where it was 16 percent.[9] In the North, the free black population, negligible before the war, reached almost fifty thousand by 1810.[10] Certainly life for newly freed blacks was difficult as they began to learn the difference between freedom and equality in a society convinced that blacks could not be a viable part of a republic.[11] Still these emancipations raised an important question: if, in the fluidity of hierarchy in the early republic, the meanings of race and racial boundaries could be negotiated and redefined, what implications might that have for definitions of gender?

The potential in the South to rework the racial norms of the colonial period was curtailed almost as soon as it appeared, however. Several circumstances converged to ensure the perpetuation of slavery there. The states of the Lower South reentered the transatlantic slave trade with gusto to replenish slaves lost during the war; the invention of the cotton gin in 1793 renewed the demand for slave labor that the languishing tobacco market had depressed; and the expansion of the franchise to white males ensured increasing hostility to freed blacks, whose successful integration into the republic most whites doubted. Yet while the North was no model for the South in terms of race relations, by the early nineteenth century a clear divergence between the two regions had emerged: the former was a society with slaves (although committed to eventual emancipation), while the latter was a slave society.[12] The distinction was crucial in many ways, particularly regarding the allocation of power and authority, that would have significant repercussions for women's voice as well.

Both regimes utilized force but in different ways, as Ira Berlin explained:

> Violence was an inherent part of slave society, playing a role quite different from the one it had played in a society with slaves. To be sure, the use of force and even gratuitous brutality was endemic in societies with slaves. . . . But violence was not only common in slave societies, it was also systematic and relentless; the planters' hegemony required that slaves stand in awe of their owners. Although they preferred obedience to be given rather than taken, planters understood that without a monopoly of firepower and a willingness to employ terror, plantation slavery would not long survive. The lash gained a place in slave societies that was not evident in societies with slaves.[13]

Unlike the economy of the North, which did not rely on slave labor, the southern agricultural economy had slavery as its foundation and predicated its legal, political, and social systems on it. Early in the colonial period, southern colonies developed comprehensive slave codes, patterned after those in English colonies in the West Indies, where the enslaved population far outnumbered the white.[14] These codes restrained the movements of slaves, prescribed punishments, forbade interracial sexual relations and marriage, and enacted broad parameters for white disciplinary measures and authority.[15] Such a system required force to survive, and initially colonial governments relied on private, rather than provincial, enforcement, instituting laws that allowed any whites (whether owners or not) to capture and discipline runaways.[16] Legal sanction thus fell on all white males, regardless of rank, to enforce the racial hierarchy, linking the interests even of nonslaveholding men with those of the gentry. In such a system, the discretion afforded whites was vast, and any gesture of defiance by a slave was untenable and subject to swift punishment. Indeed, eighteenth-century Americans used the term "impudence" to describe a slave's behavior that straddled the line between obstreperousness and punishable defiance, and whites could decide with impunity when that line had been crossed.[17]

The power and authority thus vested in all white men to maintain order was endowed with the legitimacy of governmental fiat, and, since eighteenth-century society's ideas about gender hierarchy preceded those of race, that authority could easily be applied to keeping order in the household as well.[18] Indeed, as southerners found themselves on the defensive about slavery, they often employed the subordination of wife to husband as a model in nature for the subjection of blacks to whites.[19] So, while in a society with slaves, as Berlin noted, "no one presumed the master-slave relationship to be exemplar," in a slave society, obedience to authority was paramount in all relationships.[20] It was no coincidence that the epithet "impudent" was frequently applied to women as well as to recalcitrant slaves. As white women throughout the Anglo-Atlantic world began to understand that their intellects were not inferior to men's, they threatened to break down barriers of gender that had seemed so embedded in nature. But in the South, those barriers were petrified by the absolute necessity to preserve the racial hierarchy. Southern men could not disprove the naturalness of these constructs because they would lose everything on which their political, economic, and social hegemony rested.

Of course, this system and its theoretical foundations were riddled with contradictions. For example, as intent on the preservation of racial separation and white hegemony as they were, many planters nonetheless engaged in interracial sex. Yet rather than being seen as a dilution of whiteness, interracial sex only reinforced planters' superiority over everyone else: enslaved women who could not refuse advances without risk, black men who could not assert a right to protect their wives, and white women, who risked the shame of exposure if they openly challenged their husbands. A further contradiction was the dilemma raised about how to explain two simultaneous "truths": white women's racial superiority and their gender inferiority.[21] A third contradiction was the development of an increasingly articulated theory of difference between whites and blacks that justified the exploitation of slaves, even as more and more southerners flocked to evangelical Christianity. In the post-Revolutionary period, planters retreated from their previous skepticism about converting slaves and embraced an image of themselves as parents to slaves they viewed as perpetual children. With royal authority toppled and theirs installed in its place, southern planters could more easily acknowledge the merits of an organic social structure, the reciprocal obligations of which demanded humanitarian treatment of their inferiors. In this way, planters could assent to evangelical views of the humanity of slaves without undermining the legitimacy of their claims to own them.[22] (In return, evangelical churches, uninterested in being the religion solely for poor whites, women, and slaves, responded to the wishes of their wealthier male members and by the beginning of the nineteenth century retreated from egalitarian teachings and practices.)[23] Thus although many women found in religion a source of authority for themselves, men also appropriated it, transforming the harsher patriarchal face of pre-Revolutionary slavery to the softer one of paternalism after the war, yet never relinquishing their right of control—over their slaves or over their female family members.

Gender, Race, and the Social Order

Thus the dynamic of rule that white men established to perpetuate slavery and white hegemony infused and perpetuated their hegemony over women as well and explains the limits of southern women's thought and writing. Loath to be identified with the passions southerners associated with the unrestrained bestiality of black women, white women also feared the derisive label "masculine" applied to females who flaunted the breadth of their reading and the height of their mental acuity. Mary Ambler's notation of Fordyce's admonition that she never be found guilty "of contradicting bluntly, of asserting positively, of debating obstinately, of affecting a superiority to any present" precisely addressed that fear.[24] A forward woman challenged the fundamental premise of southern societal organization: white male authority. Affecting to assume that mantle herself, she forfeited the protections her sex could claim. Citing one of the foremost authorities on female behavior, Ambler thus urged her daughter to imitate her subscription to gender-safe reading practices. Careful, then, to eschew neither their race nor their sex by their speech, demeanor, or behavior, southern women walked a tightrope of female respectability that is reflected in their attitudes toward courtship and marriage, education, and their role in society. They may have protested, squirmed, and struggled; nonetheless they acknowledged, however grudgingly, the hierarchy of authority on which they depended for security against the workforce the South enslaved.

One of the chief ways in which white southern women sought to preserve the privileges of race was in their exercise of reason over passion, especially during courtship. Decades before Thomas Jefferson wrote his famous poem to Maria Cosway about the battle between his heart and his head, Elizabeth Cocke Pratt documented hers in both poetry and prose to her suitor, Thomas Jones.[25] In a stunningly frank presentation of herself, Pratt admitted both her passionate attraction to him and her deep anxiety about surrendering to what she called a "poison'd Cup." A beautiful young widow with two children in the small town of Williamsburg in the 1720s, Pratt had apparently been at the center of female gossip when an older suitor, whom she had rejected, subsequently married her mother. Begging reason to "calm those wild disorders of my breast," Pratt knew the surest way to protect her reputation was to follow the path directed by "Heavenly thought" and "Wisdom." A life of decorous widowhood, marked by virtue and propriety, would be both "peacefull" and slander-free, but her "Captive will" rejected the counsel of "reason[,] faithful guide [, who] forever warns / my drowsy Soul to shun impending danger." Nonetheless, her outward indifference to Jones's courtship bespoke the tight rein she was able to impose on her conduct, even as her feelings churned behind the facade. To yield to her passions subjected her to the recriminations of both class and race: the backlash of "slanderous toungs" of white women "some whom I thought my friends," and the blurring of the distinction between the sexual restraint of elite white women and the sensuality of enslaved ones, so crucial to the construction of racial difference in the eighteenth century. While it is true that Pratt experienced the rule of patriarchy through the censure of gossiping women,[26] what is striking is the power of patriarchy to impose a definition of femininity that Pratt herself felt compelled to uphold, even to the point of denying herself. Female passion in white women was disdained; indeed, Pratt saw it as an evil, something she had suffered as a "sorrow Guilt or disappointment." She did not deny her feelings, but neither did she believe she could honor them, if she was to measure up to the standard of female virtue and respectability.

Passion and reason rival one another as well in Maria Carter's commonplace book, which offers a rare connection between the English belles lettres literary canon and the mind and heart of a young girl in Virginia in 1763. She copied a fragment of Alexander Pope's "Heloisa to Abelard," in which Heloisa extols heaven for first teaching letters as a gift for "some banish'd Lover, or some captive Maid." On the simplest level, this is both thanks and plea for the gift of words and of the ability to read and write them. Living in an elite household, Carter was blessed with these gifts, but she must have realized her good fortune: these skills were denied to at least half of her sex in her own day. She copied further. Words "live, they speak, they breathe what Love inspires," and allow "the Virgin's wish without her fears impart, Excuse the blush, and pour out all the Heart [and] Speed the soft Intercourse from Soul to Soul."[27] It was a dream of a loving, communicative partner, and perhaps Carter felt that "letters" (whether defined as missives or the alphabet) implied a distance between lovers that protected a woman's virtue. As Pratt had used poetry to reveal herself to her suitor, even as she fought mightily to protect her reputation, Carter may have believed that in a letter, a woman could forge the closest of connections, between one soul and another, without risking a surrender to physical passion that would be her undoing. Satisfying the cravings of the soul while maintaining a safe distance may well have been Maria Carter's eighteenth-century adaptation of the medieval ideal of courtly love. Balancing reason and passion, her formulation was both respectable and safe, the appeal of which the example of Abelard and Heloise would certainly have confirmed.[28] It was surely no coincidence that only two pages later she copied the warning implicit in so many novels: "[D]o bad men caress you? Beware for your lap dog is shewing his Love for you [and] may foul you with his paws."[29]

PATRIARCHY AND MARRIAGE

In spite of the dangers of courtship, it was a delightful fiction, to which men and women in early America assented, that a suitor's happiness—indeed, his very life—lay in the power of the lady he courted. But it was a hard reality that women of all regions of early America knew only the negative power of refusal—that is, they could reject the proffered hand but never initiate a romance. This was especially true in the South, where ingenues and older widows alike made the most of this illusion of power, weighing prospective suits, keeping men waiting, and putting off the moment when at last they must surrender their liberty. Anne Miller was sixteen in 1759 when she caught Robert Bolling's attention. Taking advantage of the "many Freedoms" that were possible "between Relations in this Colony" (they were both great-grandchildren of Colonel Robert Bolling, 1646–1709), Bolling's courtship style alternated among poses of indifference, designs calculated to inspire jealousy, and "raptures" and "transports" of passion (in which at least one fan and a necklace were casualties). Miller returned his affections, yet she was caught between a father determined to return to his native Scotland and a suitor equally determined to keep her in Virginia. In tears she explained her hapless position to the friend who served as Bolling's go-between that "tho her Father shou'd object to her return to Virginia, she was determined to tell him, as soon as he should be once settled [in Scotland], that Mr. Bolling was the only Man in the World, that shou'd be her Partner for Life." She declined a request to put her assurance in writing, as "Virgin Modesty made a Struggle on the Point of her writing," but promised that as long as her Father objected she "was determined to wait, til *she* only had a Negative, and then she wou'd bestow her Hand where her Heart had taken it's Abode."[30] There may have been a reason she refused to commit to Bolling in writing; barely three weeks later, she received him with a "constrained Kind of Civility," and he could not help but note that "the little Cupids no more sparked in her eye" when she saw him. When the *Peggy* set sail in October 1760, Anne Miller was on it, leaving her dejected lover behind. Whether she was bound by her father's will or her own, the contours of gender conventions are clear in Bolling's recounting of their courtship: her feelings of helplessness in the tug-of-war between two men and his emotions, first of prideful entitlement and then anger when his will was thwarted.[31]

Older women may have had more leverage when suitors came to call, as St. George Tucker discovered when he applied for the hand of Frances Randolph. Initially, Tucker's suit did not go well, for while she accepted his proposal, at the same time she withheld her affections. "The same Instant that made me the happiest, rendered me the most miserable Being in the universe," he recalled, "And whilst I lash'd you to my Breast with an exstatic Tenderness, which Love, Joy and Exultation had inspired, my Bliss was destroyed by finding that you would not partake with me in the Raptures I enjoyed." Her hand was his but not her heart. "The remembrance of the violent Agitation of your Mind" the evening he proposed thus compelled him "to absolve you from the secured Engagement you have made," despite "every fond wish, every pleasing hope, every joyful Expectation [that] was excited by the Thoughts of calling you mine."[32] What Frances Randolph's doubts were we cannot know for sure (the surviving courtship correspondence is almost completely one-sided), but her response to Tucker's ardor bears a striking resemblance to Elizabeth Pratt's struggles. A wealthy widow who lived on Matoax plantation in Chesterfield County, Virginia, with her three children, Randolph had no pressing reason to remarry. Indeed, her hesitation is easier to understand than her consent: financially comfortable, she was managing Matoax competently enough without a husband's guiding direction. She *had* said yes, but "in the same Instant" that she gave herself into his power, she removed herself by withholding what he wanted most: dominion over her heart. Like Pratt, she would not surrender to "raptures" and risk her reputation; instead she maintained such an indifferent exterior that Tucker began to wonder if he should withdraw his offer.

There were few moments of power in most eighteenth-century

women's lives. As a wealthy widow, however, Frances Randolph had more than most, for she was bound neither by economic dependence nor vows of obedience. The inducement to relinquish such freedoms would have to be great indeed, and that she consented to Tucker's proposal suggests that she loved him but was unwilling to lose what leverage she may have had by her admission. So the path of love did not run smoothly for him, as she began a period of testing, exercising the powers that the rituals of courtship granted, however temporarily, to women. First, she made sure that she knew that he had a rival for her affections and then made him even more miserable by banishing him from her. "In obedience to your Desire I am now preparing to leave you," he wrote dejectedly, "I leave you with the full Conviction that I have a rival whom I can not but esteem—I am apprised of his Merit and his imense attachment to you." His only chance, as he saw it, was to be able to convince her that she had nothing to dread by uniting their futures. But she would not permit him any opportunity to speak to her.[33]

In many ways, the Randolph-Tucker courtship followed traditional patterns: the lovesick suitor begging for relief; the doubtful lady, unwilling to submit immediately and impeccably discrete when at last she did; the last flexing of muscle before vowing forever to be obedient. But Frances Randolph was not a naïve young girl, pressured by parents, friends, or even financial straits to accept Tucker's suit. Hers was not the tremulous hesitation of fictional heroines. Read in the context of her situation, Tucker's letters reveal a woman determined to make no mistake; she would test this gentleman's intentions and his motives. After all, he was not even from Virginia. Bermuda-born, he had been sent to the College of William and Mary for his education, so he had no ready references to reassure her.[34] A widow with three children dependent on her, she was responsible for decisions she made for them as well as herself. At a time when the ideal of companionate marriage was more commonplace than its practice, Randolph had to be as cautious as Pratt had been fifty-five years earlier.

Charles Carter ran into the same resistance when he wooed a Virginia widow after the death of his wife. Telling his brother Landon of his determination "to know my fate," he also had to admit he was being kept waiting. Although the lady was "quite easy and unafectedly Sincere," she also told him that she "has not the least inclination to change her Condition." He hoped to counter her hesitation by "raising a flame in her breast."[35] Like Tucker's, Carter's campaign for his lady's hand depended on a surrender of reason to emotion; once her heart was engaged, her fortune would be also, and his conquest would be complete. The refusal of Carter's widow was less tart, however, than that of Ann Butler Spotswood, who, annoyed by the persistence of a suitor, told him, "Its Certain two years is a sufficient space of time for any Person [to know] there own mind. I have often told you mine, tho to little purpose."[36]

Understanding that this space of time in which they ruled was brief, while the time under the yoke of marriage was long, both northern and southern women viewed marriage warily. As Marylander Peggy Caldwell explained to her suitor, James McHenry, "Sir in the contriving of a connection on which so much will depend—you will excuse me for acting cautiously and deliberately—& for taking time to consult my own breast— before I form a decisive conclusion."[37] Virginian John Blair borrowed a ubiquitous phrase when he referred in 1780 to his niece's wedding as "the last Act of Betsey's Liberty."[38] The *Virginia Gazette* urged fathers to allow their daughters latitude of choice to be the "sole disposer of their own liberty."[39] Suffering from prewedding jitters, a friend spilled out her relief to Catherine Dulany Belt that her feelings were not unique, "the apprehension that my feelings were peculiar to myself, that no one ever knew such fear & dread as at times distressed me, was very painful, I even thought myself unfortunate & unjust in having made an engagement for life that seemed to wear so unfavorable an aspect. But the assurance that you, who are not yet quite so far gone in the scrape [almost married], experience the same sensations, has revived all my most sanguine hopes."[40] Indeed, there are indications that Belt had also feared wedded life. While she awaited the arrival of a doctor to pull an abscessed tooth, Peggy Murdock wrote to Belt of her fear of the operation: "I don't believe, you dreaded your wedding day, more than I do tomorrow, nor was more frightened, the 24th of July, than I shall be, the 8th of December."[41] New Englander Elizabeth Smith Shaw referred to the decision to accept a proposal of marriage as "*the* Crisis upon which our Fate depends," while in Maryland Elizabeth Maynadier admitted that she was trying to avoid "too much retrospect of the past or anticipation of the future," as she tried to cope with the pain of failed pregnancies and the loneliness of plantation life.[42] But when Virginian Anne Stuart dismissed the rumors that she had "determined to take W J for my Lord and Master," she used a phrase that resonated much more deeply in the slave South, where both a white wife and enslaved black women were subject to a common master, than it would have in Massachusetts.[43] White fathers, husbands, brothers, and sons all enjoyed unlimited sexual access to enslaved women's bodies, a feature of a slave society about which some white women agonized privately in their journals but were otherwise constrained to remain silent.[44]

This is not to say that companionate marriage was unknown in the South; indeed, letters reveal plenty of instances of affectionate relationships. But the ideal of companionate marriage, however attractive, rarely implied an equal partnership. It was clear that men expected to take the initiative and women to follow. Frances Randolph acknowledged that she ignored prevailing convention when she admitted to St. George Tucker during their courtship that "I have not stood on the Punctilio of your writing first." But, she excused herself, nothing could "prevent my giving you the satisfaction of knowing I am well & that I think of you with the tenderest affection."[45] Margaret Parker of Norfolk wrote plainly of her longing and affection for her husband in 1760. "I can tell you with a great deal of truth that the moon has never made her appearance Since you left me," she mused, "but what I have looked at her & thought of you, & often wished to know whether or not when you was going to bed it would not have been rather more agreeable to have had me with you." Yet even within this loving marriage, she apologized for her lengthy letters, depending "on your sense to make allowances for the imperfections of a poor foolish Girl, whose Study & greatest pleasure always has & shall be to please you."[46]

Frances and John Baylor enjoyed a loving relationship, but she, too, prefaced a letter by asking her husband to "excuse the liberty of addressing you as I have done," before continuing with great exasperation, "you appear to be so totally ignorant of my intention. . . . I must now tell you that myself and children are in the primitive state of Christians . . . we are very sensible of pressing wants—which you however appear to be insensible to—so wholly engross'd are your tho'ts on adding to your territory."[47] Similarly, in the early national period, Elizabeth and William Wirt spent their lives trying to craft a companionate marriage. Yet Elizabeth's wishes were frustrated repeatedly, as her officeholding husband sympathetically acknowledged her complaints about his absences from home yet continued to pursue his political career.[48] Affection may have enabled more frank expression of feeling, whether of love or frustration, but it did not alter the essential power structure of eighteenth-century marriages, especially in the South. Frances Baylor and Elizabeth Wirt spoke their minds but nonetheless remained completely dependent on their husbands.

It is significant that the Revolution did so little to change the politics of patriarchy in southern households, even as Elizabeth Wirt alerts us to the changing hopes and expectations southern women may have had for their marriages. In many ways, they experienced the same perils of courtship and marriage that northern women did. Still, there was an additional overlay of authority over them, as southern planters aligned their defense of slavery with the ideological changes of the post-Revolutionary world and elaborated a theory of gender suitable for southern women in the new republic. This was clear even in public expressions of patriotism: genteel balls, in which individual women could exert their influence, were replaced by militia musters and parades, masculine rituals of military prowess. Elite women and their children waved from stands; literally side-lined, they were visible symbols of those who required the protections on display in the parades.[49] Republican motherhood thus offered women roles in the republic that differed from those of men; women could par-ticipate in the polity in this way without ever claiming the rights of men.[50] Indeed, their presence in patriotic observances of Independence Day ac-tually reinforced the trope of their dependence, a posture women as-sumed even when they were politically conscious enough to approach state legislatures with formal petitions.[51] Thus while northern women would begin, albeit with ambivalence, explorations of the mind that would eventually lead to the affirmation of individual identity, the experi-ence of Republican motherhood in the South would confirm women's identity as a subordinate member of a patriarchal system.

This development is all the more ironic because it occurred *after* the Revolution. Southern women had not always retreated into the shadows of domesticity, consistently obedient to the dictates of men; truculent fe-male voices in court records throughout the century show that they did not. In 1722 Easter Chinn, the wife of prominent Raleigh Chinn, "being by the Sd Rawleigh's Unsufforable Cruelty and Severity towards her forced to leave him," approached the chancery court in Lancaster County, Virginia, to intervene against her husband's intention to "convey away his Estate with Design to Defraud her of her Sd Alimony."[52] She would have disagreed with North Carolina judge Jon Jacocks, who in 1801 placed "the great quantity of petitions for divorce" in the same category as "other triffles" and "nothing of moment."[53] Mary Horton sued James Pinkard in 1751 for failing to honor his agreement to teach her daughter, indentured to his service, "Reeding or soen [sewing] or [how to] knit as a woman ought to do."[54] In 1762 Elizabeth Gilbert, threatened with a law-suit by Rawleigh Shearman for title to one-third of her land, spiritedly re-torted, "so he might, for that she hoped there was Law for her as well as him."[55] In the late 1780s, Benjamin Powell was forced to sue his intransi-gent daughter, Ann Burwell, when she refused to vacate the property he wanted to sell as executor of her husband's will. Her answer to her fa-ther's complaint was unadorned and uncompromising: she "admits . . . that the complainant hath applied to this defendant for the sale . . . [and] that she hath refused and still doth refuse her consent to such sale."[56] While Chinn and Horton looked upon the law as a father, relying on its protective arm, Gilbert and Burwell claimed the law as their own instrument, stridently refusing to be cowed by men who would use its weight against them.

Nonetheless, a form of patriarchy peculiar to the slave society of the South developed throughout the century, shaping the contours of women's authority and resisting derailment, even by Revolution. As in the North, it was not unheard of for women in the colonial South to run businesses; widows often did. But unlike male masters, who exerted over their slaves their own personal authority and administration of punishments, women relied on the strong arm of the court to discipline their recalcitrant slaves (who unerringly had targeted the weak link in Virginia's racial hierarchy). When two women, each abandoned by her husband and living in a legal limbo, applied to the Virginia House of Burgesses for feme sole status, the legislature agreed to press their cases forward to the king's Privy Council. It is doubtful that the burgesses meant to support female autonomy. Rather, it is more likely that they desired to assert provincial autonomy over local concerns: the post-Revolutionary legislature passed laws enabling men to sell both land and slaves more easily, circumscribing further women's efforts to retain their control over their property.[57]

Reviewing the extant legal history of the colonial South, historian Terri L. Snyder observed that during the first half of the eighteenth century "there occurred a restructuring of patriarchal authority from an earlier authoritarian model . . . to a somewhat more paternalistic model." But a critical change in the property law in 1705 suggests a shift in degree, rather than in kind, at least for women. The change in the status of slaves from personal property (which could be bequeathed for women's ownership) to real (which a woman could only hold for her use) kept valuable property in men's hands. "Placing property interests of widows squarely in the service of the family," Snyder pointed out, was an important way to "perpetuate planter hegemony."[58] The point was not lost on St. George Tucker, a lawyer and judge, who, in a tug-of-war exchange of letters with his future son-in-law, had insisted on a marriage settlement to protect his daughter before he would allow the wedding to take place.[59]

This context may well explain the hostilities that broke out in 1806 between Susanna Wilcox and her son-in-law, whom she infuriated with her tight rein over her daughter Susan's money, money he clearly intended to control himself upon his marriage. In a tight-lipped exchange with Wilcox, James Hubard began, "I little suspected at the time that I married into your family that in consequence of the marriage contract or settlement between my Wife & myself that any right was vested in you of controuling the use of the funds or money belonging to my dear Wife." Gradually it dawned on Hubard that, indeed, that was precisely Wilcox's intention. "At the time that I married, I certainly had a right to expect pecuniary or money assistance, Susan was wealthy and her funds quite sufficient; But what assistance have they afforded me?" he fumed, "—None." He complained that he had seen little more than one hundred dollars from Susan's estate but that Wilcox had received considerably more. "Does her estate belong to you? or who does it belong to?" he asked her furiously. The inversion of conventional gendered allocations of power was more than he could stand: "Can you suppose for one moment that I would submit to your control or directions?"[60]

Hubard's fury at being financially stymied by his mother-in-law makes an important point about the expectations of men and women about marriage after a century of change. While courtship in the eighteenth century became freer on both sides of the Atlantic and the ideal of companionate marriage acquired greater currency as well, neither development signaled any fundamental change in the balance of power within marriage.[61] Hubard's rage at being "misled" speaks eloquently to the social and legal norms that remained in place in the South at the turn of the nineteenth century. As he put it bluntly, he had a *right* to financial assistance from his family. Wilcox's iron determination, on the other hand, bespeaks women's willingness to make the most of Virginia law to protect themselves against grasping husbands (and sons-in-law).

Limits of Female Intellectual Autonomy

These examples denote neither latent feminism nor resistance to the racial and gender hierarchy. Though they were significant struggles for the women involved, they never embraced goals beyond that of the immediate situation and participants. That is to say, they were not protests against the system on behalf of women at large but concerted efforts on their particular behalf to wrest from the law what little protection it might afford. Like South Carolina's Alice Izard, southern women would have rejected the ideas of Mary Wollstonecraft, who criticized the "false system of education . . . by men who consider[ed] females rather as women than human creatures."[62] Izard, who agreed with her husband's assessment of Wollstonecraft as a "vulgar, impudent Hussy," had little patience with *Vindication of the Rights of Woman*, having "just finished reading the rights of Women . . . as much of it as I could read, for I was often obliged to stop, & pass over, & frequently to cough & stammer &c." Izard emphatically asserted the innate differences between the sexes, explaining to her daughter that the "great author Nature has stamped a different character on each sex, . . . [so that a woman] frequently guides, where she does not govern."[63] One doubts whether Sophy Bland, who "was not at all pleased" with *Vindication*, was persuaded by her brother's argument that there was much in it that "ought to be followed—as for example cleanliness—Sincerity—and the necessity to acquire knowledge in order that we may form a correct judgment of things—These I am sure are articles in which Mrs. Woolstoncroft might easily be followed by every woman without endangering her effeminancy or delicacy in the least."[64] Margaret Caldwell also refused to step beyond that which was suitable for women's consumption. As she explained to her suitor, James McHenry of Maryland, "Content with little, I am not anxious to go abroad in quest for more. By tasting of the tree of good and evil, our first mother lost her peace, by abstaining from it I may preserve mine.—I do not find that conquerers have increased their happiness, by extending their conquests. . . . I tremble therefore at the thought of an experiment involving consequences equally doubtful [as the Fall]."[65] For southerners, a well-ordered society preserved distinctions of gender and race. To insist on a common humanity and an education that blurred those distinctions was not only ludicrous but could lead to results as disastrous as Eve's prideful sin.

That women should receive a different education than men was thus clear to southerners and explains the popularity throughout the eighteenth century of writers like Allestree, Halifax, and Fordyce, who in all ways understood and promoted female subordination in an organic society. This remained true even when opportunities for female education increased after the Revolution. By the antebellum period, as female curricula had broadened to include science, for example, an area usually reserved to men, only astronomy and botany were understood to be appropriate for young girls to study.[66] And even when women's reading preferences changed in favor of novels, they read those that portrayed women as creatures of piety, sensibility, and virtue, that is, as women whose innately female attributes distinguished them from men. These works, combined with the imperatives of evangelical Christianity, educated women for their roles as southern republican mothers, responsible for their families, including their slaves. For example, since literacy was forbidden to slaves, evangelical white mistresses instructed them in Christian principles (primarily of obedience and submission). Of course, enforced slave illiteracy was a crucial tactic that shored up the racialized hierarchy separating white women from black and benefited white men most of all.

Slave labor allowed a degree of gentility that would have been impossible if white women had had to labor in the fields. When, during the antebellum period, writers would idealize southern women as having reached the pinnacle of civilization, it was clear that they referred to slaveholding women who devoted their time to Christian works of benevolence and duty to their families.[67] Slavery, then, underwrote a system not only of race, but of class. Slaveholding women were well aware of how their own fortunes were embedded in that system. It is striking that Alice Izard should be such a determined supporter of an organic order, for, although she married an Izard from South Carolina, she herself was a New Yorker from the illustrious DeLancey family. Yet she was able to accommodate herself readily to slavery, even advising her son how to use his books to avoid its horrors.[68] Perhaps her ready acceptance was a function of her whiteness; a generation before her, British traveler Janet Schaw had been appalled at first but then came to accept punishments meted out to slaves, since their "Natures seem made to bear it."[69] Izard would not have been a stranger to slavery, at any rate; one-fifth of New York City's households held slaves in the 1780s. The likely explanation for her easy acceptance of slavery, however, must lie in her own elite roots and her belief in a hierarchical society in which "our well bred Gentleman must set the example, & so must our well educated Ladies. They are the reformers of the world. To them society has always been indebted for elegance, & refinement."[70]

"The reformers of the world" also had an obligation to their slaves. When traveling through North Carolina in 1794, Alice Izard had been dismayed at "the very disagreeable situation in which we find the Black People at most of the Houses we stop at."[71] Their own enlightened treatment of their slaves both differentiated them from less Christian slaveowners and justified their slaveholding in an age of increasing manumissions and abolition. The elite of the South, the Izards believed, knew well the difference between mastery and tyranny. Indeed, son Ralph wrote of his delight with "the character of Sir William Wallace. I am constantly wishing that Heaven made me such a man," referring to the hero of Jane Porter's *Scottish Chiefs*, who led Scotland's rebellion against English tyranny, rendering assistance to the weak, poor, and downtrodden along the way.[72] Of course, Eliza Foote Washington wrote of her sense of Christian responsibility to her slaves in the 1780s, decades before Ralph Izard wrote his observations to his mother in 1810. Well-educated southern women also crafted an idealized identity as owners of slaves, as did Washington and Alice Izard, but understood that they could be teachers of slaves and children without that mastery.[73]

Ultimately, then, southern women rarely asserted a woman's right to an education for the purpose of self-sufficiency, as did Massachusetts's Judith Sargent Murray;[74] economic independence was decidedly masculine, as was the citizenship that self-mastery conferred. They could assent to the value of educating the female intellect but only while maintaining the boundaries of separate spheres. In some ways, of course, many northern men and women agreed: republican motherhood effectively kept women out of the polity. Brief forays into politics, such as Philadelphia women marching in parades supporting the French Revolution or wearing the red, white, and blue stockades, were just that—brief.[75] Yet such active female patriotic displays did take place in the North, and it was the North that would produce women like Lucretia Mott and Elizabeth Cady Stanton; statements such as the "Declaration of Sentiments," written and proclaimed in 1848; and probably the most eloquent statement against coverture, Stanton's 1892 speech, "The Solitude of Self." In the North the Grimké sisters from South Carolina would find their abolitionist voices, within the walls of the Quaker Arch Street Meeting House in Philadelphia. Of course, these developments were years in the offing, but the point is that they were possible in the North. In a region devoted to the proposition that people exist in an organic order, however, there could be no elaboration of a theory of individual identity for women. As Eliza Mackay of Charleston was told in 1813, "you don't belong to yourself but to your family."[76] Peggy Caldwell's remark that "[w]e are not all destined for mothers" was a rare admission for a southern woman. And while she even saw that "[n]either can the best pilot [husband] ensure a safe passage or guard against the elements" (exactly the point Stanton made in her "Solitude of Self" speech), she nonetheless retreated to safer ground: "I am afraid to venture beyond the boundaries of my own knowledge."[77] Accepting the eighteenth-century redefinition of women as feeling, pious, and virtuous mothers, southern women retreated to the protection of men.[78]

THE COALE SISTERS: A BALTIMORE CASE STUDY

The Writings of the Coale Sisters

Perhaps a more useful comparison would be one fortuitously situated between the North and the South but representative of neither: early national Baltimore, a society with slaves, to be sure, but not a slave society. There, two young sisters, Anna Maria Coale and Mary Abigail Willing Coale, seemed less willing to accept gender hierarchies as formulated by a natural or divine plan (even as they acknowledged the inferiority of their sex's position in the world), and more willing to engage in discussions about "the Sex" and to celebrate female friendship and the single life—even in writing, even with men.[79] Indeed, there is even a tantalizing suggestion that, living with the complexity of the slave system in early national Baltimore, Anna Coale may have expanded her questions about natural hierarchies to slavery as well.

At age fourteen, Anna Coale kept a commonplace book in 1792; just over a decade later, her younger sister, Mary Coale, would enter into a correspondence with a male friend of their elder brother's and later keep a commonplace book of her own. Their books and letters make clear that they understood both the constructed character of gender and the double injury women suffered in following male prescriptions: the derogation of their intellects in their quest for beauty and the resulting male rebukes of female frivolity. While their writings preserve all the traditional forms of style, address, and etiquette, their content reveals ways in which the sisters diverged from the dominant prescriptions for the roles for which their female nature cast them. In the range of their subjects it is possible to detect a wider latitude of expression than usually obtained in women's writings in the plantation South. In urban Baltimore, the writings of the Coale sisters recognize what writers such as Judith Sargent Murray and Mary Wollstonecraft had also discovered: the inferiority of women was culturally created and perpetuated. Products of a unique society, neither plantation South nor urban North, the Coale sisters occupied an interstitial space both geographically and intellectually. This context was crucial to the development of their insights, as were their reading and writing. In the process of editing the words of others, they advanced their own thinking, and, as they wrote, they realized their own sense of themselves, cultivating autonomy of thought and expression about gender, female friendship, and even slavery.

Anna Coale's commonplace book, a thin volume bound in cardboard and dated May 1792, in which she recorded her treasury of literary keepsakes, is a mix of both the traditional view that female happiness is best to be found in marriage and the few encomiums in that literature to the respectability of the single life. For while she copied English bluestocking Hester Chapone's advice that "you have the fairest chance of attaining the best blessings this world can afford in a faithful and virtuous union with a worthy man—who may direct your steps in safety and honour through this life and partake with you the rewards of virtue in that which is to come," she also used her book to record those assurances she could find that the single woman was not to be despised but loved and even respected. "Do not be afraid of the single life," Chapone urged, "A worthy woman is never destitute of friends. . . . Nay she must be honoured by all

persons of sense and virtue for preferring the single state to union un-
worthy of her."[80] Coale's emphasis on the respectability of the single life
stands in marked contrast to the diatribe printed in a 1790 North Carolina newspaper that described spinsters as "ill-natured, maggoty, peevish,
conceited, disagreeable, hypocritical, fretful, noisy, jibing, canting, censo-
rious . . . good for nothing creatures."[81] Indeed, by her selective act of notation, Coale highlights the single life in a way that diverges even from
Chapone, who generally urged young women toward lives of pious compliance to God and husband.[82] The second of eight children, Anna Coale
watched as her mother's "delicate frame for breeding" was tested every
other year.[83] Perhaps she had already determined, at age fourteen, to
avoid such a fate. Or perhaps the fragility of her own health, on which
family letters comment after 1800, was already a feature of her life and
she foresaw, with a prescience beyond her years, that she would never
marry.

Anna Coale's sister, Mary, kept a letter book in addition to the precious
correspondence of friends and relatives over the years 1803–13. In it she
preserved a record of three letters she had written to her older brother's
Philadelphia friend, a Mr. Ewing, who had opened the correspondence
with her in the summer of 1803, when she was fourteen. Although initially shy about "writing to a Gentlemen," she gracefully expressed to her
friend, "the gratitude I feel for your attention in writing to a little girl
whose letters I fear will give you no other pleasure than that which you
may derive from the knowledge that you are of great improvement to
her. . . . I am much very much gratified to find that you think me worth
writing to."[84] Ewing thought her "apprehensions to be proper and pru-
dent." Young girls should acknowledge the wider and worldly experience
of older male correspondents. But further, he warned her, "whatever you
may find in Novels, or whatever may be whispered by the Gentleman, a
young Lady can not bestow too much deliberation" about where and to
whom to bestow her writings.[85] They both knew she must take care in
choosing her correspondents to avoid the betrayal of confidences, inscribed on paper and innocently entrusted to friends who later would
prove faithless.

A respectable literary connection thus established between them, however, Ewing lectured his young correspondent about the female character
and proper behavior. "It is necessary occasionally that you should be reminded that you *positively are not angels*—You should also be taught humility while you are single, that, when the holy gates of wedlock close upon
you and shut you out from all the gay amusements of younger years, you
may be able with greater felicity to practice it—For you know, *my sweet little*

idol, that you are all bound not only to *love* and to *honour,* but emphatically, to *obey* your *Lords*—that you are the *weaker vessels*—that, as Burns says, '*one of two must still obey.*' "[86]

Uncowed by the authority vested in him by virtue of his age and sex, Mary Coale replied smartly, "I supose tho' you had so much to say against our sex a great part of it was meant for me, if not, why should you write so unless indeed you wish'd me to publish your letter for the good of women in general, if it is for me alone. . . . I think you rather severe." She saw right through his attempts to sugarcoat his teachings: "[Y]ou did not wish me to find fault with your letter [and] therefore threw in a handsome compliment here and there, and for fear they should have the effect of exciting my vanity you reminded me I was not an Angel, how kind it was of you—," she finished with some acerbity.[87]

In the same letter, she questioned the logic of his conventional male view of the chains by which marriage bound men. A bachelor, Ewing had written of his hope to visit Baltimore unless prevented by the "Fetters" of marriage. "I hope you will not be fettered very soon as your visit to B[altimore] depends on that," she replied, "tho' I do not know how it should unless you are to be governed instead of governing," an inversion of power to which she could not envision Ewing submitting.[88] Three decades earlier, replying to his wife's request for legal protections for married women, John Adams had protested that "[w]e [men] have only the Name of Masters."[89] But Mary Coale did not believe that a wife ruled, any more than Abigail Adams had. Indeed, her comment pierced the fallacy of overweening female influence on men, perceiving full well where position, power, and authority lay.

"I am pleased that my letters have compelled you to become a defender of your sex," Ewing responded, since, he admitted, nothing he could say about women would be "very serviceable to them."[90] But while Mary Coale asserted that "[y]ou are much mistaken if you think I wish to take up the cause of the generality of my sex," she could not distance herself from that project. Rejecting his characterization of woman as either angel or temptress, she explained that "I think much of their misconduct originates with yours [men] . . . Those females . . . who dress fashionably and in short one what you may call fashionables undoubtedly for all this to please the ungrateful Beaux who requite them by paying them [,] when with them [,] the most anxious attentions, but no sooner are they out of their company than they rail against the whole sex and say they are disgusted with every thing which they had before affected to admire." A decade earlier, her sister, Anna, had transcribed words to the same effect: "Profligates first betray to infamy all the women they can deceive—and then by a double injustice Judge the rest of the sex by the examples they have made."[91] Pressing her point, Mary Coale insisted, "Now you must acknowledge that this behaviour in our own sex proceeds from the dissimulation of yours who disapprove in their hearts, what they are apparently pleased with."[92]

The Coales were surely acquainted with both the religious and scientific foundations of gender: it is likely that they knew Gregory's *A Father's Legacy to His Daughters*, which had enjoyed sixty-nine printings in America from 1775 on; Anna Coale drew many excerpts from Hannah Chapone's *Letters on the Improvement of the Mind*, which underwent thirty-seven editions; Benjamin Franklin had recommended the older *The Ladies Library* for intensive reading for his daughter.[93] Their mother, Anne Hopkinson Coale, owned a copy of Fordyce's *Sermons*, which also appeared in numerous lending, as well as private, libraries throughout the country.[94] As we have seen, all these works reinforced conservative trends in the 1790s, steering women from public and civic displays toward enclosure in idealized sites of domesticity. Yet Anna Coale had recorded Milton's fair description of Eve, as well as passages praising female friendship, virtue, and the single life, while Mary Coale's insightful response to Ewing revealed her belief that females were not formed by nature to be dim-witted, flighty, frivolous creatures. Like Judith Sargent Murray, who argued "if opportunity of acquiring knowledge hath been denied us, the inferiority of our sex cannot fairly be deduced from thence," Mary Coale understood women's intellectual inferiority was created.[95] Women simply did not have access to the same educational opportunities men enjoyed. And those who indulged their love of reading had been warned, as had the daughters of Dr. John Gregory in 1774, to keep any learning "a profound secret."[96] Far from being an exemplar, a "learned woman" was a label of opprobrium even after the Revolution, signifying a willful rejection of one's sex.[97] Finally, Mary Coale had asked pointedly, trained to compete for male attention by enhancing their external beauty, how could women be blamed for neglecting their minds?

Early National Baltimore

The Coale sisters' notations and correspondence suggest that the thriving urban environment of Baltimore enabled a degree of freedom in thought and expression that more closely resembled cities such as Philadelphia to the north, than the slave society of the tidewater Chesapeake immediately to the south. Indeed, early national Baltimore was unique, distinguishing itself from all other American cities in its meteoric growth. From a hamlet of "nine miserable log houses," in 1750, Baltimore had mushroomed to 564 houses and almost six thousand people by 1774, and presented to a traveler a "new and promising scene of industry. Wharfs were constructed, elegant and convenient habitations rapidly erected; marshes were drained; spacious fields were occupied."[98] Its inauspicious beginnings had hardly foreshadowed this precipitous growth. An unattractive site compared with the lower Chesapeake, the land was hilly, with "short go-nowhere rivers," and it never drew the critical mass of landed gentry who found the flatlands of the tidewater better suited to tobacco farming. Nor did Baltimore County see leading families cohere into a governing elite commanding the deference of their neighbors. The early years were characterized by investments of time, money, and energy that often were agonizingly futile, as more fortunes foundered than were founded. By the 1760s, however, that picture had begun to change. Scotch-Irish and German immigrants began to flow into the town, lending it ethnic diversity. But more significant for Baltimore's growth was their ability as merchants to channel the grain trade through the port to the West Indies. The booming shipbuilding trade at Fells Point supported the city's expansion as a commercial center.[99] By 1790, Baltimore was the fourth-largest city in the United States, with a population of 13,503 that doubled yet again by 1800.[100] Visitors now exclaimed over the city's assembly room, pronouncing it "the most elegant dancing Assembly Room in the United States," or over the "noble prospect" commanded by St. Paul's Protestant Episcopal Church's hilltop perch.[101] An Irish gentleman was impressed by the vibrant commerce of the city, exemplified in its three banks, while an Irish actor was impressed by the townspeople's fondness for political controversy, even among women.[102] Francis Baily, a founder of the Royal Astronomical Society, noted with pleasure in 1796 that Baltimore's library and two daily newspapers "encourage a taste for literature and reading amongst themselves."[103] Twenty years later, the famous itinerant bookseller Parson Weems, who never took time to dust off his shoes in one place if there were books to be sold in another, spent almost two months in Baltimore.[104]

In this growing city, newly married Dr. Samuel Stringer Coale set up his medical practice in 1775. One of ten physicians, he quickly distinguished himself as a leader in the medical community and as a humanitarian, helping to establish an almshouse and fees proportionate to wealth and providing care to the poor through epidemics and the particularly frigid winter of 1779.[105] He served as both church warden and vestryman for St. Paul's Church, which, together with the Presbyterian Church, attracted well-heeled Baltimoreans by the turn of the century.[106] His bride, Anne

Hopkinson, was from the illustrious Philadelphia Hopkinson family, the daughter of Thomas Hopkinson, judge of the admiralty in Delaware and Pennsylvania, and sister of Francis Hopkinson, signer of the Declaration of Independence.[107] Her sister, Emily, married the Reverend Jacob Duché, Anglican rector of Christ Church and St. Peter's Church in Philadelphia, who served as chaplain to Congress in 1776. In short, Anne Hopkinson Coale was a devout Anglican, well connected to the city's Revolutionary elite and to relatives and dear friends with whom she maintained her ties even after her removal to Maryland.[108]

It is clear that "a taste for literature and reading" and learning formed an integral part of this family's life.[109] In 1790, Dr. Coale had delivered a public lecture in an organized effort to interest the city in establishing a medical college.[110] Anne Hopkinson Coale's brother, Francis Hopkinson, was secretary and sometime purchaser for the Library Company of Philadelphia, and had supplied her with a copy of Fordyce's *Sermons*.[111] The Coales attended a church that would have fed its congregation intellectual as well as spiritual fare. Eight of nine rectors of St. Paul's between 1790 and 1830 were doctors of divinity; the earlier rector, William West (1779–91), had died possessed of a considerable library.[112] The Coales' firstborn, Edward Johnson Coale, subscribed to the city's Library Company as early as 1800, and succumbing to the charm of books, had forsaken the career in law for which he had trained, to become a publisher and bookseller in the city.[113] Among his many publications was *The Portico*, a weekly that printed the original works of the Delphian Club, a small group of elite men who perceived themselves as "male muses," devoted to advancing the literary culture of the city.[114] Anna Coale's commonplace book reveals both her novel reading and her devotion to bluestocking Hester Chapone. When second son William Coale was preparing to set sail for the West Indies, his mother sent "a Sett of books" as companions for his journey. Books—provided, perhaps, by her brother Edward—relieved the tedium of travel when Mary Coale visited relatives in Philadelphia and New Jersey, as is clear in a list prepared by one of her cousins of items she had inadvertently left behind.[115] During one Philadelphia stay, when a visit to a cousin had to be postponed because of the weather, Hopkinson took her to the library, where they happily "staid untill it was quite dark—I could not but be pleased."[116]

Not only did the Coale sisters read but they also wrote. The Coale and Hopkinson families shared the post-Revolutionary interest in female education. Francis Hopkinson's satire, "Nitidia," demonstrated how a woman's domestic obligations interfered with her ability to nurture an intellectual life, which, given the chance, would likely have proven more productive than that of her bumbling amateur scientist husband.[117] In 1810 Edward Johnson Coale collected subscriptions for his publication *The American Lady's Preceptor*; from Boston, his cousin Esther Duché Hill requested three copies.[118] Designed for use in female academies, *The American Lady's Preceptor* compiled biographies of notable women including Margaret of Anjou, Catherine of Aragon, Anne Boleyn, Marie Antoinette, and even Philadelphia writer and salonniere Elizabeth Graeme Fergusson.[119] Esther Hill no doubt intended to put the book to use in her own household; as she wrote to her cousin, "I wil reply to dear Nancy's sweet letters as soon as I can command leisure. But I pay close attention to my darlings being desireous their Father may find them improved on his return."[120]

The existence of Anna and Mary Coale's commonplace books indicates a purposeful program of education, although whether they attended a formal school (either in Baltimore or in Philadelphia) or were educated at home is unclear. In the early national period, Susan Miller observed, writers of commonplace books "took writing to be a function of acquisitive self-development, a process that constituted and confirmed their class status."[121] As we have seen, girls, too, had begun to keep commonplace books by the latter half of the eighteenth century, citing such literary luminaries as John Milton and Alexander Pope in the colonial period but increasingly shifting after the Revolution to novelists and female writers such as English bluestocking Hester Chapone and evangelical Hannah More.[122] Adopting a form of discourse prized in male education, women imitated the dominant mode, but by the early national period they had begun to craft it to suit their own purposes.[123] While their commonplace books assuredly linked their individual identities with a larger, privileged class identity, they also confirmed for women their participation in a world of letters that, from time out of mind, had been almost exclusively masculine. Further, by partaking of this discipline, women of the early republic proved their ability to counteract their passionate natures with rational discourse, thereby demonstrating their worthiness for the blessings of liberty and the rights of citizenship.[124] Indeed, Hannah W. Foster's *The Boarding School* (1798), an account of an idealized female academy, recommended the keeping of commonplace books "for materials to supply the pen" by which the mind "imperceptibly treasures up the ideas."[125] Singled out as wisdom to be read and reread, then, the entries in the Coale sisters' commonplace books could be as revelatory of their thinking as a letter or diary of their own words. In the Coale family, keeping such books was a clear priority for the girls, as they created, both materially and intellectually, their own literary property. Anna Maria Coale's simply bound book was treasured lovingly after her death in 1813; Mary Coale had hers bound in leather, her embossed name on the cover proclaiming her pride of ownership.

Female Networks

Though the contours of the girls' educations are unclear, the family papers plainly reveal a female network of shared wisdom over space and time, at the apex of which stood Mary Johnson Hopkinson, mother of Anne Hopkinson Coale. Widowed with seven children (the eldest was fourteen), Mary Hopkinson managed to "carefully educate [them], genteely, but frugally, out of the income of a small estate," observed Benjamin Franklin, who had assiduously crafted for himself a reputation for frugality, "without much diminishing their portions."[126] As a child she had been left in the care of a guardian who neglected her education and squandered her inheritance, and she may well have been determined to protect her daughters from such a fate. When she died, she distributed shares of stock among her grandchildren in addition to Bibles (and her collection of books and bookcase to grandson and bookseller Edward Johnson Coale).[127]

   In the letters written between Philadelphia and Baltimore, we can see the essence of the education transmitted from one generation to the next and echoed in the pages of their commonplace books and letters. The strength of female friendship is a strong current: despite the intense heat of a July day, Philadelphian Abigail Willing sat down to "chatter" to her friend, Anne Hopkinson Coale. "I am delighted to the finding Writing So Easy to you," Willing wrote. "I always dreaded a Seperation Still more than I Shoud have done; Coud I but believ'd that you woud have been Such a faithfull Corespondant. But w[h]ere Persons Love as Afectionately as we doe Trifles won't Interfere with real pleasure, Such I hope it is & Ever *Will* be to you to write."[128] In a letter to Anne Hopkinson Coale, a New Jersey friend recalled with pleasure the "Worthy Circle of friends who were accustim'd to meet at your dear Momma's," women with whom Mary Johnson Hopkinson had surrounded herself.[129] Although she could no longer convene with that circle herself, Anne Hopkinson named her youngest daughter after her dearest friend, Abigail Willing. And the commonplace books of Anna and Mary Coale ring with the praises of female friendship: "The first attachment of young hearts is friendship—the noblest and happiest of affections," Anna Maria extracted from Hester Chapone. In later years, the Coale women expressed the depth of their attachments to one another in the most poignant of ways: Anne Hopkinson Coale devised a single share of her stock in the Union Bank of Maryland to be held in the name of her daughter, Anna Maria, who had predeceased her. In 1816, Mary Coale Proud named her first-born child Anna Maria, and in the pages of her commonplace book copied sister Eliza's eulogizing poem, "[I]s it for Friendships sacred flame / we wake the slumbring lyre / yes by her own celestial flame . . . there adoration pay."[130] Over four generations, female friendship transcended separations imposed by both distance and death, disproving notions that women, lacking the restraints of reason, were unable to know true friendship.

Yet writing was pregnant with danger as well as pleasure. Mary Coale's concern about the propriety of her correspondence with a man has antecedents in a letter from her mother's friend, Abigail Willing. In July 1775, concerned about her association with a Mrs. Mercer, Willing had asked her friend's opinion of the woman, noting "You know Nancy it is a delicate thing the Company a Lady keeps & more particularly With Whom she Corresponds."[131] Anna Coale had copied Hester Chapone's caution: "It has been supposed a duty of friendship to lay open every thought and every feeling of the heart to our friend.—[But there are instances] in which this is not only unnecessary but wrong." Both writers show their keen awareness of the need for self-control, a discipline denoted masculine in the eighteenth century. Each implicitly rejected the characterization of women as unboundedly passionate creatures, as each realized the necessity of caution informed by rational judgment. The question of female associations, in writing and in person, persisted into the early national period, as in Hannah W. Foster's novel, *The Coquette* (1797), which examined the fatal consequences of notes exchanged and read in secret and confidences entrusted to false friends. Foster's *The Boarding School*, published the following year, told the story of Celia and Cecilia, close friends at boarding school, whose whispered exchanges became written ones after graduation separated them. Committing her confidences about her lover to paper, Celia was undone when he intercepted, read, and circulated her letters.[132] Aware of these dangers, Margaret Caldwell had forced herself to overcome her reticence about writing to her suitor, both because she knew about "those men who only write to betray" and "because I must intrust what I said to chance for the conveyer."[133] Mary Coale's ambivalence about writing to Ewing could well have sprung from the warnings of her female network, but those warnings were also part and parcel of female novelists' depictions of the gender experience in the early republic.

The significance of committing one's thoughts to paper, especially to a man, can be more fully appreciated when we recall the significance for women of letter writing. Girlhood writing lessons had focused on the elegant formation of their letters, rather than on content; their handwriting, then, was as much a presentation of themselves as their dress and deportment.[134] That explains why, in a less than perfect hand, Henrietta Tilghman (of Maryland's Eastern Shore) begged her friend Polly Pearce, "As you value either yourself or me burn this when you read, for you are too apt to be careless of your Letters."[135] When Mary Coale wrote from Philadelphia to her sister Anna, she pleaded, "[P]ray don't read this in the presence of any person and don't let any one see it I think not Brother if he does tell him to make allowances for stiff fingers bad pen— headache and the confusion of just arrived."[136]

Beyond the consideration of one's handwritten presentation, however, were lurking dangers, as Mary Coale's cousin, Esther Hopkinson, warned her in 1809. "It appears to me my cousin you have got into a pretty sentimental dilemma, so much for writing your feelings. It would have been much better to have 'relieved your mind' and body in any other way, You recollect Sternes Commentations after his remarks that got into a french womans head, You must do as he did, that is, do nothing, the more that is said or written upon such a business only makes it worse . . . [but] Never mind my dear Mary," Hopkinson consoled, "those who know you as I do, will know how I excuse all the expressions of your letter, however it will be advisable whenever you want to *relieve* yourself to do it upon any thing but paper."[137] Private though these exchanges were meant to be, they were— or could become, if seen by eyes other than those for whom they were intended—public performances.[138] Female modesty dictated reticence in speech and deportment, disregard of which was easily construed as promiscuity.[139]

In spite of the risks, however, some women were quite deliberate in committing their thoughts to paper. A friend of Catherine Dulany Belt wrote to her a lengthy letter about her prewedding jitters, even though she intended to arrive at Belt's home the next morning early enough to awaken her with a kiss and to devote the entire day's conversation to the subject.[140] And despite the defensive posture with which she ended her final letter, Mary Coale's parries with Ewing displayed her courage in writing. He had warned her of the dangers of a "young girl entering on a correspondence with a gentleman who has no claims from relationship" upon her. In itself, he pointed out, "it is an act at which the sober part of the world will frown, and in its consequences, it may involve your dearest interests."[141] Her letters, methodically written, addressed, and sent, risked exposure of the gravest kind. The boldness of her accusation could be used to threaten her "dearest interests"; she might one day face the spectacle of her own hand turned against her. Yet, even after Mary apologized that "What I had to say on this subject I have expressed in as few words as I could and yet I have said more than I intended," she would not "abridge it so it must e'en Go." She even concluded, "It is but a poor one [excuse for women's behavior], to say it is their appreciating so highly the opinion of such insignificant animals as the generality of the Beaux are."[142] Even so, mindful perhaps of the advice of the Countess of Carlisle to "preserve a copy of every letter you write, or receive; this exactitude will secure you against future accusations and misinterpretation," Mary kept her copies.[143]

Deeper still than questions of propriety and reputation, however, were questions of the soul. Here, too, we see the strength of the influence of Mary Hopkinson on the younger generations. Her will authorized the expense of "4 Dollars apiece" to provide Bibles for her granddaughters "as handsome as they can be got of," but the children were not to receive them until "they [are] of an age to take care of them."[144] A staunch Anglican, Mary vigorously opposed the Deist teachings of the late eighteenth century, asking her daughter to relay her concern about an acquaintance for whom she "had always an affection . . . which made me very uneasy to hear that he had commenced a disciple of that miserable creature Paine."[145] Even as she wrote two years later to condole with her daughter's anxiety about Samuel Coale's failing health, she wrote, "I wish the Doc would read that Book I sent[.] I mean the appeal to the Deists . . . if you should not understand it at first, give it another reading."[146] She visited her steadfast Anglicanism upon her daughter, who in turn inculcated that faith in her children, as seen in son William Coale's mischievous assurance that, even in her absence, he was "going to church like a good boy."[147] Upon Mary Hopkinson's death, a granddaughter wrote to Anne Hopkinson Coale that "the loss of so inestimable a woman will be strongly felt by all. . . . She was all goodness; ten thousand sermons upon charity . . . could not have the effect as *one* such example—If I have not profited by it, it is my own fault and I lament it."[148]

Ultimately, the writings of these women underscore the value of this female network as teacher and exemplar over the best scholars and clerics. Faithful adherents to the Anglican (later Episcopal) Church; capable and strong, if not hard-headed, in the face of the challenges of widowhood (Dr. Samuel Coale died in 1798, when their youngest, Mary, was barely nine); and devoted to friendships sustained over the miles that separated them, grandmother and mother modeled the power of the female intellect, soul, and spirit for the younger generations in ways that were more effective than any sermon could have been.

Transplanted from Philadelphia to Baltimore, Anne Hopkinson Coale carried her mother's passion for reading, reflecting, and writing: her supervision of her daughters' writing endeavors is evident in a son's letter. Reporting on the home front while she was visiting in Philadelphia in spring 1801, William informed his mother, "Mary has been a very good girl, I have daily Supply'd her with pens which She has used in writing to Eliza Henrietta."[149] Likely enclosed in that same packet to Philadelphia was eleven-year-old Mary's letter, in which she dutifully listed for her mother's approbation the many letters she had written within her own corresponding network. While she began with formulaic formality—"I thank my D[ea]r Mama for taking so much notice of me in her letter"— she was already so comfortable with the medium of letter writing that she slipped easily into a conversational mode, immediately bridging the miles between them. "Miss Mc Causlin is a going to have a party next Saterday I am not invited I do not care for she is very affected and it always disgusted me to look at her," Mary confided to her mother, before concluding brightly, "[G]ive my love to my D[ea]r GrandMama and tell her I want to see her very much."[150] That the Baltimore Coales were embraced by the Philadelphia network of women is clear in the family correspondence. The sisters made extended visits to Philadelphia relatives and indeed may have even received some formal education there.[151] Reinforced, then, by books, letters, and the extended network of women between Philadelphia and Baltimore, the younger generation learned from the strong female models before them.[152]

Philadelphia Connections

Their connections with Philadelphia may well have offered the Coale sisters another view of female influence in the early national period that they did not see in Baltimore. Because of its history of rapid growth, with all the attendant risks and failures, Baltimore had never developed an entrenched gentry elite such as had appeared in the tidewater Chesapeake. Nor could it approach the glitter and sophistication of post-Revolutionary Philadelphia, which as the national capital in the 1790s, had attracted the nation's political and social elite. Alice Izard and her daughter Margaret Izard Manigault, for example, found Philadelphia the perfect ground for the preservation of a genteel elite, combining the best of republicanism, breeding, and merit (a project made all the more pressing with the Jeffersonian-Republican triumph of 1800). Izard and Manigault surrounded themselves with like-minded Federalists, countering democratizing trends by organizing a genteel life around visits, walks, and salons that served as visible markers of elite status within the new republic.[153] In addition to southerners, the Manigault circle admitted the best Federalist Philadelphia families to their gatherings—among them the Hopkinsons.[154]

A Federalist, an Anglican, and a Hopkinson, Mary Coale fit perfectly into this Philadelphia set.[155] That she was invited into this circle is clear from a letter reprising a round of visits one day that included the celebrated Mrs. Izard.[156] Here she could see the ways in which the deficiencies of her sex might be mitigated by the advantages of class.[157] Privileged by their wealth, these elite women were expected to soften the edges of a harsh male world. Cultivated men welcomed the conversation of refined women, and in the Manigault salon one visitor recalled years later that "men of wit and science knew where they could always find congenial society of both sexes," who "ardently opposed royal tyranny, without the slightest sympathy with Democracy."[158] These gatherings between the sexes defied categorization as either private or public but were expressions of politeness in an "unofficial public sphere to which privileged women could lay legitimate claim."[159] In such a world, one might be able to speak, without recriminations or censure, about the equal intellectual capacities of men and women or about the appearance of female inferiority that is the direct consequence of a lack of education.

The Coale sisters never quoted the writings of northern women such as Judith Sargent Murray or the more radical *Vindications of the Rights of Woman* or the appeals of Philadelphia Quaker abolitionists. Even so, their work diverges from the views of many women of the plantation South, whose writings concentrated so heavily on pleasing men and scouting marriage prospects. Mary and Henrietta Tilghman lived on Maryland's Eastern Shore, still tobacco country after the Revolution. Their letters (1782–89) concern endless rounds of visiting and reports on courtships, fashion, and balls. They were, in short, accounts of societal rituals to attract male approval. Here, where more traditional ideas of gender relations prevailed, Mary Tilghman paled at the prospect of a conversation with her friend Mary (Polly) Pearce's uncle, Michael Earle, "I am almost afraid of him too, when I recollect that he has the Spectator at his fingers ends, makes such apt Quotations from it, on every occasion, and subject, that I shou'd be perfectly awed by his superior knowledge."[160] She knew well, too, how women were judged, regardless of their education. Of female beauty, she observed, "Wisdom says it is a fading flower, but fading as it is, it attracts more admiration than wit, goodness, or anything else in the World."[161] And so her conversation is full of beaux ("the only beau within my reach is the serene Hugh of Huntington");[162] of the beautiful women who attract them ("Mrs. Lloyd is more follow'd and admir'd than ever she was");[163] and of a round of visits that discuss them all ("the tea Tables at Chester Town are oblig'd to Miss Piner for furnishing them with conversation, three Weeks have beheld Mr Bordley at the feet of the languishing fair, and it is fear'd she will at last banish him").[164] No wonder Rosalie Stier, a Belgian émigré to Maryland, noted that "the women of Annapolis are very obliging about personal criticism, which is their principal occupation."[165] Competing for the attentions of men was serious business, pitting woman against woman and fragmenting female solidarity.[166] Women devoted much time to cultivating the beauty men so admired and learning the postures of willing subordination that were essential to success.

But southern women also adopted the language of inferiority even in the most affectionate of relationships, in which one might suppose those postures were not required. For example, Mary Spotswood Campbell (the widow of the son of Governor Alexander Spotswood of Virginia) sounded a plaintive tone as she begged her son's help in settling some complex financial questions. "It is a thing Improbable for me to decide by myself those weighty matters I now Inclose," she wrote to her son in 1794, "without you will come down, and appoint such gentlemen as you and myself can confide in and consult with them on these affairs [,] I can do nothing . . . as I am not a proper Judge for my self, where my worldly happiness is so concerned." Although the weight of her correspondence reveals a woman who fought to meet the challenges of living in the legal limbo of an abandoned wife, her writing assumed the expected female posture to solicit the attentions of her son (who, not incidentally, owed her money).[167] Jean Cameron sought the approval of a beloved brother, Duncan, "I have not heard a sentence from you since we left Hillsborough, but I will not complain for fear of a *rebuke*, for I can stand reproof better from any, than those I love."[168] Nor, for all the advantages of her education, was Martha Laurens Ramsay willing to "contend for the equality of the sexes" in her marriage.[169]

Dependent as women were on the approbation of men, Mary Coale understood, as Ewing did too, that the empty compliments of his earlier letters could have created a vain girl. But Mary was not so easily beguiled. Her commonplace book reveals why. "The mind that has not in itself a sufficient stock of ideas, may, by reading, be furnished with such as will promote reflection and meditation," she copied from "Burton." "It will enable us to contemplate truth in a variaty of forms and extract from thence useful principles and maxims."[170] Mary read to expose herself to a "variaty" of truths, but ultimately, she would decide what was useful, precisely because she could; her reading had informed her, educated her, and given her the tools that enabled such self-possession. Together with the strength of the female network behind her and her sense of herself cultivated during visits to Philadelphia, the authority she derived from her reading could certainly explain why she was undeterred from writing her thoughts to an older man.

The contrast between the women of the plantation South and the Coale sisters is significant, both in the different functions reading served and in the ways they responded to their reading in their writing. Anna Coale used her reading to reflect on the strength of female friendship and the respectability of the single life for women. Her sister understood that her reading opened her to a variety of truths on which she could reflect and, in an exercise of independent thought, extract for herself "useful principles and maxims." For them, the process of keeping their commonplace books was not unlike that explained by a Mount Holyoke (Massachusetts) student two generations later. "Take some book for instance," Julia Hyde instructed a friend in 1839, "and read it and form your own opinion as to its character, influence, its beauties and faults. Have an opinion about it, and then . . . find out what others think and compare your decisions with theirs."[171] The seriousness of purpose that characterized this approach to reading and writing is entirely missing in the daydreaming aspect of the woman writer in "Correspondence."[172] Everything about this portrayal of the woman writer belies the realities of writing in the eighteenth-century South: her relaxed and reflective pose that suggests quantities of time; her well-supplied table laden with large sheets of paper, two sharp pens, three inkstands, and commodious lighting; and the absence of any books from which she would draw ideas to discuss. One does not expect a learned treatise from this writer; rather, she will write whatever spontaneous thoughts occur. As a friend confessed to Letitia McKean in 1788, after wandering from her subject, "This is a specimen of my want of thought. My pen controlls me and fancy often takes the reigns and reason is left behind."[173] Certainly this portrayal of a writing woman diminished the challenge female writers posed to men, but it could not be further from the image evoked by the Coale sisters' careful transcriptions and thoughtful letters.

Reading outside a Slave Society

The Coale sisters' understanding of women's reading thus differed in emphasis and purpose from the attitude that obtained in the plantation south. Thomas Jefferson, for example, saw married women's reading as a

Fig. 5. "Correspondence" (London, 1760). Suggestive of leisurely rather than serious scholarly or business activity, this portrayal of a writing woman diminishes the threat she might otherwise pose to male hegemony over the pen. Courtesy of the John D. Rockefeller, Jr. Library, Colonial Williamsburg Foundation.

diversion of low priority. "Nothing is so engaging as the little domestic cares into which you appear to be entering," he wrote to his daughter, Martha Jefferson Randolph, newly married and mistress of her own household, "and as to reading it is useful for only filling up the chinks of more useful and healthy occupations."[174] A far better choice, Jefferson thought, was needlework, which would relieve the tedium of "dull company and dull weather."[175] When she was a child, Jefferson had sketched out a plan of education that groomed her to take her place in his plantation home of Monticello. The daily program of study for Martha followed the traditional paradigm for a late-eighteenth-century elite female education. Her day began with two hours of music instruction at eight, followed by a three-hour and one-hour block of dance or drawing (reversed on alternate days), an hour of French, another of music, and then reading and writing in English from five until bedtime. The question is what purpose this education, noteworthy more for its rigorous hourly discipline than its more ornamental content, was intended to serve.

With Scottish Enlightenment thinkers like Lord Henry Home Kames and Adam Smith, Jefferson believed that men and women shared "a love of others, a sense of duty to them, a moral instinct."[176] But that moral instinct had to be practiced. One way in which to do that was by a program of right reading, anything "that contributes to fix us in the principles and practice of virtue." The mind, like the body, requires exercise, Jefferson believed; "exercise produces habit; and . . . the exercise . . . of the moral feelings, produces a habit of thinking and acting virtuously."[177] Of course, the definition, application, and exercise of virtue would change and varied enormously for men and women in early republic, but the idea of education as praxis was what was important.[178] For Jefferson, education for girls meant inculcating discipline rather than developing intellectual or economic autonomy. For example, when fourteen-year-old Martha complained from her convent school in Paris that "Titus Livius puts me out of my wits. I can not read a word by myself," her father replied, "It is a part of the American character to consider nothing as desperate . . . consider therefore the conquering your Livy as an exercise in the habit of surmounting difficulties."[179] Reading as a practice of self-discipline, rather than reading for content, reflection, critical analysis, or even imitation (as for example, in boys' study of rhetoric) rendered the subject matter almost irrelevant. Certainly Martha Jefferson must have thought so when her father's admonition came to hand and she turned reluctantly back to her text. But the point was to persist, to practice self-discipline and to overcome the obstacle, and in so doing, prepare for life's future challenges. Years later, Martha's cousin, Judith Randolph, would complain to her that the slim opportunity for even a "tolerable education" was "one of the greatest disadvantages which the Virginia girls are attended with."[180] Longing for a good education, Randolph, like other southern women, was constrained by the exigencies of plantation life and by the men who controlled it. The result of this approach to female education was even more apparent years later, when Jefferson's granddaughters would lament the futility of their genteel upbringing in earning a living when necessity dictated.[181]

On the Eastern Shore of Maryland, Mary Tilghman used both reading and letter writing to relieve the isolation of plantation life. She longed for the company of her friend, Polly Pearce. "How often my dear Polly do I wish for you, particularly when the walking hour arrives, and I sally out by myself," but, she acknowledged, "It is a selfish wish in me too for, what signifies lying—this place is cruelly lonesome."[182] In February 1787 she promised that on her next visit to Pearce, she would be accompanied by "all my Books" that filled her empty hours.[183] Mary Huger of Georgia read "for amusement in my solitary hours."[184] For these readers, then, books were amusements whose chief usefulness lay in the diversion they offered from the tedium and isolation of plantation existence. Reading as amusement could not be justified when there was work to be done, as diary entries by women north and south noted how they read only after their chores were done.[185] In the North, women found ways to combine the two: one might read as others sewed or cooked.[186] From Philadelphia, Mary Coale happily reported to her sister Eliza that "we have some delightful plans in contemplation some for improvement *all* for amusement we shall soon commence reading I am to read aloud whilst Cousin E[mily] works."[187] But in the isolation of southern plantation life, such community reading was rare, and even individual reading was constrained by limits imposed by fathers and husbands.

The consequences of these views of female reading in the plantation South is clear in Thomas Jefferson's remark about the dinner conversation at a Philadelphia salon that turned to the horror of the execution of French King Louis XVI in 1793. The dinner guests included women "of the first circle," who were "all open-mouthed against the murders of a sovereign, and they generally speak those sentiments which the more cautious husband smothers."[188] Mary Coale's independence of mind, formed as a result of her reading, was just the result Jefferson feared.

But perhaps most startling of all the entries in the sisters' commonplace books was that which occupied pride of place on the first page of Anna Coale's book. Laurence Sterne's words filled the page: " 'I can't get out. I can't get out: said the Starling I stood looking at the bird—and to every Person who came into the Passage—it ran fluttering to the side towards which they approach'd it, with the same lamentation of its Captivity—I can't get out—said the Starling.' " The narrator struggles in vain to free the starling from its cage, but beaten, says bitterly, "Disguise thyself as thou wilt—still—Slavery—said I—still thou are a bitter draught." The copybook continues: "The Bird in his cage pursued me into my Room. . . . I sat down close to my table—and leaning my head upon my hand—I began to figure to myself the miseries of confinement."[189] Unable to imagine the sufferings of millions, the narrator begins, affectingly (this is, after all, his *Sentimental Journey*), to describe the misery of one. Anna Coale's pen follows, until her transcription ends abruptly in midsentence—the next four pages are torn from the book.

Did Anna Maria apply this transcription, extracted from its original context in the novel, to the racial slavery to which daily she was a witness?[190] It is certainly possible, for there are clues that the Coale family was troubled by the conventional southern notions and practice of slavery. Samuel Coale owned at least three male slaves during his lifetime; he seems to have used them to clear and cultivate "Morven," acreage he owned in neighboring Anne Arundel County. Yet his will provided for their eventual manumission, seven and ten years after his death in 1798.[191] His wife ordered the eventual manumission of her female slaves and their issue as well.[192] The Coales' wills conform to a pattern of slaveholding and manumission in this period in Baltimore. Baltimore's rapid growth had not come about solely on the efforts of white labor. While the pre-Revolutionary black population was negligible, the Revolution spurred the growth of slavery. By 1783, there were about 1,000 slaves in the city; less than thirty years later, that number had grown to 4,672, nearly 13 percent of Baltimore's overall population.[193] At the time of Dr. Coale's death, 61 percent of Baltimore slaveholders were merchants, traders, and professionals, whose average holding of three slaves was a sign of gentility, an overall pattern in which Coale is a perfect fit. But it was expensive in this urban setting; indeed, for most, "slave owning was an unaffordable luxury," so frequently slaveholders hired out their slaves in contracts that offered both employer and slave great flexibility of terms.[194] Under these circumstances, slave owning in Baltimore began to diminish after 1810, and by 1830 four-fifths of Baltimore's blacks were legally free, the largest group of free people of color in any American city.[195]

What explains the Coales' manumission of their slaves and their daughter's attention to Sterne's caged starling? Certainly their actions allow a glimpse, within a single Baltimore household, of larger patterns that were, in part, economically driven: by age thirty-five, both male and fe-

male slaves are past their prime productive years and thus more easily released. Moreover, it hardly bespeaks an abolitionist temperament or even
Christian benevolence to free slaves from the grave, when their service is
no longer required to make one's own life comfortable. Indeed, the terms
of the Coales' wills enabled them to have the satisfaction of "freeing" their
slaves while simultaneously providing the slaves' continued service for
their survivors. Anne Hopkinson Coale's Philadelphia connections may
help explain her sympathies: her family connections and antislavery sentiments certainly overlapped. Her brother, Francis Hopkinson, was part of
a circle of Federalists in Philadelphia that included Benjamin Rush, who
had helped write the constitution of the Pennsylvania Abolition Society
(PAS) and served as its secretary. Revived after the war, the work of the
PAS drew the attention of the city's Federalists elites; only two members
were affiliated with the Jeffersonian Republicans.[196] Hopkinson also revived the American Philosophical Society, which published Samuel Stanhope Smith's *Essay on the Causes of the Variety of Complexion and Figure in the
Human Species,* which argued the common humanity of all human beings,
no matter what their skin color.[197] The swirling currents toward manumission were particularly strong in the Upper South and Delmarva penin-
sula in the 1790s as well.[198] Dr. George Buchanan, with whom Coale had
worked on the medical college project, was also a member of the American Philosophical Society and, no doubt influenced by Rush's antislavery
orations, gave a speech to the Anti-Slavery Society of Maryland in 1791.[199]
The Coale family's professional connection with Buchanan was cemented
in 1815 with the marriage of Edward Johnson Coale to Buchanan's
daughter, MaryAnn, and Edward Coale would later serve as the first president of Maryland's Colonization Society.[200]

These layered connections and evolving sympathies surely form the
context for Anna Coale's commonplace book entry, completed the year
after Buchanan's speech and, significantly, preceding her father's will by
six years. It is notable that at fourteen she chose the particular words of
Sterne's *Sentimental Journey* to memorialize; something about them struck
a chord within her, so she extracted them, carefully and deliberately copying them into a book she would read over and over again.[201] Perhaps she
understood that it was of no consequence how gilded was the cage in
which the starling was imprisoned: confinement, in and of itself, produces
the chief misery. The relative latitude Baltimore slaves experienced and
the hope many harbored for the freedom their negotiated contracts
seemed to offer constituted but a gloss to slavery's essence. Even beyond
Baltimore, Anna could see that the material circumstances of slavery were
improving slightly in the post-Revolutionary period. No matter that slave-

holders recognized their Christian paternal duty to better house, feed, and clothe their slaves; or that the legal system no longer condoned the mutilation and murder of one's slaves with complete impunity; or that by the mid-eighteenth century, slaves were able to construct the family and religious structures that were to be the pillars of a developing African American culture.[202] However significant these improvements in the material and spiritual conditions of slave life may have been, they could never atone for a life one lived but could never own.

Whatever the stirrings that prompted her transcriptions, it is remarkable that this outright condemnation of slavery should appear in the copybook of a young girl in the upper South as early as 1792. No outpouring of frustration at a recalcitrant slave or a husband's nocturnal visits to the slave quarters, these words were a moral condemnation that struck at slavery's very essence. In her copybook, Sterne's words had become her own. It is a marked contrast to the silence on the subject in the memoir, kept during the same period, of Martha Laurens Ramsay, whose father, Henry Laurens, was one of the largest importers of slaves in South Carolina.[203] Perhaps Coale was influenced by her father's benevolent ministrations to the poor. Perhaps she knew of Dr. Buchanan's speech and of the antislavery arguments being debated among Philadelphia Federalists. Perhaps she felt a sense of responsibility conveyed by her elite status and enhanced by her religious sensibilities. Or perhaps her notation was her subscription to eighteenth-century notions of female sensibility that did not emphasize the moral wrong of slavery but rather "validated the moral authority of those who look on with sympathy."[204] Indeed, while this passage of *Sentimental Journey* has often been cited as a satire on the absurd heights (or depths) sentimental literature could reach, the sympathies it aroused may have been all a fourteen-year-old girl needed as evidence of her identity and moral authority to arrive at her own judgment, years before her father arranged for the gradual manumission of his slaves.

That Anna and Mary Coale *wrote* their reading speaks volumes for the active way they approached their books. No mere diversion, their books opened them to a "variaty of truths," a bountiful board of ideas from which they sampled eagerly. It is easy to imagine them seated at their reading. Captured by an image or pondering a phrase, they stop, seeing the momentary confluence of their world with the world they hold in their hands. Then, selecting the passages they found so striking, they edit and copy them in their neatest hand. At the last, they bind their treasures, inscribing name and date, thus fixing into perpetuity the insights of those moments. That they delighted in their reading as well is clear in Mary

Coale's exclamation, "Reading may truly be call'd the luxury of the mind."[205]

The Coale sisters' commonplace books are suggestive of how young women processed advice of various types. It is significant that in her neat, careful hand, Anna Coale selected passages about the captivity of both the free and the enslaved within slavery (the free narrator no more able to effect the freedom of the caged bird than the bird itself) and the choices a woman should be empowered freely to make. Whether Anna Coale was thinking of the confinements of slavery or of her sex as she copied Sterne's words, it is impossible to know. Her thoughts may have focused quite literally on slavery. Or she could have seen, as did Sarah Grimké in her *Letters on the Equality of the Sexes* (1837), that the societal incapacities imposed on both slaves and women (especially married women) were sufficiently alike as to defy analytical separation. Coale's celebration of the single life supports that possibility as well. Yet single or married, women continued to be governed by Enlightenment ideas of female sensibility that appeared to enhance women's moral authority over men but in fact confined them to their biologically determined weakness of nerves and temperament. Coale may well have chafed under the limitations imposed by a solicitous family vainly hoping to preserve her delicate health. Regardless, in neither subject did she conform to the prevailing conventions of the society of the early republic that excluded both slave and woman from the idea and practice of owning oneself.

Yet in such a space as early national Baltimore, with its practice of term slavery, it was possible to question the "natural" hierarchies of gender and race.[206] Boundaries were not yet fixed in the 1790s: not in the diverse and rapidly growing city of Baltimore or in the forms slavery or gender would take in the new republic. Neither was the character of a fourteen-year-old girl fixed: it could still be formed by carefully supervised reading and the keeping of a commonplace book. For the Coale sisters, writing was both agent of their learning and expression of their own agency. The measured deliberation of their transcriptions was a short, but perhaps necessary, step to the written expression of their own ideas, as in Mary Coale's correspondence with Ewing. The very act of writing presumed an authority not understood to be female, as the "intruding upon the rights of men" exclamation of Anne Finch, seventeenth-century Countess of Winchelsea, had recognized.[207] That the Coale sisters copied the words of others does not lessen the independence of their thought. Rather, copying examples of original female writing, they were emboldened to take the leap from transcription to creation.

Indeed, years after Mary Coale's correspondence with Ewing began, she filled her commonplace book not only with the writings of published authors but also with those of female family members and friends: prayers written by Anna Maria Coale and the poems of her sister, Eliza, commemorating the death of their brother, William, in 1807 and, in 1813, the exemplary life and death of Anna herself.[208] In their original writings, the younger Coales may have followed an example set among Anglican and Quaker women in Philadelphia like Elizabeth Graeme Fergusson or Hannah Griffitts.[209] Or they may have been at the beginning of a trend, noticeable by midcentury, of what Mary Louise Kete has called "sentimental collaboration," a process both "conservative and generative" that both restored the essence of the person lost to death and was generative of something tangible and new—the poetry—created by these female authors.[210] "Your characters during life, and even when you shall sleep in the dust," Hannah Foster reminded her readers, "may rest on the efforts of your pens."[211] In their writing, these young women created something "for futurity," work that contrasted mightily with the products of domestic labor that daily were consumed or worn to disintegration.[212] In any event, the effect of their writing was the same: binding the generations together across space and time, life and death, in a densely woven fabric of female bonds.

These bonds have drawn a lot of attention from historians who studied the rise of female academies and the friendships formed within them in the antebellum period and saw in them the beginning of a female consciousness that was crucial to the eventual development of feminism.[213] Here as well, the Coale sisters occupy a middle space between the rather more sporadic and isolated education of colonial American girls and the structure and fellowship of antebellum female schools.[214] The Coales' wide and layered female network developed and grew without the geographic and intellectual cohesion that later female academies provided. The very existence of those academies disproved the notion that women's reading and writing were nonproductive uses of time, since women were sent away to school to do just that. But in this earlier transitional period, the Coales' cousin, Esther Duché Hill, would excuse herself for taking time away from her duties to write a letter, even as she dreamed in that same letter about editing a publication of her father's letters, complete with an introduction she would write.[215] Yet clearly this early community of female readers and writers was doing what historian Mary Kelley observed of her antebellum academy student subjects: they made of the rich female network of grandmother, mother, sisters, cousins, and friends "models of womanhood in which learning was consonant with more traditional gender conventions."[216] That is, they remade the image of a learned woman from an object of opprobrium to one of admiration.

One last example underscores the importance of cultural context to reading, writing, and identity. Perhaps the most privileged young woman in the early republic was Eleanor Parke Custis (later Lewis), granddaughter of Martha Washington and adopted daughter of George Washington. Raised with all the advantages the love, devotion, and money of her grandparents could lavish on her, she received the best education they could provide. During her grandfather's tenure as president, Nelly (as she was called) lived with him in New York and Philadelphia, where she established connections she would maintain the rest of her life. Unlike the Coale sisters, however, she did not come to question conventional attitudes toward gender as a result of those experiences. Returning to plantation life at Mount Vernon in 1797, Nelly wrote to her Philadelphia friend, Elizabeth Bordley, letters that, like the Tilghman correspondence, elaborated the details of balls and beaux and beat back false rumors of engagements. Although she swore, at age eighteen, that until she met the man whom she could love "with all my Heart" she would "remain E P Custis Spinster for Life," when she met Lawrence Lewis, her views on marriage mirrored popularly held expectations. Reporting to Bordley her marriage in 1799, she assured her that she had "not a wish beyond domestic retirement, and complying with every wish of my Husband."[217]

As she raised her daughters at Woodlawn, her plantation three miles from Mount Vernon, she lamented both her flaws as an "instructress" and the limits of what they could accomplish without good teachers, even as she insisted on schooling them at home. When she relented and sent her eldest, Parke, to Madame Rivardi's school in Philadelphia, she begged Bordley to "make Parke play on the Piano . . . & inform me how she performs, also sound her a little on the subject of her French." The attentive mother was fairly satisfied with recent samples of Parke's drawing and painting but wanted Bordley to remind Parke to keep "open her chest, & hold her neck well." In short, Lewis visited the ornamental education she had received as a child upon her daughter, emphasizing the graces of her sex and her social standing to attract a husband. Notwithstanding the developments of the early republican era all around her and her solid contacts with Philadelphia, Lewis remained committed to a hierarchically ordered world in which education was firmly gendered, women gave themselves over to the care of their husbands, and the labor of slaves made possible the genteel life she enjoyed at Woodlawn.[218]

Resisting Reading

It is well to remember Kathryn Shevelow's admonition that even though women were becoming increasingly visible as subjects, readers, and writers in this period, their "access to the mechanisms of print" could signify "restriction and containment" as much as, if not more than, "enfranchisement and inclusion."[219] While many women reading in the slave society of the plantation South exemplify the former, the Coale sisters and their circle show how much more was possible in the unique, in-between space of a society with slaves. But wherever women read—urban Britain, Quaker Philadelphia, expanding Baltimore, or the plantation South—they read in a world dominated (albeit, to varying degrees) by men, although they did not necessarily adopt for their own everything they read. The competing and contradictory views of womanhood—indeed, of humanity itself—in the Revolutionary era made it impossible to distill coherent messages: How could women be both irrational and capable of education? How could women claim spiritual authority and be inferior to men? How could women be called on to ensure the virtue of the republic if they were the weaker sex? How could women be educated to self-sufficiency and remain legal dependents, deprived of the full benefits of citizenship? Yet, as historian Anne Clark Bartlett has suggested in her study of medieval Englishwomen, it is precisely within disparate views of womanhood that the seeds for "resisting reading" lie. True, many women recognized and even aspired to be the women Fordyce's *Sermons* urged them to be. But we have also seen how some southern women reformulated white femininity, for how was it possible to be an effective republican mother or a model of evangelical womanhood if one kept demurely silent? Such questions made possible further questioning of the dominant discourse of patriarchy, creating space for women to "alter drastically the contents of a given work" they had read.[220]

The sites and range of resistance varied widely, of course. In Britain, a group of literate, educated women known as "bluestockings" formed salons, spurred by their belief that the conversation and civil manners of enlightened men and women could transform the world.[221] Here, in a venue of sociability that integrated public and private, men and women could mix freely in private homes, a setting of civility that recognized each sex's claim to the rational enterprise of the commerce of ideas.[222] That is, intellectual conversation with women was cultivated and celebrated as a civilizing influence on men and on society in general.[223] Indeed, noted writer Mary Wortley Montague praised "the frequency of mixed Assemblies" as "a kind of Public Education, which I have always considered as necessary for girls as for boys."[224] Anachronistic barriers of gender thus appeared to give way before refined conversation in this enlightened age.[225] Some women even participated in debating societies, which from the 1770s discussed questions such as "does the clause of obedience in the Marriage ceremony, bind a Wife to obey her Husband at all times?"

Historian Roy Porter counted at least "four dozen sets of rooms in the metropolis [that] were hired out to such societies," despite the dour disapproval of London newspapers.[226]

In Philadelphia, the residual cultural influence of the Quakers encouraged women to more explicit resistance, most notably in their celebration of the single life in verse and prose. Hannah Griffitts was so awed by the example of her aunt Elizabeth Norris that she wrote a long poem in tribute to her life at Fairhill.[227] The poem lays out both the ideal of the Quaker marriage relationship and a critique of its declension in eighteenth-century life in Philadelphia. It praises her aunt Norris's solution (that is, her female retreat) to the dilemma posed by contemporary Quaker practices that fell so far short of the ideal of partnership and ends by suggesting that men's abuse of power would be punished by God Himself on Judgment Day. It skewered notions of divine assignment of sovereignty to men—"That law Divine,-(A Plausible Pretence)," as Susanna Wright called it—that men "rejoyc[ed] to fullfill" and asserted that "No Right, has man, his Equal, to controul, Since, all agree, there is no Sex in soul."[228] In her freedom, however, Norris reigned a "Queen," happily resistant to the seductive flattery that had drawn many a weaker woman into matrimony and all the bonds, legal as well as social, that state entailed. Recognizing that "He only Rules Those, who of choice obey," Norris chose the course recommended decades earlier by seventeenth-century English writer Mary Astell: the single life.[229] Nor were these ideas limited to an elite circle of wealthy Quaker women. Historian Karin A. Wulf has found that "students' surviving school copybooks . . . show that generations of girls educated in Quaker schools were introduced to the unpublished poetry" of writers such as Susanna Wright and Hannah Griffitts. Unlike the manuscripts in seventeenth- and eighteenth-century England, which were privately shared and tended to foster the exclusivity of aristocratic circles by admitting access only to a select few, Philadelphia women's writings were distributed, read, marked, and digested by schoolgirls who had never even met the women who authored their texts.[230]

We have observed at length the ways that the absence of a strong gentry and the fluidity of term slavery in Baltimore made room for liberties of thought, even for adolescent girls. But in the plantation South, the sociability of English and Philadelphia salons was absent (with the exception of the all-male "Tuesday Club" of Annapolis), and the hospitality of southern planters was no substitute. Ornamental in their husbands' extension of hospitality, plantation wives were part of a social and racial hierarchy on display rather than educated participants in the refined conversation of the salons.[231] As historian David Shields explains, "Whereas sociability promoted the free and friendly conversation of persons meeting in public space, hospitality organized social exchange under the auspices of a family in its household. Whatever hierarchy of authority governed the family was reinforced by a hierarchy among host and guests based on property."[232] Libraries, which in the North facilitated women's increasing participation in print culture, were scarce in the South; in its very organization and collection, the best known of these, the Charleston Library Society, secured the cultural and legal dominance of elite men rather than enabling a wider reading public.[233] Nor did religion provide a means to question natural hierarchies, as even evangelical churches retreated from their earlier egalitarian messages. And, of course, by contrast with Baltimore, the "term" of slavery on the plantations was life, and theories of race and slavery became ever more definitive rather than fluid in the antebellum South. Nevertheless, even in the South, where resistance to patriarchy was problematic on many different levels, we have seen women, hitherto unsung and unpublished, reject notions of female inferiority, spiritual and intellectual.[234]

Ultimately, however, their resistance was circumscribed by the cultural context of the slave society in which they read and the rigid boundaries of race and gender to which they subscribed. Even in the antebellum period, when southern women were publishing advice books and novels and assuming the duties of evangelical motherhood to their families (white and black), they lived in what historian Joan Cashin has called a "culture of resignation." Unlike fourteen-year-old Mary Coale's spirited defense of her sex to an older man, antebellum women rarely confronted inequities.[235] So powerful was their commitment to this model of southern womanhood they had helped forge that even the financial failures and professional disappointments of the post-Revolutionary generation of men failed to dislodge it.[236]

The early national period offered a brief opportunity for redefining liberty, equality, and identity, as Americans struggled to figure out what a commitment to the principles of liberty and equality meant in practice. But in spite of Thomas Jefferson's ringing phrase in the Declaration of Independence that "all men are created equal," southern women never made the mistake of assuming his conflation of freedom and equality for themselves. They could understand, perhaps better than most, the difference between the two. Even as Americans were engaging Jefferson's fundamental premise of human equality, "historically new forms of inequality" spurred by an emerging capitalist system arose at the same time.[237] Neither producers of wealth like men nor property like slaves, southern women negotiated their position in this system by creating their own model of femininity. They could participate in the commerce of ideas and produce their own advice. But, as Catherine Allgor quipped, they remained "astute enough to appear politically null," offering no challenge to gender conventions.[238] And in their exercise of reason over passion, they protected their racial boundaries.

In her industrious intellectual pursuits, Ellen Randolph Coolidge was a perfect example of elite southern femininity in full flower by the 1820s. She was a product of the culture of learning her mother and grandfather had created in the household at Monticello. In many ways, it looked like an Enlightenment model with its emphasis on learning and the cultivation of a rational, disciplined self. Offered to both sons and daughters, this regimen could have threatened to break through gender conventions (all the more significant when one considers increasingly elaborate defenses of slavery based on the infinitely older paradigm of "natural" gender relations). That it did not is due in no small part to southern women themselves. In the different meanings they crafted of female self-discipline, learning, and industry, southern women of the early republic gave a distinctively southern cast to the Enlightenment and post-Revolutionary conversations about women, reason, and self-government. No mere submissive receptacles for the traditional lessons of Anglo-Atlantic print culture, southern women were actors in the cultivation of a regional identity from which, in alliance with their powerful colonizers, they hoped to profit.

Conclusion

The Enduring Problem of Female Authorship and Authority

We should not be surprised that, after surveying the intellectual landscape of the eighteenth-century South, historians concluded that women were absent from it. William J. Scheick ruefully admitted the frustration of his fruitless search for "pre-Revolutionary southern women authors," explaining this dearth of evidence as the result of the demographic majority of men and of the arduous labor of survival in the seventeenth century that deprived southern women of time and opportunity for reading and writing.[1] This book has tried to insert women into that landscape. But to construct this history, we must think in new ways and look in new places—to prescriptive literature rather than to the classics; to women's letters and diaries rather than to published tracts and weighty learned texts; to women's homes as impromptu classrooms rather than to the College of William and Mary or Grey's Inn, London (where so many gentry sons read law); to their kin and friends rather than to schoolmates. We must begin to think what "a literary history [would] look like that tried to make familiar letters the textual web out of which significance is woven."[2]

"Rare it is to see a Female Bard / Or that my Sex in Print have e're appear'd," Mary Wadsworth Brewster lamented in her collection of poems printed in Boston in 1758.[3] Women in the South had particular cause to complain, since southern bookshops were stocked with male-authored advice. That advice altered over the eighteenth century, reflecting changes in English society to which patriarchal structures had adapted. The traditional advice of the Restoration period, in which women's virtue needed protection against the assault of aristocratic rogues, had been augmented at the end of the century by sermons that cajoled women to feminine compliance designed to promote domestic harmony. The English Civil War had offered unprecedented opportunities for the rethinking of gender relations and power within the family and the polity. For the English, the period from one revolution (the Glorious, of 1688) to another (the infamous French, of 1789) encompassed enormous political and social change. The restoration of the English monarchy and its firm commitment to Protestantism ushered in a period of accommodation in which sentiment prevailed over reason for women as they were wooed by patriarchy's softer words. That the seventeenth-century advices of Richard Allestree and Lord Halifax continued to be printed in many editions throughout the social and political changes of the century, however, suggests that all was not proceeding smoothly with that transition. Indeed, women's increasing presence in English public spaces—including print—clearly unnerved many men.

The colonial and early national South may not have had the urban context that gave rise to the public culture of theaters, assemblies, parks, and salons of eighteenth-century London, but it did import English advice literature, which comprised the bulk of what girls read, in educations that were vastly circumscribed. Of course, education was uneven in the colonial period for both boys and girls, but John Trumbull's arch query, "Why should girls be learnd or wise / Books only serve to spoil their eyes" (an opinion about the usefulness of female education that was almost universally shared), explains why it was worse for girls.[4] With such meager intellectual fare, advice literature loomed even larger in importance in a girl's education, for it aimed to refine her understanding of the female nature and its limitations.

These educational disadvantages were compounded by the broader contexts in which southern women lived. In the eighteenth century southern men faced a different set of challenges to the structures they had been trying to create out of the chaotic conditions of the seventeenth century. Within a southern world divided by race as well as gender, meticulous adherence to a strictly delineated hierarchy was even more critical: rebellion by blacks, women, or nonelite men could topple the whole precarious structure. The traditional advice of the Restoration era served male purposes well in the South as it fostered a patriarchal ethic in a society that constantly threatened to refute it. Indeed, the expansion of print throughout the century reinforced the traditional ideas of gender that were available to all ranks of people from tidewater Virginia to the Carolina backcountry.

It was within this context that white women learned what it meant to be female. With advice literature as their texts, they learned of a natural and divine order by which their world and everything in it was arranged. Their books, whether Scripture, devotional materials, or English advice, assumed a definition of humanity as masculine.[5] Subordination to men was a woman's natural state; women degraded themselves when they stepped out of it.[6] No wonder that even eminent New England poet Anne Bradstreet believed that "Men doe best, and Women know it well."[7]

While the canon remained consistent in its insistence on women's essential inferiority, women read and internalized it in different ways. Eliza Lucas accepted her female inferiority, although she criticized Samuel Richardson's formulation of virtue and its rewards. The stalwart Mildred Smith resisted the charms of the Frenchmen in Yorktown, Rachel Warrington succumbed to them, and Betsey Ambler teetered giddily and might have fallen but for her father's attention to her substantial education. Caroline Clitherall reworked her own quiet courtship into the stuff of novels, while Nancy Johns Turner blamed novels' pernicious influence for her disastrous first marriage. The evidence of some women's acceptance of the male articulation of the gender order is clear in self-deprecating letters. Yet there is also evidence enough to show a reformulation of traditional advice and to suggest the strong influence of the new, even within the strictures of a patriarchal slave society. The definitions of female and feminine were still being worked out in the eighteenth century; the fact that those terms were used interchangeably is significant, since the separation of the biology of sex from the construction of gender was only beginning to be suggested, particularly with respect to women's education. Southern women redefined those words for themselves, never forgetting their respectability and virtue but taking notions of the female nature and turning them to their own advantage.

There are distinct limitations, of course, in trying to discern readers' understandings of their books. In a now classic study of reading and readers' *mentalité*, historian Carlo Ginzburg discovered that he could not assume he understood the thinking of sixteenth-century Italian miller Menocchio simply because he read the same books Menocchio had read. For example, reading a book in which the word "predestination" appeared, Ginzburg might have assumed Menocchio subscribed to that doctrine. However, in his trial for heresy, Menocchio testified that he did not even know what the word meant. Indeed, further complicating his project, Ginzburg found a layer of oral tradition in Menocchio's trial testimony that operated as a kind of filter between Menocchio and his books, resulting in what villagers called his "fantastic opinions." Thus while the

miller identified Mary the mother of Christ as a virgin (an orthodox belief) because one of his books told of her lodging as a young girl "with the
other virgins who had been dedicated to God," he nonetheless denied the
doctrines of the Virgin birth and Christ's divinity.[8] As a reader, then,
Menocchio certainly drew information from the orthodox authority represented in the printed word, but he also incorporated it into his own belief system in a way that made sense to his worldview.

Similarly, women in the eighteenth-century South, marginalized from
the dominant discourse, also adapted their ideas to it. It was in the convergence of religious with secular themes that women found their authority to pick up their pens and become producers of their own advice literature. William J. Scheick has pointed out that within early American
culture, in which writing was presumed to be masculine, "colonial women
who approached writing as an activity in itself were probably very self-
conscious in their undertaking."[9] Religion and sentiment were the filters
through which southern women read, allowing them to block out lessons
that could not be reconciled with their experience. Elizabeth Foote Washington's rules of conduct for herself and her infant daughter, for instance, are most significant viewed in this light.

There were some "resisting readers" in the South, although none as formidable as Mary Wollstonecraft and Jane Austen of England.[10] There
were women who wrote against the tide, examining, for instance, the tensions between the dual callings of mother and writer. Most notable is the
poem written by Margaret Page, the New York wife of Virginian John
Page. Circulating her poetry among a group of writers gathered around
St. George Tucker in Williamsburg after the Revolution, Page wrote, "A
Country Wife has much to do; / No moment finds of peaceful leisure[e] /
To ope the Muses sacred treasure / From Books and Poetry, must turn /
to mark the *Labours of the Churn* . . . Ah yes! 'tis true, upon my Life! / No
Muse was ever yet a *Wife*."[11] Judith Lomax, her niece by marriage, responded in kind in verses that acknowledged the rounds of chores of a
wife and mother, but she nonetheless pointed out that Margaret Page had
in fact created the time to write: "Yes,—Madam may her cotton weigh,
/ . . . / May poultry feed, and cream prepare, / . . . This she may do, perhaps still more, / and yet Apollo's power adore. / And that I judge most
truly sage, / Lo! *Proof* behold in—*Mrs. Page.*"[12] Indeed, poetry was a fitting
mode for women's writing, since, unlike an essay or rhetorical address, it
did not require a classical education to construct. As a mode of expression that connected people to one another "in a rule of civility," it could
even be denoted a service, in which women could rightly participate.[13] Yet
both content and extensive classical allusions distinguish the poetry of

both Page and Lomax, the polish of their style perhaps as subversive as the feelings they expressed.

By and large, however, the southern women presented here did not pursue subversive tactics but rather—like the bourgeois Englishwomen studied by Terry Lovell who "negotiated rather than confronted the terms of feminine domesticity" because of their "distinct interest in the maintenance of class privileges and powers"—upheld the social order.[14] They would be neither victims of patriarchy nor marginalized as women-who-would-be-men. Of course, class was crucial in the South, particularly among women, whose dress and behavior conveniently maintained distinctions of rank even as those distinctions were being blurred among white men.[15] But more important than class was a configuration of race that propped up an economic and social structure that served white women as well as white men. There were protections and material comforts, as well as status, to be had for women who adhered to gender conventions. As Sabina Lovibond has asked, "Whoever wants to claim that conventional femininity, even at its most abject, cannot be *pleasurable* for women?"[16] Even inheriting widows of eighteenth-century South Carolina, who had opportunity enough to cultivate autonomy with their newfound freedom and wealth, chose instead to put the interests of a patriarchal family ahead of their own, preserving estates for male heirs.[17] Eliza Lucas Pinckney, who at age sixteen managed her father's plantation in his absence and in her long widowhood launched her sons into public careers, taught her daughter that her highest aim should be pleasing her husband.[18]

Instead, southern women used religion and reading and writing as a way to carve out their niche in the republic, although in different ways than northern women. Certainly this does not diminish their accomplishments, especially when considering the boundaries—social, legal, political, and religious—erected around their experiences. But it does show the importance of cultural contexts. David Shields recently asked whether "one's powerlessness in early American society registered in the restriction of the number of roles one could play? Or was power an obdurate insistence on the primacy of a single identity?"[19] My study leads me to incline toward the latter. White southern women expanded the roles they could play because ultimately their access to all other degrees of power was absolutely limited by the insistence on white male authority and its enforcing legal apparatus. Thus, for example, even though the premise of the necessity of an education for girls was accepted, it did not flower into a human rights argument (as it would in the thought of Judith Sargent Murray and later antebellum women like the Grimké sisters and Elizabeth

Cady Stanton) but was itself put to the service of a social organization that was repressive to so many.

Nor was this repression a rural phenomenon; it was present in southern cities as well. Martha Laurens Ramsay lived in Charleston, the daughter of a prominent slaver and one-time president of the Continental Congress; her uncle James Laurens imported religious books;[20] her husband was in the center of an active intellectual elite in the city. Yet even the experience of a city-bred woman, with access to a library of books and a husband with keen intellectual pursuits, cannot be compared with the experience of northern women, so isolated was Martha from that intellectual milieu. Excluded from the Enlightenment project of forming a community of thought of which her husband was a part, she did not form a salon or gather an intellectual elite around her but rather focused inward, developing her spiritual life.[21] Even when the South developed schools for young girls in the nineteenth century, they advertised how different they were from northern ones; they meant to attach their pupils to "home, its duties and association," unlike northern schools, which encouraged women to roam abroad.[22] The cultural context of a slave society could even overwhelm prior training from educations received elsewhere. Alice Delancey Izard and Margaret Lowther Page, educated in New York, and Caroline Burgwin Clitherall and Eliza Lucas, educated in England, nonetheless adapted remarkably to slavery upon their move (or return) to the South, despite having spent most or all of their childhoods elsewhere.

The scarcity of southern women's writings relative to men's before the end of the century demonstrates the results of the imbalance in educational opportunity. Marginalized in their education and living in a slave society that depended on the dominance of white male authority, southern women were "colonized" by instruction emphasizing their inferiority. While not overtly challenging ideas of female subordination to men, southern women nonetheless began to build a sense of the legitimacy of their claims to moral authority, founded on religion and their novels. Of course, this development took more than a century. As Robert Shoemaker has pointed out, "gender roles often change very slowly, one often needs to look at such long and turbulent periods of time to detect significant changes."[23] What prompted change in the lives of eighteenth-century southern women was less the Revolution as a defining event than broader developments spaced over time, such as evangelical Christianity (even for Anglican women) and the increased production and accessibility of print.

We should not be impatient that the process was so slow in the South. Century after century, women have laboriously worked their way to the same insights about the culturally constructed inferiority of women: Christine de Pizan's *The Book of the City of Ladies* in 1405; Mary Astell in England in the 1690s; Mary Wollstonecraft a century later; American Elizabeth Cady Stanton's "Declaration of Sentiments" in 1848; Betty Friedan's identification of the "problem that has no name" in *The Feminine Mystique* in 1963; Vivian Gornick's 1990 description of the exhilaration of feminism's second wave in the 1970s.[24] Denied education, women lacked voice and authority; denied their history, they repeated the painful process in isolation. They have expended much intellectual energy in recognizing how educational deprivation explained women's "inferiority" and in pleading for and justifying women's access to education.[25]

Indeed, women still feel the effects of this educational disadvantaging today. "What does a woman need to know?" feminist Adrienne Rich once asked.[26] The answer, it turned out, could not have been more fundamental: interviews conducted by the four authors of *Women's Ways of Knowing* convinced them "that every woman, regardless of age, social class, ethnicity, and academic achievement, needs to know that she is capable of intelligent thought, and she needs to know it right away."[27] What is so striking about these findings is that they appeared in 1986, a full twenty momentous years after the renewal of the women's movement in the 1960s, an epoch one historian described as a time when the "world split open."[28] Yet women still had not learned that they were intellectually capable.

"The educational deprivation of women," Gerda Lerner pointed out, was one form of "male hegemony over the [cultural] symbol system."[29] For many feminists since Mary Wollstonecraft, the battle for female access to the same kind of educational opportunities open to men seemed to be the way to achieve equality of the sexes. Even so, some theorists questioned whether, in fact, such a goal was even desirable. "This access to a male dominated culture may equally be felt to bring with it alienation, repression, division," Mary Jacobus believes, "a silencing of the 'feminine,' a loss of women's inheritance."[30] Historically, secondary and postsecondary schools had been created for male students. Thus the intellectual canon has been the predominantly male-produced literature, history, art, music, and scholarship of Western civilization.[31] As women clamored for admission to this intellectual system, they had to learn how to learn in this environment: how to think critically and to demolish an opponent's argument, skills that have become the benchmark of a quality education.

Should women try to counter male dominance of culture by generating a literature of their own? When pondering the desirability of that alternative, Elaine Showalter warned that "the theory of a female sensibility revealing itself in an imagery and form specific to women always runs dangerously close to reiterating the familiar stereotypes. It also suggests permanence, a deep, basic, and inevitable difference between male and female ways of perceiving the world." Instead, she argues, the female literary tradition comes from "the still-evolving relationships between women writers and their society."[32] This is not to argue that women should follow the centuries-old teachings that drew on culture, science, and religion to prove their biologically determined inferior intellectual capabilities. Twentieth-century studies have shown that women have different ways of knowing and learning and writing than do men. As Cheri Register concluded, "Feminists do not deny that women exhibit group characteristics. However, they do not accept the thesis that similarities in female behavior are biologically determined."[33]

Significant work has been done on how men and women grow, mature, and learn. In a classic study, Michelle Rosaldo showed how boys, taught to differentiate themselves from their mothers, grow away from them, learning how to be separate. Girls, on the other hand, continue to identify and develop deep attachments with the figure who raised them; indeed, they measure their value, their identity, and their success in life in terms of their relationships. When girls are socialized in this way, it is hardly surprising to discover that there are male and female ways of learning within academic structures; but it is essential to note that they are *learned* ways of knowing. Still, when girls approach secondary and college campuses, they must adjust (if not totally abandon) their way of learning for a different one. To use Elaine Showalter's example, "a woman studying English literature is also studying a different culture, to which she must bring the adaptability of the anthropologist."[34]

These considerations about gendered ways of learning are very recent, of course; until the 1970s psychologists categorized gender-related behaviors, leading one to draw inferences from a subject's behavior about his or her relative masculinity or femininity. An assertive woman, for example, was thought to have adopted a "masculine" trait that demonstrated her rejection of her female role. Psychological testing instruments based on these "masculine" and "feminine" traits presumed a continuum, in which men would cluster at one end and women at the other.[35] Even though psychologists rejected as nonsensical nineteenth-century warnings that too much study could cause physical trauma to women's reproductive systems, they continued to argue that men and women differed in temperamental qualities.[36]

The intellectual community of the late twentieth century has only begun to struggle with these issues, to wrest cultural constructs from biological determinism, to question assumptions about gender roles that have prevailed for millennia, even to find the language that will enable us to break out of patriarchal systems of thought. The changes wrought in the last three decades have been significant, yet as British literary historian Janet Todd commented, "The arrival of a few women in academic high places has no more transformed the establishment of culture—not to mention the material condition of women's lives—than the arrival of the odd prime minister in Number 10 has transformed the social establishment."[37] In the United States, where approximately 70 percent of women between the ages of fifteen and sixty-four are in the workforce,[38] and the relative pay scale (seventy-six cents for every (white) female hour worked to one dollar for every male hour) is more favorable than it has ever been; and where (in the last Congress of the twentieth century) there were nine women in the Senate and fifty-six in the House of Representatives, traditional gender views remain resilient.[39] Even as the number of doctoral degrees earned by women is estimated to almost equal the number that will be earned by men by 2005, female academics are still viewed as nurturers: students use phrases like "nice lady" to evaluate female faculty, while no comparable categories exist for male faculty. Female authority is still an oxymoronic concept in a variety of areas: witness religious groups who continue to resist female ordination or the gendered division of labor that still obtains in American homes, where women do 80 percent of household tasks.[40]

Thus we come full circle back to the question of how women are best served in their struggle to realize their own authority and voice: by claiming the rights of men or by constructing an alternative model? The example of William Byrd II shows how men based their assertions of power and authority in their literacy and education. And while education was widely touted as foundational to financial success in the industrialized period of the nineteenth century, how closely connected the two were in fact was a complicated question. Indeed, one scholar has described the idea that literacy would translate into economic gain and status as a "myth."[41] In their fight for access to such bastions of male power, perhaps women, too, sought the economic gain and status literacy might confer, although the inequalities of gendered work and pay make clear that those hopes have not yet been entirely realized. The experiences of women in this book teach us that as diverse as the American experience has been, it has been unable to reject entirely the gender attitudes and practices of centuries.

Less clear, but no less true, is that men continue to reap benefits from the Enlightenment into the twenty-first century, particularly in terms of how reason and emotion, male and female, continue to be defined and understood. Here, too, the hopes of post-Revolutionary women were also disappointed. Though its economic potential for women like Judith Sargent Murray was significant, literacy also had the potential to reconfigure women's nature as rational and thus capable of political participation. Constitutionally defined out of the polity,[42] however, southern women found in their religion and their reading an authority born of sentiment that was uniquely theirs and empowered them to pick up their pens to write and teach. Yet more than two hundred years later, women's writings still do not carry the same authoritative weight as men's writing. The same essay will receive positive or negative reviews, respectively, depending on the readers' perspective of male or female authorship; an authoritative account of the rise of the novel failed to include an account of women's participation in that development; and feminist literary criticism is marginalized as deviant and unintelligible to men, even as female writers fail to find a fair hearing in mainstream literary circles.[43] This lopsided scale obtains even in conversations between men and women. As Dale Spender reported, "Again and again I have asked people to rate transcripts [of conversations between men and women] and the very same speech can be rated as positive or negative, depending on the presumed sex of the speaker. When I have indicated, for example, that a lengthy expression of opinion is the pronouncement of a man, it has invariably been rated as impressive, thoughtful, informative, and useful; the same speech, when attributed to a woman has been dismissed as rambling, irrational, tedious, and (once)—'a waste of words.' "[44]

So while we may consider ourselves light years removed from the prevailing ideas about writing women in the eighteenth century, connections between that time and ours are real, rendering this study all the more pressing. The telling of this story pushes back the parameters of southern women's intellectual history but does not presume to have the last word, just a suggestive first.[45] Searching for fragments of southern women's writing in the eighteenth century, I have followed an approach similar to Jacqueline Jones Royster's in her study of nineteenth-century African American women, and "[kept] the eyes and the mind open for the imaginable, that is, for opportunities to make connections and draw out likely possibilities."[46] By looking beyond the traditional male experience of schoolrooms, classical texts, and authorial voices in the press, to female venues—advice manuals, scribal publication, letters, commonplace books, and journals—it is possible to recover for women another piece of their intellectual history.

Postscript

Iam a late bloomer. It was not until I returned to school after a sixteen-year hiatus that I discovered the new social history, colonial Virginia, and women's history. My utter delight in all three combined to direct my research interests to eighteenth-century southern women. A seminar in the history of the book, the influence of Cathy Davidson's *Revolution and the Word: The Rise of the Novel in America,* and the absorbing letters of two Yorktown girls began to narrow that focus further still. Then a friend suggested I apply the analytical approach of my work on those letters to a larger study: a book-length intellectual history of early southern women. Yet, late bloomer that I am, it was not until I was well into the final stages that I fully realized why this project has been so compelling for me: as was true of the women in this book, discovering that I had something to say and then taking up the pen to say it has been the project of a lifetime. In seeking to understand women who lived and died two centuries ago, I have learned why my own journey was long and arduous.

Yet my subjects would envy the access American women today have to books, pen, and print. Women's literacy rates in the colonial South (measured in terms of the ability to sign one's name) always lagged substantially behind men's, although more women could read than write. In a time when reading and writing were not taught in tandem as they are now, writing was understood to be a necessity for males, who were expected to go into trade and support families. Generally, however, it was thought that informal transmissions of housewifery skills and just enough rudimentary reading ability to read the Bible were all women needed to know. Gendering education in this way reinforced a hierarchy of being in which women were taught that their subordinate status was instituted by divine and natural law and that because of their nature, they were best suited to domestic duties. Neither the intellectual nor the physical equal of men, women simply did not require more.

These ideas of female inferiority are ancient and continue to retain currency even today. Aristotle, one of the great philosophers of Western thought, regarded women as imperfect or incomplete men. The noted twentieth-century theorist Jacques Lacan described woman as "an empty set."[1] Clearly there is little point in teaching "an empty set" to write, since by definition she would have nothing to say. Thus writing, as a masculine privilege, was much more than vocational skill; it was the ultimate signifier of authority, and the deprivation of that ability for women (or the poor or slaves) was willful and calculated to incapacitate. The predictable consequence of this way of thinking has been the educational disadvantaging of women, one of innumerable aspects of human existence that gender has prescribed.

Another consequence has been the difficulty women have had to claim the right to read and write. As Carol J. Singley has observed, "Text after text in western culture claims that women, lacking adequate selfhood, can neither read nor write; women who do so, then, must confront female textuality on male grounds." Thus women today who enter secondary and postsecondary schools, which were created originally for male students to teach a predominantly male intellectual canon, must learn how to learn in this environment: how to think critically and to excel in argumentative debate. For a woman, then, to read and write intelligibly in this world in which the very language she must use perpetuates her subordination (as for example, the use of the word "man" instead of "humanity," effectively erasing the female experience), she has had to "internalize male desire and imagine herself as men imagine her."[2] That is, women have to learn to think like men as they read in this canon, to identify with the masculine, which is portrayed as universal and normative, and to see themselves as the observed deviant from that norm—ironically, an intellectual maneuver of such incredible complexity that it would evoke admiration in any other context were it not so costly to female identity.

If reading presented a conundrum for women, writing was an even bigger challenge. Just picking up the pen assumed an authority understood to be masculine. In the early modern period, women were admonished to modesty in all their behavior: in the way they dressed, looked, walked, and talked. Critics of writing women excoriated their lack of modesty, accusing them of exposing themselves as wantonly as any prostitute. Since female reputations were made or broken on the imputation of chastity, female writers risked everything by placing their words before a lecherous and hostile world. Rejecting their sex by the very act of writing, female authors abandoned the protections afforded by respectable men and rendered themselves vulnerable to all manner of assaults.

Women today still struggle to claim voice and authority. Despite the stereotype of women as the talkative sex, those who strive for equal time in conversations with men will find themselves characterized as aggressive and domineering (and worse), even if they command only a third of the conversation. An essay will receive admiring commentary or scathing critique, depending on the readers' perception of the sex of the author.[3] In my own profession, the ancient bias against female authority is reflected in women's standings in American universities: in 1998, women still had not reached parity with men in earning doctoral degrees; they comprised only one-third of full-time faculty and 16 percent of university presidents;[4] and they are paid less, at all levels, than their male colleagues.[5]

Against such a backdrop, my own experience became much more comprehensible. In company with my long-dead subjects, I read the books they did, reflected with them on the teachings of Scripture and science, and marveled at the wit, creativity, and courage they nonetheless summoned to pick up their pens and write. I am grateful for all they have taught me.

Abbreviations

CWF Special Collections, John D. Rockefeller, Jr. Library, Colonial Williamsburg Foundation
CWM Manuscripts and Rare Books Department, Earl Gregg Swem Library, The College of William and Mary
LVA State Library of Virginia
MHS H. Furlong Baldwin Library, Maryland Historical Society
MSA Maryland State Archives
SHC Southern Historical Collection, Wilson Library, University of North Carolina at Chapel Hill
UVA Albert and Shirley Small Special Collections, University of Virginia
VHS Virginia Historical Society
WMQ *William and Mary Quarterly*

All quotations from manuscript and published primary sources preserve the original spelling and punctuation.

Notes

1. Toward an Intellectual History of Early Southern Women

1. Louis B. Wright and Marion Tinling, eds., *The Secret Diary of William Byrd of Westover 1709–1712* (Richmond, Va.: Dietz Press, 1941), December 30, 1711, 461–62. On the Dunns, see 82–83n2.

2. Joseph Swan to Lady Jean Skipwith, 1819, box IX, folder 75, Skipwith Family Papers, CWM.

3. Mildred K. Abraham, "The Library of Lady Jean Skipwith: A Book Collection from the Age of Jefferson," *Virginia Magazine of History and Biography* 91 (1983): 303, 296.

4. Rhys Isaac, "Books and the Social Authority of Learning: The Case of Mid-Eighteenth-Century Virginia," in *Printing and Society in Early America*, ed. William Joyce, David D. Hall, Richard D. Brown, and John B. Hench (Worcester, Mass.: American Antiquarian Society, 1983), 228–49.

5. Wright and Tinling, *Secret Diary*, July 12, 1710, 203; Kevin Hayes, *The Library of William Byrd of Westover* (Madison, Wis.: Madison House, 1997), 38.

6. Louis Wright, *The First Gentlemen of Virginia: Intellectual Qualities of the Early Colonial Ruling Class* (San Marino, Calif.: Huntington Library, 1940), 123. On Byrd's library, see Hayes, *Library of William Byrd*, 38. Wright argues strongly for the status Byrd derived from his library collection, while Richard Beale Davis emphasizes Byrd's use of his books. Richard Beale Davis, *Intellectual Life in the Colonial South 1585–1763* (Knoxville: University of Tennessee Press, 1978), 2:556. Of course, these viewpoints are not mutually exclusive; both the appearance of and the learning derived from the books upheld Byrd's claims to authority.

7. William Byrd to Charles, Earl of Orrey, July 5, 1726, quoted in Rhys Isaac, *The Transformation of Virginia 1740–1790* (1982; repr., Chapel Hill: University of North Carolina Press, 1999), 40–41.

8. Jean Skipwith's papers contain several bills from book binders. See, for example, box I, folder 58, 1781, and box IX, folder 54, 1817, Skipwith Family Papers, CWM.

9. Abraham, "Library of Lady Jean Skipwith," 305.

10. While historians have advanced significant correctives to that view in the past thirty years, they have focused almost entirely on male literary culture. For example, Davis, *Intellectual Life in the Colonial South*; Jay Fleigelman, *Prodigals and Pilgrims: The American Revolution against Patriarchy* (Cambridge: Cambridge University Press, 1982); David D. Hall, *Cultures of Print: Essays in the History of the Book* (Amherst: University of Massachusetts Press, 1996).

11. James Raven, *London Booksellers and American Customers: Transatlantic Literary Community and the Charleston Library Society, 1748–1811* (Columbia: University of South Carolina Press, 2002), 17.

12. Both presses were set up by the enterprising William Parks. Calhoun Winton, "The Southern Book Trade in the Eighteenth Century," in *A History of the Book in America: The Colonial Book in the Atlantic World*, ed. Hugh Amory and David D. Hall (New York: Cambridge University Press, 2000), 1:226, 228. For Governor Berkeley's quote, see William Waller Hening, *The Statutes at Large; Being a Collection of all the Laws of Virginia*, 2d ed. (New York, 1819–1823), 2:517.

13. Indeed, historians had often portrayed Virginia as devoid of intellectual life because of its lack of a press. While conceding Virginians' contributions to law and politics, and perhaps agriculture, Henry Adams denied them any other intellectual creativity. Richard Beale Davis, *Literature and Society in Early Virginia, 1608–1840* (Baton Rouge: Louisiana State University Press, 1973), xiii. In 1939 Perry Miller described Puritanism as "the most coherent and most powerful single factor in the early history of America"; in the 1954 reprinting of his book *The New England Mind*, he declared that the intervening fourteen years had "confirmed my youthful insight." Perry Miller, *The New England Mind: The Seventeenth Century* (Cambridge, Mass.: Harvard University Press, 1954), viii, xii. For a general corrective to the New England model see Jack Greene, *Pursuits of Happiness: The Social Development of Early Modern British Colonies and the Formation of American Culture* (Chapel Hill: University of North Carolina Press, 1988).

14. Philip Alexander Bruce, *Institutional History of Virginia in the Seventeenth Century* (New York: G. P. Putnam's Sons, 1910), 1, pt. 2, 293–459; Bruce, *Virginia: Rebirth of the Old Dominion* (Chicago: Lewis Publishing, 1929); Julia Cherry Spruill, *Women's Life and Work in the Southern Colonies* (1938; repr., New York: W. W. Norton, 1972), 208–31; and Wright, *First Gentlemen of Virginia*; Louis B. Wright and Marion Tinling, eds., *The London Diary of William Byrd, 1717–1721* (New York: Oxford University Press, 1958); Wright and Tinling, *Secret Diary of William Byrd*; Wright, ed., *Letters of Robert Carter, 1720–1727: The Commercial Interests of a Virginia Gentleman* (San Marino, Calif.: Huntington Library, 1940).

15. See, for example, Amory and Hall, *History of the Book in America*; Richard D. Brown, *Knowledge Is Power: The Diffusion of Information in Early America, 1700–1865* (New York: Oxford University Press, 1989), 42–64; and Kevin J. Hayes, *A Colonial Woman's Bookshelf* (Knoxville: University of Tennessee Press, 1996); Kenneth Lockridge, *Literacy in Colonial New England: An Inquiry into the Social Context of Literacy in the Early Modern World* (New York: W. W. Norton, 1974).

16. Cathy Davidson, *Revolution and the Word: The Rise of the Novel in America* (New York: Oxford University Press, 1986); Linda Kerber, *Women of the Republic: Intellect and Ideology in Revolutionary America* (New York: W. W. Norton, 1980); Mary Beth Norton, *Liberty's Daughters: The Revolutionary Experience of American Women, 1750–1800* (New York: Harper Collins, 1980); Spruill, *Women's Life and Work in the Southern Colonies*; Cynthia Kierner, *Beyond the Household: Women's Place in the Early South, 1700–1835* (Ithaca: Cornell University Press, 1997).

17. Christie Anne Farnham, *The Education of the Southern Belle: Higher Education and Student Socialization in the Antebellum South* (New York: New York University Press, 1994); Michael O'Brien, ed., *An Evening When Alone: Four Journals of Single Women in the South, 1827–67* (Charlottesville: University Press of Virginia, 1993).

18. John Alden, *The First South* (Baton Rouge: Louisiana State University Press, 1961), 3–32; Thad Tate, "Defining the Colonial South," in *Race and Family in the Colonial South*, ed. Winthrop D. Jordan and Sheila L. Skemp (Jackson: University Press of Mississippi, 1987), 3–20.

19. A classic example is the diary of a New Jersey Presbyterian hired as a tutor in a Virginia Anglican plantation home. Hunter Dickinson Farish, ed., *Journal and Letters of Philip Vickers Fithian 1773–1774: A Plantation Tutor of the Old Dominion* (Charlottesville: University Press of Virginia, 1993).

20. Catherine Kerrison, "By the Book: Eliza Ambler Brent Carrington and Conduct Literature in Late Eighteenth-Century Virginia," *Virginia Magazine of History and Biography* 105, no. 1 (1997): 27–52.

21. Miller, *New England Mind*, viii, xii.

22. Bruce, *Institutional History of Virginia*, 1:440–41.

23. Richard Allestree, *The Whole Duty of Man Laid Down in a Plain and Familiar Way for the Use of all but Especially the Meanest Reader with Private Devotions for Several Occasions* (London, 1657).

24. For Virginia, see Hall, *Cultures of Print*, 121. For Maryland, see Joseph Towne Wheeler, "Books Owned by Marylanders, 1700–1776," *Maryland Historical Magazine* 35 (1940): 338–43.

25. Wright, *First Gentlemen of Virginia*, 239–41, 149.

26. William Byrd is the classic example of this trend. On this point, see also Isaac, *Transformation of Virginia*; Richard L. Bushman, *The Refinement of America: Persons, Houses, Cities* (New York: Vintage Books, 1993); T. H. Breen, "Creative Adaptations: Peoples and Cultures," in *Colonial British America: Essays in the New History of the Early Modern Era*, ed. Jack P. Greene and J. R. Pole (Baltimore: Johns Hopkins University Press, 1984), 221; Cary Carson, Ronald Hoffman, and Peter J. Albert, *Of Consuming Interests: The Style of Life in the Eighteenth Century* (Charlottesville: University Press of Virginia, 1994).

27. James Raven, "The Importation of Books in the Eighteenth Century," in Amory and Hall, *History of the Book in America*, 1:186. Raven reports these findings in the context of a comparison with imports to New England. Between 1701 and 1780, 23 percent of English book exports to North America and the Caribbean went to New England, and 19 percent to Virginia and Maryland, combined. The balance of trade shifted, however, by the latter part of the century, so that while imports to New England declined between 1769 and 1770, imports to Virginia and Maryland increased "markedly" in the years 1768–71 (185–86). The volume of book exports was measured in hundredweights (112 pounds), not actual numbers of books. Books were valued at a standard median rate of £4 per hundredweight (cwt) (184).

28. Winton, "The Southern Book Trades," in Amory and Hall, *History of the Book in America*, 1:232.

29. Quoted in William David Sloan and Julie Hedgepeth Williams, *The Early American Press* (Westport, Conn.: Greenwood Press, 1994), 99.

30. Robert Manson Meyers, "The Old Dominion Looks to London," *The Virginia Magazine of History and Biography* 54 (1946): 195; Gregory A. Stiverson and Cynthia Z. Stiverson, "Books Both Useful and Entertaining: A Study of Book Purchases and Reading Habits of Virginians in the Mid-Eighteenth Century," research report no. 25, (unpublished report of the Colonial Williamsburg Foundation, 1977). Colonial book-

sellers also found that false English imprints could sell local publications. Stephen Botein, "The Anglo-American Book Trade before 1776," in Joyce et al., *Printing and Society in Early America*, 79.

31. Quoted in Lawrence C. Wroth, *The Colonial Printer* (1931; repr., Charlottesville: University Press of Virginia, 1964), 236.

32. David Rawson, "'Guardians of their own Liberty:' A Contextual History of Print Culture in Virginia Society" (Ph.D. diss., College of William and Mary, 1998), 147. Alexander Purdie joined with John Dixon in a partnership that lasted until 1775, when Purdie went solo and Dixon partnered with William Hunter Jr. In the meantime, William Rind began a third paper (at the behest of Thomas Jefferson to print the protesting resolutions of the House of Burgesses against the Stamp Act) and published it from 1766 until his death in 1773. His widow, Clementina, printed the paper for a year until her death. Robert Weir, "Newspaper Press in the Southern Colonies" in *The Press and the American Revolution*, ed. Bernard Bailyn and John B. Hench (Boston: Northeastern University Press, 1981), 109.

33. *Virginia Gazette*, January 28, 1737, 4.

34. Rawson, "Guardians of their Liberty," 148.

35. Brown, *Knowledge Is Power*, 46–47, 255–56, 350.

36. Meyers, "Old Dominion Looks to London," 197.

37. *Virginia Gazette*, December 10, 1736, 2.

38. Meyers, "Old Dominion Looks to London," 200–207. Meyers refers to Alexander Pope as "an arbiter of literary taste" in Virginia.

39. The *Virginia Gazette* advertised available titles, and two account books from the tenures of William Hunter (1750–52) and Joseph Royle (1764–66) list both titles and prices and, in many instances, the purchasers. Stiverson and Stiverson, "Books Both Useful and Entertaining"; and Cynthia Z. Stiverson and Gregory A. Stiverson, "The Colonial Retail Book Trade: Availability and Affordability of Reading Material in Mid-Eighteenth-Century Virginia," in Joyce et al., *Printing and Society in Early America*, 132–73. Other studies confirm the Stiversons' conclusions: John Edgar Molnar, "Publication and Retail Book Advertisements in *The Virginia Gazette*, 1736–1780" (Ph.D. diss., University of Michigan, 1978). While the Stiversons focused only on elite purchasers (those who had bought more than four books), David Rawson's study counted *all* purchasers recorded in the daybooks but reached essentially the same conclusions. This trend, Rawson argued, persisted through the early national period. Rawson, "Guardians of Their Liberty," 501–2.

40. Stiverson and Stiverson, "Books Both Useful and Entertaining," 21. Indeed, the customer base at the print shop, which doubled as a post office, trebled over the era recorded in the office's daybooks. In such ways did the Williamsburg printing office link Virginians with one another, the other colonies, and England. Rawson, "Guardians of their Liberty," 148.

41. John Gemit, employed by William Hunter, bought twenty-four books from him on June 3, 1751. Of the twenty-four books, eighteen were religious titles (including six catechisms). None of the books cost more than two shillings. Rawson, "Guardians of Their Liberty," 148. A middling-class annual income was approximately £40, so 2-shilling books were affordable. Almanacs cost 7 pence, equivalent to one dollar today.

42. "Books in Colonial Virginia," *Virginia Magazine of History and Biography* 7 (1900): 299–303.

43. Inventory, John Broster [1706]; Inventory, Thomas Gibbins, November 29, 1707; Inventory, Armiger Wade, March 3, 1709, York County Deeds, Orders, and Wills, 1706–1710, M-1.6, M-1.8–9, CWF. York County's boundaries overlapped the city of Williamsburg in the colonial period and therefore would be a place in which, be-

cause of its accessibility to the Atlantic trade and the city print shop, one might expect to find considerable and enumerated book holdings. However, from the beginning of the eighteenth century to the end, the predominant citation is "one parcell of old books." See also "Books in Colonial Virginia," *Virginia Historical Magazine* 10 (1902–3): 389–405, for listings of books drawn from inventories of many counties scattered across the colony.

44. Inventory, Henry Tyler, January 17, 1729/30, York County Deeds, Orders, and Wills, 1729–1732, M-1.6, M-1.8–9, CWF.

45. Jon Butler, "Thomas Teackle's 333 Books: A Great Library on Virginia's Eastern Shore, 1697," *WMQ*, 3d ser., 49 (1992): 462. Divided into four lots and assigned numbers (the fourth being medical books that the executors apparently hoped to sell), the books were bequeathed to Teackle's son John (numbers 1–89) and daughters Elizabeth (90–178) and Catherine (179–282).

46. "Inventory of Ralph Wormeley II," *WMQ*, 1st ser., 2 (1893–94): 169–175. By the time of his death in 1777, William Byrd III had expanded the library to four thousand volumes, which were housed in twenty-three "double presses of black walnut." *Virginia Gazette*, Dixon, December 19, 1777, 2.

47. Will, Edward Moseley, in *North Carolina Wills and Inventories Copied from Original and Recorded Wills and Inventories in the Office of the Secretary of State*, ed. J. Bryan Grimes (1912; repr., Baltimore: Genealogical Publishing, 1967), 317.

48. Farish, *Journal & Letters of Philip Vickers Fithian,* July 11, 1774, 119; letter to Rev. Enoch Green, December 1, 1773, 26.

49. *Virginia Gazette,* Purdie & Dixon, August 29, 1771, 3. An earlier ad requesting the return of books appeared in *Virginia Gazette,* Rind, December 15, 1768, 2.

50. David Hackett Fischer, *Albion's Seed: Four British Folkways in America* (New York: Oxford University Press, 1989), 92.

51. On the development of North Carolina see Harry R. Merrens, *Colonial North Carolina in the Eighteenth Century: A Study in Historical Geography* (Chapel Hill: University of North Carolina Press, 1964); Hugh T. Lefler and William S. Powell, *Colonial North Carolina: A History* (New York: Scribner, 1973); Roger Ekirch, *"Poor Carolina": Politics and Society in Colonial North Carolina, 1729–1776* (Chapel Hill: University of North Carolina Press, 1981).

52. Wroth, *Colonial Printer,* 48.

53. Inventory, John Luttrell, 1782, Orange County Inventories Sales and Accounts of Estates, 1758–1809, in Grimes, *North Carolina Wills and Inventories,* 368–69. Luttrell's wife, Susanna, compiled the inventory in 1782. That she recorded the books by their short titles indicates a degree of familiarity with them that was remarkable for a woman in the North Carolina backcountry; certainly her handwriting bespeaks a good education.

54. Davis, *Intellectual Life in the Colonial South,* 567. Davis incorrectly refers to Milner as John instead of James.

55. Inventory, James Milner, December 17, 1773, in Grimes, *North Carolina Wills and Inventories,* 514–22. I am indebted to James P. Whittenburg and Sheila Phipps for providing copies of the Luttrell and Milner inventories.

56. See, for example, David D. Hall, *Worlds of Wonder, Days of Judgment: Popular Religious Belief in Early New England* (Cambridge: Harvard University Press, 1989) and Carson, Hoffman, and Albert, *Of Consuming Interests,* on the closing of the gap between elite and popular culture. On the European side, see Carlo Ginzburg, *The Cheese and the Worms: The Cosmos of a Sixteenth-Century Miller,* trans. John and Anne Tedeschi (1980; repr., New York: Penguin Books, 1982). Eamon Duffy shows the ways in which English Catholics actively participated in the pre-Reformation Church's rich theology, as man-

ifested in liturgical and seasonal rituals, without benefit of reading skills. Eamon Duffy, *The Stripping of the Altars: Traditional Religion in England 1400–1580* (New Haven: Yale University Press, 1992).

57. Lockridge, *Literacy in Colonial New England,* 72–101. Lockridge's figures for female literacy have been challenged in more recent studies, however. See Jennifer Monaghan, "Literacy Instruction and Gender in Colonial New England," *American Quarterly* 40 (1988): 18–41, and Linda Auwers, "Reading the Marks of the Past: Exploring Female Literacy in Colonial Windsor, CT," *Historical Methods* 13 (1980): 204–14, who argues for 90 percent signature literacy level among women born in the 1740s.

58. Isaac, "Books and the Social Authority of Learning," 230.

59. See ibid. for an extension of this point in his analysis of the Virginia court system, which was presided over by the gentry, whose authority was legitimated by their learning.

60. Frederick Douglass, *Narrative of the Life of Frederick Douglass, An American Slave,* ed. David W. Blight (Boston: Bedford Books, 1993), 57.

61. Gerald W. Mullin, *Flight and Rebellion: Slave Resistance in Eighteenth-Century Virginia* (London: Oxford University Press, 1972), 76, 80–81, 93–94, 114, 121.

62. Alan Watson, *Slave Law in the Americas* (Athens: University of Georgia Press, 1989), 71. In 1739, between fifty and one hundred (estimates varied) slaves launched a violent uprising twenty miles from Charles Town, South Carolina, killing twenty-five whites. Although quickly suppressed, the Stono Rebellion stunned white settlers and prompted a swift legal backlash in the slave codes. Peter H. Wood, *Black Majority: Negroes in Colonial South Carolina from 1670 through the Stono Rebellion* (New York: W. W. Norton, 1974), 308–26.

63. Lawrence A. Cremin, *American Education: The Colonial Experience 1607–1783* (New York: Harper & Row, 1970), 351–52.

64. Janet Duitsman Cornelius, *"When I Can Read My Title Clear": Literacy, Slavery, and Religion in the Antebellum South* (Columbia: University of South Carolina Press, 1991), 14.

65. Edgar W. Knight, ed., *A Documentary History of Education in the South Before 1860* (Chapel Hill: University of North Carolina Press, 1949), 1:152.

66. Cornelius, *"When I Can Read My Title Clear,"* 32–33.

67. Peter Kolchin, *American Slavery 1619–1877* (New York: Hill and Wang, 1993), 142.

68. Raven, *London Booksellers and American Customers,* 35. On mulattoes in colonial America, see Philip D. Morgan, *Slave Counterpoint: Black Culture in the Eighteenth-Century Chesapeake and Lowcountry* (Chapel Hill: University of North Carolina Press, 1998), 10, 12, 17.

69. Quoted in Spruill, *Women's Life and Work in the Southern Colonies,* 195. This phenomenon was not limited to the South, of course. Laurel Thatcher Ulrich observed that in New England, poor boys were apprenticed four times as often as poor girls; while boys and girls learned to read, only boys learned "to write a Ledgable hand & cypher" or "to keep a Trademan's Book." Coffin Papers, quoted in Ulrich, *Good Wives: Image and Reality in the Lives of Women in Northern New England 1650–1750* (1980; repr., New York, 1991), 44.

70. Abigail Adams to John Adams, June 30, 1778, in *Adams Family Correspondence* (Cambridge: Harvard University Press, 1963), 1:52.

71. Farish, *Journal and Letters of Philip Vickers Fithian,* 247–48n159; 240n6. James Marshall was Fithian's predecessor; John Peck, Fithian's friend and Princeton classmate, succeeded him.

72.. Ibid., 33, 149.

73. Jessica Kross, "Mansions, Men, Women, and the Creation of Multiple Publics in Eighteenth-Century British North America," *Journal of Social History* 33, no. 2 (1999): 388–89, 399.

74. *Virginia Gazette,* Purdie and Dixon, March 25, 1773, 3.

75. *Virginia Gazette,* Dixon, December 20, 1776, 4.

76. *Virginia Gazette,* Purdie and Dixon, December 22, 1768, 4.

77. Eliza Jaquelin Ambler Brent Carrington to Ann (Nancy) Ambler Fisher (undated but probably early 1809), Manuscript DMS 54.5, Elizabeth Jaquelin Ambler Papers, CWF. Eliza Carrington was recalling her childhood education; she was born in Yorktown in 1765.

78. Mason v. Pinckard, May 10, 1751, Lancaster County Chancery Court Records, LVA.

79. Tamara Thornton, *Handwriting in America: A Cultural History* (New Haven: Yale University Press, 1996), 23.

80. Ibid., 6–7, 38.

81. *Virginia Gazette,* Purdie and Dixon, February 20, 1772, 3.

82. The most famous case of cross-dressing as an expression of gender has been analyzed by Kathleen Brown, *Good Wives, Nasty Wenches, and Anxious Patriarchs: Gender, Race, and Power in Colonial Virginia* (Chapel Hill: University of North Carolina Press, 1996), 75–104. Examples of satires of women in eighteenth-century England appear in Linda Colley, *Britons: Forging the Nation 1707–1837* (New Haven: Yale University Press, 1992), 243, 247.

83. Susan Stabile, *Memory's Daughters: The Material Culture of Remembrance in Eighteenth-Century America* (Ithaca: Cornell University Press, 2004), 99, 101, 103.

84. *Virginia Gazette,* Purdie and Dixon, November 26, 1772, 2.

85. *Virginia Gazette,* Purdie and Dixon, February 20, 1772, 3.

86. Thornton, *Handwriting in America,* 8.

87. Madame Johnson, "A New And Easy Introduction to the Art of Writing," in *Madame Johnson's Present, or the Best Instructions for Young Women* (London, 1754), quoted in Stabile, *Memory's Daughters,* 92. For needlework as literacy training in New England, see Laurel Thatcher Ulrich, *The Age of Homespun: Objects and Stories in the Creation of An American Myth* (New York: Alfred A. Knopf, 2001), 148–49.

88. Robert Shoemaker, *Gender in English Society 1650–1850: The Emergence of Separate Spheres?* (London: Longman, 1998), 131. There is a voluminous literature on female education in England. The best places to begin are Anne Laurence, *Women in England 1500–1760: A Social History* (New York: St. Martin's Press, 1994), 165–71, and Anthony Fletcher, "Educating Girls," in *Gender, Sex, and Subordination in England 1500–1800* (New Haven: Yale University Press, 1995), 364–75. On education for upper-class women see Amanda Vickery, *The Gentleman's Daughter: Women's Lives in Georgian England* (New Haven: Yale University Press, 1998); for daughters of the middling class, see Margaret Hunt, "To Read, Knit, and Spin: Middling Daughters and the Family Economy," in *The Middling Sort: Commerce, Gender, and the Family in England 1680–1780* (Berkeley: University of California Press, 1996), 73–100. On women's literacy in England, see David Cressy, *Literacy and the Social Order: Reading and Writing in Tudor and Stuart England* (Cambridge: Cambridge University Press, 1980). On the vigorous protestations by Englishwomen for access to education, see Angeline Goreau's annotated excerpts in *The Whole Duty of a Woman: Female Writers in Seventeenth-Century England* (Garden City, New York: Doubleday, 1985) and Hilda Smith, *Reason's Disciples: Seventeenth-Century English Feminists* (Urbana: University of Illinois Press, 1982).

89. Lockridge, *Literacy in Colonial New England,* 72–73, 97; Hall, *Cultures of Print,*

124; Rawson, "Guardians of Their own Liberty," 49. Male literacy rates in New England in 1750 were approximately 75 percent and by the 1790s had risen to above 90 percent; in Virginia, male literacy reached approximately 67 percent and remained there to the end of the century. Lockridge, *Literacy in Colonial New England*, 74–78.

90. Thornton, *Handwriting in America*, 58.

91. William J. Scheick, *Authority and Female Authorship in Colonial America* (Lexington: University Press of Kentucky, 1998), 18–19.

92. On education in early America, see Cremin, *American Education*; Sol Cohen, ed., *Education in the United States: A Documentary History* vol. 1 (New York: Random House, 1974). On women's education in America, see Kerber, *Women of the Republic*, 185–232, and Norton, *Liberty's Daughters*, 256–94. For women's education in the colonial south, see Spruill, *Women's Life and Work*, 185–207.

93. *Virginia Gazette*, May 20, 1737, 1. Whether the author was English or Virginian is irrelevant; the important point is that the writer drew completely from English ideas of women's conduct and rewrote them for consumption in Virginia.

94. Quoted in Joan Hoff-Wilson, "The Illusion of Change: Women and the American Revolution," in *The American Revolution: Explorations in the History of American Radicalism*, ed. Alfred F. Young (DeKalb: Northern Illinois University Press, 1976), 431.

95. Kenneth Lockridge makes this point for the American colonial period in Virginia in *Literacy in Colonial New England*, 83–101. Keith Wrightson came to a similar finding for literacy and society in early modern England in *English Society 1580–1680* (1982; repr., New Brunswick, N.J.: Rutgers University Press, 1992), 183–99.

96. Brown, *Knowledge Is Power*, 175.

97. Nancy Cott, "Passionless: An Interpretation of Victorian Sexual Ideology, 1790–1850," *Signs* 4 (1978): 223.

98. Englishmen tended to look askance at all things French; this was true particularly of the freedoms they saw French women take in Parisian salons. "The minority of Frenchwomen who had acquired pretensions to intellectual autonomy," Linda Colley found, were excoriated by the conservative evangelical Thomas Gisborne as the "least eligible of wives." Colley, *Britons*, 251. The backlash to the rise of salons in England is a good indicator of the helplessness of conservatives to suppress them. David Shields has described a culture of sociability in colonial America; however, with the notable exception of the male "Tuesday Club" of Annapolis, Maryland, it remained a northern phenomenon. The most prominent women included Elizabeth Magawley of Philadelphia in the 1730s and Elizabeth Graeme Fergusson a generation later, also in Philadelphia. David Shields, *Civil Tongues and Polite Letters in British America* (Chapel Hill: University of North Carolina Press, 1997), 99–104, 120–40.

99. Margaret Hunt makes this point of Englishwomen in *The Middling Sort*, 75.

100. P. Joy Rouse, "Cultural Models of Womanhood: Practices of Colonization and Resistance," in *Nineteenth-Century Women Learn to Write*, ed. Catherine Hobbs (Charlottesville: University Press of Virginia, 1995), 236. Rouse is describing a model elaborated by Bonnie Cook Freeman, "Female Education in Patriarchal Power Systems," in *Education and Colonialism*, ed. Philip G. Altback and Gail P. Kelley (New York: Longman, 1978), 207–42.

101. See chapter 5 for a discussion of commonplace books.

102. Copybook, Maria Carter of Cleve, Armistead-Cocke Papers, CWM. Maria Carter was the daughter of Charles Carter of Cleve, King George County. She married William Armistead in 1765. "Some Colonial Letters," *Virginia Historical Magazine* 15 (1908): 435.

103. Copybook, Maria Carter. All quotations are from Carter's unpaginated copybook. The "book" itself is a collection of slips of paper of different sizes. No inch of

paper was wasted. Judging by the letter that was used as a front and back cover, the whole was not bound before 1792.

104. Maria Carter (daughter of Landon Carter) to her cousin Maria Carter (daughter of Charles Carter), March 25, 1756, Armistead-Cocke Papers, CWM.

105. The endlessly repetitious nature of women's work has been a predominate theme in women's history. A 1904 history of Augusta, Maine, dismissed much of the diary of midwife Martha Ballard (1785–1812) as "trivial and unimportant . . . being but a repetition of what has been recited many times." Even a 1970s feminist history of midwifery commented, "Like many diaries of farm women, it is filled with trivia about domestic chores and pastimes." But Laurel Thatcher Ulrich understood that the "real power" of Ballard's diary lay in just that "exhaustive, repetitious dailiness"; she won a Pulitzer Prize for her analysis of the diary. Laurel Thatcher Ulrich, *A Midwife's Tale: The Life of Martha Ballard, Based on Her Diary, 1785–1812* (New York: Random House, 1991), 8–9.

106. Letter, Ann Stuart to Eliza Lee, June 29, 1806, Richard Bland Lee Papers, VHS.

107. M. Williams to Ann Eaton Johnson, December 10, 1805, no. 380, William Johnson Papers, SHC.

108. Diary, Judith Anna Smith, May 3, 1789, Katherine Heath Hawes Papers, VHS.

109. Sir Richard Steele, *The Ladies Library, Written by a Lady*, 6th ed. (London, 1751), 61.

110. Mary Astell, *Serious Proposal to the Ladies for the Advancement of Their True and Greatest Interest* (London, 1694), in Goreau, *Whole Duty of Woman*, 254, 246. Goreau has assembled a superb collection of excerpts of these writings.

111. Smith, *Reason's Disciples*.

112. Julia Cherry Spruill, "Southern Lady's Library, 1700–1776," *South Atlantic Quarterly* 34 (1935): 23–41; "Books in Williamsburg," *WMQ* 15 (1906): 100–113; Library of Robert Carter of Nomini Hall, listed in Farish, *Journal and Letters of Philip Vickers Fithian*, 221–29; Edwin Wolf, 2d, "The Dispersal of the Library of William Byrd of Westover," *Proceedings of the American Antiquarian Society* 68 (1958): 19–106; Edwin Wolf, 2d, "More Books from the Library of the Byrds of Westover," in *Proceedings of the American Antiquarian Society* 88 (1978): 51–82. Nor have any works of this nature appeared in any private inventories in the present study.

113. Sheila L. Skemp, *Judith Sargent Murray: A Brief Biography with Documents* (Boston: Bedford Books, 1998), 144–49, 162–68.

114. Mercy Otis Warren, *History of the Rise, Progress, and Termination of the American Revolution, Interspersed with Biographical, Political and Moral Observations* (Boston, 1805).

115. Kerber, *Women of the Republic*, 277; Abigail Adams to Abigail Adams Smith, May 13, 1809, in Phyllis Lee Levin, *Abigail Adams: A Biography* (New York: St. Martin's Press, 1987), 427.

116. Judith Sargent Murray, *The Gleaner*, in Skemp, *Judith Sargent Murray*, 146, 109. Mary Wollstonecraft, *A Vindication of the Rights of Woman*, ed. Carol H. Poston (New York: W. W. Norton, 1988), 149.

117. "To Sophronia. In answer to some Lines she directed to be wrote on my Fan. 1769," in Karin Wulf, *Milcah Martha Moore's Book: A Commonplace Book from Revolutionary America* (University Park: Pennsylvania State University Press, 1997), 173.

118. Single women were not a rarity in colonial Philadelphia. Robert Wells has estimated that in the early Quaker families he studied, of the children still alive at age fifty, fully 16 percent of the daughters (and 12 percent of the sons) never married. Robert Wells, "Quaker Marriage Patterns in a Colonial Perspective," *WMQ*, 3d ser., 39 (1972): 426–28. See also Karin Wulf, *Not All Wives: Women of Colonial Philadelphia* (Ithaca: Cornell University Press, 2000), 12–17.

119. On Quakers and society in colonial Pennsylvania, see Barry Levy, *Quakers and the American Family: British Settlement in the Delaware Valley* (New York: Oxford University Press, 1988); Richard S. Dunn and Mary Maples Dunn, eds., *World of William Penn* (Philadelphia: University of Pennsylvania Press, 1986); Frederick B. Tolles, *Quakers and the Atlantic Culture* (New York: Octagon Books, 1980).

120. See, for example, "The Invitation," in Wulf, *Milcah Martha Moore's Book*, 259. David Shields has documented the rise of belles lettres in colonial Philadelphia, where Elizabeth Magawley published a poem in Andrew Bradford's *Gazette*, "The Wits and Poets of Pennsylvania, a Poem, Part I"(there never was a part 2), in which she "challenged male wits to contend about issues of love, courtship and marriage." Her poem comments on "the entire tribe of wits then inhabiting PA" after two wits rise to her challenge. Interestingly, Shields examines her poems to understand better each male wit she describes but never comments that a woman is participating in this literary culture as early as 1730–31. David Shields, "The Wits and Poets of Pennsylvania, a Poem, Part I," *Pennsylvania Magazine of History and Biography* 59, no. 2, (1985): 99–143.

121. Quoted in Wulf, *Not All Wives*, 44.

122. *Virginia Gazette*, October 15, 1736, 3. The introduction to the poem indicated that it had been written and presented to the subscriber "some Years" earlier. *South Carolina Gazette*, August 15, 1743, 3.

123. "Reply to Ladies Complaint," *South Carolina Gazette*, August 22, 1743, 3.

124. Ignored until recently, English women writers before Jane Austen have generated a great deal of scholarly interest. For an introduction to the subject see Dale Spender, ed., *Living By the Pen: Early British Women Writers* (New York: Teachers College Press, 1992); James Fitzmaurice and Josephine A. Roberts, eds., *Major Women Writers of Seventeenth-Century England* (Ann Arbor: University of Michigan Press, 1997); Janet Todd, *The Sign of Angellica: Women, Writing and Fiction, 1660–1800* (New York: Columbia University Press, 1989); Cheryl Turner, *Living by the Pen: Women Writers in the Eighteenth Century* (London: Routledge, 1992). On the expanding boundaries of female respectability, see Vickery, *Gentleman's Daughter,* while Margaret R. Hunt's *Middling Sort* argues that the boundaries between public and private were considerably blurred for the middle class as commerce permeated the home.

125. Astell's *Serious Proposal* was first published in London in 1694; Makin's *Essay* was published in London in 1673.

126. For the intersections of race and gender, see Brown, *Good Wives*; Catherine Clinton and Michele Gillespie, *Devil's Lane: Sex and Race in the Early South* (New York: Oxford University Press, 1997). Edmund Morgan shows the intersection of race and power in *American Slavery, American Freedom: The Ordeal of Colonial Virginia* (New York: W. W. Norton, 1975); Rhys Isaac analyzes male gentry rituals emphasizing rank in *Transformation of Virginia*. For works on the gendering of racial difference in the nineteenth century see Catherine Clinton, *The Plantation Mistress: Woman's World in the Old South* (New York: Pantheon Press, 1982); Elizabeth Fox-Genovese, *Within the Plantation Household: Black and White Women of the Old South* (Chapel Hill: University of North Carolina Press, 1988); Suzanne Lebsock, *The Free Women of Petersburg: Status and Culture in a Southern Town, 1784–1860* (New York: W. W. Norton, 1985). For ways in which male economic power in Virginia was strengthened by inheritance practices, see Holly Brewer, "Entailing Aristocracy in Colonial Virginia: 'Ancient Feudal Restraints' and Revolutionary Reform," *WMQ*, 3d ser., 54 (1997): 307–46. For women and the law of property in early America, see Mary Lynn Salmon, *Women and the Law of Property in Early America* (Chapel Hill: University of North Carolina, 1986).

127. Shields, *Civil Tongues and Polite Letters*. The English coffeehouse was a male bastion of talk, one feature of which "was its obsession with news," Shields explained. That

conversation spilled over into periodicals such as the *Spectator,* the *Idler,* the *Rambler,* and the *Tatler.* These journals gave a forum to the writings of men who were schooled "in a discourse of civility [that] was renovated from its courtly exclusivity to something more demotic and applicable to the world at large," 20–22.

128. Meyers, "Old Dominion Looks to London," 197.

129. Richard Beale Davis, *A Colonial Southern Bookshelf: Reading in the Eighteenth Century* (Athens: University of Georgia Press, 1979), 119. Robert Winans noted that in Charles Evans's *American Bibliography,* "ghosts [books listed based on the basis of circumstantial evidence of their existence, such as advertisements] of English novels far outnumber those of any other category of book for the late eighteenth century." Robert Winans, "Bibliography and the Cultural Historian: Notes on the Eighteenth-Century Novel," in Joyce et al., *Printing and Society in Early America,* 176.

130. On censure of novels, Cathy Davidson, "The Life and Times of Charlotte Temple: The Biography of a Book," in *Reading in America* (Baltimore: Johns Hopkins University Press, 1989), 164.

131. Davis, *Colonial Southern Bookshelf,* 122.

132. Cathy Davidson, *Revolution and the Word: The Rise of the Novel in America* (New York: Oxford University Press, 1986), 65, 144.

133. Michael Warner, *The Letters of the Republic: Publication and the Public Sphere in Eighteenth-Century America* (Cambridge: Harvard University Press, 1990), xiii.

134. Westmoreland County Orders, reel 60, May 29, 1764, 125a, LVA.

135. Louise Belote Dawe and Sandra Gioia Treadway, "Hannah Lee Corbin: The Forgotten Lee," *Virginia Calvacade* 75 (1979): 75; Elizabeth Dabney Coleman, "Two Lees, Revolutionary Suffragists," *Virginia Calvacade* (1953): 19–21.

136. Journal of Elizabeth Foote Washington, July 1792, 58, Washington Papers, Library of Congress.

137. Kierner, *Beyond the Household,* 54–67.

138. Joanna Bowen Gillespie, "1795: Martha Laurens Ramsay's 'Dark Night of the Soul' " *WMQ,* 3d ser., 48 (1991): 68–92.

139. Michael O'Brien, *Rethinking the South: Essays in Intellectual History* (Baltimore: Johns Hopkins University Press, 1988), 19–22.

140. Tatiana van Riemsdijk, "Time and Property from Heaven: Wealth, Religion, and Reform in Chesapeake Society, 1790–1832" (Ph.D. diss., University of California, San Diego, 1999), 180.

141. Lorena S. Walsh, "Community Networks in the Early Chesapeake," in *Colonial Chesapeake Society,* ed. Lois Green Carr, Philip D. Morgan, and Jean B. Russo (Chapel Hill: University of North Carolina Press, 1988), 225–28; Darrett B. Rutman and Anita H. Rutman, *A Place in Time: Middlesex County, Virginia, 1650–1750* (New York: W. W. Norton, 1984), 103–13.

142. Joan Gundersen, "Kith and Kin: Women's Networks in Colonial Virginia," in Clinton and Gillespie, *The Devil's Lane,* 101.

143. Joanna Gillespie devoted an entire chapter in her biography of Martha Laurens Ramsay, daughter of one of the wealthiest slave traders in South Carolina, to her silence on the subject. "Slavery and Silence," in *The Life and Times of Martha Laurens Ramsay, 1759–1811* (Columbia: University of South Carolina Press, 2001), 146–85.

144. Brown, *Good Wives;* Kirsten Fischer, *Suspect Relations: Sex, Race, and Resistance in Colonial North Carolina* (Ithaca: Cornell University Press, 2002).

145. Amy L. Wink, *She Left Nothing in Particular: The Autobiographical Legacy of Nineteenth-Century Women's Diaries* (Knoxville: University of Tennessee Press, 2001), xxiv.

146. Ellen Wayles Randolph Coolidge (EWRC) (Boston) to Martha Jefferson Ran-

dolph (MJR) (Monticello), August 19, 1828, no. 9090, Ellen Wayles Randolph Coolidge Correspondence, UVA. At times, however, Ellen was critical of her own education. She wrote to her sister the following year that she had been "dazzled" by the "false glare which quick parts and the love of literature threw . . . [so that] I never knew how deficient I was in my useful qualities until called on for the exercise of them . . . my object ever since has been by pawning my jewels to procure my linen, or in other words, I am constantly trying by the sacrifice of my brilliant qualities to acquire those of ordinary usefulness, which it is equally disgraceful and uncomfortable to be without." EWRC to Virginia Jefferson Randolph Trist (VJRT), May 3, 1829. Her critique echoes that of her kinswoman, Judith Randolph, who bemoaned the useless education she received that did not prepare her for the challenges of her rapidly declining family fortunes. Cynthia Kierner, "'The Dark and Dense Cloud Perpetually Lowering over Us': Gender and the Decline of the Gentry in Postrevolutionary Virginia," *Journal of the Early Republic* 20 (2000): 189. Indeed, neither Judith Randolph's traditional ornamental education nor Ellen's more substantially intellectual one seemed to have served southern women well; nonetheless, Ellen was disdainful of her future sister-in-law's "useful education" and continued to see some kinds of labor as better relegated to servants.

147. Edmund Bacon in Hamilton W. Pierson, *Jefferson at Monticello: The Private Life of Thomas Jefferson from Entirely New Materials* (1862; repr., Freeport, N.Y.: Books for Libraries Press, 1971), 87.

148. A letter from MJR to EWRC, November 26, 1825, suggests gaps in Ellen's housewifery training at Monticello. No. 9090, Coolidge Correspondence, UVA. After Ellen's marriage, her mother recommended a recipe book to her and suggested that she bring it with her when she next visited Monticello so they could fill in the missing directions.

149. EWRC to VJRT, October 15, 1830, no. 9090, Coolidge Correspondence, UVA.

150. O'Brien, *An Evening When Alone*; Farnham, *Education of the Southern Belle*; Hobbs, *Nineteenth-Century Women Learn to Write*; Anne Firor Scott, *The Southern Lady: From Pedestal to Politics, 1830–1930* (Chicago: University of Chicago Press, 1970).

151. Ira Berlin, *Many Thousands Gone: The First Two Centuries of Slavery in North America* (Cambridge, Mass.: Harvard University Press, 1998), 97–99.

2. "The Truest Kind of Breeding"

1. "Diary of M. Ambler, 1770," *Virginia Historical Magazine* 45 (1937): 170.

2. Kevin Hayes, *A Colonial Woman's Book Shelf* (Knoxville: University of Tennessee Press, 1996), 76–77. Fordyce's *Sermons* appear in inventories of private collections from Massachusetts to North Carolina, as well as on the shelves of the New York Society Library, the Library Company of Philadelphia, and the Union Library of Hatboro, Pennsylvania.

3. Richard L. Bushman, *The Refinement of America: Persons, Houses, Cities* (New York: Random House, 1992); Kevin M. Sweeney, "High-Style Venacular: Lifestyles of the Colonial Elite," in *Of Consuming Interests: The Style of Life in the Eighteenth Century*, ed. Cary Carson, Ronald Hoffman, and Peter J. Albert (Charlottesville: University Press of Virginia, 1994), 1–58; C. Dallett Hemphill, *Bowing to Necessities: A History of Manners in America, 1620–1860* (New York: Oxford University Press, 1999).

4. "Diary of M. Ambler, 1770," 170.

5. Carville V. Earle, "Environment, Disease, and Mortality in Early Virginia," in *The Chesapeake in the Seventeenth Century: Essays on Anglo-American Society*, ed. Thad W. Tate and David L. Ammerman (New York: W. W. Norton, 1979), 96–125.

6. Edmund S. Morgan, *American Slavery, American Freedom: The Ordeal of Colonial Virginia* (New York: W. W. Norton, 1975), 108–30.

7. James Horn, "Servant Emigration to the Chesapeake in the Seventeenth Century," in Tate and Ammerman, *Chesapeake in the Seventeenth Century*, 51–95.

8. Morgan, *American Slavery, American Freedom*, 295–315.

9. Lorena S. Walsh, "'Till Death Us Do Part': Marriage and Family in Seventeenth-Century Maryland," in Tate and Ammerman, *Chesapeake in the Seventeenth Century*, 150.

10. Darrett B. Rutman and Anita H. Rutman, "'Now-Wives and Sons-in-Law': Parental Death in a Seventeenth-Century Virginia County," in Tate and Ammerman, *Chesapeake in the Seventeenth Century*, 153–82. The guarantee of a husband, and the resulting opportunity to be mistress of one's household, was an undoubted inducement for Englishwomen to migrate to a colony with a noted reputation for disease and early death. (In 1624, the king had revoked the Virginia Company's charter because of its inability to curb the colony's mortality rates.) To remain in England could well mean resignation to a lifetime in service; as many as 10 percent of Englishmen and women did not marry in seventeenth-century England. Keith Wrightson, *English Society 1580–1680* (1982; repr., New Brunswick, N.J.: Rutgers University Press, 1992), 68.

11. For example, "by the time she was ten, [Agatha Vause] had lost a father, two stepfathers, a mother, and her guardian uncle." Rutman and Rutman, "'Now-Wives and Sons-in-Law,'" 168.

12. Lois Green Carr, Philip D. Morgan, and Jean B. Russo, eds., *Colonial Chesapeake Society* (Chapel Hill: University of North Carolina Press, 1988); Darrett B. Rutman and Anita H. Rutman, *A Place in Time: Middlesex County, Virginia 1650–1750* (New York: W. W. Norton, 1984); Daniel Blake Smith, *Inside the Great House: Planter Family Life in Eighteenth Century* (Ithaca: Cornell University Press, 1980).

13. Sally Hadden, *Slave Patrol Law and Violence in Virginia and the Carolinas* (Cambridge: Harvard University Press, 2001); Peter H. Wood, *Black Majority: Negroes in Colonial South Carolina from 1670 through the Stono Rebellion* (New York: W. W. Norton, 1974); Gerald W. Mullin, *Flight and Rebellion: Slave Resistance in Eighteenth-Century Virginia* (London: Oxford University Press, 1972), 57.

14. Rhys Isaac, *The Transformation of Virginia* (1982; repr., Chapel Hill: University of North Carolina Press, 1999).

15. Quoted in Edward L. Bond, *Damned Souls in a Tobacco Colony: Religion in Seventeenth-Century Virginia* (Macon, Ga.: Mercer University Press, 2000), 240.

16. Donald G. Mathews, *Religion in the Old South* (Chicago: University of Chicago Press, 1977), 5–6.

17. Nelson, John K., *A Blessed Company: Parishes, Parsons, and Parishioners in Anglican Virginia, 1690–1776* (Chapel Hill: University of North Carolina Press, 2001), 3.

18. Bond, *Damned Souls*, 240.

19. Isaac, *Transformation of Virginia*.

20. John Winthrop quoted in Edmund S. Morgan, *The Puritan Dilemma: The Story of John Winthrop* (Boston: Little, Brown, 1958), 186. For a recent example of agreement with Winthrop, see Daniel Blake Smith, "In Search of the Family in the Colonial South," in *Race and Family in the Colonial South*, ed. Winthrop Jordan and Sheila Skemp (Jackson: University of Mississippi Press, 1987), 33.

21. Wesley M. Gewehr, *The Great Awakening in Virginia, 1740–1790* (Durham, N.C.: Duke University Press, 1930), 29–36; Isaac, *Transformation of Virginia*; Dell Upton, *Holy Things and Profane: Anglican Parish Churches in Colonial Virginia* (Cambridge, Mass.: Harvard University Press, 1986); Hunter Dickinson Farish, ed., *Journal*

and Letters of Philip Vickers Fithian, A Plantation Tutor of the Old Dominion, 1773–1774 (1957; repr., Charlottesville: University Press of Virginia, 1993), 137, 167.

22. Bond, *Damned Souls*; Nelson, *A Blessed Company.*

23. Christine Leigh Heyrman, *Southern Cross: The Beginnings of the Bible Belt* (New York: Alfred A. Knopf, 1997), 13.

24. Patricia U. Bonomi, *Under the Cope of Heaven: Religion, Society, and Politics in Colonial America* (New York: Oxford University Press, 1986), 87–92.

25. Bond, *Damned Souls*, 245.

26. Edmund S. Morgan, *Visible Saints: The History of a Puritan Idea* (New York: New York University Press, 1963), describes the Puritan conversion process, as it developed in New England.

27. Bond, *Damned Souls*, 243–50; William Byrd quoted at 250.

28. Nelson, "The Sermon," in *A Blessed Company*, 200–210.

29. Devereux Jarratt, *Sermons on Various and Important Subjects in Practical Divinity, adapted to the meanest capacities and suited to the Family and Closet,* sermon XVIII (Philadelphia: William Woodward, 1794), 3:233.

30. Ibid., sermon XXIX, 3:282.

31. Nelson, *A Blessed Company*, 200.

32. David Ramsay, "Memoirs of the Life of Martha Laurens Ramsay," quoted in *Women and Religion in America*, vol. 2, *The Colonial and Revolutionary Periods*, ed. Rosemary Radford Ruether and Rosemary Skinner Keller (San Francisco: Harper & Row, 1983), 221.

33. William K. Bottorff and Roy C. Flannagan, eds., "The Diary of Frances Baylor Hill of Hillsborough, 1797," *Early American Literature Newsletter* (1967): 15, 16, 17, 32.

34. Edmund Randolph, "Memoir" [of Elizabeth (Nicholas) Randolph], MSS 1D2278b2, Daniel Family Papers, 4–5, VHS.

35. Joseph Eggleston to Jane [Eggleston] Cocke, March 23, 1788, Cocke Family Papers, VHS.

36. In Philip Vickers Fithian's experience as a Presbyterian in New Jersey, "it is seldom in the fullest Congregations, that more sing than the Clerk, & about two others!" yet at an Anglican service, he "was surprised when the Psalm began, to hear a large Collection of voices singing at the same time . . . entirely contrary to what I have seen before." Farish, *Journal and Letters of Philip Vickers Fithian*, 195.

37. Bond, *Damned Souls*, 241, 288.

38. Ibid., 292.

39. David D. Hall concluded that the "story of readers and their books in the Chesapeake is properly a tale not of the few great libraries but of households more than half of which did without books, and of a large group of book owners satisfied with having only the Bible and a few other titles, most probably religious in their subject matter." David D. Hall, *Cultures of Print: Essays in the History of the Book* (Amherst: University of Massachusetts Press, 1996), 118–19.

40. George K. Smart, "Private Libraries in Colonial Virginia," *American Literature* 10 (1938): 32, 44. Smart studied the contents of approximately one hundred libraries that spanned three periods, 1650–1700, 1700–50, and after 1750.

41. O. M. Brack Jr., ed., *The Adventures of Telemachus, the Son of Ulysses*, trans. Tobias Smollet (Athens: University of Georgia Press, 1997). Smollet's English translation appeared for the first time in 1776. It was a popular work that most Virginia gentry could read in French. Robert Carter of Nomini Hall, for example, had a copy ("Boyer's *Telemachus*") when Philip Vickers Fithian itemized his library in 1774. Farish, *Journal and Letters of Philip Vickers Fithian*, 226. On the popularity of the work, see Smart, "Private Libraries," 35.

42. Smart, "Private Libraries," 44.

43. Richard Allestree, *The Whole Duty of Man Laid Down in a Plain and Familiar Way for the Use of all but Especially Meanest Reader with Private Devotions for Several Occasions* (1657). On its presence in the thirteen American colonies, see Kevin Hayes, *A Colonial Woman's Bookshelf*, 44; Spruill, "Southern Lady's Library," 23; Smart, "Private Libraries," 45; Richard Beale Davis, *Intellectual Life in the Colonial South, 1585–1763* (Knoxville: University of Tennessee Press, 1978), 2:502–72, 580; Richard Beale Davis, *A Colonial Southern Bookshelf: Reading in the Eighteenth Century* (Athens: University of Georgia Press, 1979), 68, 74. Davis notes that *The Whole Duty* was found in dissenting as well as Anglican households.

44. Edwin Wolf, 2d, "Catalogue of Westover Books Located," *Proceedings of the American Antiquarian Society* 68 (1958): 47.

45. Wayne Craven, *Colonial American Portraiture: The Economic, Religious, Social, Cultural, Philosophical, Scientific, and Aesthetic Foundations* (Cambridge: Cambridge University Press, 1986), 372–73.

46. Joseph Towne Wheeler, "Reading and Other Recreations of Marylanders," *Maryland Historical Magazine* 38 (March 1943): 52. These books stood side by side with William Sherlock's *Immortality of the Soul* and *The Government of the Tongue*, purchased, one suspects, for his seven children. Aubrey C. Land, *The Dulanys of Maryland: A Biographical Study of Daniel Dulany, the Elder (1685–1753) and Daniel Dulany, the Younger (1722–1797)* (Baltimore: Johns Hopkins University Press, 1955, 1968), 114–15.

47. Elizabeth Cometti, "Some Early Best Sellers in Piedmont North Carolina," *Journal of Southern History* 17 (1950): 324–37.

48. Louis B. Wright, *First Gentlemen of Virginia: Intellectual Qualities of the Early Colonial Ruling Class* (San Marino, Calif.: Huntington Library, 1940), 104.

49. Clifford K. Shipton and James E. Mooney, *National Index of American Imprints through 1800: The Short-Title Evans* (Worcester, Mass.: American Antiquarian Society and Barre Publishers, 1969), 1:16.

50. *South Carolina Gazette*, March 24, 1739, 3.

51. Indeed, it was still being published in the nineteenth century. [Richard Allestree] *The Whole Duty of Man*, with a preface by William Bentinck Hawkins (London: William Pickering, 1842), v–xiv. Parks's bookshop in Williamsburg always had copies on hand. On its English publication history, see Donald Wing, compiler, *Short Title Catalogue of Books Printed in England, Scotland, Ireland, Wales, and British America, and of English Books Printed in Other Countries, 1641–1700*, 2d ed. (New York: Modern Language Association of America, 1994), 1:49–50.

52. Wright, *First Gentlemen of Virginia*, 237.

53. Hayes, *Colonial Woman's Bookshelf*, 63.

54. Julia Cherry Spruill, *Women's Life and Work in the Southern Colonies* (1938; repr., New York: W. W. Norton, 1972), 208–9; Hayes, *Colonial Women's Bookshelf*, 61.

55. "Books Advertised in the Virginia Gazette 1775," *WMQ*, 1st ser., 15 (1902–3): 100–113.

56. Richard Grafton to Mary Grafton, September 3, 1737, box 1, MS 1919, Dulany Family Papers, MHS.

57. Will, Edward Moseley, New Hanover County, 1745, proved 1749, in *North Carolina Wills and Inventories Copied from Original and Recorded Wills and Inventories in the Office of the Secretary of State*, ed. J. Bryan Grimes (1912; repr., Baltimore: Genealogical Publishing, 1967), 313–20.

58. Davis, *Intellectual Life in the Colonial South*, 567. At his death, Milner's library contained almost 650 titles by Richard Beale Davis's count, 182 of them law books. It was a library of a gentleman, including history, philosophy, belles lettres, music, and

numerous reference works, all encased in walnut bookcases. (Davis incorrectly refers to Milner as John instead of James.)

59. Kevin Hayes, *The Library of William Byrd of Westover* (Madison: Madison House, 1997); Louis B. Wright and Marion Tinling, eds., *The Secret Diary of William Byrd of Westover* (Richmond: Dietz Press, 1941), 211.

60. Copybook, Maria Carter of Cleve, Armistead-Cocke Papers, CWM. The book, a collection of loose papers bound together, is unpaginated. Maria Carter was the daughter of Charles Carter of Cleve, King George County. She married William Armistead in 1765. "Some Colonial Letters." *Virginia Historical Magazine* 15 (1908): 435.

61. "Book of Sermons" volumes 1 through 3 are lost. The surviving book, volume 4, begins on page 563 and finishes on page 860; it was discovered at Peckatone, her married home, in the 1880s, before the house was destroyed by fire. The letters deal with matters ranging from the nature of original sin and free will to proving that Judas was not at the Lord's Supper. Lee Family Library, Stratford Hall, Virginia.

62. Elizabeth Foote Washington, "Journal, 1779–96," 29, MS-56408-3, Washington Family Papers, Library of Congress.

63. Joanna Bowen Gillespie, "1795: Martha Lauren Ramsay's 'Dark Night of the Soul' " *WMQ*, 3d ser., 48 (1991): 68.

64. C. John Sommerville, *Popular Religion in Restoration England* (Gainesville: University Press of Florida, 1978), 29. Between 1701 and 1800, there was an edition of *The Whole Duty of Man* printed in England in each of fifty-six years. In sixteen of those years, two or three editions were printed. *The Eighteenth Century: Guide to the Microform Collection* (Woodbridge, Conn.: Research Publications, [1983–]).

65. On the links between restoration of monarchical and familial authority, see Gordon J. Schochet, *The Authoritarian Family and Political Attitudes in 17th Century England: Patriarchalism in Political Thought* (1975; repr., New Brunswick, N.J.: Transaction Books, 1988), 56–57.

66. [Allestree], *The Whole Duty of Man* (1842 ed.), 259, 260, 261.

67. *The Ladies Calling* was enormously influential, riding the wave of popularity set in motion by *The Whole Duty of Man*. Four years after its initial printing it was in its fifth edition; by 1787, it had been through at least twelve editions. Robert Shoemaker, *Gender in English Society 1650–1850: The Emergence of Separate Spheres?* (London: Longman, 1998), 22. Whole sections of it were integrated ("plagiarized" would be a better word) into a hack work, *The Whole Duty of Woman*, and into the more respectable *The Ladies Library*.

68. Anthony Fletcher, *Gender, Sex, and Subordination, 1500–1800* (New Haven: Yale University Press, 1995), 384.

69. [Allestree], *The Ladies Calling In Two Parts by the Author of the Whole Duty of Man*, 5th ed. (London: At the Theatre in Oxford, 1677), 33.

70. [Allestree], *The Ladies Calling* (1677 ed.), 88, 71, 53.

71. [Allestree], *The Ladies Calling*, quoted in Angeline Goreau, *The Whole Duty of a Woman: Female Writers in Seventeenth-Century England* (Garden City, N.Y.: Dial Press, 1985), 43, 44.

72. Ibid., 44.

73. Goreau, *Whole Duty of Woman*, 10.

74. [Allestree], *The Ladies Calling*, in Goreau, *Whole Duty of Woman*, 44.

75. Goreau, *Whole Duty of Woman*, 9.

76. Of course, there were practical concerns as well. The insistence on a woman's chastity was critical to ensure their children were the offspring of their husbands, and not, as Margaret Cavendish, Duchess of Newcastle, wryly observed, "branches from the wrong stock." Quoted ibid., 9.

77. Wright, *First Gentlemen of Virginia*, 237.

78. See Isaac, *The Transformation of Virginia*; T. H. Breen, *Tobacco Culture: The Mentality of the Great Tidewater Planters on the Eve of Revolution* (Princeton: Princeton University Press, 1985); Michal J. Rozbicki, *The Complete Colonial Gentleman: Cultural Legitimacy in Plantation America* (Charlottesville: University Press of Virginia, 1998).

79. Peter Kolchin, *American Slavery, 1619–1877* (New York: Hill and Wang, 1993), table 1, 240.

80. Kathleen Brown, *Good Wives, Nasty Wenches, and Anxious Patriarchs: Gender, Race, and Power in Colonial Virginia* (Chapel Hill: University of North Carolina Press, 1996).

81. For contemporary views of African women, see Jennifer L. Morgan, " 'Some Could Suckle over Their Shoulder': Male Travelers, Female Bodies, and the Gendering of Racial Ideology, 1500–1770," *WMQ*, 3d ser., 54 (1997): 167–92.

82. Brown, *Good Wives*, passim.

83. Craven, *Colonial American Portraiture*, 227.

84. Paula A. Treckel, " 'The Empire of My Heart': The Marriage of William Byrd II and Lucy Parke Byrd," *Virginia Magazine of History and Biography* 105 (1997): 125–56; Kenneth A. Lockridge, *The Diary, and Life, of William Byrd II of Virginia, 1674–1744* (Chapel Hill: University of North Carolina Press, 1987); David Hackett Fisher, *Albion's Seed: Four British Folkways in America* (New York: Oxford, 1989), 287–92; Daniel Blake Smith, *Inside the Great House: Planter Family Life in Eighteenth-Century Chesapeake Society* (Ithaca: Cornell University Press, 1980), 163–68; Michael Zuckerman, "William Byrd's Family," *Perspectives in American History* 12 (1979): 255–311.

85. Wright and Tinling, *Secret Diary of William Byrd*, eyebrows: February 5, 1711, 296; purchases: July 9, 1710, 202; slave: December 31, 1711, 462; "over by her submission": April 9, 1709, 19.

86. Louis G. Locke, *Tillotson: A Study in Seventeenth-Century Literature* (Copenhagen: Rosenkilde and Bagger, 1954), 103 (quotation), 143, 154, 160, 165.

87. Wright and Tinling, *Secret Diary*, June 18, 1709, 192; July 30, 1709, 210–11; James Moffatt, ed., *The Golden Book of Tillotson: Selections from the Writings of the Rev. John Tillotson, D.D. Archbishop of Canterbury* (1926; Westport, Conn.: Greenwood Press, 1971), 102–3.

88. Moffatt, *Golden Book of Tillotson*, 83–84.

89. Wright and Tinling, *Secret Diary of William Byrd*, September 10, 1710, 228–29.

90. Samuel Shellabarger, *Lord Chesterfield and His World* (Boston: Little, Brown, 1951), 13. The famous Lord Chesterfield was Halifax's grandson.

91. Kathryn Shevelow, "Fathers and Daughters: Women as Readers of the *Tatler*," in *Gender and Reading: Essays on Readers, Texts, and Contexts*, ed. Elizabeth A. Flynn and Patrocinio P. Schweickart (Baltimore: Johns Hopkins University Press, 1986), 111.

92. John Kenyon, ed., *Halifax Complete Works* (Baltimore: Penguin Books, 1969), 270. The French translations appeared in 1692, 1748, 1752, and 1757; the Italian in 1734.

93. Lord Halifax, *The Lady's New Year's Gift; or, Advice to a Daughter* (London, 1700), 3–9.

94. Kenyon, *Halifax*, 277.

95. Ibid., 278, 279.

96. Ibid., 279, 280.

97. Ibid., 281, 285, 286, 281.

98. Ibid., 297.

99. Ibid., 299–300.

100. Ibid., 301–2.

101. See Mary Beth Norton, *Founding Mothers and Fathers: Gendered Power and the*

Forming of American Society (New York: Alfred A. Knopf, 1996) and Brown, *Good Wives,* for a discussion of the theory that underpinned patriarchal society in colonial Virginia and the tensions that arose in the diversions between theory and practice.

102. Kenyon, *Halifax,* 278.

103. It was said that Elizabeth Savile kept her father's gift on her dressing table; nonetheless, there is some question about its influence on her. The indulged daughter of a famous courtier, she apparently chafed at the quiet country life preferred by her husband, Philip Stanhope, Lord Chesterfield. Her copy of her father's book bears the comment her husband—or perhaps her impatient father-in-law—scrawled across it: "Wasted effort!" Kenyon, *Halifax,* 270; Shellabarger, *Lord Chesterfield and His World,* 16, 18–19.

104. Hayes, *Colonial Woman's Bookshelf,* 2; Spruill, "Southern Lady's Library," 23. Portions of both Allestree's and Halifax's work appeared in Richard Steele's *The Ladies Library,* widening further still their circles of influence. *The Lady's New Year's Gift* was printed twice in 1688 and went through at least ten more printings by 1756. French editions appeared in 1752 and 1756 and an Italian edition was printed in 1734. Library of Congress online catalog.

105. See Amanda Vickery, *The Gentleman's Daughter: Women's Lives in Georgian England* (New Haven: Yale University Press, 1998), 225–29.

106. Jürgen Habermas defined the public sphere as "a domain of our social life in which such a thing as public opinion can be formed . . . [for example] every conversation in which private persons come together to form a public." This formulation breaks down the theoretical barriers between a masculine public and a feminine private. Steven Seidman, ed., *Jürgen Habermas on Society and Politics: A Reader* (Boston: Beacon Press, 1989), 231.

107. Kathryn Kirkpatrick, "Sermons and Strictures: Conduct-Book Propriety and Property Relations in Late Eighteenth-Century England," in *History, Gender, and Eighteenth-Century Literature,* ed. Beth Fowkes-Tobin (Athens: University of Georgia Press, 1994), 198; Hayes, *Colonial Woman's Bookshelf;* Jane Austen, *Pride and Prejudice,* ed. Donald Gray (New York: W. W. Norton, 2001), 47.

108. Paul Langford, *A Polite and Commercial People, England 1727–1783* (Oxford: Oxford University Press, 1992), 606; James Fordyce, *Sermons for Young Women* (Philadelphia, 1809) Early American Imprints, 2d ser., no. 17522, ed. Clifford K. Shipton (Worcester, Mass.: American Antiquarian Society, 1967–1974), 1:iv.

109. Fordyce, *Sermons,* 1:iii; 2:26.

110. Ibid., 1:50–51.

111. Ibid., 1:88–89.

112. Ibid., 1: 113, 106.

113. Ibid., 1:84.

114. Ibid., 1:40.

115. Ibid., 1:84.

116. Hemphill, *Bowing to Necessities,* 107; Joseph Towne Wheeler, "Booksellers and Circulating Libraries in Colonial Maryland," *Maryland Historical Magazine* 34 (June 1939): 124. The book enjoyed the rare distinction of being printed in three American cities in 1775: New York, Philadelphia, and Annapolis. Jay Fliegelman, *Prodigals and Pilgrims: The American Revolution Against Patriarchal Authority, 1750–1800* (Cambridge: Cambridge University Press, 1982), 278n9.

117. John Gregory, *A Father's Legacy to his Daughters* (1774; repr., London, 1793), 23, 24–25, 74, 71.

118. Fordyce, *Sermons,* 1:137.

119. Thomas Laqueur, *Making Sex: Body and Gender from the Greeks to Freud* (Cam-

bridge, Mass.: Harvard University Press, 1990), 28–30, 1–10, 149–51. See also Tim Hitchcock, *English Sexualities, 1700–1800* (New York: St. Martin's Press, 1997), especially "The Body, Medicine and Sexual Difference," 42–57. Hitchcock agrees with Laqueur's analysis regarding science as a cultural construct but sees medical tracts more as reflective of social change than as agents of it.

120. Fletcher, *Gender, Sex and Subordination*, 61.

121. See Christopher J. Berry, *Social Theory of the Scottish Enlightenment* (Edinburgh: Edinburgh University Press, 1997), 30–33, for the Scots' refutation of Locke's theory of contract government.

122. Rosemarie Zagarri, "Morals, Manners, and the Republican Mother," *American Quarterly* 44 (June 1992): 192–215.

123. Quoted ibid., 199, 201.

124. William Smellie, *Philosophy of Natural History* (1790/1799), quoted in Patricia Howell Michaelson, *Speaking Volumes: Women, Reading and Speech in the Age of Austen* (Stanford: Stanford University Press, 2002), 25–26.

125. Langford, *Polite and Commercial People*, 606.

126. The historiography of separate spheres in England is rich. English historians have discerned separate spheres in nineteenth-century English gender relations and have looked back for its origins to industrialization in the late eighteenth century. See, for example, Bridget Hill, *Women, Work, and Sexual Politics in Eighteenth-Century England* (Oxford: Basil Blackwell, 1989). But historians have disagreed on the utility of this model as well. Robert Shoemaker concluded that in fact the "spheres were never truly separate"; instead he saw an accentuation of gender roles, both male and female. Shoemaker, *Gender in English Society*, 316–318. Margaret Hunt argued that her evidence transcended the model entirely; her study of the market and the middling class showed that public commerce pierced the privacy of the family. Not that separate spheres was implausible, Hunt acknowledged; she did fear, however, that this approach glossed over the intricate ways in which men's and women's lives overlapped. Hunt, *The Middling Sort: Commerce, Gender, and the Family in England 1680–1780* (Berkeley: University of California Press, 1996), 8–9. Linda Colley's study of the development of "Britishness" between 1707 and 1837 saw that the stridency of the English press against women's political activism revealed how very permeable the boundaries separating men and women actually were: "increasingly prescribed in theory," Colley observed, "yet [they were] increasingly broken through in practice." Colley, *Britons: Forging the Nation 1707–1837* (New Haven: Yale University Press, 1992), 250. Amanda Vickery rejected the model outright in her study of elite women in northern England. Although her book was a "reconstruction . . . of lives lived within the bounds of propriety," she argued that those bounds were wider than has been previously acknowledged, since men and women shared in the books, salon gatherings, and assemblies fostered by a culture of politeness. Vickery, *Gentleman's Daughter*, 12. In her attention to these venues, Vickery's conception of "public" mirrors the eighteenth-century usage Lawrence Klein has described and considerably expands on our understanding of women's prominent place within it. Lawrence E. Klein, "Gender, Conversation and the Public Sphere in Early Eighteenth-Century England," in *Textuality and Sexuality: Reading Theories and Practices*, ed. Judith Still and Michael Worton (Manchester: Manchester University Press, 1993), 112. Patricia Howell Michaelson believes the model works with mixed success, taking her cue from the eighteenth-century sources. Michaelson, *Speaking Volumes*.

127. Erin Mackie, *Market a la Mode: Fashion, Commodity, and Gender in The Tatler and The Spectator* (Baltimore: Johns Hopkins University Press, 1997), 116.

128. "The Conversation Group," English, c. 1775, CWF.

129. On the genre and meaning of conversation pieces, see Marcia Pointon, *Hanging the Head: Portraiture and Social Formation in Eighteenth-Century England* (New Haven: Yale University Press, 1993), 159–75.

130. "Books in Williamsburg," *WMQ*, 1st ser., 15 (1906): 112. This story was so popular, that the conversation piece of Queen Charlotte, 1764, depicted her eldest son in a Telemachus costume. Onlookers would have readily understood its symbolism. Pointon, *Hanging the Head*, 166–68.

131. "An Essay on Women," *Virginia Gazette*, Purdie and Dixon, March 4, 1773, 2.

132. Ibid.

133. Theodorick Bland to Sophia Bland, December 10, 1799, MS 134, box 4, MS 134, Bland Papers, MHS.

134. Frances Randolph Tucker (Matoax) to St. George (Williamsburg), May 25, 1779, Tucker-Coleman Papers, CWM.

135. The entire advertisement is reprinted in "Books in Williamsburg," 100–113.

136. All terms defined in *Oxford English Dictionary*, 2d ed., s.v.

137. Cynthia Z. Stiverson and Gregory A. Stiverson, "The Colonial Retail Book Trade: Availability and Affordability of Reading Material in Mid-Eighteenth-Century Virginia," in *Printing and Society in Early America*, ed. William Joyce, David D. Hall, Richard D. Brown, and John B. Hench (Worcester, Mass.: American Antiquarian Society, 1983), 170.

138. This image is discussed in chapter 4.

139. Susan Miller, *Assuming the Positions: Cultural Pedagogy and the Politics of Commonplace Writing* (Pittsburgh: University of Pittsburgh Press, 1998), 22–23.

140. Kenneth A. Lockridge, *On the Sources of Patriarchal Rage: The Commonplace Books of William Byrd and Thomas Jefferson and the Gendering of Power in the Eighteenth Century* (New York: New York University Press, 1992), 4.

141. Kevin Berland, Jan Kirsten Gilliam, and Kenneth Lockridge, eds., *The Commonplace Book of William Byrd II of Westover* (Chapel Hill: University of North Carolina Press, 2001), 79–82, 90–93.

142. Maria Carter, Copybook.

143. Journal of Elizabeth Foote Washington, 1–2.

144. Ibid., 21.

145. Christian Moore to Bishop Richard Channing Moore, August 1794, Price Family Papers, VHS.

146. David Ramsay, "Memoirs," 222.

147. Gillespie, "1795: Martha Laurens Ramsay's 'Dark Night of the Soul,'" 68–92.

148. Ibid.

149. Laurel Thatcher Ulrich, *Good Wives: Image and Reality in the Lives of Women in Northern New England 1650–1750* (1980; repr., New York: Vintage Books, 1991), 113–17.

150. George F. Sensabaugh, *Milton in Early America* (Princeton: Princeton University Press, 1964), 43–48.

151. Robert Feke, "Grizzell Eastwick Apthorp," 1748, de Young Museum, San Francisco (image available online).

152. Jan Lewis, "The Republican Wife: Virtue and Seduction in the Early Republic," *WMQ*, 3d ser., 44 (1987): 689–721.

153. Commonplace book, Anna Maria Coale, box 4, MS 248, Coale Collection, MHS.

154. "Books in Williamsburg," 111; *Virginia Gazette*, Dixon, November 25, 1775, 1.

155. Sensabaugh, *Milton in Early America*, 200, 206–7, 212–13, 215.

156. Farish, *Journal and Letters of Philip Vickers Fithian*, 123–25.

157. Randolph, "Memoir," 4.

158. Fordyce, *Sermons*; Thomas Jefferson to daughter Martha Jefferson, December 22, 1783, in *The Family Letters of Thomas Jefferson*, ed. Edwin Morris Betts and James Adam Bear Jr. (Charlottesville: University Press of Virginia, 1966), 21–22.

159. Memoir of Peter Vivian Daniel of his wife Lucy Nelson (Randolph) Daniel, 1847, MSS 1D2278b2, Daniel Family Papers, VHS.

160. Journal of Elizabeth Foote Washington, Summer 1784, 23.

161. Edmund Randolph, "Memoir," 7, MSS 1D2278b2, Daniel Family Papers, VHS.

162. Ibid.

163. W. Ronald Cocke, "Genealogical Notes," *WMQ*, 2d ser., 11 (1931): 125.

164. "Diary of M. Ambler," passim; quotations, 156, 168.

165. *Virginia Gazette*, Purdie and Dixon, February 4, 1768, 3.

166. "Diary of M. Ambler," 154, 161, 163.

3. Religion, Voice, and Authority

1. Gen. 1:27, *New Oxford Annotated Bible, Revised Standard Version* (New York: Oxford University Press, 1977).

2. Clare Drury, "Christianity," in *Women in Religion*, ed. Jean Holm (New York: Pinter Publishers, 1994), 33. The earlier story, attributed by Bible scholars to author "J," dates to approximately 900 BCE; the later, attributed to "P," the priestly writer, about 400 BCE.

3. Ibid., 34.

4. Gen. 3:6, *New Oxford Annotated Bible, RSV*.

5. 1 Tim. 2:13–14, ibid. Although this epistle is frequently attributed to St. Paul, biblical scholars have shown that it was written about sixty years after Paul's death. By the time this epistle was written, the Church was coping with fears of sexual excesses in the late Roman Empire; women were consciously linked with Eve, offering by their beauty temptations of "the forbidden fruit of sex." Karen Armstrong, *The Gospel according to Woman* (New York: Anchor Press/Doubleday, 1986), 60–61.

6. Tertullian, *De Cultu Feminarum*, quoted in Elaine Pagels, *Adam, Eve, and the Serpent* (New York: Vintage Books, 1989), 63.

7. Augustine, *de Trinitate*, quoted in Drury, "Christianity," 36.

8. Thomas Aquinas, *Summa Theologica*, quoted in Drury, "Christianity," 36.

9. John Calvin, *Commentaries*, quoted in Gerda Lerner, *The Creation of Patriarchy* (New York: Oxford University Press, 1986), 183.

10. Martin Luther, *Lectures on Genesis*, quoted in Drury, "Christianity," 39.

11. Lerner, *Creation of Patriarchy*, chaps. 1, 2, and 5. Lerner defined patriarchy as "the manifestation and institutionalization of male dominance over women and children in the family and the extension of male dominance over women in society in general. It implies that men hold power in all the important institutions of society and that women are deprived of access to that power," 239.

12. Thomas Laqueur, *Making Sex: Body and Gender from the Greeks to Freud* (Cambridge, Mass.: Harvard University Press, 1990), 28–30, 40. See also Tim Hitchcock, *English Sexualities, 1700–1800* (New York: St. Martin's Press, 1997), especially "The Body, Medicine and Sexual Difference," 42–57. Hitchcock agrees with Laqueur's analysis regarding science as a cultural construct but sees medical tracts as reflecting rather than facilitating social change.

13. Anthony Fletcher, *Gender, Sex and Subordination in England 1500–1800* (New Haven: Yale University Press, 1995), 60.

14. James Fordyce, *Sermons for Young Women* [1765] (Philadelphia, 1809), Early American Imprints, 2d ser., no. 17522, ed. Clifford K. Shipton (Worcester, Mass.: American Antiquarian Society, 1967–74), 2:26.

15. Charles B. Cross Jr., ed., *Memoirs of Helen Calvert Maxwell Read* (Chesapeake: Norfolk County Historical Society of Chesapeake, Virginia, 1970), 41.

16. Eliza Jaquelin Ambler Carrington to Ann Ambler Fisher, January 1, 1807, Elizabeth Jaquelin Ambler Papers, DMS 54.5, CWF. Rebecca Burwell Ambler's biographical information is in a letter to Ann Ambler Fisher, October 10, 1796. Rebecca Burwell was taken in by William Nelson of Yorktown, president of the King's council, "who had married her fathers only sister."

17. Catherine Belt, Windsor, to sister-in-law, Mrs. Dulany, March 8, 1792, box 1, MS 1919, Dulany Family Papers, MHS.

18. Journal of Elizabeth Foote Washington, Summer 1784, 6, 9, Washington Family Papers, Library of Congress.

19. Edmund Randolph, "Memoir" of Elizabeth Nicholas Randolph, 7, 9, MSS 1D2278b2, Daniel Family Papers, VHS. Randolph credited his wife with teaching him "oeconomy," a trait he had resisted cultivating until "a mistaken tenderness for [his] slaves" nearly "ruined" him and he could no longer afford to "neglect her admonition to sell them."

20. For those who argue for the Great Awakening's powerful influence, see John Wesley Brinsfield, *Religion and Politics in Colonial South Carolina* (Easley, S.C.: Southern Historical Press, 1983); Patricia Bonomi, *Under the Cope of Heaven: Religion, Society, and Politics in Colonial America* (New York: Oxford University Press, 1986); Nathan Hatch, *The Democratization of American Christianity* (New Haven: Yale University Press, 1989). For those who argue a relatively lower influence, particularly in the South, see John Boles, *The Great Revival 1787–1805* (Lexington: University Press of Kentucky, 1972), 6; Ned C. Landsman, *From Colonials to Provincials: American Thought and Culture, 1680–1760* (New York: Twayne Publishers, 1997), 99; Jon Butler, *Awash in a Sea of Faith: Christianizing the American People* (Cambridge: Harvard University Press, 1990). For a useful way of conceptualizing the Awakening in Virginia, see Mark A. Beliles, "The Christian Communities, Religious Revivals, and Political Culture of the Central Virginia Piedmont, 1737–1813," in *Religion and Political Culture in Jefferson's Virginia*, ed. Garrett Ward Sheldon and Daniel L. Dreisbach (Lanham, Md.: Rowman & Littlefield, 2000), 3–40. Beliles divides the First Great Awakening into the Presbyterian phase, 1743–60; Baptist phase, 1767–77; and Anglican/Methodist phase, 1764–80.

21. Christine Heyrman, *Southern Cross: The Beginnings of the Bible Belt* (New York: Alfred A. Knopf, 1997), 5, 12. The postwar revivals yielded a rich harvest: by the early 1790s, there were approximately fifteen thousand Methodists and twenty thousand Baptists in Virginia. Thomas C. Thompson, "Perceptions of a 'Deist Church' in Early National Virginia," in Ward and Dresibach, *Religion and Political Culture in Jefferson's Virginia*, 45.

22. John K. Nelson, *A Blessed Company: Parishes, Parsons, and Parishioners in Anglican Virginia, 1690–1776* (Chapel Hill: University of North Carolina Press, 2001), 282–89; Kathleen M. Brown, *Good Wives, Nasty Wenches, and Anxious Patriarchs: Gender, Race, and Power in Colonial Virginia* (Chapel Hill: University of North Carolina Press, 1996), 140–44.

23. Patricia Tracy, *Jonathan Edwards, Pastor: Religion and Society in Eighteenth-Century Northampton* (New York: Hill and Wang, 1980).

24. Harry S. Stout, *The Divine Dramatist: George Whitefield and the Rise of Modern Evan-*

gelicalism (Grand Rapids, Mich.: William B. Eerdmans, 1991); Wesley M. Gewehr, *The Great Awakening in Virginia, 1740–1790* (Durham, N.C.: Duke University Press, 1930).

25. Robert M. Calhoon, *Evangelicals and Conservatives in the Early South, 1740–1861* (Columbia: University of South Carolina Press, 1988), 13.

26. These developments are described in Rhys Isaac, *Transformation of Virginia, 1740–1790* (1982; repr., New York: W. W. Norton, 1988).

27. Examples of Anglican repression of the Baptists are recounted by Gewehr, *Great Awakening in Virginia,* 119–26.

28. Bonomi, *Under the Cope of Heaven,* 182.

29. On persecution of Baptists in Virginia see Isaac, *Transformation of Virginia,* 162–63; Lewis Peyton Little, *Imprisoned Preachers and Religious Liberty in Virginia* (Lynchburg: J.P. Bell, 1938), 41–71; Garnett Ryland, *The Baptists of Virginia, 1699–1926* (Richmond: Virginia Baptist Board of Missions and Education, 1955), 60–91; Robert B. Semple, *The History of the Rise and Progress of the Baptists in Virginia* (Richmond: Pitt & Dickinson, 1894), 29–54; Leon McBeth, *The Baptist Heritage: Four Centuries of Baptist Witness* (Nashville: Broadman Press, 1987), 270–73; Robert M. Calhoon, "The Evangelical Persuasion," in *Religion in a Revolutionary Age,* ed. Ronald Hoffman and Peter J. Albert (Charlottesville: University Press of Virginia, 1994), 159.

30. Isabel Rivers, *Reason, Grace, and Sentiment: A Study of the Language of Religion and Ethics in England, 1660–1780* (Cambridge: Cambridge University Press, 1991), 168. Both men were moderate Calvinists whose wide-ranging influence was owing to their written works and teaching of other dissenting ministers.

31. Samuel Davies made a point of visiting Doddridge's widow on a visit to England after Doddridge's death. George William Pilcher, ed., *The Reverend Samuel Davies Abroad: The Diary of a Journey to England and Scotland, 1753–55* (Urbana: University of Illinois Press, 1967), 119.

32. Sarah Jones to Mr. Lloyd, *Devout Letters: Or, Letters Spiritual and Friendly,* quoted in Cynthia Lynn Lyerly, "Passion, Desire, and Ecstasy: The Experiential Religion of Southern Methodist Women, 1770–1810" in *The Devil's Lane: Sex and Race in the Early South,* ed. Catherine Clinton and Michele Gillespie (New York: Oxford University Press, 1997), 175.

33. Paul C. Nagel, *The Lees of Virginia: Seven Generations of an American Family* (New York: Oxford University Press, 1990), 55.

34. Westmoreland County Deeds and Wills 13, 265–67, LVA. Corbin's will is quoted in full in Edmund Jennings Lee, *Lees of Virginia, 1642–1892* (1895; repr., Baltimore: Johns Hopkins University Press, 1974), 87–88. The practice of a husband's imposing limitations on his wife's widowhood was addressed by Joan Gundersen and Gwen Victor Gampel in "Married Women's Legal Status in Eighteenth-Century New York and Virginia," *WMQ,* 3d ser., 39 (1982): 114–34. In their Virginia sample for 1700–80, 6 percent of husbands imposed penalties for their widows' remarriage.

35. Will, Richard Lingan Hall, reel 13, Will Book One, proved July 25, 1774, Fauquier County Records, LVA. Hall's will names his children "born of Mrs. Hannah Corbin." It was customary in eighteenth-century Virginia to use the same baptismal names when there were different fathers or mothers. Ethel Armes, *Stratford Hall: The Great House of the Lees* (Richmond: Garrett and Massie, 1936), 212.

36. Hannah Lee Corbin Correspondence, section 12, Peckatone Papers, VHS.

37. L. Rees Watkins, "They Made It Happen" (Richmond: Baptist General Association of Virginia, 1974), 5. Watkins asserts that "much proof indicates that Hannah Corbin and Richard Hall had a perfectly moral dissenter's marriage ceremony." Nagel also follows the Baptist line, describing Hall as one of the "Northern Neck's early converts." Nagel, *Lees of Virginia,* 56.

38. Paul Verduin, "New Light on Hannah Lee Corbin," speech to the Lee Family Society, June 1995, Stratford Hall Library; Armes, *Stratford Hall*, 209–11; Louise Belote Dawe and Sandra Gioia Treadway, "Hannah Lee Corbin: The Forgotten Lee," *Virginia Cavalcade* 29, no. 2 (1979): 73.

39. Reel 60, May 29, 1764, 125a, Westmoreland County Orders, VHS.

40. Hall owned property in Fauquier County before moving to Peckatone. Dawe and Treadway, "Hannah Lee Corbin," 74; Nagel, *Lees of Virginia*, 57. On the work and influence of David Thomas see Robert B. Semple, *The History of the Rise and Progress of the Baptists in Virginia* (Richmond: Pitt & Dickinson, 1894), 378–90; Little, *Imprisoned Preachers*, 38–9; Ryland, *Baptists of Virginia*, 15–36.

41. John S. Moore and William L. Lumpkin, "Meaningful Moments in Virginia Baptist Life, 1715–1972" (prepared for the Sesquicentennial Celebration of the Baptist General Association of Virginia, 1973), 7.

42. Register, Chappawamsic Baptist Church, Stafford County, Virginia, Minute Books, 1766–1919, 2 vols., VHS; Register, Hartwood Baptist Church, Potomac Association (organized 1771 as Potomac Church), Virginia Baptist Historical Society. Both churches were in Stafford County.

43. Register, Chappawamsic Baptist Church; Register, Hartwood Baptist Church.

44. For example, on June 10, 1775, the congregation excluded Hugh Black, who was accused of "drinking to excess from time to time." On March 8, 1776, William Weeks, accused of "wrangling, quarreling, and attempting to fight his neighbors," was also excluded. Register, Hartwood Baptist Church.

45. Arthur Lee to Richard Henry Lee, quoted in Paul Verduin, "New Light on Hannah Lee Corbin," speech to the Lee Family Society, June 1995, transcript held by Stratford Hall Library.

46. Hannah Lee Corbin to Alice Shippen, n.d., c. 1780, Shippen Family Papers, Library of Congress.

47. Robert Carter's "List of places preachers, and texts. 14 Sep. 1777—4 Jul 1779," Robert Carter Papers, vol. 12, Duke University. Photocopy of typescript, Virginia Baptist Historical Society.

48. While Tillotson in Anglican fashion urged his hearers to get right with each other, James Downey has noted that "evangelicals exhorted men to get right with God." James Downey, *The Eighteenth-Century Pulpit: A Study of the Sermons of Butler, Berkeley, Secker, Sterne, Whitefield, and Wesley* (Oxford: Clarendon Press, 1969), 131.

49. Hannah Lee Corbin to Alice Shippen, n.d., Shippen Family Papers, Library of Congress.

50. Diary, Judith Anna (Smith) Smith, May 3, 1789, Katherine Heath Hawes Papers, VHS. "Mr. Lacy" may have been Drury Lacy, a Presbyterian minister actively preaching in concert with Baptist and Methodist ministers by 1788. Gewehr, *Great Awakening in Virginia*, 168.

51. Diary, Judith Anna (Smith) Smith, May 5, 1789.

52. Ibid.

53. Quoted in Heyrman, *Southern Cross*, 19, 34.

54. Diary, Judith Anna (Smith) Smith, May 7, 1789, VHS.

55. Ibid., September 8, 1789.

56. Journal of Elizabeth Foote Washington, 6, 10, 13–14.

57. Ibid., 14.

58. Heyrman, *Southern Cross*, 165–66. Indeed, the language itself had a leveling effect, as all regarded one another as members of the same family, regardless of race or sex.

59. Quoted in Frank Lambert, *The Founding Fathers and the Place of Religion in America* (Princeton: Princeton University Press, 2003), 151–52.

60. Hatch, *Democratization of American Christianity*; Bonomi, *Under the Cope of Heaven*, 161–86.

61. Lambert, *Founding Fathers and the Place of Religion*, 177–78.

62. Linda K. Kerber, *Women of the Republic: Intellect & Ideology in Revolutionary America* (1980; repr., New York: W. W. Norton, 1986), 15–32, 245. Many women disagreed with the convention's assessment, however, and attempted to claim access to the political process. See Catherine Allgor, *Parlor Politics: In Which the Ladies of Washington Help Build a City and a Government* (Charlottesville: University Press of Virginia, 2000); Cynthia Kierner, "Parades and Genteel Balls: Gender and Early Southern Civic Rituals," *Virginia Magazine of History and Biography* 104, no. 2 (1996): 184–210; Susan Branson, *Those Fiery, Frenchified Dames: Women and Political Culture in Early National Philadelphia* (Philadelphia: University of Pennsylvania Press, 2001).

63. Leonard L. Richards, *Shays's Rebellion: The American Revolution's Final Battle* (Philadelphia: University of Pennsylvania Press, 2002); Thomas Slaughter, *The Whiskey Rebellion: Frontier Epilogue to the American Revolution* (New York: Oxford University Press, 1986); Alan Taylor, *Liberty Men and the Great Proprietors: The Revolutionary Settlement on the Maine Frontier, 1760–1820* (Chapel Hill: University of North Carolina Press, 1990).

64. Gary Nash, *Race and Revolution* (Madison, Wis.: Madison House, 1990), 57–87. Ultimately it would take the Civil Rights Act of 1964 and the willingness of the federal government to enforce it to finally secure the vote for African Americans, a right that had been granted, on paper at least, to newly freed black men by the Fifteenth Amendment in 1870.

65. Kerber, " 'Why Should Girls Be Learnd or Wise?': Education and Intellect in the Early Republic," in *Women of the Republic*, 185–231; Barbara Miller Solomon, *In the Company of Educated Women: A History of Women in Higher Education in America* (New Haven: Yale University Press, 1985), 7–16. Quaker schools in colonial Philadelphia and its environs constitute an exception to the traditional patterns of female education that obtained in colonial America. See Karin Wulf, *Not All Wives: Women of Colonial Philadelphia* (Ithaca: Cornell University Press, 2000), 25–83.

66. Kerber, *Women of the Republic*, 146–48.

67. Marylynn Salmon, *Women and the Law of Property in Early America* (Chapel Hill: University of North Carolina Press, 1986.

68. Lambert, *Founding Fathers and the Place of Religion*, 230; Thomas Buckley, *Church and State in Revolutionary Virginia* (Charlottesville: University Press of Virginia, 1977).

69. Heyrman, *Southern Cross*, 25.

70. Catherine A. Brekus, "The Revolution in the Churches: Women's Religious Activism in the Early American Republic," in *Religion and the New Republic: Faith in the Founding of America*, ed. James H. Hutson (Lanham, Md.: Rowman & Littlefield Publishers, 2000), 115–36.

71. Elizabeth R. Varon, *We Mean to Be Counted: White Women and Politics in Antebellum Virginia* (Chapel Hill: University of North Carolina Press, 1998). These efforts would extend to colonization, the project of relocating newly freed Christian slaves to Africa. Tatiana van Riemsdijk, "Time and Property from Heaven: Wealth, Religion, and Reform in Chesapeake Society, 1790–1832" (Ph.D. diss., University of California, San Diego, 1999).

72. Nancy Armstrong, "The Rise of the Domestic Woman," in *The Ideology of Conduct: Essays on Literature and the History of Sexuality*, ed. Nancy Armstrong and Leonard Tennenhouse (New York: Methuen, 1987), 97. As we shall see in chapter 4, the novel remedies this defect.

73. Fordyce, *Sermons for Young Women*, Sermon 7, 1:151; Sermon 3, 1:52; Sermon 3, 1:55.

74. Kathryn Kirkpatrick, "Sermons and Strictures: Conduct-Book Propriety and Property Relations in Late Eighteenth-Century England," in *History, Gender, and Eighteenth-Century Literature,* ed. Beth Fowkes-Tobin (Athens: University of Georgia Press, 1994), 205–12. Kirkpatrick links Fordyce's suppression of female individuality with the developing capitalist ethos of middle-class Englishmen; men hardly wanted the competition of the marketplace to infect their domestic relations at home.

75. Terry Lovell, "The Reading Public in Eighteenth-Century England" in *The Consumption of Culture, 1600–1800 : Image, Object, Text,* ed. Ann Bermingham and John Brewer (London: Routledge, 1995), 3.

76. Dale Spender, *Mothers of the Novel: 100 Good Women Writers before Jane Austen* (London: Pandora, 1986), 3. On the gendering of writing as masculine, see William J. Scheick, *Authority and Female Authorship in Colonial America* (Lexington: University Press of Kentucky, 1998), 14–16. Scheick's study is exclusively about the northern colonies, "since southern women had far fewer opportunities than their northern sisters for their writings to be published," 19.

77. See, for example, the *Virginia Gazette,* February 16, 1739, 4; October 11, 1751, 4; September 5, 1777, 3; Dixon, April 20, 1776, 3.

78. Cynthia Z. Stiverson and Gregory A. Stiverson, "The Colonial Retail Book Trade: Availability and Affordability of Reading Material in Mid-Eighteenth-Century Virginia," in *Printing and Society in Early America,* ed. William Joyce, David D. Hall, Richard D. Brown, and John B. Hench (Worcester, Mass: American Antiquarian Society, 1983), 170.

79. Calhoun Winton, "The Southern Book Trade in the Eighteenth-Century," in *The Colonial Book in the Atlantic World,* ed. David D. Hall and Hugh Amory (Cambridge: Cambridge University Press), 229—30.

80. Leona M. Hudak, *Early American Women Printers and Publishers 1639–1820* (Metuchen, N.J.: Scarecrow Press, 1978), 131, 144; *South Carolina Gazette,* March 24, 1739, 3.

81. Peggy Murdock to Catherine Dulany Belt, n.d., c. 1770–80, box 1, MS 1919, Dulany Family Papers, MHS.

82. Mary Abigail Willing Coale to Eliza Coale, n.d., c. 1810–15, box 4, MS 1530, Redwood Collection, MHS.

83. Susan M. Stabile, *Memory's Daughters: The Material Culture of Remembrance in Eighteenth-Century America* (Ithaca: Cornell University Press, 2004), 77.

84. Frances Tanner Archer to Jane Cocke, n.d., c. 1790s, section 10, Cocke Family Papers, VHS.

85. Charlotte Balfour to Elizabeth Whiting, November 10, 1789, Blair, Braxton, Braxton, Horner, and Whiting Papers, 1765–1890, CWM.

86. Jean Blair [Williamsburg] to Mary Braxton [Newington], October 14, 1769, BBBHW Papers, CWM.

87. Courteny Norton [Philadelphia] to John Norton, January 7, 1791, MSS 1M4618d, Nannie Norton Collection of the Meade Family Papers, VHS.

88. Peggy McHenry to James McHenry, January 13, 1789, box 1, MS 647, McHenry Family Papers, MHS.

89. Mary Abigail Willing Coale [Philadelphia] to Eliza Coale [Baltimore], n.d., c. 1806–10, MS 1530, Redwood Collection, MHS.

90. Eliza Key to Catherine (Kitty) Dulany, June 1780, box 1, MS 1919, Dulany Family Papers, MHS.

91. Jessica Kross, "Mansions, Men, Women, and the Creation of Multiple Publics in Eighteenth-Century British North America," *Journal of Social History* 33 no. 2 (1999): 385–408.

92. Diary, Judith Anna (Smith) Smith, May 4 and May 5. Smith's May 4, 1789, entry mentions "returned to College[.] conversed with A[lexis] all the way." Her reference to the college suggests Hampden-Sydney, which was experiencing, at precisely this moment, a revival among the student body, from which many Presbyterian ministers would be raised before the revival was over. Drury Lacy, Presbyterian preacher, "was always one of the most prominent preachers at large gatherings" of this revival, which would reach its height in October 1789. Gewehr, *Great Awakening in Virginia,* 182; on the Presbyterian revival, 177–85.

93. Joanna Bowen Gillespie, *The Life and Times of Martha Laurens Ramsay, 1759–1811* (Columbia: University of South Carolina Press, 2001), 186.

94. Diary, Judith Anna (Smith) Smith, May 6, 1789.

95. Memoir of Peter Vivian Daniel of Lucy Nelson (Randolph) Daniel, 9, MSS 1D2278b2, Daniel Family Papers, VHS.

96. Catherine Fullerton Diary, June 18, 1798—September 10, 1798, 1, 2, 8, no. 2, DeRossett Papers, SHC.

97. Ibid., 4.

98. Richard Rankin, *Ambivalent Churchmen and Evangelical Churchwomen: The Religion of the Episcopal Elite in North Carolina, 1800–1860* (Columbia: University of South Carolina Press, 1993), 27–48.

99. Ibid., 45, quoting letter from Catherine DeRossett to her mother, July 28, 1820.

100. Ibid., 102, 59.

101. Ibid., 52–73.

102. Gillespie, *Life and Times of Martha Laurens Ramsay,* 188, and chap. 8, 186–201.

103. Ibid., 61. Martha Laurens's mother died in 1770. Some of the books that she read included Isaac Watts, *Divine and Moral Songs for Children*; Richard Allestree, *The Whole Duty of Man*; Jeremy Taylor, *Holy Living and Holy Dying*; and Law, *A Serious Call to a Devout and Holy Life,* 283, n. 3.

104. Gillespie, *Life and Times of Martha Laurens Ramsay,* 60, 64–65.

105. She may have begun the diary with motherhood; in 1791 she recorded an incident in which she saved her second child, born 1789, from a fall into a fireplace. Ibid., 226.

106. Ibid., 193, 191.

107. Ibid., 135, 99, 223, 120.

108. Ibid., 191, 285–86n45.

109. Journal of Elizabeth Foote Washington, Summer 1784, 25.

110. Ibid., September 1788, 29–31.

111. Ibid., Spring 1789, 45–46.

112. Ibid., 33, 48.

113. Felicity Nussbaum, *The Autobiographical Subject: Gender and Ideology in Eighteenth Century England* (Baltimore: Johns Hopkins University Press, 1989), 133.

114. Journal of Elizabeth Foote Washington, Spring 1789, 46–47.

115. Ibid., September 1788, 29.

116. Ibid., 28.

117. Eliza Jaquelin (Ambler) Brent Carrington to Ann A. Fisher, January 1, 1807, Ambler Family Papers, CWF.

118. Caroline Eliza Clitherall Diaries, 1751–1860, no. 158, 3d ser., vol. 1-1, 29, SHC. The Clitherall diaries are seventeen manuscript volumes that have been transcribed and compiled into three typescript volumes. Clitherall wrote all the diaries quoted here before 1850. In my references to the diaries, the first volume number indicates the typescript volume; the second volume number indicates the original manuscript volume; the page references refer to the typescript.

119. Clitherall Diary, I-I, 40, 2.

120. Richard Ambler to Edward and John Ambler, August 1, 1748, Elizabeth Barbour Ambler Papers, UVA.

121. Elizabeth Ambler to Edward Ambler, October 23, 1749, Elizabeth Barbour Ambler Papers, UVA.

122. Martha Laurens Ramsay to David Ramsay Jr., August 1810, in Gillespie, *Life and Times of Martha Laurens Ramsay,* 214.

123. Catherine Dulany Belt to her brother, October 5, 1807, Dulany Family Papers, MHS.

124. Fordyce, *Sermons,* Sermon VIII, 2:8.

125. Nancy L. Rhoden, *Revolutionary Anglicanism: The Colonial Church of England Clergy during the American Revolution* (New York: New York University Press, 1999), 134.

126. van Riemsdijk, "Time and Property from Heaven, 128–30.

127. Ibid., 136.

128. See, for example, Allgor, *Parlor Politics.*

129. Kerber, *Women of the Republic;* Mary Beth Norton, *Liberty's Daughters: The Revolutionary Experience of American Women, 1750–1800* (New York: Harper Collins, 1980).

130. "The Planter's Wife," *Virginia Gazette,* Rind, August 7, 1774, reprinted September 15, 1774.

131. *Virginia Gazette,* Purdie & Dixon, June 9, 1774, 3.

132. Alice Lee of Blenheim, Charles County, Maryland, written from Annapolis to Anne Galloway of Tulip Hill, who was staying in Philadelphia. Box 21, MS 1994, Cheston-Galloway Papers, MHS (n.d., but the *Peggy Stewart* was burned by its owner, Anthony Stewart on October 19, 1774.) Aubrey Land, *Colonial Maryland: A History* (Millwood, N.Y.: KTO Press, 1981), 301–03.

133. *Virginia Gazette,* Dixon, September 21, 1776, 2.

134. Judith Sargent Murray, *The Gleaner,* in *Judith Sargent Murray: A Brief Biography with Documents,* ed. Sheila L. Skemp (Boston: Bedford Books, 1998), 144–49, 162–68.

135. Quoted in Catherine A. Brekus, "The Revolution in the Churches: Women's Religious Activism in the Early American Republic," in Hutson, *Religion and the New Republic, 115.*

136. Letters of Eliza Wilkinson, c. 1779, excerpted in Mary Louise Weaks and Carolyn Perry, *Southern Women's Writing, Colonial to Contemporary* (Gainesville: University Press of Florida, 1995), 26.

137. Kerber, *Women of the Republic,* 110–11.

138. Indeed, St. John's fell on such hard times that in the 1790s the vestry met at the state capitol building for its triennial elections. J. Staunton Moore, ed., *Annals and History of Henrico Parish, Diocese of Virginia and St. John's P[rot].E[piscopal]. Church* (Baltimore: Genealogical Publishing, 1979), 27.

139. Letter, E. J. A. B. Carrington to Frances Caines, 1792, Ambler Family Papers, CWF. On March 31, 1785, Jaquelin Ambler "having subscribed to be conformable to the doctrine, discipline & worship of the Protestant Episcopal Church, entered on the office of vestryman." On June 28, 1785, Ambler was appointed treasurer of the church and on May 23, 1789, Edward Carrington was appointed chairman of the vestry. *Vestry Records of St. John's Church, 1785–1887,* March 31, 1785; June 28, 1785; May 22, 1789, miscellaneous reel no. 423, LVA.

140. Van Riemsdijk, "Time and Property from Heaven," 150–53. Bishop Meade promoted women's anonymity even as he promoted women's giving.

141. Ibid., 121–24.

142. C[harles] W[esley] Andrews, *Memoir of Mrs. Ann R. Page* (New York: Garland Publishing, 1987), 9.

143. Donald G. Mathews, *Religion in the Old South* (Chicago: University of Chicago Press, 1977), 116.

144. Van Riemsdijk, "Time and Property from Heaven," 120.

145. In addition to William, there were two other sisters, Susannah Meade and Lucy Meade, who were deeply involved in the Sunday School and colonization movements.

146. Rankin, *Ambivalent Churchmen*, 8, 14, 72–73.

147. Printer Ann Timothy printed their "Rules." Hudak, *Early American Women Printers and Publishers*, 489.

148. Suzanne Lebsock, *The Free Women of Petersburg: Status and Culture in a Southern Town, 1784–1860* (New York: W. W. Norton, 1984), 64, 196–215.

149. For Eliza Carrington's story, see Catherine Kerrison, "By the Book: Eliza Ambler Brent Carrington and Conduct Literature in the Eighteenth Century," *Virginia Magazine of History and Biography* 105 (1997): 27–52, and chapter 4. No doubt her girlhood experience of watching an orphaned friend's seduction and near ruin explains her deep interest in helping unprotected girls.

150. "Memorial Foundation for Children, History, 1965," typescript manuscript, 2–3, LVA.

151. Ibid., 3.

152. On the incorporation of the Female Humane Association of Richmond, see *Constitution and Bylaws of the Female Humane Association of the City of Richmond* (Richmond: John Warrock, 1833), accession no. 26532 a-c, LVA. A female asylum was similarly incorporated in Petersburg two years later. On the significance of the asylum's incorporation and female organizations generally, see Lebsock, "Women Together: Organizations," in *Free Women of Petersburg*, 195–236.

153. An 1843 edition of the 1833 *Constitution and Bylaws* recounts the "gloom and despondency" hanging over poorly attended meetings that yielded little revenue for the great work that had to be done. Constitution and Bylaws of the Female Humane Association of the City of Richmond (Richmond: Shepherd and Colin, 1843), 3, accession no. 26532 a-c, LVA; *Constitution and Bylaws*, 1833, 7–8.

154. "Memorial Foundation for Children," 4. Petersburg women also instituted their first fund-raising fair in May 1829, raising an astonishing $2,000 in their first attempt. Lebsock, *Free Women of Petersburg*, 211.

155. "Memorial Foundation for Children" 3. Suzanne Lebsock made this point for the Petersburg women's efforts. Lebsock, *Free Women of Petersburg*, 205.

156. Eliza (Ambler) Carrington, "Variety or the Vicissitudes of Long Life," 3, Ambler Family Papers, CWF.

157. Varon, *We Mean to Be Counted*, 11, 20–24, 30.

158. Van Riemsdijk, "Time and Property from Heaven," 182–83.

159. As late as 1840, only 6 percent of Virginia women lived in cities. Ibid., 180.

160. Heyrman, *Southern Cross*, 191–92.

161. Varon, *We Mean to Be Counted*, 43.

162. Van Riemsdijk, "Time and Property from Heaven," 283.

163. Varon, *We Mean to Be Counted*, 26.

164. Mathews, *Religion in Old South*, 112–113.

165. Amanda Porterfield, *Female Piety in Puritan New England : The Emergence of Religious Humanism* (New York: Oxford University Press, 1992).

166. Heyrman, *Southern Cross*, 193.

167. Dee Andrews, *The Methodists and Revolutionary America, 1760–1800: The Shaping of an Evangelical Culture* (Princeton: Princeton University Press, 2000), 115, 117.

168. Jerald C. Brauer, "Regionalism and Religion in America," in *Protestantism and Regionalism*, ed. Martin E. Marty (Munich: K.G. Saur, 1992), 12; Edward L. Bond,

Damned Souls in a Tobacco Colony: Religion in Seventeenth-Century Virginia (Macon, Ga.: Mercer University Press, 2000), 241–44, 284, 290–93.

169. Jan Lewis, *The Pursuit of Happiness: Family and Values in Jefferson's Virginia* (Cambridge: Cambridge University Press, 1983), 43–46.

170. Letters of Eliza Wilkinson, c. 1779, in Weaks and Perry, *Southern Women's Writing*, 26.

171. Mary Ellis to William Wirt, April 9, 1802, Baylor Family Papers, UVA.

172. This point is more fully developed in chapter 5, "Reading, Race, and Writing."

173. Hilda Smith, *All Men and Both Sexes: Gender, Politics and the False Universal in England, 1640–1832* (University Park: Pennsylvania State University Press, 2002), 197.

174. See, for example, Daniel B. Shea, ed., "Some Account of the Fore Part of the Life of Elizabeth Ashbridge," in *Journeys into New Worlds: Early American Women's Narratives*, ed. William Andrews (Madison: University of Wisconsin Press, 1990), 117–80.

175. Heyrman, *Southern Cross*, 162, 173.

176. Bonnie Cook Freeman, "Female Education in Patriarchal Power Systems," in *Education and Colonialism*, ed. Philip G. Altbach and Gail P. Kelly (New York: Longman, 1978), 207–42.

177. P. Joy Rouse, "Cultural Models of Womanhoood," in *Nineteenth-Century Women Learn to Write*, ed. Catherine Hobbs (Charlottesville: University Press of Virginia, 1995), 237.

178. Joan Hoff Wilson, "The Illusion of Change: Women and the American Revolution," in *The American Revolution: Explorations in the History of American Radicalism*, ed. Alfred F. Young (DeKalb: Northern Illinois University Press, 1976), 409.

179. Journal of Elizabeth Foote Washington, 45–46, 9.

180. Harold Love, *The Culture and Commerce of Texts: Scribal Publication in Seventeenth-Century England* (Amherst: University of Massachusetts Press, 1998), 54–58, 202.

181. Spender, *Mothers of the Novel*, 4. Indeed, as her title suggests, Spender argues that women and not men were the creators, "mothers," of the novel in eighteenth-century England.

182. Margaret Ripley Wolfe, *Daughters of Canaan: A Saga of Southern Women* (Lexington: University Press of Kentucky, 1995), 6. See also on this point, Cynthia Kierner, *Beyond the Household: Women's Place in the Early South, 1700–1835* (Ithaca: Cornell University Press, 1998), 36–68; Elizabeth Fox-Genovese, *Within the Plantation Household: Black and White Women of the Old South* (Chapel Hill: University of North Carolina Press, 1988); Catherine Clinton, *The Plantation Mistress: Woman's World in the Old South* (New York: Pantheon Press, 1982).

183. Love, *Culture and Commerce of Texts*, 56. Scribal publication in the northern and Middle Atlantic colonies was slightly more developed. See Esther Edwards Burr's correspondence with Sarah Prince in Carol F. Karlsen and Laurie Crumpacker, *The Journal of Esther Edwards Burr, 1754–1757* (New Haven: Yale University Press, 1984), and Carla Mulford, *Only for the Eye of a Friend: The Poems of Annis Boudinot Stockton* (Charlottesville: University Press of Virginia, 1995). The friend for whom Stockton compiled her volume was Elizabeth Graeme Fergusson, the center of a late eighteenth-century literary circle in the Middle Atlantic. Karin Wulf documents the publications, both scribal and in the press, of Philadelphia women in *Not All Wives: Women of Colonial Philadelphia* (Ithaca: Cornell University Press, 2000).

4. Reading Novels in the South

1. William K. Bottorff and Roy C. Flannagan, eds., "The Diary of Frances Baylor Hill of Hillsborough, King and Queen County, VA (1797), *Early American Literature* 2

(Winter 1967): 45 (first and second quotations), 48 (third quotation); Frances Burney, *Evelina, or, a young lady's entrance into the world* (London 1778).

2. Cathy Davidson, *Revolution and the Word: The Rise of the Novel in America* (New York: Oxford University Press, 1986), 83–101.

3. Bottorff and Flannagan, "Diary of Frances Baylor Hill," 45 (first quotation), 16–18 (second quotation). The full titles of the books Hill read are James Blair, *Our Savior's divine Sermon on the Mount . . . explained: and the practice of it recommended in divers sermons and discourses* (London, 1740) and John Gregory, *A Father's Legacy to his Daughters* (London, 1774; reprinted at least twenty-three times before 1877). "Letters on Education" probably was Catherine Macaulay's work of the same name, written and published in London in 1790; Hill did not specify an author or comment further.

4. By Skipwith's death in 1826, novels, poetry, and drama titles number 197 out of the 384 titles we know she owned; of religious texts, she owned but 6. Mildred K. Abraham, "The Library of Lady Jean Skipwith: A Book Collection from the Age of Jefferson," *Virginia Magazine of History and Biography* 91, no. 3 (1983): 310–11.

5. George Savile, Marquis of Halifax, *The Lady's New Year's Gift; or, Advice to a Daughter* (London, 1688). Kevin J. Hayes, *A Colonial Woman's Bookshelf* (Knoxville: University of Tennessee Press, 1996), 2; Julia Cherry Spruill, "Southern Lady's Library, 1700–1776," *South Atlantic Quarterly* 34 (1935): 23. Portions of both Allestree's and Halifax's work appeared in Richard Steele's *The Ladies Library* (first published in London in 1714), widening further still their circles of influence. *The Lady's New Year's Gift* was printed twice in 1688 and went through at least ten more printings by 1756. Library of Congress online catalog.

6. *Virginia Gazette*, May 20, 1737, 1.

7. *Virginia Gazette*, Purdie and Dixon, March 4, 1773.

8. Dale Spender, ed., *Living by the Pen: Early British Women Writers* (New York: Teachers College Press, 1992), 32.

9. "Essay on the Modern Novel," *Virginia Gazette*, Purdie and Dixon, June 11, 1772, 1.

10. Elizabeth Cometti, "Some Early Best Sellers in Piedmont North Carolina," *Journal of Southern History* 17 (1950): 324–37. Their offerings notwithstanding, Johnston and Bennehan split their inventory of novels between them in 1779, since they did not appeal to their customers as well as the steady sellers did.

11. Alice Izard to Mrs. Joseph Allen Smith, November 1, 1811, quoted in Jeffrey Robert Young, *Domesticating Slavery: The Master Class in Georgia and South Carolina, 1670–1837* (Chapel Hill: University of North Carolina Press, 1999), 140.

12. "Books in Colonial Virginia," *Virginia Historical Magazine* 10 (1903): 403.

13. Richard Beale Davis, *Intellectual Life in the Colonial South* (Knoxville: University of Tennessee Press, 1978), 2:509.

14. This is a common complaint of anyone who has tried to study this subject in the South. See Julia Cherry Spruill, "The Southern Lady's Library," 38; Davis, *Intellectual Life in the Colonial South*, 2:498–500. "Inventories of books for many counties of these seaboard colonies simply do not exist," Davis discovered. Many were lost during the course of wars and in accidental fires.

15. "Books in Colonial Virginia," 401.

16. Davis, *Intellectual Life in the Colonial South*, 2:543–61.

17. Kevin J. Hayes, *The Library of William Byrd of Westover* (Madison, Wisc.: Madison House, 1997), 307, 302, 311.

18. "Catalogue of Library of Robert Carter compiled by Philip Fithian," in *Journal and Letters of Philip Vickers Fithian: A Plantation Tutor of the Old Dominion, 1773–1774*, ed. Hunter Farish (1943; repr., Charlottesville: University Press of Virginia, 1993), 221–29. Of course, the list Fithian produced records only the books at the Nomini Hall

plantation on the Northern Neck in 1774–75; it does not touch the more than four hundred books Carter kept at his town house in Williamsburg. Undoubtedly Carter continued to add to his library until his death in 1804.

19. "Books in Colonial Virginia," 404–5.

20. Inventory, John Luttrell, 1782, Orange County Inventories Sales and Accounts of Estates, 1758–1809, 368–69; Inventory, James Milner, December 17, 1773, in *North Carolina Wills and Inventories, Copied from the Original and Recorded Wills and Inventories in the Office of the Secretary of State,* ed. J. Bryan Grimes (1912; repr., Baltimore: Genealogical Publishing, 1967), 514–22.

21. Jack Greene, *Pursuits of Happiness: The Social Development of Early Modern British Colonies and the Formation of American Culture* (Chapel Hill: University of North Carolina Press, 1988), 147; George C. Rogers Jr., *Charleston in the Age of the Pinckneys* (1969; repr., Columbia: University of South Carolina Press, 1980), 3. Before the Revolution, Charleston was known as Charles Town.

22. Elizabeth Timothy took over the reins of the *South Carolina Gazette* in December 1738 after her husband's death. She ran the paper so successfully in spite of numerous personal tragedies (she buried four children) that Benjamin Franklin included a tribute to her in his autobiography. She apparently left South Carolina in 1749, after gradually easing her son, Peter, into the trade. After his death, Peter's widow, Ann Timothy, published the *South Carolina Gazette* from 1783 until her death in 1792. Martha J. King, "Making an Impression: Women Printers in the Southern Colonies in the Revolutionary Era" (Ph.D. diss., College of William and Mary, 1992), 176–95, 258–59.

23. Henning Cohen, *The South Carolina Gazette 1732–1775* (Columbia: University of South Carolina Press, 1953), 133.

24. Lucas commented on *Pamela* after she had finished reading it; see notes 58 and 59 below. For a different perspective, see Carol F. Karlsen and Laurie Crumpacker, eds., *The Journal of Esther Edwards Burr 1754–1757* (New Haven: Yale University Press, 1984), in which Burr comments on the book to her friend, Sarah Prince, as she is reading it.

25. Christopher Gould and Richard Parker Morgan, comps., *South Carolina Imprints 1731–1800: A Descriptive Bibliography* (Santa Barbara, Calif.: ABC-Clio Information Services, 1985), 37. The Rules were published by Peter Timothy.

26. James Raven, *London Booksellers and American Customers: Transatlantic Literary Community and the Charleston Library Society, 1748–1811* (Columbia: University of South Carolina Press, 2002).

27. Gould and Morgan, *South Carolina Imprints,* 96. Since there were no further announcements about *The Beggergirl,* it is uncertain whether it actually was published, 295.

28. David A. Rawson, "'Guardians of Their Own Liberty': A Contextual History of Print Culture in Virginia Society, 1750–1820" (Ph.D. diss., College of William and Mary, 1998), 433. This practice was confined neither to Virginia printers nor to the colonial period.

29. These books are housed at CWM.

30. Davis, *Intellectual Life in the Colonial South,* 2:624.

31. Anne Blair to Frances Randolph (later Tucker), April 17, 1778, Tucker-Coleman Papers, CWM.

32. Davidson, *Revolution and the Word,* 73.

33. Halifax warned his daughter that a wife's reproaches of her husband's infidelity would provoke rather than reform him; indeed, he wrote, "such an indecent complaint makes a wife more ridiculous than the injury that provoketh it." Halifax, *The*

Lady's New Year's Gift, in John Kenyon, *Halifax: Complete Works* (Baltimore: Penguin Books, 1969), 279–80.

34. Mary Priestley, ed., *The Female Spectator, Being Selections from Mrs. Eliza Heywood's* [*sic*] *Periodical (1744–1746)* (London, 1929), 11–16, 16–26, 66–72. Not all criticisms of male sexual codes of conduct came from women. Samuel Richardson's rake, Lovelace (pronounced Love-less), in *Clarissa: Or, the History of a Young Lady: Comprehending the Most Important Concerns of Private Life; and Particularly Shewing the Distress that May Attend the Misconduct Both of Parents and Children, in Relation to Marriage* (London, 1748), excited pity rather than envy as his amorous adventures cost him the love of a virtuous woman.

35. Elizabeth Bergen Brophy, *Women's Lives and the 18th-Century English Novel* (Tampa: University of South Florida Press, 1991), 39–40.

36. The use of this phrase rebuked men who abused the privileges of their sex. See Hannah Woolley, *The Gentlewoman's Companion; or, A Guide to the Female Sex* (London, 1675), and Mary Astell, *Some Reflections Upon Marriage* (London, 1706), excerpted in Angeline Goreau, *The Whole Duty of a Woman: Female Writers in Seventeenth-Century England* (Garden City, N.Y., 1985), 27, 156. Southern women also used this expression in their letters. See, for example, *Letters of Eliza Wilkinson, During the Invasion and Possession of Charleston, S.C., by the British in the Revolutionary War* (1839; repr., New York: New York Times, 1969), 26.

37. "Lady's Toilette: The Wig," English, c. 1802, CWF.

38. Janis Bergman-Carton, *The Women of Ideas in French Art, 1830–1848* (New Haven: Yale University Press, 1995), 16–17.

39. Mildred Smith to Betsey Ambler (Eliza Jaquelin Ambler), Letter No. 1, c. 1781 (erroneously dated 1780), Elizabeth Jaquelin Ambler Papers, DMS 54.5, CWF.

40. Halifax, *Lady's New Year's Gift*, in Kenyon, *Halifax*, 302.

41. This story is recounted in detail in Catherine Kerrison, "By the Book: Eliza Ambler Brent Carrington and Conduct Literature in Late Eighteenth-Century Virginia," *Virginia Magazine of History and Biography* 105, no. 1 (1997): 27–52. Ambler's father had followed a "plan of education" that suggests a considered purposefulness that did not normally characterize girls' education in Virginia. He composed various handwriting, composition, and arithmetic lessons for his daughters (Betsey Ambler's sister, Mary, later married the future chief justice of the Supreme Court, John Marshall). He also had them read the two-volume *Preceptor* (a work directed to boys) containing sections on geography, natural history, logic, and moral philosophy. R[obert] and J. Dodsely, *The Preceptor: Containing a General Course of Education. Wherein the First Principles of Polite Learning are Laid Down in a Way most suitable for trying the GENIUS and advancing the Instruction of YOUTH* (London, 1763). Eliza Jaquelin (Ambler) Brent Carrington to Ann (Ambler) Fisher, c. 1807–9, Ambler Papers, CWF.

42. Davidson, *Revolution and the Word*, 66.

43. Priestley, *The Female Spectator*, 56. One of Haywood's devices in her *Female Spectator* was to write letters from fictitious readers, allowing her to raise whatever issues she wished in her publication and dispensing with the necessity of a staff. Patricia Meyer Spacks, ed., *Selections from* The Female Spectator *by Eliza Haywood* (New York: Oxford University Press, 1999), xiii.

44. Mildred Smith to Betsey Ambler, Letter No. 1. [1781].

45. Ros Ballaster, "Gender and Genre in Early Theories of Narrative," in Spender, *Living by the Pen*, 195. In this way, Ballaster points out, women's writings do not conform to the idea of "realism" found in eighteenth-century male-authored novels—or in twentieth-century analyses of those novels, such as Ian Watt, *The Rise of the Novel: Studies in Defoe, Richardson and Fielding* (Berkeley: University of California Press, 1962).

46. Linda K. Kerber, *Women of the Republic: Intellect and Ideology in Revolutionary America* (New York: W. W. Norton, 1980), 263–64.

47. Bottorff and Flannagan, "Diary of Frances Baylor Hill," 12, 45, 50: Elizabeth Helme, *Louisa the Lovely Orphan; or, The cottage on the moor* (Boston, 1795); *Letters of the Right Honourable Lady M[ar]y W[ortle]y M[ontag]u, written during her travels in Europe, Asia and Africa to persons of distinction* (London, 1763).

48. Catherine Fullerton Diary, 1798, folder 141, ser. 3, 9, DeRosset Family Papers, SHC, referring to John Moore, *A View of Society and Manners in France, Switzerland, and Germany; with Anecdotes Relating to Some Eminent Characters* (London, 1783). Travel literature, in fact, could be seen as a form of fiction. For example, *The Travels of Sir John Mandeville*, first published around 1360, described a magical world of Amazonian women, cannibals, and sea monsters. Nonetheless, it continued to be published into the eighteenth century. Although fictional, it was taken as truth for centuries; hence travel narratives, as a genre, continued to be tainted as fiction. See *The Travels of Sir John Mandeville* [1499 ed., from 1725 text], ed. A. W. Pollard (London, 1900), and Barbara Korte, *English Travel Writing from Pilgrimages to Postcolonial Explorations*, trans. Catherine Matthias. (New York: St. Martin's Press, 2000), 23–30.

49. Quoted in Margaret Law Callcott, ed., *Mistress of Riversdale: The Plantation Letters of Rosalie Stier Calvert 1795–1821* (Baltimore: Johns Hopkins University Press, 1991), 9. A young girl upon her arrival in Maryland in 1794, Rosalie Stier apparently took quickly to American ways. In 1803, as her father reflected on her often-stated wish that the family might be reunited, in Europe if necessary, he remarked, "I don't know if you yourself, having left at so young an age and having become used to other ways, would find life here [in Belgium] more pleasant than there." Ibid., 69.

50. Richard Brinsley Sheridan, *The Rivals* [1775], ed. Alan S. Downer (New York: Appleton-Century-Crofts, 1953), 10.

51. "Maternal Advice," London, 1795. An alternative reading, suggested by her drooping muff, might be that the daughter's plans to meet her suitor have been foiled by her mother's lesson; whatever the case, the generation gap is clear.

52. Will, Sarah Allen, 1761, proved 1763, in J. Bryan Grimes, *North Carolina Wills and Inventories*, 9–13.

53. Charles B. Cross Jr., ed., *Memoirs of Helen Calvert Maxwell Read* (Chesapeake, Va.: Norfolk Historical Society, 1970), 43–44.

54. Diary of Elizabeth Drinker, June 20, 1795, quoted in Kerber, *Women of the Republic*, 238. Kerber's analysis of women's reading in the early national period relies heavily on this wonderful source. American women's commentaries on their reading are few before the rise of women's academies in the nineteenth century, even in the North.

55. Samuel Richardson, *Pamela: Or, Virtue Rewarded* (London, 1740). Esther Edwards Burr to Sarah Prince, March 12, 1755, and April 8, 1755, in Karlsen and Crumpacker, *The Journal of Esther Edwards Burr,* 209 (first quotation), 99 (second quotation), 107 (third quotation).

56. Kerber, *Women of the Republic*, 249.

57. Elise Lucas Pinckney, ed., *The Letterbook of Eliza Lucas Pinckney, 1739–1762* (Chapel Hill: University of North Carolina Press, 1972), xv–xvi.

58. Letter, Eliza Lucas to Mary Bartlett, c. June or July 1742, ibid., 47–48.

59. Ibid.

60. Cathy Davidson, ed., *Charlotte Temple*, by Susanna Haswell Rowson. (New York: Oxford University Press, 1986), xix.

61. Eliza Lucas to Mary Bartlett, n.d., in Pinckney, *Letterbook*, 48.

62. *Virginia Gazette*, Purdie and Dixon, December 22, 1752, 1.

63. "For the Perusal of our Female Readers," *Virginia Gazette*, Purdie and Dixon, March 28, 1771, 2. It is not known whether these criticisms were written by English or American writers. Regardless of their origins, however, the significant point is that they were printed by a Virginia press for consumption in that colony.

64. "Essay on the Modern Novel," 1.

65. Kathleen Brown makes the point that the distinctions of class among women enabled the freer association of all ranks of white men. Kathleen Brown, *Good Wives, Nasty Wenches, Anxious Patriarchs: Gender, Race, and Power in Colonial Virginia* (Chapel Hill: University of North Carolina Press, 1996), 317.

66. "Essay on the Modern Novel," 1.

67. The rise of the companionate marriage has been the subject of much study by social historians in the last two decades. See Lawrence Stone, *The Family, Sex, and Marriage in England, 1500–1800* (New York: Harper & Row, 1977), and Anthony Fletcher, *Gender, Sex, and Subordination in England, 1500–1800* (New Haven: Yale University Press, 1995). On the phenomenon in Virginia, see Daniel Blake Smith, *Inside the Great House: Planter Family Life in Eighteenth-Century Chesapeake Society* (Ithaca: Cornell University Press, 1980). Linda Kerber has documented evidence of these heightened expectations of marriage in her study of post-Revolutionary divorce suits in Kerber, *Women of the Republic*, 167, 175–77.

68. Jack Greene, ed. *Diary of Landon Carter of Sabine Hall, 1752–1778* (Charlottesville: University Press of Virginia, 1965), 2:720 (first quotation), 763 (second quotation), 814 (third quotation), 868 (fourth and fifth quotations), 795 (sixth quotation), 1146 (seventh quotation). Carter no doubt referred to John Dryden's *All for Love* or *The World Well Lost*, a 1677 tragedy based on Shakespeare's *Antony and Cleopatra*.

69. Nancy Johns Turner, "The Imaginationist or Recollections of an old lady, a native of one of the southern States, now a resident of the State of Ohio in the Year 1844," typescript, 18 (all quotations), VHS. The books that Turner named, all European imports, were among the most popular novels of the colonial period: Tobias George Smollet, *The adventures of Peregrine Pickle. In which are included, Memoirs of a lady of quality* (London, 1751) and *The adventures of Roderick Random* (London, 1748); and Alain René Lesage, *The Adventures of Gil Blas of Santillane. A New translation from the best French edition* (London, 1749). She would have read these novels sometime before 1808, the date of her first marriage.

70. Ibid., 25 (first quotation), 31–32 (second and third quotations).

71. Ibid., 25.

72. *Virginia Gazette*, Purdie & Dixon, July 14, 1775, 4.

73. Accounts of Hannah Lee Corbin, section 13, Peckatone Papers, VHS. Receipts dated from October 21, 1766, through July 10, 1772, show her purchase of books; some receipts list titles, others list merely "books."

74. *The History of Charlotte Summers, The Fortunate Parish Girl* (London, 1750), listed in "An Inventory and Appraisement of the Personal Estate Of Mrs. Hannah Corbin," January 13, 1783, Accounts, section 13, Peckatone Papers, VHS; receipt dated October 21, 1766, for the purchase of Jean Digard de Kerguette, *True Merit, True Happiness; Exemplified in the Entertaining and Instructive Memoirs of Mr. S—* (London, 1757), in Accounts, section 13, Peckatone Papers, VHS.

75. Receipt dated October 21, 1766, for the purchase of [Anne-Louise Elie de Beaumont], *The History of the Young Lady of Distinction. In a Series of Letters* (London, 1754), in Accounts, section 13, Peckatone Papers, VHS.

76. [Beaumont], *History of a Young Lady of Distinction*, 1:5–6 (first quotation), 8 (second and third quotation), 11–12 (fourth quotation).

77. Paul C. Nagel, *The Lees of Virginia: Seven Generations of an American Family* (New York: Oxford University Press, 1990), 121.

78. [Beaumont], *History of a Young Lady of Distinction*, 1:43–53, 98–99, 108–9, 156–69.

79. Ibid., 1:80–81 (first, second, and third quotations), 87 (fourth quotation), 92–97.

80. Rhys Isaac, *Transformation of Virginia 1740–1790* (1982; repr., New York: W. W. Norton, 1988), 58–65; Dell Upton, *Holy Things and Profane: Anglican Parish Churches in Colonial Virginia* (Cambridge: Harvard University Press, 1986); Farish, *Journal and Letters of Philip Vickers Fithian*, 137, 167.

81. [Beaumont], *History of a Young Lady of Distinction*, 1:161 (first quotation), 168 (second quotation).

82. Letter, Hannah Lee Corbin to Alice Lee Shippen, c. 1780, Shippen Family Papers, Manuscripts Division, Library of Congress. In this same letter Corbin wrote, "Your niece has also enlisted herself amongst the poor despised Baptists. . . . Elisha delights much in the Religious society [the young Baptist women], but the Lord has never yet revealed himself to him."

83. Doreen Rosman, *Evangelicals and Culture* (London: Croom Helm, 1984), 167.

84. Landon C. Bell, *Cumberland Parish, Lunenburg County, Virginia 1746–1818; Vestry Book 1746–1818* (Richmond: William Byrd Press, 1930), 132–43. Cameron, born and ordained in Scotland, served in Bristol Parish from 1784 to 1793.

85. Peyton Skipwith to Jean Miller, September 7, 1788, Skipwith Family Papers, CWM.

86. Quoting Agnes Maria Bennett, *Agnes De-Courci: A Domestic Tale*, 2d ed. (London, 1797), 1:92, 100. Receipt from William Potts, 1807, Skipwith Family Papers, CWM. The citation and all punctuation are Jean Skipwith's.

87. See list of Corbin's orders, notes 90 and 91. On female authorship in England, see Dale Spender, *Mothers of the Novel: 100 Good Women Writers before Jane Austen* (London: Pandora, 1986). Spender's book is a corrective to the idea of the novel as a solely male creation and endeavor, as portrayed in Watt, *The Rise of the Novel* and Michael McKeon, *The Origins of the English Novel 1600–1740* (Baltimore: Johns Hopkins University Press, 1987). Long after the Revolution, American women were still reading English novels. Richard D. Brown, *Knowledge Is Power: The Diffusion of Information in Early America, 1700–1865* (New York: Oxford University Press, 1989), 175.

88. Janet Todd, *The Sign of Angellica: Women, Writing and Fiction, 1660–1800* (New York, Columbia University Press, 1989), 3.

89. Ruth Bloch, "Gendered Meanings of Virtue," *Signs: Journal of Women in Culture and Society* 13 (1987): 37–58. Laurel Ulrich describes how the controls over sexual behavior changed from external to internal ones, with the demise of church authority in New England. Laurel Ulrich, *Good Wives: Image and Reality in the Lives of Women in Northern New England, 1650–1750* (1982; repr., New York: Vintage, 1991), 97, 103.

90. Inventory, Hannah Lee Corbin, October 21, 1782, and January 13, 1783, Accounts, section 13, Peckatone Papers, VHS. The full titles are *The History of a Young Lady of Distinction. In a Series of Letters* (London, 1754); *The History of Charlotte Summers, The Fortunate Parish Girl* (London, 1750); Charles de Fieux Mouhy, *The Fortunate Country Maid. Being the entertaining memoirs of the present celebrated Marchioness of L.V. who from a cottage . . . Became a lady of the first quality in the court of France* (Dublin, 1741); *The country cousins: or, a journey to London* (London, 1767).

91. Receipt from Nathaniel Young, Bookseller in London, October 21, 1766, and from T. Cadell, London, June 19, 1772, Accounts, section 13, Peckatone Papers, VHS. Unfortunately for historians, books were infrequently itemized in early American inventories, even in estates of wealthy people. George K. Smart, "Private Libraries in Colonial Virginia," *American Literature* 10 (1938): 28n15. The incompleteness of

Corbin's inventory is suggested by the additional titles in her accounts. The full titles are *The Rival Mother: or, the history of the Countess De Salens, and her Two Daughters* (London, 1755); *True Merit, True Happiness; Exemplified in the Entertaining and Instructive Memoirs of Mr. S—* (London, 1757); *The Curate of Coventry: a tale* (London, 1771).

92. Quoted in Todd, *The Sign of Angellica*, 112.

93. Catherine Craft-Fairchild, *Masquerade and Gender: Disguise and Female Identity in Eighteenth-Century Fictions by Women* (University Park: Pennsylvania State University Press, 1993), 166.

94. Mitzi Myers, "Daddy's Girl as Motherless Child: Maria Edgeworth and Maternal Romance; An Essay in Reassessment," in Dale Spender, *Living by the Pen*, 147; Abraham, "Library of Lady Jean Skipwith," 331–32.

95. Abraham, "Library of Lady Jean Skipwith," 327 (Bennett), 341 (Roche), 345 (West), 339–340 (Porter), 338 (Opie), 326 (Burney), 340 (Radcliffe), 340 (Reeve).

96. William Parks, the Williamsburg printer of the *Virginia Gazette*, opened a bookstore in 1742 and stocked it with a hundred two-volume sets of Samuel Richardson's wildly popular novel *Pamela*, supplied by Philadelphia printer Benjamin Franklin. Calhoun Winton, "The Southern Book Trade in the Eighteenth Century," in *A History of the Book in America: The Colonial Book in the Atlantic World*, ed. Hugh Amory and David D. Hall (New York: Cambridge University Pres, 2000), 1:230.

97. Abraham, "Library of Lady Jean Skipwith," 306; account slips, Skipwith Family Papers, CWM.

98. Felicity Nussbaum, *The Brink of All We Hate: English Satires on Women, 1660–1750* (Lexington: University Press of Kentucky, 1984), 161.

99. Macaulay argued that "the great difference now beheld in the external consequences which follow the deviations from chastity in the two sexes, did in all probability arise from the women having been considered as the mere property of the men; . . . that policy adopted this difference, when the plea of property had been given up; and it was still preserved in society from the unruly licentiousness of the men, who . . . by mutual support and general opinion [continue] to use their natural freedom with impunity." Catherine Macaulay, *Letters on Education* (London, 1790; repr., Oxford: Oxford University Press, 1994), 220. See also Alice Browne, *The Eighteenth-Century Feminist Mind* (Detroit: Wayne State University Press, 1987), 150; and Todd, *Sign of Angellica*, 208.

100. Cynthia Kierner makes this point, noting that Mary Beth Norton's study, *Liberty's Daughters*, which begins in 1750, missed these trends started long before the Revolutionary era. Mary Beth Norton, *Liberty's Daughters: The Revolutionary Experience of American Women, 1750–1800* (New York: Harper Collins, 1980). Cynthia Kierner, *Beyond the Household: Women's Place in the Early South, 1700–1835* (Ithaca: Cornell University Press, 1998), 238–39n73.

101. Richard Henry Lee [Chantilly] to Hannah Lee Corbin, March 17, 1778, in *The Letters of Richard Henry Lee, 1762–1794*, ed. James Curtis Ballagh (New York: Macmillan, 1911–14), 1:392–94. For other views of this letter, see Louise Belote Dawe and Sandra Gioia Treadway, "Hannah Lee Corbin: The Forgotten Lee," *Virginia Calvacade* (Autumn 1979): 75; Elizabeth Dabney Coleman, "Two Lees, Revolutionary Suffragists," *Virginia Calvacade* (Autumn 1953): 19–21.

102. Virginia Historical Society, "The Balfours of 'Little England,'" *An Occasional Bulletin*, no. 17 (October 1968): 4; *Virginia Gazette*, Purdie & Dixon, June 28, 1770. James Balfour's portrait, also at the Virginia Historical Society, shows a well-established man holding a letter addressed to him as agent of Hanbury and Company at Little England, Virginia. Yet, like his wife, he eschews the pretensions of the British elite and is portrayed with his arm falling affectionately around the toddler son who has inter-

rupted his father's work with his exuberant drumming. Although usually attributed to Cosmo Alexander, the paintings were probably done by Philadelphian Matthew Pratt. He advertised for business in the *Virginia Gazette* in March 1773. Little George Pratt's age matches that time frame. *Virginia Gazette,* Purdie and Dixon, March 18, 1773, 3. In addition, the background of Mrs. Balfour's portrait matches exactly the description of Pratt's preferred background: "a tenebrous atmosphere and often [with] dark colors in the clothing and drapery." "Matthew Pratt, 1734–1805," in John Caldwell and Oswaldo Rodrigues Rogue, *American Paintings in the Metropolitan Museum of Art* (Princeton University Press, 1994), 1:55–56.

103. Portrait, Mrs. Charles Cotesworth Pinkney (Sarah Middleton), c. 1773, Gibbes Museum of Art, Charleston, South Carolina (image available online).

104. Aileen Ribeiro, "Muses and Mythology: Classical Dress in British Eighteenth-Century Female Portraiture," in *Defining Dress: Dress as Object, Meaning and Identity,* ed. Amy de la Haye and Elizabeth Wilson (Manchester: Manchester University Press, 1999), 104–13.

105. Stephanie Grauman Wolf, "Rarer Than Riches: Gentility in Eighteenth-Century America," in *The Portrait in Eighteenth-Century America,* ed. Ellen G. Miles (Newark: University of Delaware Press, 1993), 96.

106. Kierner, *Beyond the Household,* 59.

107. Cynthia Kierner, "Genteel Balls and Republican Parades: Gender and Early Southern Civic Rituals, 1677–1826," *Virginia Magazine of History and Biography* 104 (1996): 186–210; Susan Branson, *These Fiery Frenchified Dames: Women and Political Culture in Early National Philadelphia* (Philadelphia: University of Pennsylvania Press, 2001); Catherine Allgor, *Parlor Politics: In Which the Ladies of Washington Help Build a City and a Government* (Charlottesville: University Press of Virginia, 2001). For southern gentility in Philadelphia in the early national period, see Daniel Kilbride, "Cultivation, Conservatism, and the Early National Gentry: The Manigault Family and Their Circle," *Journal of the Early Republic* 19 (1999): 221–56.

108. Linda Kerber argues in *Women of the Republic* that women's status was worse. See esp. chaps. 5, 6, and 9.

109. Brown, *Knowledge Is Power,* 163.

110. Anna Cameron to Duncan Cameron, July 6, 1790, no. 133, Cameron Family Papers, SHC.

111. Ralph Izard Jr. to Alice Izard, July 6, 1801; Alice Izard to Ralph Izard Jr., January 5, 1803, Ralph Izard Sr. Papers, Library of Congress.

112. Jane Randolph to Mary Harrison, November 24, 1805, Harrison Family Papers, VHS.

113. James Fordyce, *Sermons to Young Women* (London, 1765). Women's "true interests," Fordyce believed, did not "require reasoning or accuracy. . . . It is not the argumentative but the sentimental talents . . . that lead to your principal ends as Women." *Sermons,* Early American Imprints, 2d ser., no. 17522, ed. Clifford K. Shipton (Worcester, Mass.: American Antiquarian Society, 1967–1974), 1:138.

114. I am indebted to Robert Gross for this insight. Private correspondence, Spring 1995.

115. Priestley, *The Female Spectator,* 56.

116. Spender, *Mothers of the Novel,* 117. Actually, this count of female authors is a conservative one, given the number of anonymous publications. Indeed, since anonymity was a female virtue, Spender observes that it may not be too much to suggest that women wrote half of the two thousand published.

117. Juliet Mitchell, "Femininity, Narrative, and Psychoanalysis," in *Feminist Literary Theory: A Reader,* ed. Mary Eagleton (Oxford: Oxford University Press, 1986), 100. See

also Ellen Moers, "Literary Women," ibid., 96–98, linking the rise of the novel with "the rise of women to professional literary status." Ros Ballaster's "Romancing the Novel," in Spender, *Living by the Pen*, 188–200, argues that women's writings were labeled (derisively) romances, because of their flight-of-fancy plots and characters; men's writings were called novels because of the male monopoly on reason and realism.

118. Feminist literary theory has questioned whether there is a "female imagination"—that is, a tradition of female experience that is expressed in a distinctively female literature. Patricia Meyer Spacks, *The Female Imagination* (New York: Alfred A. Knopf, 1975), first posed this question. While Elaine Showalter discovered a female subculture of women fiction writers in the nineteenth century in *A Literature of Their Own: British Women Novelists from Brontë to Lessing* (Princeton: Princeton University Press, 1977), Mary Daly's *Beyond God the Father: Toward a Philosophy of Women's Liberation* (Boston: Beacon, 1973) asserted that women had yet to recover the language men stole from them in the book of Genesis. Janet Todd describes these early efforts at feminist literary criticism in America in *Feminist Literary Theory* (New York: Routledge, 1988), 17–33. "Although I do not believe there is a female identity that can somehow be known outside the patriarchy in which we and women of the past have all lived," Todd concluded, "I can accept a difference in male and female experience and I do not regard it as essentialist in any pejorative way to stress it" (p. 138). For many viewpoints conveniently located in one volume, see Eagleton, *Feminist Literary Theory: A Reader* (Oxford, 1986).

119. See chapter 3 for Elizabeth Foote Washington.

120. Eliza Jaquelin Ambler Brent Carrington to Ann Ambler Fisher, October 10, 1796, Ambler Papers, CWF.

121. Eliza Jaquelin Ambler to Mildred Smith, Letter No. 2, c. 1781, Ambler Papers, CWF.

122. Kerrison, "By the Book," 48–50.

123. Caroline Eliza Clitherall Diaries, 1751–1860, no. 158, 3d ser., vol. 1-1, 14–18, SHC.

124. Ibid., 1-1, 26 (first quotation), 29 (second quotation), 14 (third quotation).

125. Ibid., 1-4, 12. Clitherall's diaries do not provide the dates of her first romance, her return to America, or her courtship with George Clitherall. She was born in 1784 and married in 1802, so it is probably safe to estimate that these events occurred between 1800 and 1802. Clitherall Diaries Inventory Abstract, SHC.

126. Clitherall Diaries, 1-4, 33–38, 1 (first quotation), 3 (second quotation), 3–4 (third quotation), 4 (fourth quotation), 6 (fifth and sixth quotations).

127. Ibid., 1-5, 7. Burgwin grudgingly gave his consent shortly thereafter and the two wed.

128. Ibid.

129. Ibid., 6–7.

130. Ibid., 6.

131. Ibid., 1-1, 29 (first quotation), 30 (second quotation).

132. On realism as a distinctive attribute of the novel, see Watt, *Rise of the Novel*, 11. Dale Spender has pointed out that letter writing also allowed a construction of self that was "worthy of esteem." In these centuries of British colonial expansion, a woman correspondent could easily imagine a cluster of people gathered about her letter. In those letters, Spender notes, "it is not difficult to detect yet another influence working to transform the letter into the epistolary novel," either in its gloss over dangers or its supply of entertaining stories. *Living by the Pen*, 6.

133. M. Klotz to Jane Charlton, August 18, 1783, Robinson Family Papers, VHS.

134. Mildred Smith to Betsey Ambler, Letter No. 1.

135. Betsey Ambler to Mildred Smith, Letter No. 2.

136. October 12, 1822, Preface to *Exercises in History, Chronology, and Biography,* quoted in Davidson, *Charlotte Temple,* xxvii.

137. John Richetti, *Popular Fiction before Richardson: Narrative Patterns 1700–1739* (Oxford: Clarendon Press, 1969), 13.

138. Hayes, *Colonial Women's Bookshelf,* 50.

139. Jan Lewis, *The Pursuit of Happiness: Family and Values in Jefferson's Virginia* (1983; repr., Cambridge: Cambridge University Press, 1988), 243n42.

140. Steven Stowe, *Intimacy and Power in the Old South: Ritual in the Lives of the Planters* (Baltimore: Johns Hopkins University Press, 1987), 252.

141. Ruth Bloch, "Religion, Literary Sentimentalism, and Popular Revolutionary Ideology," in *Religion in a Revolutionary Age,* ed. Ronald Hoffman and Peter J. Albert (Charlottesville: University Press of Virginia, 1994), 308–30.

142. Ned C. Landsman, *From Colonials to Provincials: American Thought and Culture, 1680–1760* (New York: Twayne Publishers, 1997), 132; Richard Rankin, *Ambivalent Churchmen and Evangelical Churchwomen: The Religion of the Episcopal Elite in North Carolina, 1800–1860* (Columbia: University of South Carolina Press, 1993), 128.

143. Young, *Domesticating Slavery,* 151.

144. Women's worlds did not extend very far beyond their own plantations. Darrett and Anita Rutman found that at the turn of the eighteenth century in Middlesex County, 36 percent of marrying couples married someone who lived within a half mile of their homes. Darrett B. Rutman and Anita H. Rutman, *A Place in Time: Middlesex County, Virginia 1650–1750* (New York: W. W. Norton, 1984), 121. By mid- to late century, gentry patterns of visiting, especially for women, widened geographically, but because visits tended to be restricted to kin, women's circles of influence remained domestic. Daniel Blake Smith, *Inside the Great House: Planter Family Life in Eighteenth-Century Chesapeake Society* (Ithaca: Cornell University Press, 1980), 194–230. Laurel Thatcher Ulrich has observed the differences in the cycles of the lives of men and women in agricultural communities, noting that while men's were bound by the agricultural seasons, women's were bound by "personal seasons of pregnancy and lactation." Ulrich, *Good Wives,* 135.

145. Men claimed the public spaces of courthouse, militia muster, and parades for civic rituals that became increasingly masculinized after the Revolution. Isaac, *Transformation of Virginia;* Joan R. Gundersen, "Kith and Kin: Women's Networks in Colonial Virginia," in *The Devil's Lane: Sex and Race in the Early South,* ed. Catherine Clinton and Michele Gillespie (New York: Oxford University Press, 1997), 101. See also Karin Wulf, *Not All Wives: Colonial Women of Philadelphia* (Ithaca: Cornell University Press, 2000), on the exclusion of women from public civic rituals in Revolutionary Philadelphia.

146. Theodorick Bland [Jonesborough, TN] to Sophy Bland, [Port Royal, Virginia], August 5, 1799, Bland Family Papers, box 4, MS 134, MHS.

147. Alice Izard to Henry Izard, October 18, 1807, quoted in Young, *Domesticating Slavery,* 133.

148. Amanda Vickery, *The Gentleman's Daughter: Women's Lives in Georgian England* (New Haven: Yale University Press, 1998), 12. Vickery's study of eighteenth-century elite women of northern England observed a culture of politeness that women shared with men in a world of reading, letter writing, and lives lived in the public terrain of assemblies, concerts, plays, and other entertainments.

149. David Shields, *Civil Tongues and Polite Letters in British America* (Chapel Hill: University of North Carolina Press, 1997), 119. Shields rightly contrasts the northern culture of sociability with Virginia's. Virginia and Carolina planters developed a social life built

around entertaining guests, but the result was hospitality, not sociability: "Whereas sociability promoted the free and friendly conversation of persons meeting in public space, hospitality organized social exchange under the auspices of a family in its household. Whatever hierarchy of authority governed the family was reinforced by a hierarchy among host and guests based on property," Shields, *Civil Tongues and Polite Letters*, 301. The point is a crucial one for the place of southern women in both the hierarchy and the resulting exchanges of conversation. Kathleen Brown has described the place of elite southern women within the spaces of the plantation household in *Good Wives, Nasty Wenches, and Anxious Patriarchs*, 260–72. Contrast with Cynthia Kierner, "Hospitality, Sociability, and Gender in the Southern Colonies," *Journal of Southern History* 52 (1996): 449–80, who uses the terms "hospitality" and "sociability" interchangeably. Yet elite women struggled to retain some control over these public and social spaces as they were pushed out of public displays of patriotism in the reconfiguration of citizenship and patriotism in the early republic. See Allgor, *Parlor Politics*; Kierner, "Genteel Balls and Republican Parades"; and Kilbride, "Cultivation, Conservatism, and the Early National Gentry."

150. Craft-Fairchild, *Masquerade and Gender.*

151. Carroll Smith-Rosenberg, "Domesticating 'Virtue': Coquettes and Revolutionaries in Young America," in *Literature and the Body*, ed. Elaine Scarry (Baltimore: Johns Hopkins University Press, 1988), 178.

5. Reading, Race, and Writing

1. Jeffrey Robert Young, *Domesticating Slavery: The Master Class in Georgia and South Carolina, 1670–1837* (Chapel Hill: University of North Carolina Press, 1999), 111–12.

2. Eric Foner, *America's Unfinished Revolution, 1863–1877* (New York: Harper & Row, 1988), 6.

3. Paul Finkelman, *Slavery and the Founders: Race and Liberty in the Age of Jefferson*, 2d ed. (Armonk, N.Y.: M.E. Sharpe, 2001), 14.

4. Peter Kolchin, *American Slavery 1619–1877* (New York: Hill and Wang, 1993), 30.

5. Ira Berlin, *Generations of Captivity: A History of African-American Slaves* (Cambridge, Mass.: Harvard University Press, 2003), 18.

6. Kolchin, *American Slavery*, 78.

7. Ira Berlin, *Many Thousands Gone: The First Two Centuries of Slavery in North America* (Cambridge, Mass.: Harvard University Press, 1998), 232–33.

8. Philip Morgan, *Slave Counterpoint: Black Culture in the Eighteenth-Century Chesapeake and Lowcountry* (Chapel Hill: University of North Carolina Press, 1998), 490.

9. Kolchin, *American Slavery*, 78, 81–82, on Delaware and the Upper South; Morgan, *Slave Counterpoint*, on Maryland, 490.

10. Berlin, *Generations of Captivity*, 104.

11. Ibid., 102–11.

12. Ibid., 9; Berlin, *Many Thousands Gone*, 97–99.

13. Berlin, *Many Thousands Gone*, 98.

14. Sally E. Hadden, *Slave Patrols: Law and Violence in Virginia and the Carolinas* (Cambridge, Mass.: Harvard University Press, 2001), 28. South Carolina, settled largely by colonists from Barbados, enacted its code in 1696. Virginia lagged behind; its code was drawn up in 1705 and, with only minor alterations, served for the remainder of the colonial period. On the development of slavery in the Caribbean, see Richard Dunn, *Sugar and Slaves: The Rise of the Planter Class in the English West Indies, 1624–1713* (1972; repr., Chapel Hill: University of North Carolina Press, 2000).

15. For North Carolina, see Marvin L. Michael Kay and Lorin Lee Cary, *Slavery in North Carolina, 1748–1775* (Chapel Hill: University of North Carolina Press, 1995), 61–69; for South Carolina, see Peter Wood, *Black Majority: Negroes in Colonial South Carolina from 1670 through the Stono Rebellion* (New York: W. W. Norton, 1974), 271–84; for Virginia, see Philip Schwarz, *Slave Laws in Virginia, 1705–1865* (Athens: University of Georgia Press, 1996), and Schwarz, *Twice Condemned: Slaves and the Criminal Laws of Virginia* (Baton Rouge: Louisiana State University Press, 1988); Gerald W. Mullin, *Flight and Rebellion: Slave Resistance in Eighteenth-Century Virginia* (New York: Oxford University Press, 1972); James Hugo Johnston, *Race Relations in Virginia and Miscegenation in the South, 1776–1860* (1937; repr., Amherst: University of Massachusetts Press, 1970).

16. Hadden, *Slave Patrols*, 29–38.

17. Alex Bontemps, *The Punished Self: Surviving Slavery in the Colonial South* (Ithaca: Cornell University Press, 2001), 121–24.

18. Kirsten Fischer, *Suspect Relations: Sex, Race, and Resistance in Colonial North Carolina* (Ithaca: Cornell University Press, 2002), 5. The subordinate position of women, Eleanor Miot Boatwright observed of Georgia women, "fitted into the concept of a stratified society and became an inalienable part of the defense of slavery. The philosophers of this ideal state continued to romanticize women of the upper classes and to forget those of the lower." Eleanor Miot Boatwright, *Status of Women in Georgia, 1783–1860* (Brooklyn: Carlson Publishing, 1994), 123.

19. Cynthia Lynn Lyerly, "Passion, Desire, and Ecstasy: The Experiential Religion of Southern Methodist Women, 1770–1810," *The Devil's Lane: Sex and Race in the Early South,* ed. Catherine Clinton and Michele Gillespie (New York: Oxford University Press, 1997), 169.

20. Berlin, *Generations of Captivity*, 9.

21. Marli Weiner, *Mistresses and Slaves: Plantation Women in South Carolina, 1830–1880* (Urbana: University of Illinois Press, 1998), 135, 57. On the different ways in which colonial Virginians, South Carolinians, and West Indians viewed miscegenation, see Richard Godbeer, *Sexual Revolution in Early America* (Baltimore: Johns Hopkins University Press, 2002), 208–23.

22. Young, *Domesticating Slavery*, 111–12.

23. Christine Leigh Heyrman, *Southern Cross: The Beginnings of the Bible Belt* (New York: Alfred A. Knopf, 1997), 193–94; Richard Rankin, *Ambivalent Churchmen and Evangelical Churchwomen: The Religion of the Episcopal Elite in North Carolina, 1800–1860* (Columbia: University of South Carolina Press, 1993), 137–38.

24. Diary of M. Ambler, 1770, in *Virginia Historical Magazine* 45 (April 1937): 170.

25. Roger Jones Family Papers, Library of Congress. Kathleen Brown has analyzed Pratt's poem, written c. 1724, in *Good Wives, Nasty Wenches, and Anxious Patriarchs: Gender, Race, and Power in Colonial Virginia* (Chapel Hill: University of North Carolina Press, 1996), 313–17.

26. Brown, *Good Wives, Nasty Wenches, and Anxious Patriarchs*, 318.

27. Copybook, Maria Carter of Cleve, Armistead-Cocke Papers, CWM. Alexander Pope's poetry was found in many respectable southern colonial libraries. Felicity A. Nussbaum described his poetry's views of women: while his women "exhibit universal characteristics of inconstancy, pride, and self-love," Pope revealed "an unusual awareness of the control that custom and tradition have over women's lives, while he encourages women to act as models of good humor and good sense in spite of their unavoidable difficulties." Nussbaum, " 'The Glory, Jest, and Riddle of the Town': Women in Pope's Poetry," in *The Brink of All We Hate: English Satires on Women, 1660–1750* (Lexington: University Press of Kentucky, 1984), 137.

28. Courtly love was the love of a gentleman for a married woman. It was necessar-

ily platonic, therefore, but its beauty and appeal were in the constant striving for an unattainable object, a striving that remained pure, unsullied by any physical contact. The true story of Abelard and Heloise is a famous one of forbidden love that did lapse into a physical affair, producing a child. In retaliation, Heloise's enraged uncle arranged for Abelard's castration. Although Abelard and Heloise did marry, they lived out their lives separately in religious communities.

29. Maria Carter Copybook, Armistead-Cocke Papers, CWM.

30. J. A. Leo Lemay, ed., *Robert Bolling Woos Anne Miller: Love and Courtship in Colonial Virginia, 1760* (Charlottesville: University Press of Virginia, 1990), 52, 13, 59. Although sharing the same great-grandfather, the lovers were descended from different great-grandmothers.

31. Ibid., 66, 72. When next Bolling saw her, four years later, she was married to one of his friends, Peyton Skipwith—a choice more acceptable to her father, perhaps. Anne Miller Skipwith died the day after the birth of her fourth child in 1779. Her husband remarried; for his wife he chose Anne Miller's sister, Jean. Ibid., 31.

32. St. George Tucker to Frances Bland Randolph, c. 1778, Tucker-Coleman Papers, CWM.

33. Ibid.

34. The rest of his family remained in Bermuda. The College of William and Mary was a more affordable alternative than an English university education.

35. Charles Carter to Landon Carter, April 26, 1758, Landon Carter Correspondence, UVA.

36. Ann Butler Spotswood to Rev. John Thompson, July 29, 1742, Spotswood Family Papers, VHS.

37. Margaret Caldwell [signed "Dorothy Broadbottom"] to James McHenry, January 21, 1779, MS 647, McHenry Family Papers, MHS.

38. John Blair [Williamsburg] to his sister Mrs. Mary Burwell, October 3, 1780, Blair, Banister, Braxton, Horner, and Whiting Papers, CWM.

39. *Virginia Gazette*, Purdie & Dixon, July 14, 1768.

40. Letter to Catherine Dulany Belt, n.d., Dulany Family Papers, MHS.

41. Peggy Murdock to Catherine Dulany Belt, c. December 1783, Dulany Family Papers, MHS.

42. Elizabeth Smith Shaw to her niece Abigail Adams Smith, November 27, 1786, quoted in Mary Beth Norton, *Liberty's Daughters: The Revolutionary Experience of American Women, 1750–1800* (New York: Harper Collins, 1980), 42. Elizabeth Maynadier to Catherine Belt, August 9, 1786 (quotation), and May 14, 1785, Dulany Family Papers, MHS.

43. Anne Stuart to Eliza Lee, June 29, 1806, Richard Bland Lee Papers, VHS.

44. See C. Vann Woodward, ed., *Mary Chesnut's Civil War* (New Haven: Yale University Press, 1981), 29.

45. Frances Randolph to St. George Tucker, July 10, 1778, Tucker-Coleman Papers, CWM.

46. Margaret Parker to James Parker, September 5, 1760, and August 12, 1760, quoted in Daniel B. Smith, *Inside the Great House: Planter Life in Eighteenth-Century Chesapeake Society* (Ithaca: Cornell University Press, 1980), 161–62.

47. Frances Baylor to John Baylor, November 8, 1802, Baylor Family Papers, UVA.

48. Anya Jabour, *Marriage in the Early Republic: Elizabeth and William Wirt and the Companionate Ideal* (Baltimore: Johns Hopkins University Press, 1998).

49. Cynthia Kierner, "Republicanism," in *Beyond the Household: Women's Place in the Early South, 1700–1835* (Ithaca: Cornell University Press, 1998), 102–38. Kierner describes the ways in which rituals of civic participation became masculine, with the dis-

appearance, for example, of colonial balls celebrating imperial events, and the increasing lionization of the military. Karin Wulf, *Not All Wives: Women of Colonial Philadelphia* (Ithaca: Cornell University Press, 2000) describes a similar process in post-Revolutionary Philadelphia. Linda Kerber's *Women of the Republic: Intellect and Ideology in Revolutionary America* (New York: W. W. Norton, 1980) stands as the classic description of the formulation of "Republican Motherhood," which connected, however tenuously, female domesticity to participation in the polity.

50. Young, *Domesticating Slavery*, 118.

51. See post-Revolutionary petitions for financial relief in Cynthia Kierner, *Southern Women in Revolution, 1776–1800: Personal and Political Narratives* (Columbia: University of South Carolina Press, 1998), 167–90.

52. Chinn v. Chinn, September 12, 1722, Lancaster County Chancery Court Records, LVA.

53. Jon Jacocks to Elizabeth Jacocks, December 4, 1801, no. 372, Jonathan Jacocks Papers, SHC.

54. Mary Horton v. James Pinkard, May 1751, Lancaster County Court Records, LVA.

55. Deposition of Martin George in Rawleigh Shearman v. Elizabeth Gilbert, 1762, Lancaster County Chancery Court Records, LVA.

56. Bill of Complaint, undated, Robinson Family Papers, VHS. John Burwell, Ann's husband, died in 1788.

57. Linda L. Sturtz, *Within Her Power: Propertied Women in Colonial Virginia* (New York: Routledge, 2002), 101, 62–66.

58. Terri L. Snyder, "Legal History of the Colonial South: Assessments and Suggestions," *WMQ* 50 (1993): 27.

59. St. George Tucker and Joseph Cabell correspondence, October and November 1806, no. 38-111, Joseph Cabell Carrington Papers, UVA.

60. James T. Hubard to Susanna Wilcox, November 20, 1806, no. 360, Hubard Family Papers, SHC. The exchange of letters (of which we have only his) culminated in a lawsuit several years later, which she won. Both Hubard and his mother-in-law died in 1812. Hubard left his family in dire financial straits, both from his wife's failure to inherit and from his debts. His wife was forced to apply to her brother for help to avoid eviction from her home. Survey book, no. 360, Hubard Family Papers, SHC.

61. The rise of the companionate marriage has been the subject of much study by social historians in the last two decades. See, for example, Lawrence Stone, *The Family, Sex, and Marriage in England, 1500–1800* (New York: Harper & Row, 1977), and Anthony Fletcher, *Gender, Sex, and Subordination in England, 1500–1800* (New Haven: Yale University Press, 1995). On companionate marriage in the South, see Jabour, *Marriage in the Early Republic*; Jane Turner Censer, *North Carolina Planters and Their Children, 1800–1860* (Baton Rouge: Louisiana State University Press, 1984); and Daniel Blake Smith, *Inside the Great House: Planter Family Life in the Eighteenth Century Chesapeake* (Ithaca: Cornell University Press, 1980).

62. Mary Wollstonecraft, *Vindication of the Rights of Woman: An Authoritative Text, Backgrounds, the Wollstonecraft Debate, Criticism*, ed. Carol H. Poston, 2d ed. (New York: W. W. Norton, 1988), 7.

63. Alice Izard to Margaret Izard Manigault, May 29, 1801, quoted in Young, *Domesticating Slavery*, 117.

64. Theodorick Bland [Sullivan Courthouse, Tennessee] to Sophy Bland [Chotank, Virginia], February 7, 1801, box 4, MS 134, Bland Papers, MHS.

65. Margaret Caldwell to James McHenry, January 28, 1779, MS 647, McHenry Family Papers, MHS.

66. Ann B. Shteir, *Cultivating Women, Cultivating Science: Flora's Daughters and Botany in England 1760–1860* (Baltimore: Johns Hopkins University, 1996), 35. The only early American example of a female botanist was New York's Jane Colden in the 1750s, 52. A female academy in North Carolina began to offer astronomy in 1823 and botany three years later. Kim Tolley, "Science for Ladies, Classics for Gentlemen: A Comparative Analysis of Scientific Subjects in the Curricula of Boys' and Girls' Secondary Schools in the United States, 1794–1850," *History of Education Quarterly* 36 (1996): 136, table 1.

67. Marli Weiner, "Expectations of White Womanhood," in *Mistresses and Slaves*, 53–71.

68. See chapter 4, "Reading Novels in the South."

69. Evangeline W. Andrews and Charles M. Andrews, eds., *Journal of a Lady of Quality; Being a Narrative of a Journey from Scotland to the West Indies, North Carolina, and Portugal, in the Years 1774 to 1776* (New Haven: Yale University Press, 1934), 127.

70. Alice Izard to Margaret Manigault, March 31, 1811, in Young, *Domesticating Slavery*, 155.

71. Alice Izard to Ralph Izard, November 21, 1794, in Young, *Domesticating Slavery*, 110–11.

72. Ralph Izard Jr. to Alice Izard, October 25, 1810, in Young, *Domesticating Slavery*, 135–36.

73. But see Kirsten E. Wood, *Masterful Women: Slaveholding Widows from the American Revolution through the Civil War* (Chapel Hill: University of North Carolina Press, 2004), for when women become masters upon the deaths of their husbands.

74. Lee Virginia Chambers-Schiller observed that the pattern of choosing careers and the single life among women in the Northeast did not begin in the South until the generation born in the 1840s and 1850s. Chambers-Schiller, *Liberty a Better Husband: Single Women in America, the Generations of 1780–1840* (New Haven: Yale University Press, 1984), 5.

75. Susan Branson, *Those Fiery Frenchified Dames: Women and Political Culture in Early National Philadelphia* (Philadelphia: University of Pennsylvania Press, 2001).

76. Mr. Carnochen to Eliza Mackay, August 18, 1813, Eliza Anne McQueen Mackay Papers, Duke University.

77. Margaret Caldwell [signed "Dorothy Broadbottom"] to James McHenry [addressed as "Mr Richard Honest"], January 21, 1779, MS 647, McHenry Family Papers, MHS.

78. Hilda Smith, *All Men and Both Sexes: Gender, Politics, and the False Universal in England 1640–1832* (University Park, Pa.: Pennsylvania State University Press, 2002), 137–39. From her readings of *The Lawes Resolutions* (1632) and *The Laws Respecting Women* (1777), both published in England, Smith traced the changing views of woman, from "threatening spectre of public women during the mid-seventeenth century" to the eighteenth-century woman, who "became more attached to qualities of helplessness, of needing protection, of requiring separation from public venues, of a greater focus on dress and cosmetics." Her description of Englishwomen is strikingly applicable to southern women as well.

79. Hereinafter, Anna Coale and Mary Coale.

80. Coale Copybook, MS 248, Coale Collection, MHS.

81. Quoted by Linda Grant de Pauw and Conover Hunt, *Remember the Ladies: Women in America, 1750–1815* (New York: Viking Press, 1976), 12. Lee Virginia Chambers-Schiller, in a study of one hundred northeastern women, explores the increasing rejection of "the ties that bind" by women after the Revolution. Southern women, she admits, were much more constrained in their search for independence,

living as they did in a slave society, which applied that concept to white men only. Chambers-Schiller, *Liberty a Better Husband,* 4–5.

82. Indeed, another quote from Hester Chapone in Anna Coale's book reads, "That ready compliance—that alertness to assist and oblige whilst demonstrate[ing] true affection must animate your behaviour and endear your most common actions." Coale Copybook, MHS.

83. The description comes from her mother's Philadelphia friend, Abigail Willing, in a letter to Anne Hopkinson Coale, March 15, 1789, MS 1530, Redwood Collection, MHS.

84. Mary Coale to L. Ewing, August 23, 1803, MS 1530, Redwood Collection, MHS.

85. L. Ewing to Mary Coale, September 3, 1803, ibid.

86. L. Ewing to Mary Coale, June 3, 1804, ibid. "Burns" is probably Richard Burn, *The Justice of the Peace and Parish Officer* (London, 1755), a classic legal text. Mary Coale's elder brother, Edward Johnson Coale, had trained for the law; Ewing clearly assumes her familiarity with the existence of this text.

87. Mary Coale to L. Ewing, Letterbook, Letter 2, undated, MS 1530, Redwood Collection, MHS.

88. Ibid.

89. John Adams to Abigail Adams, April 14, 1776, in *Adams Family Correspondence,* ed. L. H. Butterfield (Cambridge: Harvard University Press, 1963–1973), 1: 382.

90. L. Ewing to Mary Coale, July 24, 1804, MS 1530, Redwood Collection, MHS.

91. Anna Coale Copybook, MS 248, Coale Collection, MHS.

92. Mary Coale to L. Ewing, Letterbook, Letter 3, undated, MS 1530, Redwood Collection, MHS.

93. C. Dallett Hemphill, *Bowing to Necessities: A History of Manners in America, 1620–1860* (New York: Oxford University Press, 1999), 107. Annapolis bookseller William Aiken reported to his customers that five thousand copies of the first edition of Gregory's *Legacy* had been sold in London in three weeks. Joseph Towne Wheeler, "Booksellers and Circulating Libraries in Colonial Maryland," *Maryland Historical Magazine* 34 (June 1939): 124.

94. Kevin Hayes, *A Colonial Woman's Book Shelf* (Knoxville: University of Tennessee Press, 1996), 76–77.

95. Judith Sargent Murray, "On the Equality of the Sexes" (1790), in *Judith Sargent Murray,* ed. Sheila Skemp (Boston: Bedford Books, 1998), 177–78.

96. John Gregory, *A Father's Legacy to his Daughters* (London, 1774; repr., 1793), 74.

97. Kerber, *Women of the Republic,* 26, 198–99.

98 Christopher Phillips, *Freedom's Port: The African American Community of Baltimore, 1790–1860* (Urbana: University of Illinois Press, 1997), 12, quoting William Eddis (the surveyor of customs in Annapolis), 1777.

99. Charles G. Steffen, *From Gentlemen to Townsmen: The Gentry of Baltimore County, Maryland 1660–1776* (Lexington: University Press of Kentucky, 1993), 11–14.

100. Phillips, *Freedom's Port,* 14.

101. Raphael Semmes, ed., *Baltimore as Seen by Visitors, 1783–1860* (Baltimore: Maryland Historical Society, 1953), 27–28, taken from James Kent, "A New Yorker in Maryland: 1793 and 1831," in *Maryland Historical Magazine* 47 (1952): 135–45.

102. Semmes, *Baltimore as Seen by Visitors,* 25, taken from Isaac Weld Jr., *Travels through the States of North America, and the Provinces of Canada during the Years 1795, 1796 and 1797* (London, 1799), and John Bernard, *Retrospections of America, 1797–1811* (New York, 1887). On women's need to be politically informed, Mary Coale

transcribed the following excerpt into her commonplace book: "Madam De Stael's character of Napoleon . . . I saw him one day approach a French lady distinguished for her beauty, her wit, and the ardour of her opinions. He placed himself straight before her, like the stiffest of the German Generals, and said to her Madam, I don't like women to meddle with politics. You are right, General, replied she; but in a country where they lose their heads, it is natural for them to desire to know the reason. Bonaparte made no answer. He is a man who is calmed by an effective resistance; those who have borne his despotism deserve to be accused as much as he himself."

103. Semmes, *Baltimore as Seen by Visitors*, 13, taken from Francis Baily, *Journal of a Tour in the Unsettled Parts of North America in 1796 and 1797* (London, 1856). In the 1790s, the number of printers, publishers, and booksellers rose from four or five to nineteen, a rate of increase, Sherry H. Olson noted, greater than that in Philadelphia, New York, or Boston. Sherry H. Olson, *Baltimore: The Building of an American City*, rev. ed. (Baltimore: Johns Hopkins University Press, 1997), 28.

104. Ronald Zboray, *A Fictive People: Antebellum Economic Development and the American Reading Public* (New York: Oxford University Press, 1993), 44.

105. John R. Quinan, *Medical Annals of Baltimore from 1608–1880, Including Events, Men and Literature* (Baltimore: Press of Isaac Friedenwald, 1884), 14–20.

106. Bill and Martha Reamy, eds., *Records of St. Paul's Parish* (Westminster, Md.: Family Line Publications, 1988), 1:157. On religion and status in Baltimore, see Terry D. Bilhartz, *Urban Religion and the Second Great Awakening: Church and Society in Early National Baltimore* (Rutherford, N.J.: Fairleigh Dickinson Press), 24–25.

107. Hopkinson also served as an executor of Benjamin Franklin's estate. Notes from the Library of Congress, Mary (Coale) Redmond Files, MHS.

108. The Reverend Duché's unfortunate—if not infamous—letter, transmitted by Elizabeth Graeme Fergusson during the British occupation of Philadelphia and urging George Washington to relinquish the fight to British might, did nothing to diminish those ties of affection. Visits and correspondence continued after the Duchés returned to Philadelphia in 1790 from their exile. "Jacob Duché," typescript taken from *Lamb's Biographical Dictionary*, vol. 2, 532, Redwood Genealogical Files, MHS.

109. The Coale family papers and records do not contain any lists of their book holdings. Dr. Coale's will devises real property rather than personal and mentions no books. Anne Hopkinson Coale's will provides a Bible for each child and mentions no further books. There are no inventories of either estate surviving in the Baltimore City or Baltimore County records.

110. Quinan, *Medical Annals of Baltimore*, 17.

111. Albert J. Edmunds, "The First Books Imported by America's First Great Library: 1732," *Pennsylvania Magazine of History and Biography* 30 (1906): 300, 302.

112. Bilhartz, *Urban Religion*, 41–44. On the intellectual and cultural leadership of Maryland Anglican clergy in the pre-Revolutionary period see Steffen, *From Gentlemen to Townsmen*, 123–26.

113. L. Ewing to Mary Coale, June 3, 1804, MS 1530, Redwood Collection, MHS.

114. Rollo G. Silver, *The Baltimore Book Trade* (New York: New York Public Library, 1953), 4. For more on the Delphian Club, see John E. Uhler, "The Delphian Club," *Maryland Historical Magazine* 20 (1925): 305–45. On Coale as publisher of *The Portico*, see Olson, *Baltimore*, 93. Among the club's members was William Gwynn, publisher of the *Federal Gazette*, ibid., 44.

115. This family was considerably more bookish than the Maryland gentlemen-turned-townsmen described by Charles G. Steffen. His chart, "Value of Bookholdings of Baltimore Elite 1660–1776," makes plain the lack of elite enthusiasm for book own-

ership; only 11 of 181 owned books valued at between £5 and £20. Steffen, *From Gentlemen to Townsmen,* 127.

116. Mary Coale [Philadelphia] to Anna Maria Coale [Baltimore], June 17, [no year], MS 1530, Redwood Collection, MHS.

117. Ibid., 257.

118. Esther Duché Hill [Boston] to Edward Johnson Coale [Baltimore], December 11, 1810, MS 1530, Redwood Collection, MHS.

119. Kerber, *Women of the Republic,* 249, 259. Indeed, the edition cited by Kerber was printed in Baltimore in 1810. The book's subtitle reveals its purpose: *A compilation of observations, essays, and poetical effusions, designed to direct the female mind in a course of pleasing and instructive reading.*

120. Esther Duché Hill to Edward Johnson Coale, December 11, 1810, MS 1530, Redwood Collection, MHS.

121. Miller, *Assuming the Positions,* 7, 48–49. Indeed, Noah Webster, promoter of a new American program of education, believed that the goal of an education was the preservation of past wisdom, not individual growth or advancement. William J. Gilmore, *Reading Becomes a Necessity of Life: Material and Cultural Life in Rural New England, 1780–1835* (Knoxville: University of Tennessee Press, 1989), 37.

122. Kevin Berland, Jan Kirsten Gilliam, and Kenneth A. Lockridge, eds., *The Commonplace Book of William Byrd II* (Chapel Hill: University of North Carolina Press, 2001), 22–29.

123. June Hadden Hobbs describes Carlo Ginzburg's theoretical model in which "socially subordinate groups read and express themselves through a filter that effectively blocks what lacks meaning for them or does not accord with their experience." June Hadden Hobbs, "His Religion and Hers," in *Nineteenth-Century Women Learn to Write,* ed. Catherine Hobbs (Charlottesville: University Press of Virginia, 1995), 122.

124. Michael Kann, *On the Man Question: Gender and Civic Virtue in America* (Philadelphia: Temple University Press, 1991), 249. Kann points out that American women were not understood to have been born with rights but instead had to earn them by sublimating passions to reason.

125. Hannah W. Foster, *The Boarding School* (Boston: Thomas and Andrews, 1798), 30, quoted in Janet Carey Eldred and Peter Mortensen, "Gender and Writing Instruction in Early America: Lessons from Didactic Fiction," *Rhetoric Review* 12, no. 1 (1993): 36.

126. Benjamin Franklin to James Burrow, May 10, 1765, typescript, Redwood Genealogical Files, MHS.

127. Will of Mary Hopkinson, January 21, 1799, typescript, Redwood Genealogical Files, MHS.

128. Abigail Willing [Philadelphia] to Anne Hopkinson Coale [Baltimore], July 14, 1775, MS 1530, Redwood Collection, MHS.

129. Rebecca Frazier [Trenton] to Anna Coale [Baltimore], November 24, 1790, MS 1530, Redwood Collection, MHS.

130. Anne Hopkinson Coale divided her shares in the Union Bank of Maryland between her two surviving daughters, with the exception of one share, bequeathed to Edward Johnson Coale to be kept in the name of Anna Maria Coale. Will, Anna [Anne] Coale, May 28, 1817, Baltimore City Wills, book 10, 285, MSA.

131. Abigail Willing [Philadelphia] to Anne Hopkinson Coale [Baltimore], July 14, 15, 1775, MS 1530, Redwood Collection, MHS.

132. Foster, *Boarding School.* An excerpt from this book, recounting this story, appears as an appendix in Eldred and Mortensen, "Gender and Writing Instruction in Early America," 51–53.

133. Margaret Caldwell to James McHenry, November 17, 1783, MS 647, McHenry Family Papers, MHS.

134. E. Jennifer Monaghan, "Literacy Instruction and Gender in Colonial New England," in *Reading in America: Literature and Social History,* ed. Cathy Davidson (Baltimore: Johns Hopkins University Press, 1989), 59–60.

135. H. M. Tilghman [Chester Town, Maryland] to Polly Pearce, April 28, c. 1783 or 1784, *Maryland Historical Magazine* 21, no.1 (1926): 29.

136. Mary Coale [Philadelphia] to Anna Coale [Baltimore], December 27, 1806, MS 1530, Redwood Collection, MHS.

137. Emily Hopkinson to Mary Coale [Baltimore], April 26, 1809, MS 1530, Redwood Collection, MHS.

138. Colonial women writing letters back to their friends and relatives in England were very conscious of their writing as public performance, understanding that their letters would be shared and read aloud. Dale Spender, *Living by the Pen: Early British Women Writers* (New York: Teachers College Press, 1992), 6.

139. Indeed, seventeenth-century English women writers circulated their letters, poems, and other texts in manuscript form to avoid the stigma that associated appearing in print with sexual promiscuity. Harold Love, *The Culture and Commerce of Texts: Scribal Publication in Seventeenth-Century England* (Amherst: University of Massachusetts Press, 1998), 54–59, 202. On the redefinition of "modesty" to encompass a sexual significance, see Angeline Goreau, *The Whole Duty of Woman: Female Writers in Seventeenth-Century England* (Garden City, N.Y.: Dial Press, 1985).

140. Unsigned letter to Catherine Dulany Belt, c. 1780–1783, box 1, Dulany Family Papers, MHS.

141. L. Ewing to Mary Coale, September 3, 1803, MS 248, Coale Collection, MHS.

142. Mary Coale Letterbook, Letter 3, MS 1530, Redwood Collection, MHS.

143. Countess of Carlisle, *Thoughts in the form of maxims addressed to young ladies, on their first establishment in the world* [1789], 94, quoted in Jennifer Claire Georgia, "Polite Literature: Conduct Books and the Novel in Eighteenth-Century England" (Ph.D. diss., Harvard University, 1994), 265. But more than prudence dictated Mary's practice of keeping copies; she intended her writings to be permanent. As she wrote home to her sister Anna about her travels, Mary Coale begged her "Do take care of my letters as on my return home, I shall want them, I am going to begin a journal if you lose one of the letters I am lost." Mary Coale to Anna Maria Coale, June 17 [no year], MS 1530, Redwood Collection, MHS.

144. Addendum to will of Mary Hopkinson, July 3, 1802, Redwood Genealogical Files, MHS.

145. Mary Hopkinson [Philadelphia] to Anne Hopkinson [Baltimore], May 23, 1795, Redwood Genealogical Files, MHS. Hopkinson was referring to Thomas Paine's pamphlet "The Age of Reason."

146. Mary Hopkinson [Philadelphia] to Anne Hopkinson Coale [Baltimore], September 25, 1797, Redwood Genealogical Collection, MHS.

147. William Coale [Baltimore] to Anne Hopkinson Coale [Philadelphia], April 26, 1801. Mary Abigail Willing Coale Proud and her elder sister, Eliza Sophia Coale Proud, were not just members but full communicants of St. Paul's Episcopal Church. Typescript, Records of family Bible of John Greene Proud [husband of Eliza Sophia Coale Proud], Redwood Genealogical Files, MHS.

148. Emily Hopkinson [Philadelphia] to Anne Hopkinson Coale [Baltimore], November 14, 1804, MS 1530, Redwood Collection, MHS.

149. William Coale to Anne Hopkinson Coale [Philadelphia], April 26, 1801, MS 1530, Redwood Collection, MHS. Left in charge of the household in her absence, he

assured her that "we do extremely well without you therefore don't hurry home to see if we are not dead." Supervision of his younger sister's writing—and making her pens—was clearly one of the household responsibilities with which he was entrusted.

150. Mary Abigail Willing Coale [Baltimore] to Anne Hopkinson Coale [Philadelphia], April 29, 1801, MS 1530, Redwood Collection, MHS.

151. When Mary was only five, her father wrote to decline an offer for her to come to Philadelphia. Already suffering from the consumption that would kill him in 1798, he was loath to part from his daughter, believing it best to provide for her education himself. His letter suggests the expectations of the Philadelphia relatives that Anne's daughter should stay with them. Letter, Dr. Samuel Coale to Mrs. [Emily Hopkinson] Duché, December 2, 1794. In addition to the letters sent home to Baltimore by Anna Coale and Mary Coale, there is evidence that the boys also made trips to Philadelphia. Dr. Samuel Coale wrote to his wife that he was "very glad you let our D[ea]r little Will go to Philad[elphi]a" in August 1793. Typescript, Redwood Genealogical Files, MHS.

152. On kinship links fortified in the mid-nineteenth century by "the physical object of the book and its associations," see Ronald J. Zboray and Mary Saracino Zboray, "Books, Reading, and the World of Goods in Antebellum New England," *American Quarterly* 48, no. 4 (1996): 592–97.

153. Izard and Manigault exemplify a southern version of republican womanhood: the preservation of female influence in elite circles. Kierner, *Beyond the Household*, 109.

154. Daniel Kilbride, "Cultivation, Conservatism, and the Early National Gentry: The Manigault Family and Their Circle," *Journal of the Early Republic* 19 (1999): 221–56.

155. Indications of the Coale family's Federalist sympathies (in addition to the Hopkinson connection) include the obituary of John Greene Proud, the husband of Mary Coale's sister Eliza, that extolled his loyalty to the memory of George Washington and Alexander Hamilton. Redwood Genealogical Files, MHS.

156. Emily Hopkinson to Mary Coale, April 26, 1809, MS 1530, Redwood Collection, MHS.

157. The women who populate Catherine Allgor's *Parlor Politics* similarly use their elite position to participate in the new government. Ironically, Allgor concluded, their use of "old-fashioned court behaviors to create the new structures" resulted in a democracy of men from which they were further marginalized. Catherine Allgor, *Parlor Politics: In Which the Ladies of Washington Help Build a City and a Government* (Charlottesville: University Press of Virginia, 2000), 240.

158. Kilbride, "Cultivation, Conservatism, and the Early National Gentry," 245.

159. Amanda Vickery, *The Gentleman's Daughter: Women's Lives in Georgian England* (New Haven: Yale University Press, 1998), 197. Vickery points out that though Englishwomen never attained the significant roles Frenchwomen did in their salons, their refining influence on men was assumed. On sociability in colonial and early national America see Hemphill, *Bowing to Necessities*, and David S. Shields, *Civil Tongues and Polite Letters in British America* (Chapel Hill: University of North Carolina Press, 1997).

160. Mary Tilghman to Mary (Polly) Pearce, April 13, 1786, in *Maryland Historical Magazine* 21, no. 2 (1926): 138.

161. Mary Tilghman to Mary (Polly) Pearce, c. 1783–84, in *Maryland Historical Magazine* 21, no. 1 (1926): 34.

162. Mary Tilghman to Mary (Polly) Pearce, August 5, 1785, in *Maryland Historical Magazine* 21, no. 2 (1926): 131.

163. Mary Tilghman to Mary (Polly) Pearce, c. 1783–84, 34.

164. Mary Tilghman to Mary (Polly) Pearce, August 5, 1785, 132.

165. Rosalie Stier to her brother Charles Stier, February 19, 1796, in Margaret Law

Caldicott, ed., *Mistress of Riversdale: The Plantation Letters of Rosalie Stier Calvert 1795–1821* (Baltimore: Johns Hopkins University Press, 1991), 11.

166. This is a classic behavioral model in oppressive social regimes, as studies of slavery have made manifestly clear. See, for example, Morgan, *Slave Counterpoint.*

167. Mary Spotswood Campbell to Colonel John Spotswood, December 23, 1794, Spotswood Family Papers, VHS.

168. Jean Cameron to Duncan Cameron, February 8, 1797, no. 133, Cameron Family Papers, SHC.

169. David Ramsay, "Memoirs," in *Women and Religion in America*, vol. 2, *The Colonial and Revolutionary Periods*, ed. Rosemary Radford Ruether and Rosemary Skinner (San Francisco: Harper & Row, 1983), 222.

170. Mary Coale Commonplace Book, MS 248, Coale Collection, MHS.

171. Julia Hyde to Lucy Goodale, September 26, 1839, quoted in Mary Kelley, "Reading Women/Women Reading: The Making of Learned Women in Antebellum America," *Journal of American History* (1996): 415.

172. "Correspondence," London, 1760, CWF.

173. Anna [?] to Letitia McKean, September 7, 1788, box 4, MS 1530, Redwood Collection, MHS.

174. Thomas Jefferson to Martha Jefferson Randolph, February 2, 1791, in *The Family Letters of Thomas Jefferson*, ed. Edwin Morris Betts and James Adam Bear (1966; repr., Charlottesville: University Press of Virginia, 1986), 71. As Barbara Miller Solomon commented, "The leaders [of the Revolutionary generation] did not want their wives and daughters to be intellectuals. . . . Although Franklin, Jefferson, and [John] Adams had enjoyed the company of English Bluestockings and French *femmes savants*, these leaders retained a homegrown model of American womanhood." Barbara Solomon, *In the Company of Educated Women: A History of Women and Higher Education in America* (New Haven: Yale University Press, 1985), 11.

175. Thomas Jefferson to Martha Jefferson, March 28, 1787, in Betts and Bear, *Family Letters of Thomas Jefferson*, 35. Yet in spite of the limitations of Jefferson's prescription for female education, he did educate Martha more rigorously, in case she needed to supplement the earnings of a "blockhead" husband who was unable to provide for his family. Solomon, *In the Company of Educated Women*, 12. More commonly, however, needlework served male purposes better than it did female. In promoting needlework, whether in private counsel or in school curricula, southern men promoted female isolation and kept their world as divided by gender as it was by race. Cynthia Kierner points out that needlework survived the transition of post-Revolutionary education of women from ornamental to academic because of its usefulness in filling in time on Southern plantations. Nor was needlework a social activity in the South as it was frequently in the North. Alice Delancey Izard of South Carolina was so struck by the novelty of a group of Pennsylvania women working together in a bee that she described the phenomenon in detail to her daughter. Kierner, *Beyond the Household*, 155, 178.

176. Ibid., quoted p. 51.

177. Thomas Jefferson to Robert Skipwith, August 3, 1771, in *The Papers of Thomas Jefferson*, ed. Julian P. Boyd (Princeton: Princeton University Press, 1950), 1:76–77.

178. The idea of education as praxis was a product of the Enlightenment and became a cornerstone of the early German Romantic philosophy of *bildung*, the view of education as self-formation, a task that concentrated on one's interior, spiritual self rather than on improving the world. W. H. Bruford, *The German Tradition of Self-Cultivation: 'Bildung' from Humboldt to Thomas Mann* (Cambridge: Cambridge University Press, 1975), 17; John H. Smith, *The Spirit and Its Letter: Traces of Rhetoric in Hegel's Philosophy of Bildung* (Ithaca: Cornell University Press, 1988), 45–47.

179. Martha Jefferson to Thomas Jefferson, March 25, 1787, in Betts and Bear, *Family Letters*, 33; Thomas Jefferson to Martha Jefferson, March 28, 1787, ibid., 35.

180. Judith Randolph to Martha Jefferson, February 12, 1785, quoted in Cynthia Kierner, "'The Dark and Dense Cloud Perpetually Lowering over Us': Gender and the Decline of the Gentry in Postrevolutionary Virginia," *Journal of the Early Republic* 20 (2000): 189.

181. Jan Lewis, *The Pursuit of Happiness: Family and Values in Jefferson's Virginia* (Cambridge: Cambridge University Press, 1983), 149–50.

182. Mary Tilghman to Polly Pearce, August 5, 1785, in *Maryland Historical Magazine* 21, no. 2 (1926): 130–31.

183. Mary Tilghman to Polly Pearce, February 18, 1787, ibid.,148.

184. Mary Huger to Eliza Mackay, April 4, 1812, no. 470, Mackay and Stiles Family Papers, SHC.

185. See Diary of Elizabeth Drinker [Philadelphia] and of Frances Baylor Hill [Virginia] for but two examples. June 20, 1795, and February 29, 1796, in *The Diary of Elizabeth Drinker*, ed. Elaine Forman Crane (Boston: Northeastern University Press, 1991); and William K. Bottorff and Roy C. Flannagan, eds., "The Diary of Frances Baylor Hill of Hillsborough, King and Queen County, VA (1797)," *Early American Literature* 2 (1967): 45.

186. On the combination of needlework and reading, see Ronald J. Zboray and Mary Saracino Zboray, "Books, Reading, and the World of Goods," *American Quarterly* 48, no. 4 (1996): 599–602. The Zborays observed that even in the more densely populated antebellum North, "[r]eading and sewing alone, in short, commonly signified loneliness," 601.

187. Mary Coale [Philadelphia] to Eliza Sophia Coale [Baltimore], undated, MS 1530, Redwood Collection, MHS.

188. Letter, Thomas Jefferson to James Madison, March 1793, in Branson, *These Fiery Frenchified Dames*, 138–39.

189. The words quoted by Anna Maria Coale can be found in Laurence Sterne, *A Sentimental Journey Through France and Italy by Mr. Yorick*, ed. Gardner D. Stout Jr. (1768; repr., Berkeley: University of California Press, 1967), 195–202.

190. The captivity that Mr. Yorick faced was incarceration in the Bastille if he, as an English citizen, was caught in revolutionary France without his passport.

191. Last Will and Testament of Dr. Samuel Stringer Coale, September 3, 1798, typescript, Redwood Genealogical Files, MHS.

192. Coale spelled out the terms of their manumission: "I give to Mary my Negro Woman Dolley to serve my said Daughter, her heirs and assigns for the term of ten years from the first of Jan last and to be henceforth absolutely free and to my daughter Eliza I give my mulatto girl Harriet to serve my said Daughter her heirs and assigns until the said Harriet shall arrive at the age of thirty five years and that thence forth she shall be absolutely free and I desire that my said Daughter will take all means in their power so that the off spring of said Dolly and Harriet should they have any shall not be in servitude by the age of thirty five years." Will, Anna Coale, May 28, 1817, Baltimore City Wills, MSA.

193. Phillips, *Freedom's Port*, 14.

194. Ibid., 19–23.

195. T. Stephen Whitman, *The Price of Freedom: Slavery and Manumission in Baltimore and Early National Maryland* (Lexington: University Press of Kentucky, 1997), 1. Between 1799 and 1830, residents of Baltimore County had freed at least 2,448 slaves. Phillips, *Freedom's Port*, 37.

196. On Rush and the Pennsylvania Abolition Society, see Gary Nash, *Race and Rev-*

olution (Madison, Wis.: Madison House, 1990), 32–33, and Nash, *Forging Freedom: The Formation of Philadelphia's Black Community, 1720–1840* (Cambridge: Harvard University Press, 1988), 105. On the connection between Philadelphia elites and post-Revolutionary antislavery movements, see Richard S. Newman, *The Transformation of American Abolitionism: Fighting Slavery in the Early Republic* (Chapel Hill: University of North Carolina Press, 2002), 21–22, 29, and Nash, *Forging Freedom*, 105–6. On Federalist antislavery sentiments, see Paul Finkelman, *Slavery and the Founders: Race and Liberty in the Age of Jefferson*, 2d ed. (Armonk, N.Y.: M.E. Sharpe, 2001), 115–25. According to Nash, "Philadelphia owners freed at least 269 slaves from 1781 to 1790. Several hundred more slaves secured their freedom through the work of the PAS in these years." Nash, *Forging Freedom*, 72.

197. Nash, *Forging Freedom*, 106.

198. Sylvia Frey, *Water from the Rock: Black Resistance in a Revolutionary Age* (Princeton: Princeton University Press, 1991), 248–49; Morgan, *Slave Counterpoint*, 665.

199. Joanna Bowen Gillespie, *The Life and Times of Martha Laurens Ramsay* (Columbia: University of South Carolina Press, 2001), 180. Dr. Buchanan had married a Philadelphian, who returned to the city after her husband's death. "A Short Biographical Sketch of Edward Johnson Coale," Redwood Genealogical Files, MHS.

200. "A Short Biographical Sketch of Edward Johnson Coale."

201. That *A Sentimental Journey* has been seen as a work that "criticizes sentimental indulgence" does not negate the significance of these words to Anna Coale. Indeed, the book "applaud[s] natural benevolence . . . and reprove[s] . . . self-indulgence," views with which Coale would have agreed. Barbara M. Benedict, *Framing Feeling: Sentiment and Style in English Prose Fiction 1745–1800* (New York: AMS Press, 1994), 88.

202. Berlin, *Many Thousands Gone*; Morgan, *Slave Counterpoint*; Alan Kulikoff, *Tobacco and Slaves: The Development of Southern Cultures in the Chesapeake, 1680–1800* (Chapel Hill: University of North Carolina Press, 1986); Young, *Domesticating Slavery*; Weiner, *Mistresses and Slaves*.

203. As Ramsay's biographer, Joanna Gillespie, has noted, "The actual work of slaves in their owners' households . . . remains uniformly invisible in polite literature, including family letters. Slaves were primarily visible in the amazingly exact and complete business accounts kept by Martha's merchant father." Gillespie, *Life and Times of Martha Laurens Ramsay*, 39. See also chap. 7, "Slavery and Silence," 146–85.

204. Claudia L. Johnson, review of Janet Todd, *Sensibility: An Introduction* (1986), quoted in G. J. Barker-Benfield, *The Culture of Sensibility: Sex and Society in Eighteenth-Century Britain* (Chicago: University of Chicago Press, 1992), 225. Barker-Benfield points out that sentimental novels of the period were concerned with imprisonment, both "real and metaphorical" of women by men.

205. Mary Coale, Commonplace book, MS 248, Coale Collection, MHS.

206. The culture of urban slavery that developed in the city during the explosive expansion years favored inducements rather than punishments to ensure the cooperation of its slaves. Hence "term slaves," those promised freedom within a fixed number of years, became more the rule than the exception. T. Stephen Whitman notes that many slaves "seized the opportunities to make money in this explosive growth . . . buying themselves and others out of slavery." Whitman, *The Price of Freedom*, 1 and passim.

207. Anne Finch, Countess of Winchelsea, quoted in *Major Women Writers of Seventeenth-Century England*, ed. James Fitzmaurice and Josephine A. Roberts (Ann Arbor: University of Michigan Press, 1997), 336.

208. Mary Coale Commonplace book, MS 248, Coale Collection, MHS.

209. Wulf, *Not All Wives*, chaps. 1–2. Indeed, Milcah Martha Moore collected the writings of this circle of women in her commonplace book in the 1770s, producing a

far livelier work than the collection of advice she produced during the post-Revolutionary period. Comprised mostly of the writings of male didactic authors, the latter book was published for consumption of students. Catherine La Courreye Blecki and Karin A. Wulf, eds., *Milcah Martha Moore's Book: A Commonplace Book from Revolutionary America* (University Park: Pennsylvania State University Press, 1997), 56.

210. Mary Louise Kete, *Sentimental Collaborations: Mourning and Middle-Class Identity in Nineteenth-Century America* (Durham: Duke University Press, 2000), 52–53.

211. Foster, *Boarding School*, 33. Quoted in Eldred and Mortensen, "Gender and Writing Instruction in Early America," 36.

212. Indeed, the lack of material evidence has been one of the biggest challenges for historians of women. See, for example, Laurel Thatcher Ulrich, *A Midwife's Tale: The Life of Martha Ballard, Based on Her Diary, 1785–1812* (New York: Vintage Books, 1990), 100.

213. The literature emphasizing the positive impact of separate spheres (a topic that has generated a huge literature in itself) begins with Nancy Cott's *The Bonds of Womanhood: "Woman's Sphere" in New England, 1780–1835* (New Haven: Yale University Press, 1977). For a review of this literature, see Linda K. Kerber, "Separate Spheres, Female Worlds, Woman's Place: The Rhetoric of Women's History," *Journal of American History* 75 (1988): 9–39.

214. For the contrasting levels of female education and literacy in New England in 1790 and 1830, see Richard D. Brown, "Daughters, Wives, and Mothers," in *Knowledge Is Power: The Diffusion of Information in Early America, 1700–1865* (Oxford: Oxford University, 1989), 160–96.

215. Esther Duché Hill [Boston] to Edward Johnson Coale [Baltimore], December 11, 1810, MS 1530, Redwood Collection, MHS. Of course, the notion that reading is a nonproductive use of women's time has never been eradicated fully. Even into the twentieth century, Martyn Lyons commented, the reading woman is incompatible with the idealized housewife, who has more useful ways to spend her time. Martyn Lyons, "New Readers in the Nineteenth Century: Women, Children, and Workers" in *A History of Reading in the West*, ed. Guglielmo Cavallo and Roger Chartier, trans. Lydia G. Cochrane (Amherst: University of Massachusetts Press, 1999), 321.

216. Mary Kelley, "Reading Women/Women Reading: The Making of Learned Women in Antebellum America," *Journal of American History* (1996): 424.

217. Patricia Brady, ed., *George Washington's Beautiful Nelly: The Letters of Eleanor Parke Custis Lewis to Elizabeth Bordley Gibson, 1794–1851* (Columbia: University of South Carolina Press, 1990), 39 (first quotation); 61 (second quotation).

218. Brady, *George Washington's Beautiful Nelly*, 69, 72–73 (on education); 80 (quotations). Like Martha Laurens, Lewis rarely mentioned her slaves in her letters; when she did, it was to inquire about the legal consequences of bringing them with her when she visited Philadelphia. (She left them home.) Letter of March 1, 1815, 77.

219. Kathryn Shevelow, *Women and Print Culture: The Construction of Femininity in the Early Periodical* (New York: Routledge, 1989), 1.

220. Anne Clark Bartlett, *Male Authors, Female Readers: Representation and Subjectivity in Middle English Devotional Literature* (Ithaca: Cornell University Press, 1995), 21.

221. As David Allan explained, the "free exchange of information and opinion represented an unparalleled opportunity to spread moral insight and mutual understanding." David Allan, *Scotland in the Eighteenth Century: Union and Enlightenment* (London: Longman Ltd., 2002), 130.

222. On the origins and program of the Bluestockings, see Elizabeth Eger, *Bluestocking Feminism: Writings of the Bluestocking Circle, 1738–1785* (London: Pickering & Chatto, 1999), ix–xi. Vickery, *Gentleman's Daughter*, 197.

223. "By this view," Amanda Vickery points out, "'politeness' was a way of conceptualizing an unofficial public sphere to which privileged women could lay legitimate claim." Vickery, *Gentleman's Daughter*, 197.

224. Quoted in Roy Porter, *The Creation of the Modern World: The Untold Story of the British Enlightenment* (New York: W. W. Norton, 2000), 570n32.

225. Barker-Benfield, *Culture of Sensibility*, 85–89; Porter, *Creation of the Modern World*, 325; Erin Mackie, *The Commerce of Everyday Life: Selections from the Tatler and the Spectator* (Boston: Bedford St. Martin's, 1998).

226. Porter, *Creation of the Modern World*, 325–36. This topic was debated in November 1798. Indeed, on the continent, Englishwomen had a reputation for their relative freedom of mobility and expression.

227. Karin A. Wulf has analyzed Griffitts's poem at some length. Karin A. Wulf, "'My Dear Liberty': Quaker Spinsterhood and Female Autonomy in Eighteenth-Century Pennsylvania," in *Women and Freedom in Early America*, ed. Larry D. Eldridge (New York: New York University Press, 1997), 83–108.

228. Quoted in Wulf, "'My Dear Liberty,'" 92.

229. Mary Astell's *Some Reflections upon Marriage* (1700) suggested the liberty of a single life for Englishwomen wealthy enough to afford it, because when a wife "elects a monarch for life [she] gives him an Authority she cannot recall however he misapply it." Astell's *A Serious Proposal to the Ladies for the Advancement of their True and Greatest Interest* (1694) proposed a female college where women of means could withdraw from the world and study. Norris may have been acquainted with Astell's writings as she created her female retreat in Fairhill.

230. Harold Love, *The Culture and Commerce of Texts: Scribal Publication in Seventeenth-Century England* (Amherst: University of Massachusetts Press, 1993); Wulf, *Not All Wives*, 47.

231. Brown, *Good Wives, Nasty Wenches, Anxious Patriarchs*, 262–63, 267–75.

232. David Shields, *Civil Tongues and Polite Letters*, 301.

233. James Raven, *London Booksellers and American Customers: Transatlantic Literary Community and the Charleston Library Society, 1748–1811*, Carolina Lowcountry and the Atlantic World Series (Columbia: University of South Carolina Press, 2002).

234. Jacqueline Pearson, *Women's Reading in Britain 1750–1835* (Cambridge: Cambridge University Press, 1999), 47–48.

235. Joan Cashin, ed., *Our Common Affairs: Texts from Women in the Old South* (Baltimore: Johns Hopkins University Press, 1986), 22–24.

236. Lewis, *Pursuit of Happiness*; Kierner, "'Dark and Dense Cloud.'"

237. James Oakes, "Slavery as an American Problem," in *The South as an American Problem*, ed. Larry J. Griffin and Don H. Doyle (Athens: University of Georgia Press, 1995), 92.

238. Allgor, *Parlor Politics*, 31.

Conclusion

1. William J. Scheick, *Authority and Female Authorship in Colonial America* (Lexington: University Press of Kentucky, 1998), 23–24, 18–19.

2. David S. Shields, "Questions, Suspicions, Speculations," *Journal of Southern History* 24, no. 2 (2004): 339.

3. Martha Wadsworth Brewster, *Poems on Divers Subjects* (Boston: Edes and Gill, 1758), quoted in Scheick, *Authority and Female Authorship*, 20.

4. John Trumbull, "The Progress of Dulness," quoted in Linda Kerber, *Women of*

the Republic: Intellect and Ideology in Revolutionary America (New York: W. W. Norton, 1980), 185.

5. Felicity Nussbaum, *The Autobiographical Subject: Gender and Ideology in Eighteenth-Century England* (Baltimore: Johns Hopkins University Press, 1989), 127.

6. Miss C. Palmer, *Letters upon Several Subjects from a Preceptress to her Pupils who have left School* (1797), quoted in J. M. Tompkins, *The Popular Novel in England 1770–1800* (Lincoln: University of Nebraska Press, 1961), 146–47.

7. Quoted in Scheick, *Authority and Female Authorship*, 20.

8. Carlo Ginzburg, *The Cheese and the Worms: The Cosmos of a Sixteenth-Century Miller*, trans. John and Anne Tedeschi (New York: Penguin Books, 1982), 32, 34.

9. Scheick, *Authority and Female Authorship*, 21.

10. The phrase comes from Jacqueline Pearson, *Women's Reading in Britain 1750–1835* (Cambridge: Cambridge University Press, 1999), 43, 46–47. Wollstonecraft and Austen were two examples of Pearson's resisting readers.

11. *Journal and Letters of Margaret Lowther Page* (New York, c. 1790), CWM (title page missing).

12 Judith Lomax, *Notes of An American Lyre*, Early American Imprints, 2d ser., no. 28971 (Richmond: Samuel Pleasants, 1813)

13. Daphne Hamm O'Brien, "From Plantation to Parnassus: Poets and Poetry in Williamsburg, Virginia 1750–1800" (Ph.D. diss., University of North Carolina, Chapel Hill, 1993), 169.

14. Terry Lovell, "Subjective Powers? Consumption, the Reading Public, and Domestic Woman in Early Eighteenth-Century England," in *The Consumption of Culture, 1600–1800: Image, Object, Text*, ed. Ann Birmingham and John Brewer (London: Routledge, 1995), 37.

15. Kathleen Brown, *Good Wives, Nasty Wenches, and Anxious Patriarchs: Gender, Race, and Power in Colonial Virginia* (Chapel Hill: University of North Carolina Press, 1996).

16. Sabina Lovibond, "Feminism and Postmodernism," *New Left Review* 178 (1988): 27, quoted in Lovell, "Subjective Powers?" 38.

17. Cara Anzilotti, "Autonomy and the Female Planter in Colonial South Carolina," *Journal of Southern History* 63, no. 2 (1997): 239–68; Lori Glover, *All Our Relations: Blood Ties and Emotional Bonds Among the Early South Carolina Gentry* (Baltimore: Johns Hopkins University Press, 2000).

18. Anzilotti, "Autonomy and the Female Planter," 250.

19. Shields, "Questions, Suspicions, Speculations," 337.

20. Joanna Bowen Gillespie, *The Life and Times of Martha Laurens Ramsay, 1759–1811* (Columbia: University of South Carolina Press, 2001), 29.

21. David Moltke-Hansen, "The Expansion of Intellectual Life: A Prospectus," in *Intellectual Life in Antebellum Charleston*, ed. Michael O'Brien and David Moltke-Hansen (Knoxville: University of Tennessee Press, 1986), 3–44; Arthur H. Shaffer, "David Ramsay and the Limits of Revolutionary Nationalism," ibid., 47–84. Indeed, slaves likewise adopted this same "turning inward" strategy to construct their own culture on the terrain of their master's plantation. Ira Berlin, *Many Thousands Gone The First Two Centuries of Slavery in North America* (Cambridge, Mass.: Harvard University Press, 1998), 107.

22. Limeston Springs Female High School, Spartanburg, South Carolina, 1845, quoted in P. Joy Rouse, "Cultural Models of Womanhood: Practices of Colonization and Resistance" in *Nineteenth-Century Women Learn to Write*, ed. Catherine Hobbs (Charlottesville: University Press of Virginia, 1995), 232.

23. Robert Shoemaker, *Gender in English Society 1650–1850: The Emergence of Separate Spheres?* (London: Longman, 1998), 5.

24. Vivian Gornick, "Who Says We Haven't Made a Revolution?" *New York Times Magazine,* April 13, 1990, 24, 27, 52–53.

25. Gerda Lerner, *The Creation of Feminist Consciousness from the Middle Ages to Eighteen-Seventy* (New York: Oxford University Press, 1993), 10–12.

26. Adrienne Rich, *On Lies, Secrets, and Silence: Selected Prose 1966–78* (New York: W. W. Norton, 1979), quoted in *Women's Ways of Knowing: The Development of Self, Voice, and Mind,* ed. Mary Field Belenky et al. (New York: Basic Books, 1986), 193. I am indebted to Wendy Hamilton Hoelscher for this reference. Ten years later, the authors reexamined their feminist theories about knowledge, power, and authority, in an updated book that expanded and confirmed the original premise. Nancy Rule Goldberger et al., eds., *Knowledge, Difference, and Power: Essays Inspired by Women's Ways of Knowing* (New York: Basic Books, 1996).

27. Belenky et al., *Women's Ways of Knowing,* 193. The authors' interviews of 135 women produced five thousand pages of text; the subjects were recent college graduates, college students, and "students" in what the authors called "invisible college," that is, "human service agencies supporting women in parenting their children," 11–12.

28. Ruth Rosen, *The World Split Open: How the Modern Women's Movement Changed America* (New York: Penguin Books, 2000).

29. Lerner, *The Creation of Patriarchy* (New York: Oxford University Press, 1986), 219.

30. Mary Jacobus, quoted in Belenky et al., *Women's Ways of Knowing,* 198.

31. See, for example, the "great books" curriculum for St. John's College, Annapolis, Maryland.

32. Elaine Showalter, "The Female Tradition," in *Feminisms: An Anthology of Literary Theory and Criticism,* ed. Robyn R. Warhol and Diane Price Herndl (New Brunswick: Rutgers University Press, 1991), 273.

33. Cheri Register, "American Feminist Literary Criticism: A Bibliographical Introduction," in *Feminist Literary Criticism: Exploration in Theory,* ed. Josephine Donovan (Lexington: University Press of Kentucky, 1989), 13.

34. Elaine Showalter, "Women Writers and the Double Standard," in *Women in a Sexist Society,* ed. Vivian Gornick and Barbara K. Moran (New York: Basic Books, 1971), 324.

35. Janet T. Spence, "Changing Conceptions of Men and Women: A Psychologists' Perspective," in *A Feminist Perspective in the Academy: The Difference It Makes,* ed. Elizabeth Langland and Walter Gove (Chicago: University of Chicago Press, 1981), 132.

36. Ibid., 134.

37. Janet Todd, *Feminist Literary History* (New York: Routledge, 1988), 2.

38. Linda K. Kerber and Jane Sherron DeHart, eds., *Women's America: Refocusing the Past,* 5th ed. (New York: Oxford University Press, 2000), 623.

39. Ruth B. Mandel, "Women's Leadership in American Politics: The Legacy and the Promise," in *The American Woman 2001–2002,* ed. Cynthia B. Costello and Anne J. Stone (New York: W. W. Norton, 2001), 43.

40. Kerber and DeHart, *Women's America,* 612; Rosalind Rosenberg, *Divided Lives: American Women in the Twentieth Century* (New York: Hill and Wang, 1992), 244.

41. Harvey J. Graff, *The Literacy Myth: Literacy and the Social Structure in the 19th Century* (New York: Academic Press, 1979).

42. An excellent treatment of women's relationship to American constitutional culture is Sandra F. VanBurkleo, *"Belonging to the World": Women's Rights and American Constitutional Culture* (New York: Oxford University Press, 2001).

43. Spender, *The Writing or the Sex? Or, Why You Don't Have to Read Women's Writing to Know It's No Good* (New York: Pergamon, 1989), 13, 23–39; Ian Watt, *The Rise of the*

Novel: Studies in Defoe, Richardson and Fielding (Berkeley: University of California Press, 1962); Janet Todd, *The Sign of Angellica: Women, Writing and Fiction, 1660–1800* (New York: Columbia University Press, 1989), 3.

44. Spender, *The Writing or the Sex?* 12–13.

45. Mary Louise Weaks and Carolyn Perry, eds., *Southern Women's Writing: Colonial to Contemporary* (Gainesville: University Press of Florida, 1995). The anthology assembled by Weaks and Perry contains only three examples of women's writing in the eighteenth century, 42 pages in a volume of 390 pages.

46. Jacqueline Jones Roytster, *Traces of a Stream: Literacy and Social Changes of African American Women* (Pittsburgh: University of Pittsburgh Press, 2000), 83.

Postscript

1. Quoted in Juliet Mitchell and Jacqueline Rose, eds., *Feminine Sexuality and the "École Freudienne"* (New York: W. W. Norton, 1982), 167.

2. Carol J. Singley, "Female Language, Body, and Self," in *Anxious Power: Reading, Writing, and Ambivalence in Narrative by Women*, ed. Singley and Susan Elizabeth Sweeney (Albany: State University of New York Press, 1993), 3–4.

3. Dale Spender, *The Writing or the Sex? Or, Why You Don't Have to Read Women's Writing to Know It's No Good* (New York: Pergamon, 1989), 9–10, 12–13.

4. Cynthia B. Costello and Anne J. Stone, eds., *The American Woman 2001–2002: Getting to the Top* (New York: W. W. Norton, 2001), 64, 66.

5. "Facts and Figures: What Professors Earn," *Chronicle of Higher Education*, April 19, 2002.

Index

Adams, Abigail, 22, 96
Adams, Hannah, 97
advice
    as education, 18, 106, 187
    influence of, 65–69, 116, 124–25
    and the learned lady, 126
    maternal, 34–35, 69, 93–95, 112–14,
        120–21, 128, 137, 155
    novels' challenge to, 6, 26, 105–6,
        109–10, 112, 122, 136
    popularity of, 112
    print dissemination of, 19
    persistence of, 124–25, 136, 154, 186–87
    revised, 55, 179
    Scriptural basis, 71–73
    in the South, 46–48, 186
    traditional, 34–35, 93, 104, 128
    women's views of, 63–67, 187
    See also Carrington, Eliza Jaquelin Am-
        bler Brent; Clitherall, Caroline Burg-
        win; A Father's Legacy to his Daughters;
        Hopkinson, Mary; Izard, Alice; The
        Ladies Calling in Two Parts; Lady's New
        Year's Gift to a Daughter; Ramsay,
        Martha Laurens; Randolph, Jane; Ser-
        mons for Young Women; Washington,
        Elizabeth Foote; The Whole Duty of Man
Allestree, Reverend Richard, 21, 42, 67,
    119, 122, 129, 154, 186
    women readers, 43–44, 91

See also The Ladies Calling in Two Parts;
    The Whole Duty of Man
Ambler, Eliza. See Carrington, Eliza Jaque-
    lin Ambler Brent
Ambler, Elizabeth, 94
Ambler, Jaquelin, 97
Ambler, Mary, 34–35, 57, 67–69, 74, 144
Ambler, Rebecca Burwell, 74
Ambler, Richard, 94
American Colonization Society, 100–101,
    176
American Revolution
    and authority, 81–82
    and defining citizenship, 82
    and female intellectual identity, 83–88,
        128
    and marriage, 150
    and political identity, 125–28
    and social hierarchies, 139, 141
Anglican Church
    in Baltimore, 161
    demise, 90
    evangelical women in, 80, 97–98
    structure and theology, 38–40
    worldliness of, in Virginia, 121
    See also disestablishment; Episcopal
        Church
Archer, Frances Tanner, 86
Astell, Mary, 89. See also Serious Proposal to
    the Ladies

Balfour, Charlotte, 86
Balfour, James, 119, 126–27
Balfour, Mary Jemima, 119, 126
Baltimore
  rise of, 160–61, 168
  slaveholding in, 175, 182
Baptists, 74, 88
  Anglican view of, 27, 80, 81
  Broad Run Church, 77
  and novels, 119–20, 121, 136
  persecution of, 76
  rise of, 75–76
  David Thomas, 77
Baylor, Frances and John, 150
Beale, Judith Carter, 117–18
Behn, Aphra, 138
belles lettres, 8, 10–11, 25, 57, 64, 94–95,
  107–8
Belt, Catherine Dulany, 74, 85, 95, 166
benevolence associations, 95, 99–101
bibles, 42, 167
Blair, Anne, 109
Blair, Jean, 86
Bland, Sophy, 137, 154
Bland, Theodorick, 137, 154
Bolling, Robert, 146–47
books
  advertised for sale, 60
  in Baltimore, 161–62
  bequeathed by women, 114, 164, 167
  cost of, 61–63, 109
  devotional, 40–43
  loaned by women, 109
  ownership, 7, 9–11, 107–9
  purchased by women, 1–3, 63, 119–20,
    123–24
  religious, 7, 19, 42, 74
  sizes, 60–61
  sold at Williamsburg, 9, 60–63, 124
  women's access to, 2–3, 59–60, 90, 111,
    139
  See also bibles; libraries; novels; *individual authors and titles*
book trade
  local, 1–2, 9, 60–63, 109, 124
  transatlantic, 7, 63, 119, 124
Braxton, Mary, 86
Broweder, Mary Avery, 79–80
Burgwin, Caroline. *See* Clitherall, Caroline
  Burgwin
Burgwin, Eliza Bush, 94, 130–33

Burgwin, John, 130–33
Burwell, Rebecca, 74
Burr, Esther Edwards, 115
Bush, Eliza, 94, 130–33
Byrd, Lucy, 1, 48–49, 59
Byrd, William, 38
  commonplace book, 63
  control of library, 1, 9, 18, 87
  devotional reading, 48, 59
  marriage, 48–49
  reading and identity, 11–12, 63–64, 127
  and religion, 40
  Secret History of the Dividing Line, 11

Caldwell, Margaret. *See* McHenry, Margaret
  (Peggy) Caldwell and James
Calvert, Rosalie Stier, 112, 170
Cameron, Anna, 128
Cameron, Rebecca, 98
Carrington, Eliza Jaquelin Ambler Brent
  and benevolence, 99–100
  education, 14, 74, 94, 187
  and Episcopal Church, 27–28, 97
  letter writing, 134, 137
  and novels, 110–11, 130
Carter, Charles, 148
Carter, Judith, 117–18
Carter, Landon, 117–18, 148
Carter, Maria (of Cleve), 20, 63–64,
  145–46
Carter, Maria (of Sabine Hall), 21
Carter, Robert, 10, 13
Chapone, Hester, 157–58, 160, 162,
  164–65
Charlotte Temple (Hannah Foster), 116, 129
Charlton, Jane Hunter, 133–34
Chesapeake, 36–38
Clitherall, Caroline Burgwin, 190
  courtship of 131–32
  and novels, 134–35, 137, 187
Coale, Anna Maria, 140
  commonplace book of, 157–58, 162–64
  death, 179
  and slavery, 175–77
  and writing, 178
Coale, Anne Hopkinson, 160
  Anglicanism, 161–62
  and manumission, 175
  Philadelphia relations, 162, 164–65,
    168, 176
Coale, Edward, 162–63, 176

Coale, Mary Abigail Willing, 85–86, 140
commonplace book, 165, 170–71, 177,
178–79
letter writing, 166–67, 168
reading, 174
views on gender, 158–60, 183
Coale, Dr. Samuel, 161–62, 175–76
Coale, William, 162, 167, 168, 179
colonization theory, 19–20
commonplace books
as education 63–64; 163–64, 170–71
and female writing, 177–78
See also Carter, Maria (of Cleve); Coale,
Anna Maria
Coolidge, Ellen Wayles Randolph, 31–32,
140, 184
Corbin, Gawen, 77
Corbin, Elisha. See Hall, Elisha Corbin
Corbin, Hannah Lee
conversion, 74, 77–79, 119
and novels, 119–24, 134, 137
and property taxation, 125–26
Corbin, Martha, 77
Corbin, (Baptist) Martha, 77
courtship, 114–15, 130–33, 144–49, 152–53
Custis, Eleanor Parke, 180

Daniel, Lucy Randolph, 66, 88–89
Daniel, Peter Vivian, 66, 88
Davidson, Cathy, 111
Davies, Samuel, 76, 87–88
and novels, 26
and slaves, 75
DeRossett, Dr. Armand, 89, 90
DeRossett, Catherine Fullerton, 89–90, 112
devotional reading, 64–65, 74
disestablishment, 27–28, 83–84
and female activism, 97–100
and the social order, 95–96
See also religion
Doddridge, Philip
Principles of Christian Religion, 76, 88
Rise and Progress of Religion in the Soul, 90
and spiritual journals, 92
Drinker, Elizabeth, 115
Dulany, Catherine. See Belt, Catherine Du-
lany

Edgeworth, Maria, 124
education
in colonial period, 13

gendered, 13–19, 32, 85–86, 87, 154,
186, 190
politics of, 100
religious, 74
twentieth-century, 191–92
See also female education; reading;
schools; writing
Eloisa (Jean-Jacques Rousseau), 108, 110
Enlightenment, the 2
benefits of, 193–94
and female sensibility, 177, 178
passion and reason, 145–48, 163, 165,
193–94
and reason, 103
Scottish, and women, 56–57, 59, 173
women's claim to, 102, 104, 169, 184
Episcopal Church, 83, 90, 98, 161–62. See
also Anglican Church
evangelical womanhood, 102
Eve, 71–73, 106
in southern women's writings, 64–65,
93, 103, 154
Evelina (Frances Burney), 105, 112, 125

Father's Legacy to his Daughters, A (Dr. John
Gregory), 18, 54–56, 106, 160
female education
antebellum, 179
classrooms, 13–14, 17, 185
colonization of and resistance, 19–25,
93, 103, 110, 190
consequences of, 190–94
curriculum, 106, 118, 154, 173
disparaged, 15, 126, 144
novels as, 110–11, 115–17, 127, 136
ornamental, 111
post-Revolutionary, 128–29
promoted by women, 114, 128–29
and race, 31–32
Ramsay, Martha Laurens, 91
to self-sufficiency, 96, 155–56
Female Spectator, The (Haywood, Eliza), 25,
110, 111, 124, 129, 138
Fergusson, Elizabeth Graeme, 24, 179
Fithian, Philip Vickers, 65
Fordyce, Reverend James, 53–56, 66, 95,
122, 126, 129, 144, 154. See also Sermons for Young Women
Foster, Hannah
The Boarding School, 163, 179
The Coquette, 26

Franklin, Benjamin, 85
Fullerton, Catherine, 89–90, 112

gender relations
    in Britain, 44–45, 181–82, 186
    men's views on, 158–59
    shaped by southern women, 183–84,
        187
    women's views on, 153–54, 156, 169–70,
        178, 182, 187
    See also Coale, Mary Abigail Willing
Gil Blas (Alain René LeSage), 107, 108,
    118
Great Awakening, 75, 81–82
Griffitts, Hannah, 23, 140, 179, 182

Halifax, George Lord. *See* Savile, George
    Lord Halifax
Hall, David D., 11
Hall, Elisha Corbin, 77
Hall, Martha Corbin, 77
Hall, Dr. Richard, 77
handwriting, 14–17, 85–86, 166
Heloise (Jean-Jacques Rousseau), 108, 110
Hill, Frances Baylor, 105, 111–12, 115,
    125, 136
History of a Young Lady of Distinction, The
    (Beaumont, Anne-Louise Elie de),
    120–21
Hopkinson, Esther, 166
Hopkinson, Francis, 162, 176
Hopkinson, Mary, 164, 167
hospitality, 182–83
Hubard, James, 152–53

intellectual history, 3–4
intellectuality
    limits on southern female, 30–32, 144,
        189–90
    regional contrasts, 171, 174
    and regional identity, 5–6, 139–40, 151
    transatlantic influence on, 119, 136–38
Izard, Alice, 128, 137, 155, 190
    on Mary Wollstonecraft, 153
    on Philadelphia, 168–69
Izard, Ralph, 128, 155

Jarratt, Devereux, 40–41
Jefferson, Martha, 173
Jefferson, Thomas, 74, 81, 83, 127, 144,
    183

and education, 100, 173
and women's reading, 172–74
Jones, Sarah, 76

Kerber, Linda, 111, 115
Key, Eliza, 87

Ladies Calling in Two Parts, The (Rev.
    Richard Allestree), 18, 42, 43, 45–
    46
*Lady's New Year's Gift; or Advice to a Daughter,
    A* (Savile, George Lord Halifax), 18,
    42, 43, 49–52, 106, 110, 111
Lee, Arthur, 78
Lee, Mary Custis, 100–101
Lee, Richard Henry, 78, 125–26, 127
letters
    colonial period, 94–95
    dispensing advice, 92, 94–95
    and female networks, 29–30, 164–68,
        174, 179
    as literary device, 133
    love, 132–33, 149–50
    read as advice 94, 130–31, 134
    southern writers of, 21, 78, 85, 133–34
    See also Coale, Anne Hopkinson; Coale,
        Mary Abigail Willing
Letters on Education (Catharine Macaulay),
    106, 125
libraries
    inventoried, 9, 107–9, 123–24
    as male preserve, 1, 87
    planter, 9–11, 43, 108–9
    private, 9–11, 43–44, 106, 108
    Society, in South Carolina, 109, 183
    See also Skipwith, Lady Jean Miller
literacy
    and authority, 11, 193–94
    in colonial America, 11
    and gender, 13, 17
    post-Revolutionary, 127
    and salons, 182–83, 190
    and slavery, 12
    writing, 70
Logan, Deborah, 15, 85–86
Lucas, Eliza. *See* Pinckney, Eliza Lucas
Luttrell, John, 108

Manigault, Margaret Izard, 168
marriage
    companionate, 149–50, 153, 127

essays on, 106–7
novels and, 117–18
and Revolution, 150–51
women's views on, 89, 122–23, 145–46,
149, 157–58, 181
Meade, Mary, 97–98, 100
Meade, William (Bishop), 97–98, 101
McHenry, Margaret (Peggy) Caldwell and
James, 86, 154, 156, 165
Methodists, 75, 79, 88
in North Carolina, 89–90, 98
and manumission, 102
Miller, Anne, 146–47
Miller, Jean. *See* Skipwith, Lady Jean
Miller
Milner, James, 108
Moore, Milcah Martha, 23
motherhood, 127–28, 151, 156
More, Hannah, 98, 109
Murdock, Margaret (Peggy), 85
Murray, Judith Sargent, 22–23, 96, 104,
140, 155–57, 160, 169. *See also* female
education

Norris, Elizabeth, 23–24, 182
Norton, Cortenay, 86
novels
as advice, 6, 110
appeal of, 26, 105–6, 109–11, 115, 117,
123–24, 127–28
censure of, 26, 107, 117–19
changing emphasis in, 123
and courtship, 114, 117–19, 146
and education, 111, 115
English, 123–24, 133–35
epistolary, 133–34
and female identity, 129–30
and gender conventions, 110, 123
influence on women's writing, 114,
118–19, 128–38
male readership of, 26, 107–9
purchased, 119, 124
readership of, 112–16
readership by matrons, 114–15, 118–24,
127, 129
readership in the South, 25–26, 105,
107–8, 136–38
religion and, 135–37
Revolution and, 125–28
and slavery, 174–77
Scottish, 155

sentiment in, 123–24
young readers of, 111–19, 127
See also specific titles

Page, Ann Randolph Meade, 97
Page, Margaret Lowther, 188, 190
Pamela (Samuel Richardson), 25–26, 107,
108, 109, 115–17, 124, 133, 134, 137,
187
Paradise Lost (John Milton), 65
Parks, William, 7–8, 9, 85
patriarchy, 71–73, 102
Pearce, Mary (Polly), 166, 169, 174
Peregrine Pickle (Tobias Smollett), 107, 108,
118
Pinckney, Eliza Lucas, 109, 126, 189, 190
on *Pamela*, 115–17, 134, 137, 187
Pinckney, Sarah Middleton, 126–27
Pope, Alexander, 8, 20, 43, 64, 108,
145–46
portraits, 48, 57–59, 65, 119, 126–27
Pratt, Elizabeth Cocke, 144–45, 147
Presbyterians, 75–76, 87–88, 98, 101
printing, 3, 6, 10, 124. *See also* Franklin,
Benjamin; Parks, William; Timothy,
Ann; Timothy, Elizabeth

Quakers, 68, 75
and literary culture, 23–24, 182
and marriage, 182
women preachers, 103

race
and class, 38, 155, 189
and gender, 47–48, 140, 143, 150, 154,
178
and passion, 144
and patriarchy, 30, 141–44
Ramsay, Martha Laurens, 28, 95
devotional reading, 44
and the Enlightenment, 190
on gender, 64–65, 170
spiritual journal, 64–67, 90–92
on slavery, 177
Randolph, Edmund, 66, 67
Randolph, Elizabeth, 66, 74, 88
Randolph, Frances Bland. *See* Tucker,
Frances Bland Randolph
Randolph, Jane, 128–29
Randolph, Martha Jefferson, 173
Read, Helen Calvert Maxwell, 74, 114–15

readers
as female community, 111, 136–38, 171, 174, 179
of newspapers, 7–8
reader response, 117–24, 187–88
reading
as colonized, 19–21, 63–67
devotional, 43–44, 98, 102, 122
as discipline, 173
as diversion, 174
gendered, 18–19
influence on political sensibilities, 125–27
regional contrasts, 171, 174, 180–81, 185–86
as resistance, 109–10, 180–84, 188–89
Scripture, 64–65, 93
in a slave society, 144–46, 173
southern experience of, 136–38, 139, 180
time for, 115
See also advice; commonplace books; education; novels
reason, 82, 103. *See also* Enlightenment, the
religion
and authority, 28, 81–82, 91–93, 102–4
church attendance, 38–41
clergy selection, 98
evangelical, 27, 75–81
and female activism, 28, 83–84, 97–101
and gender relations, 90, 102, 183
influence on gender ideology, 81, 89, 103–4
and novels, 120–23, 135–36, 188
private worship, 40–41, 79, 95, 98
and reason, 102–3, 104
and the self, 78–84, 88–89, 101, 102
and women's writings, 104, 135–36, 167
See also Baptists; disestablishment; Methodists; Presbyterians
Republican Motherhood, 82
and novels, 127–28
and race, 155–56
Rind, Clementina, 96
Rivals, The (Richard Sheridan), 112
Roderick Random (Tobias Smollett), 107, 118
Rowson, Susanna, 135
Royall, Anne, 101

Savile, George Lord Halifax, 122, 129, 154, 185–86. See also *A Lady's New Year's Gift; or, Advice to a Daughter*

schools, Virginia, 13–14, 15, 100
scribal publication, 104, 133
Sentimental Journey, A (Laurence Sterne), 107, 174–77
Serious Proposal to the Ladies (Mary Astell), 21–22, 24
Sermons for Young Women (Rev. James Fordyce)
British context, 53, 55–57
content, 52–56, 59, 61, 65, 69, 73, 112, 119
popularity of, 18, 34–45
southern readers, 10–11, 59, 68–69, 91, 105, 160, 180
woman as object, 84
Shippen, Alice Lee, 78, 120
Skipwith, Lady Jean Miller, 1–2, 109, 122–24, 136, 137
Skipwith, Sir Peyton, 122
slavery, 29
codes, 38, 142–43
and evangelical Christianity, 143–44, 183
and force, 142
literacy 12, 154
manumission, 141, 175–76
northern, 141, 155
as personal and real property, 152
post-Revolutionary, 176–77
as regional, 140–41
teaching slaves, 93, 94
term, 175, 176, 182, 183
trade, 141
women's views on, 155, 174–77, 190
See also Baltimore
slave society
and intellectual life, 29–30, 137–40, 189–90
male authority in, 142–44, 189–90
patriarchy in, 152
Smith, Judith Anna, 21, 79–80, 87–88
Smith, Mildred, 110–11, 130, 134, 137, 186
sociability, 182–83
South, the, 139–44, 183–84
South Carolina Gazette, 12, 24, 108–9
Spender, Dale, 84, 107, 194
Spotswood, Ann Butler, 148–49

Telemachus (François Fénelon), 59, 108
Tilghman, Henrietta, 166, 169–70, 180
Tilghman, Mary, 169–70, 174, 180

Tillotson, Archbishop John, 20, 40, 42, 43, 48–49, 59–61, 64
Timothy, Ann, 108
Timothy, Elizabeth, 85, 108
Tom Jones (Henry Fielding), 107, 108
Tristram Shandy (Laurence Sterne), 107, 108
True Merit, True Happiness (Kerguette, Jean Digard de), 120
Tucker, Frances Bland Randolph, 109, 147–48, 150
Tucker, St. George, 147–48, 152, 188
Turner, Nancy Johns, 118–19, 187

Virginia Gazette, 14
    account books, 26, 85
    advertisements for paper, 85
    advertisements for return of books, 10, 109
    advertisements for teachers 14–15
    circulation, 8
    contents 8–9
    English literary influence in, 8–9, 11
    female advice, 18, 24, 59, 106–7, 149
    and novels, 107, 117, 125

Warren, Mercy Otis, 96, 104
Warrington, Rachel, 111, 129, 134
Washington, Elizabeth Foote, 101
    advice to daughter, 28, 137, 188
    journal, 64, 67, 74, 92, 130
    religious views of, 27, 80, 92
    and slaves, 155
Washington, George, 13, 125, 127, 180
Washington, Martha, 13, 180
Watts, Isaac, 76
Whitefield, George, 75
Whiting, Eliza, 86
Whole Duty of Man (Rev. Richard Allestree) 43
    content, 18, 44–45
    popularity of 18, 42, 106
    in the South, 46–48, 59, 91, 126
widows, 34, 63, 77, 125–26, 148, 170, 189
Wilcox, Susanna, 152–53
Wilkinson, Eliza, 96, 102
Willing, Abigail, 164, 165

Wirt, Elizabeth and William, 150
Wollstonecraft, Mary, 157
    criticized, 153–54
    Vindication of the Rights of Woman, 23, 169, 191
women
    and American Revolution, 82, 96
    and the courts, 14, 151–52
    courtship, 146–49
    and disestablishment, 83–84
    and evangelical religion, 74, 80–81
    legal status of, 125–26, 127, 151
    marriage, 149–50
    and patriotism, 96–97
    and political activism, 15, 125–27
    printers, 96, 108
    and property, 152–53
    religious instruction of, 79
    salon politics, 168–69
    shaping southern regionalism, 139–40, 189–90
    and subjectivity, 84, 95, 129–30
    as teachers, 74, 94, 154–55
    writing women portrayed, 171–72
writing
    advice for daughters, 92–94
    authority of, 194
    in Baltimore, 178–79
    dangers of, 165–67
    Englishwomen's, 24–25, 93, 103–4, 129
    and female community, 179
    female publication, 183
    and female reticence, 147, 166
    gender, 85, 178
    inspired by novels, 129–35
    instruction in, 85
    memoirs, 94
    obstacles to, 84
    poetry, 188
    promoted by women, 114
    rise of, 4–5, 188–89
    and the self, 84, 91–92, 178
    southern, 29
    spiritual journals, 66–67, 79–80, 87–93
    supplies for, 15, 85–86
    time and space for, 86–87
    See also education; letters; novels